D0620932

Tuff City

Remapping Cultural History

General Editor: Jo Labanyi, New York University and University of Southampton

Published in association with the Institute of Germanic & Romance Studies, School of Advanced Study, University of London

The theoretical paradigms dominant in much of cultural history published in English tend to be derived from northern European or North American models. This series will propose alternative mappings by focusing partly or wholly on those parts of the world that speak, or have spoken, French, Italian, Spanish or Portuguese. Both monographs and collective volumes will be published. Preference will be given to volumes that cross national boundaries, that explore areas of culture that have previously received little attention, or that make a significant contribution to rethinking the ways in which cultural history is theorised and narrated.

Tuff City

Urban Change and Contested Space in Central Naples

Nick Dines

Berghahn Books
New York • Oxford

First published in 2012 by

Berghahn Books

www.berghahnbooks.com

© 2012 Nick Dines

Library of Congress Cataloging-in-Publication Data

Dines, Nick
    Tuff city: urban change and contested space in central Naples / Nick Dines.
        p. cm. — (Remapping cultural history; 13)
    Includes bibliographical references and index.
    ISBN 978-0-85745-279-5 (hbk.: alk. paper) — ISBN 978-0-85745-280-1
(ebook)
    1. Public spaces—Italy—Naples. 2. Urbanization—Italy—Naples. 3. City
planning—Italy—Naples. 4. Land use, Urban—Italy—Naples. I. Title.
    HT169.I84N3453 2012
    307.760945'731—dc23

                                                              2011032700

British Library Cataloguing in Publication Data

A catalogue record for this book is available from the British Library.

Printed in the United States on acid-free paper

978-0-85745-279-5 (hardback)
978-0-85745-280-1 (ebook)

To Bjarne

Contents

Illustrations

Maps

Abbreviations

AD	Alleanza Democratica
AN	Alleanza Nazionale
ASCOM	Associazione Commercianti
CGIL	Confederazione Generale Italiana del Lavoro
DAMM	Diego Armando Maradona Montesanto
DC	Democrazia Cristiana
DP	Democrazia Proletaria
DS	Democratici di Sinistra
FS	Ferrovie dello Stato
ISTAT	Istituto Centrale di Statistica
MSI	Movimento Sociale Italiano
PCI	Partito Comunista Italiano
PD	Partito Democratico
PDS	Partito Democratico della Sinistra
PLI	Partito Liberale Italiano
PPI	Partito Popolare Italiano
PRC	Partito della Rifondazione Comunista
PRI	Partito Repubblicano Italiano
PSDI	Partito Socialista Democratico Italiano
PSI	Partito Socialista Italiano
RAI	Radio Televisione Italiana
SDI	Socialisti Democratici Italiani
UDEUR	Unione Democratica per l'Europa
UNESCO	United Nations Educational, Scientific and Cultural Organization

Preface

This book has had a drawn-out and, at times, complicated gestation. It represents more than a decade of research, writing, conversations, and reflections, first in Naples (from 1998 to 2004), later in London (from 2004 to 2007) and most recently in Rome. Much of the original fieldwork was carried out for my PhD thesis in Italian Studies at University College London (UCL), which was presented at the end of 2001. Additional material derives from a study of the 1980 earthquake in the historic centre of Naples, conducted between 2002 and 2004 for an AHRB (Arts and Humanities Research Board)-funded oral history and documentary film project based in the Italian department at UCL, and from self-funded research on the postwar history of the Neapolitan Left, which commenced on my return to Italy in 2007. Like many, I have been engrossed by the recent trials and tribulations of Naples, but these have also convinced me of the importance of writing a critical ethnographic history of the preceding period, when the city was instead widely seen to be on the rise.

The book has been greatly shaped by the experience of studying and working in a range of disciplinary fields during my stop-start academic career. These have included (in roughly chronological order) art history, Italian studies, sociology, oral history, town planning, community health studies, geography, migration studies and cultural anthropology. I do not wish here to sing the praises of interdisciplinarity, and in fact, when not complaining about the parochial and rigid disciplinary divisions in the Italian academy, I have often found myself envying the depth and stability provided (at least in the past) by its higher education system. Rather, I can simply say that these accumulated encounters have left their mark on the book in varying ways and to varying degrees. My insistence on interweaving different strands and approaches to the study of urban phenomena often rendered the task of producing a publishable manuscript arduous and time consuming. Naples, as the main object of analysis, only made matters worse. For Naples is not just a *tuff* city characterized by the yellowish volcanic building material that has also served as the physical referent to a number of local heuristics and stereotypes, such as Walter Benjamin's notion of 'porosity', it is also a *tough* city: a tough city to govern, to live and to survive in; tough to endorse or criticize without resorting to cliché and a tough place to assert the right to indifference. But for me, over the last few years, it has been, more than anything else, tough to write about: it is a city that perpetually challenges preconceptions about urban processes and the vocabulary that we unquestioningly use to read and interpret them. For all those painful hours spent searching for a suitable prose that could capture the city's fascinating complexities, I now feel it was worth it.

Over the course of more than a decade, numerous individuals have influenced and supported this project. First, I would like to express my gratitude to the many people I was able to interview during my research on Piazza Plebiscito, Piazza Garibaldi, the Neapolitan *centri sociali* and the 1980 earthquake. Oreste Ventrone, Fabio Amato, and Luciano Brancaccio have been pillars of encouragement and have always generously shared their knowledge of Naples. I am also indebted to a number of people in the various universities of Naples for taking an interest in my work, for their advice and assistance: Amalia Signorelli, Gabriella Gribaudi, Giovanni Persico, Federica Palestino, Daniela Lepore, Antonello Petrillo, Iain Chambers and Marina di Chiara. A special mention goes to my friend Pietro Marcello for his collaboration with film work and for the times spent exploring and discovering the city together. Down the years I have benefited from many conversations about all aspects of Naples with, among others, Piero Vivenzio, Luigi Cavallo, Paola D'Onofrio, Maurizio Braucci, Jonah Hershowitz, Sara Marinelli, Mauro Forte, Sergio Vitolo, Zak Ischov, Jonathan Pratschke, Francesco Festa, Gigi Caputo and Massimiliano di Tota. In some way or another, their thoughts, observations, or simple nuggets of information have accompanied me during the writing of this book. Alfonso De Vito was a boundless source of knowledge about local social movements and provided countless links to alternative takes on Neapolitan affairs. Thanks are also due to Dario Belluccio for gaining me access to the newspaper archive in the otherwise impregnable citadel of the Soprintendenza in the Royal Palace. Francesco Soverina at the Istituto Campano per la Storia della Resistenza provided impeccable assistance, while the staff at the Emeroteca Matilde Serao and the Biblioteca Nazionale were always helpful. I am also very grateful for the invaluable help of Giovanni Laino and Nino Ferraiuolo during my research on the earthquake.

My supervisors and former colleagues at University College London have been instrumental to my academic development. Bob Lumley, John Foot, David Forgacs and John Dickie in the Italian department and Sandra Wallman in the Anthropology department have all provided fundamental guidance over the years and critically commented on early versions of my work. Thank you also to Emanuela Tandello, who supported my application for an Italian Cultural Institute grant that first got me to Naples in 1996. From the world of geography, Alastair Bonnett and Donald McNeill both offered invaluable advice and early inspiration. My return to full-time work in London in 2004 put the project on hold but in compensation gave me a contemporary British perspective on many of the issues I was studying in Naples. During this period I had the pleasure to collaborate with Vicky Cattell, Margaret Byron and Rob Imrie. In the United Kingdom I have been able to count on the friendship, care and stimulus of many, including Dan Sayer, Vittorio Bini, Becky Winstanley, Emiliano Battista, Francesco Salvini, Dimitris Papadopolous, Joel Jenkins and Elena Vacchelli. More recently, in Rome, seminars coordinated by Piero Bevilacqua at La Sapienza University and by Alessandro Simonicca at the Fondazione Basso have kept me thinking and reflecting about my own work. Thanks are due to Clara Buhr and Francesca Komel for their emergency hospitality and last-minute babysitting in Rome and to Mirna Campanella, Laura Liverani, Massimiliano Bonini and Cristiano Perruti for fun and distractions in Bologna. Also a big thank you to the editors at Berghahn for their patience when I disappeared off the radar, as well as to the anonymous referees for their helpful comments.

Every effort has been made to obtain permission to use copyright photographs included in this book. I would like to thank Stefano Fittipaldi and Magda Calabrese at the Archivo Fotografico Parisio, Gianni Fiorito, Luciano Ferrara, Marco Demarco at *Corriere del Mezzogiorno,* Antonio Stanga at the Archivio Ferrovie dello Stato in Rome, and Roberta Valerio for their kind permission to reproduce images, and also Aurelia Longo for her technical assistance.

My family has been a backbone of love and support: my father, Stephen, who allowed his house to be turned upside down during my writing spells over long summers in the late 1990s; my mother, Claire, with whom I have shared the experience of living in Italy and who got me dividing my football allegiances between Napoli and Livorno; Martin and Sergio for listening to my moans about academic life; and Kristian and Gülcin for instead being so far away from it all. Maria Donà has recently been a vital presence when times have been hard. Lastly, a very special thank you to Enrica for her love and hardheaded wisdom and for keeping me going, and to Rocco for making the whole process more difficult and completion all the more worthwhile. This book is dedicated to the memory of my brother, Bjarne, who so almost made it and whom I miss sorely.

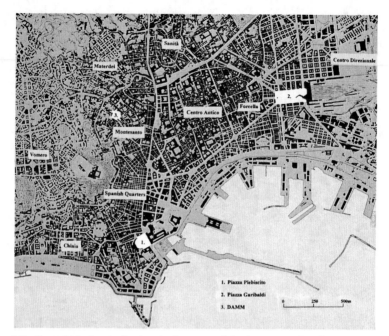

Map I.1. Central Naples, indicating the locations of the three sites of study. *Designed by Nick Dines.*

1: San Ferdinando
2: Chiaia
3: Posillipo
4: Porto
5: San Giuseppe
6: Montecalvario
7: Avvocata
8: Pendino
9: Mercato
10: Stella

11: San Carlo all'Arena
12: San Lorenzo
13: Vicaria
14a: Poggioreale
14b: Zona Industriale
15: Vomero
16: Arenella
17: S. Giovanni a Teduccio
18: Barra
19: Ponticelli

20: San Pietro a Patierno
21: Secondigliano
22: Miano
23: Scampia
24: Piscinola
25: Chiaiano
26: Pianura
27: Soccavo
28: Fuorigrotta
29: Bagnoli

Map I.2. The districts of Naples. *Designed by Nick Dines.*

Introduction[1]

An urban aporia?

> Many of us are the city's harshest critics, and yet all of us are fiercely defensive when outsiders speak ill of it, as they often do. … Visitors tell us that Naples reminds them of Bombay or Cairo, and we want to remind them that we are Europeans and secretly wish someone would mistake Naples for Stockholm or Bern. (Astarita 2005: 7)

> In my younger and more citizenship-minded days, I once told a nine- or ten-year-old boy in Calcutta not to throw rubbish in the street. 'Why not?' he asked, as he proceeded to throw the rubbish anyway. 'I suppose you like to think we live in England, don't you?' (Chakrabarty 2002: 79)

In his essay 'Of Modernity, Garbage and the Citizen's Gaze', the Indian historian Dipesh Chakrabarty discusses attitudes about the public realm in nineteenth- and twentieth-century India. Colonialists and nationalists, he argues, were similarly repelled by the dirt and disorder perceived to predominate in the bazaars and streets of Indian cities. Both held fast the modernist separation between public and private and accordingly deplored the ways in which open spaces were habitually used for domesticated pursuits such as washing, eating, sleeping and defecating. Each sought to transform these spaces of unfettered urbanism into 'benign, regulated public places' (Chakrabarty 2002: 77). But while the British were primarily concerned to quell the risk of rebellion and safeguard the health of Europeans, nationalist figures such as Mahatma Gandhi and Nirad Chaudhuri were more keen to inculcate a culture of citizenship and civic consciousness among the population. Central to the development of the modern state and Indian capitalism, this project inevitably made huge and unrealistic demands upon the social life of the city and its associated pleasures, and, as Chakrabarty wryly notes, 'People in India, on the whole, have not heeded the nationalist call to discipline, public health, and public order' (ibid.). Instead, in its management of the public realm, the Indian state would often revert to repressive action, such as the old colonial practice of *Halla,* whereby police would abruptly clear the streets of hawkers. Alongside this persistent situation of conflict, a less

---

1. Note on text: All translations from Italian are by the author unless otherwise stated.

conspicuous but equally unremitting ideological battle is waged between the sensibility of the subaltern, for whom the universal idea of public space has yet to become a self-evident fact, and that of the academic observer who inhabits a bourgeois-modern position (ibid.: 77–78). In this struggle, Chakrabarty declares, analysis is not neutral, because however sympathetic our ethnographic gaze, we always prefer health over disease, life over death and ultimately 'align ourselves with those who want to build citizen cultures' (ibid.: 69).

This book critically examines, through the study of three public spaces, the transformation and redefinition of the historic centre of Naples during the last decade of the twentieth century. Under the stewardship of a left-wing administration, the city sought to rid itself of its international notoriety as an urban outcast of Europe by reclaiming its immense cultural and architectural patrimony. Commencing with the reflections of a postcolonial theorist might appear somewhat gratuitous, and it is certainly not meant to humour those local self-flagellators, northern Italian secessionists and rival football fans who continue to consign 'Third World' status upon Italy's third largest city. Admittedly, it is difficult to resist baiting those, such as the US-based Neapolitan historian Tommaso Astarita cited above, who instead wish Naples were compared more often with northern Europe and for whom juxtaposition with a city like Calcutta would probably provoke instant irritation. I would rather respond that liberal elites in India have entertained similar desires and that, as Allan Pred's masterly montage of modern Stockholm demonstrates (1995), northern European cities have possessed their own fair share of nonconforming elements and counter-narratives. Starting with Chakrabarty is not an invitation to draw fatuous parallels between Neapolitan and Indian street life, nor is it just a call to provincialize the geographical frames of reference used to defend and imagine Naples. On the contrary, Chakrabarty's essay provides a provocative, if discomforting, entry point to thinking about the complex role that urban public space has played in modern history and in formulating images of the city.

Streets, squares, parks and other open places have long been ideally deployed as a measure of modernity and progress but have likewise been evoked to censure populations, social practices and urban traditions. They form part of a wider political discourse about citizenship that intersects questions of power, control, belonging, rights, obligations and social justice. However, between political discourse and lived experience there is always a gap. For open public space is also an unfinished process, continuously shaped by responses and disruptions from the ground. To enter it is to encounter an empirically perilous domain, not just because we are confronted with diversity (Young 1990), but because it potentially challenges the value systems with which we contemplate urban settings. It is capable of shaking up what the anthropologist Michael Herzfeld has termed our 'geographic complacency' (2006: 129). Can we, for instance, talk 'objectively' of the 'rise' and 'decline' of public space without recourse to preordained axioms about what constitutes a 'good' or 'virtuous' city? Is not describing a place as 'clean' or 'convivial' as politically charged as critiquing privatization or social exclusion? These dilemmas are more pronounced when public space becomes an expedient for reorienting the image of cities and a focus of debates about urban change. Such dilemmas also lie at the heart of this book.

Naples, the principal metropolis of the Mezzogiorno (or Italian South) with a declining population of just over one million during the 1990s and at the centre of a growing metropolitan area totalling more than three million people, has traditionally been regarded as a pathological exception: a swollen, preindustrial city of chronic social and economic problems, characterized by peculiar cultural practices, ingenious survival strategies and an apparent dearth of urban order. Grand Tour visitors to Naples in the eighteenth century were as shocked by the dirt and clamour as they were awed by the city's natural and monumental beauty (Calaresu 2007). Despite its proximity and close association with the classical ruins of Pompeii and Herculaneum, the city would be paradoxically cast on the margins, if not completely off, the historical map of European and Italian modernity. Indeed, during the course of the nineteenth century, Naples often functioned as a sort of degenerate urban template against which to countermeasure the progress of the Italian North, but at the same time its very presence was seen to impede the liberal project of building the nation-state (Moe 2002). After the Second World War, the idea of backwardness was eclipsed by the paradigm of underdevelopment. Naples was a city of blocked growth: economically dependent on the state and conditioned by a political system where personal ties and clientelism prevailed. Local society was made up of an omnipotent political and economic ruling class, an unproductive, parasitic middle class that overshadowed a small, historically defeated, enlightened bourgeoisie, a swarming mass of urban poor at the city's centre and a fragmented proletariat employed in a few heavily subsidized industrial poles on its fringes (Allum 1973).

It is important to note that the aberrant image of Naples was not always seen in a negative light. For example, both the German philosopher Walter Benjamin and the Friulan poet and filmmaker Pier Paolo Pasolini identified in Naples a primordial urbanism that provided a seductive alternative to, respectively, a northern European and Italian modernity. For Benjamin and his coauthor Asja Lacis the Naples witnessed on day visits from Capri in 1924 oozed 'porosity', where the social and built elements of the city interpenetrated in a timeless state of 'blissful confusion' (Benjamin 1978: 170); this in spite of Fascism's recent (and unmentioned) rise to power. For Pasolini, writing in 1975 a few months before his death, Naples remained 'the last plebeian metropolis, the last great village' in Italy (Pasolini 1976: 17) that had withstood the spread of consumer culture, even though during the same year his revered '*popolo*' was at the forefront of the wave of 'Organized Unemployed' protests which sought a more active participation in the city's imperfect modernity.

From the 1980s, numerous researchers, primarily historians and economists, began to critique the orthodox representations of southern Italy. It was claimed that the depiction of an undifferentiated and economically immobile Mezzogiorno had been elaborated in functional opposition to ideal-type models of a modern Italian North (Lupo 1996; Bevilacqua 1996; Gribaudi 1997). Revisionist histories set about dismantling the traditional premises of the 'Southern Question', such as the perpetuation of *ancien régime* social relations and the absence of economic change by reconsidering, for instance, the relationship between the Italian state and southern elites after Unification. They underlined the presence of 'many Souths' which had taken diverse, if mainly unsuccessful, paths to modernization. Meanwhile, the expansion during the 1980s of small-enterprise districts producing high-quality products such as furniture and footwear, often in poor agricultural regions, suggested dynamic endogenous growth in the face of the concomitant failure of state industrial policy (Trigilia 1992).

The new approach to the South produced some far-reaching, innovative scholarship and was successful in overturning timeworn stereotypes and shifting the terms of debate, but it was not without its critics. Some argued that the historical revaluation of regional and local dimensions appeared at times to countenance a top-down view of southern society and that in certain cases old formulae were replaced by more sophisticated but no less culturally determinist 'internal' constraints, such as the lack of 'civic traditions' (Davis 1998), while analyses of industrial clusters were distinguished, at least during an initial phase, by a celebratory rhetoric that highlighted efficiency and entrepreneurship but disregarded poor labour conditions and the deep inequalities that continued to exist between North and South (Rossi 2004a; Dunford and Greco 2006).

New research on Naples was conducted primarily in the fields of social and economic history and included groundbreaking studies of the development of the local bourgeoisie during the nineteenth century (Macry 1988; Caglioti 1994). The city's distinctive and complex historical geography was not, for the most part, an immediate object of analysis. In some respects this was understandable: the prior aim was to challenge the empirical certainties upon which accounts of social and economic change had hitherto rested. Moreover, urban and architectural histories of Naples already abounded, even if much of this work continued to take the form of conventional monographs and rarely crossed disciplinary boundaries.[2] Nevertheless, given the intent of mapping internal differences in the South, it is surprising that there has been little interest to explore, say, multiple experiences of urbanization or contested histories of place during the contemporary period within Naples itself (although see Gribaudi 1999). This said, it is possible to detect parallels between the objectives of the southern revisionists and public debates about Naples during the 1990s: local economic development was promoted over traditional forms of state welfarism, the emergence of a new political class was keenly and critically charted and the simplistic images of a backward Naples, although never entirely vanquished, were increasingly superseded by more positive articulations of local identity.[3] However, this ideal version of the city could only operate by drawing a line around those elements considered abject. Certain manifestations of urban life, for example the generalized lack of respect for the highway code, continued to be censured as culturally regressive and, in any case, too trite to warrant serious analysis. Anybody overly interested in the everyday minutiae and tumult of the city, especially if an outsider (Benjamin and Pasolini excused), was suspected to be under the spell of some folkloristic ruse or, worse still, in connivance with crime. In other words, irrespective of a paradigmatic turn in attitudes about the South, Naples retained an aberrant residue, but one which would now be normalized through its (attempted) ejection from interpretative discourses about the city. An urgent question that therefore needs to be posed, and one that is unlikely to have a straightforward answer, is *what* and *whose* city would emerge in urban policies and debates during the period?

---

2. Urban history in Italy traditionally had a local rather than national focus and was thus less enmeshed in North-South dualisms, although certain urban forms such as piazzas were considered quintessentially northern topics (Barbiani 1992). Research was firmly encamped either in architectural studies or social history, but there were some notable exceptions, in particular Cesare De Seta's classic biography of Naples (1981), which examined the city's development in the light of wider social and cultural processes. As Sergio Pace (2004) notes in his review of Italian urban studies, from the 1980s onwards more refined readings of the city were produced in other disciplinary fields such as town planning and sociology. Pioneering work on Naples include urban planner Attilio Belli's study of planning policies before and after the 1980 earthquake, which draws inspiration from Foucault's analysis of power (Belli 1986), and sociologist Giovanni Laino's case study of economic and housing inequalities in the Spanish Quarters in central Naples (1984).

3. In fact, some historians associated with the revisionist perspective, such as Paolo Macry and Gabriella Gribaudi, became regular columnists for Neapolitan newspapers from the second half of the 1990s.

It is partly as a result of the weighty legacy of ambiguity and aberrance, stereotypes and counter discourses, that Naples and its recent past represent a particularly fascinating focus of study. First and foremost, it encourages us to interrogate the linguistic and theoretical frameworks with which we are accustomed to reading and interpreting contemporary urban change in Europe. Through the course of the book I explore how local contexts and discourses impacted upon the production and experience of urban space. But I am also concerned to situate the transformations that occurred in Naples within wider processes of urban, social, economic and political change. Explanations of Naples have often been torn between the idea of a bewilderingly unique city and the urge to squeeze it into theories tried and tested elsewhere. One of the challenges of this book will be to find a way of integrating the particularistic and universal dimensions into a meaningful and sensitive critique of urban renewal. Helpful to this end is the concept of the 'ordinary city' developed in Jenny Robinson's postcolonial critique of urban theory. Following Robinson, Naples should be examined like any other city, because all cities, in spite of the inequalities that exist between them, 'are dynamic and diverse, if conflicted, arenas for social and economic life' (Robinson 2006: 1). All cities are historically and geographically contingent. All have been reconfigured by global capitalism but are at the same time the sites where its alternatives are hatched. And ultimately all are in some way adversely affected by labelling processes, whether as the result of being confined to a lower tier in urban hierarchies or through the exclusion of nonconforming experiences within a city from dominant definitions of place. Indeed, it is not just a matter of refuting the modern-traditional or innovative-imitative axes upon which cities are typically measured, or of bearing in mind the 'cosmopolitan' ways in which the notion of urban modernity is assembled and deployed (ibid.: 65–92), but of comprehending how evaluative grids are projected upon urban populations *from the inside*.

As this book will show, Naples is comprised by an overlapping web of imaginary and real urbanisms that respond to divergent and often incompatible needs and desires. Fathoming how and why these are differentiated and the circumstances in which they interconnect tells us far more about the nature of urban change than reconceiving the city on a new epistemological map of the Italian South. For as far as it seeks to account for complexity, this map tends to frame difference according to ideal criteria and to remove its constitutive element of conflict. A nonethnocentric analysis of a public realm that has been excessively celebrated and denigrated by outsiders over history does not, by extension, mean we should endorse local value judgements as the rightful expressions of a particular urban cultural system but rather charges us with the responsibility of acknowledging and disentangling the power relations and internal ethnocentrisms that underpin definitions about the city. As Chakrabarty concludes, this challenge also inevitably compels us as academics, commentators or simple onlookers to reconsider our own notions and presumptions about urban life.

From the Dark Ages to the Renaissance

The history of modern Naples is often read as unfolding in a near permanent state of crisis, interspersed with a few positive episodes (studies typically cite the Saredo Report which led to the 1904 law on the industrial development of Naples and the establishment of the steelworks in the western suburb of Bagnoli (Becchi 1984)) and numerous lows, of which the building speculation and unchecked expansion of the city after the Second World War particularly stands out (Allum 2003). During the 1980s and early 1990s, Naples was seen to have reached its nadir and for many in Italy and abroad the city became a synonym for urban decay. The 1980 earthquake had badly damaged the historic centre and severely disrupted the fragile informal economy upon which thousands of people depended, and the flow of reconstruction funds into the region had fed extensive corruption in the public administration and collusion between politicians, entrepreneurs and organized crime. Throughout the period, the latter – the Camorra – also waged a bloody, internecine war for the control of the drug trade, as Naples became a hub of heroin distribution in Europe as well as a major market for its consumption. Meanwhile, essential public services, from hospitals and schools to clean tap water, were either deficient, on the verge of collapse or simply nonexistent. To top it all – and to corroborate stereotypical images of its chaotic traffic – Naples possessed some of the worst noise and atmospheric pollution in Western Europe.

In his 1992 bestselling book on southern Italy, entitled peremptorily (and notwithstanding the new ideas about the Mezzogiorno) *L'Inferno*, the popular Piedmontese journalist Giorgio Bocca recounts a Naples on its knees 'resigned to the indisputable dominion of the new historic block between a political and business bourgeoisie and the Camorra' (Bocca 1992: 211), where an embattled cultural elite are presented as the last heroic line of defence to the supremacy of an unscrupulous and plebeian mindset. Bocca tours the city meeting, among others, two journalists in their small office at the heart of the Camorra-controlled Forcella neighbourhood who produce a shoestring-budgeted magazine spotlighting local political intrigues and the lawyer Gerardo Marotta, who keeps alive

the memory of the city's failed bourgeois revolution of 1799 by organizing philosophy seminars with the likes of Hans-Georg Gadamer and Karl
Popper. In another vignette, Sergio Piro, a key figurehead in the radical
psychiatry movement in Italy, is depicted gazing down at traffic from his
smart fourth-storey apartment close to the Castel dell'Ovo. He expresses
relief that a semblance of reason and solidarity still exists amidst all the
chaos:

> If an elderly person were to find themselves in the middle of the street, so frightened and
> dazed that they don't know which way to turn, the driver of the big, clapped-out public
> bus will stop and follow them at a crawl without honking the horn or hurrying them
> along, as if this person were a domesticated elephant. Respect for the weak somehow
> remains. (Bocca 1992: 198–99)

A different portrait of the era by an outsider is provided by Thomas
Belmonte, author of *The Broken Fountain* (1989), a beautiful and biting
ethnography of the urban poor in the historic centre of the city where
Belmonte had lived for a year between 1974 and 1975. On his return to
Naples almost a decade later, the American anthropologist is reunited
with the family at the centre of his original study.[4] Most noticeably, the
children had grown up: Gennaro, the eldest son had turned to religion and
exorcism; Ciro had recently been jailed as a 'soldier' for the Camorra;
Pepe had become a heroin addict; Pasquale had left for Germany to look
for work; Nina was still living in the hotel room that had been assigned to
the family after the earthquake; while Robertino, a toddler back in 1974,
had taken up boxing. The daily strains of poverty replace Bocca's sweeping canvas of moral and political decadence, and although Belmonte de-
tects a deteriorated situation compared to the city he had got to know in
the 1970s, he nevertheless noted an underlying resistance:

> Not only were former *picaros* and purse-snatchers armed now and sporadically afflu-
> ent, but organized crime had moved in to fill the political and entrepreneurial void that
> had been created by the failure of civic institutions. The family, however, appeared to
> be holding its own. The petty criminals and coke-dealers at Fontana del Re tended to be
> responsible husbands and fathers, perhaps because of the enormous sacrifices that their
> wives were willing to make during their prison terms. (Belmonte 1989: xxv–xxvi)

Belmonte's informants inhabited the same city that Bocca's enlightened minority longed to reform. As Belmonte struggled to understand
the Weltanschauung of an 'underclass', he refrained from references to
a netherworld. That Naples faced a host of severe problems during the
1980s was undeniable, but its *descent into hell* appeared anchored to a
particular morally inflected view of the world.

---

4. Belmonte's return to Naples is recounted in a new introduction and epilogue in the book's second
edition.

During the course of the 1990s, conditions in Naples appeared to significantly improve. Following systematic change in local politics and electoral reform in 1993 which introduced the direct election of the mayor, the city's new administration, headed by the former Communist Antonio Bassolino, embarked on a comprehensive programme of urban renewal. One of the administration's priorities was to harness the city's cultural and architectural heritage, building on independent initiatives that had occurred during the preceding years. Historical monuments were restored, piazzas and streets were repaved and closed to traffic, and a plethora of open-air events were organized to draw people back to what were considered neglected public spaces. This strategy aimed to overturn the negative reputation of Naples and, by attracting tourism and inward investment, lay the foundations for economic growth. In the space of a few years, a city that had been persistently portrayed in a state of interminable decline had come to nationally represent a laboratory of what in other geographic contexts was commonly dubbed 'urban regeneration'. Locally, the term 'Neapolitan Renaissance' was proffered, mainly by the media, which appeared to fit with the idea of the '*anni bui*' (dark years) of the previous decade. Although this label would often be disparaged as a slogan and disowned by the administration itself, the idea of a resurgent and rediscovered Naples was generally embraced, perhaps with soberer and less historically onerous terms such as '*riqualificazione*' (upgrading), '*recupero*' (reclamation) and '*risanamento*', a medical-sounding word deriving etymologically from the verb 'to heal', which in the past had been associated with redevelopment schemes in the old city. The extent and manner of change was open to fierce debate, but during the 1990s there was broad consensus that the city was moving in a different direction.

The idea of a 'new Naples' was closely bound with the figure of the city's mayor, Antonio Bassolino. Among a number of left-wing mayors elected in Italian cities at the end of 1993, Bassolino was seen to personify more than anyone else a new political-administrative season that emerged in the wake of *Mani Pulite* ('Clean Hands'), the anti-corruption trials that erupted in early 1992 and which wiped out a large swathe of the nation's ruling political class. Unusual for a southern politician, Bassolino, who was born in 1947 in the town of Afragola, ten miles to the north of Naples, did not possess a university degree. Instead, after joining the youth organization of the Italian Communist Party (PCI) as a teenager and abandoning early on his studies in medicine, he quickly rose through the party's ranks: in 1970, at the age of twenty-three, he was elected a councillor in the Campania regional government; in 1972 he entered the PCI's Central Committee and in 1976 was made the party's regional secretary. Throughout his career Bassolino was associated with the PCI's internal left, which championed labour and social struggles over the pursuit of political alliances, although he remained in the Democratic Party of the Left (PDS) formed in the aftermath of the PCI's dissolution in 1991, unlike other left-wingers who founded the smaller breakaway Communist Refoundation Party (PRC).[5]

After having spent a decade in central office in Rome (and becoming a member of parliament in 1987), Bassolino returned to Naples in early 1993 to rebuild the local PDS, which had been shaken by *Mani Pulite,* before being selected in the autumn of the same year as the city's mayoral candidate for the 'Alliance of Progressives' composed of the PDS, PRC, Greens, The Network (an antimafia party) as well as a small, left-leaning formation that had split from the Italian Socialist Party (PSI). His candidature came as a surprise: he was relatively unknown outside political circles, while local intellectuals and cultural associations were initially hostile to someone they regarded as a professional party politician imposed from above. But from a dour, stuttering and chain-smoking functionary, Bassolino swiftly proved himself to be an intelligent and able orator, with a clear idea of the problems besetting Naples and a realistic agenda based around the reestablishment of democratic accountability and legality in everyday life, the publicly controlled redevelopment of former industrial areas as well as investment in the city's cultural heritage. The fact that his principal adversary in the mayoral race turned out to be Alessandra Mussolini, granddaughter of *Il Duce* and candidate for the neo-Fascist Italian Social Movement (MSI), ensured that the contest attracted international media attention as the ultimate ideological clash. Bassolino eventually won the runoff in early December 1993, polling a relatively comfortable 55.6 per cent, although the MSI returned as the largest party with over 31 per cent of the vote. By the time of the following local elections in November 1997, Bassolino had become one of the most popular politicians in Naples of all time[6] and was duly returned mayor with 73 per cent of the first round ballot, which that year was by far the highest victory margin among Italy's main cities. Moreover, the PDS became the first party in all of the city's 29 administrative quarters, increasing its total vote in the space of four years from 19.8 to 33.4 per cent. For a period, Naples usurped Bologna as Italy's progressive citadel, the mayor was hailed as a future national leader of the Left, while enthusiasm for the 'Bassolino phenomenon' (Petrusewisz, quoted in Dunford

---

5. At the PCI's final congress in January 1991 Bassolino had actually presented a compromise motion that sought to reconcile the party's divisions but was supported by only 5 per cent of delegates.

6. From a survey carried out in 1996 of a representative sample of 400 inhabitants, it emerged that 80 per cent of Neapolitans considered Bassolino 'the best or one of the best mayors that the city has ever had' (Savino 1998: 44).

and Greco 2006: 11) resounded across international academic circuits and urban policy networks alike.

The Communist Left had long possessed a complicated and tormented rapport with Naples. For the orthodox ideologue, it was a city that boasted a highly organized, albeit small, industrial labour force, but was otherwise constrained by contradictory class allegiances, an apparent lack of civil society and general political deviance. For the more astute activist, Naples also possessed alternative collective and insurgent inclinations that called for a more refined understanding of local society. Crucially, the transformations that took place in Naples during the 1990s coincided with major changes on the Italian parliamentary Left. From its inception, the PDS found itself caught between the legacy of the mass party with a deep-rooted political and moral identity and the leadership's urge to embrace liberal democracy and the market economy. It still possessed a solid industrial working-class base, but like elsewhere, this had shrunk and was increasingly overshadowed by a middle-class electorate. Furthermore, since the dissolution of the PCI in the wake of the prolonged political crisis of the 1980s (and not simply precipitated by the fall of Soviet Communism after 1989), the PDS had been grappling with a new set of ideological discourses, first and foremost, that of 'citizenship'. These shifting political agendas and repertoires would not only have consequences upon the sorts of policies implemented by the Bassolino administration but would, at a more general level, frame visions about an ideal, 'regenerated' city. In other words, a genealogical analysis of the new Naples must necessarily examine the reconfiguration of the relationship between the institutional Left and the city. A key argument running through this study is that underlying the widespread contemporary praise for the 'Bassolino phenomenon' was a somewhat ambivalent notion of progressive politics, one which (inevitably) spoke of inclusion but which constructed and presumed consensus around normative and socially exclusive images of the built environment. More generally, Naples provides a seminal site for analyzing the emergence of a new municipal Left in Italy and its accompanying system of values and categories. In fact, questions such as decorum and security that dominate local left- and right-wing agendas in Italy today already lay at the core of the Bassolino project.

Locating the new city

I can remember following the mayoral results of late 1993 on television in the kitchen of my flat in Bologna, where I had recently arrived as a placement student at the local university. As my first experience of an Italian election special, I found myself absorbed by the evening's denouements and was soon registering the names of the new mayors: the youthful Green Rutelli had beaten the bespectacled leader of the Neo-Fascists Fini in Rome; Sansa, a judge, had defeated the Northern League in Genoa; a hirsute philosopher by the name of Cacciari had won Venice; the coffee baron Illy had taken Trieste, while antimafia crusader and former Christian Democrat Orlando had already stormed the first round in Palermo. Television commentators declared it an unprecedented victory for the Left, at least since the mid-1970s when the PCI, at the pinnacle of its support, headed numerous city administrations. Together with the results of local elections held earlier in the year, every major city in Italy, apart from Milan and Bari, now had a left or centre-left mayor. A few days later, Silvio Berlusconi publicly announced his entry into national politics, and over the next decade most of the victors of those memorable 1993 elections would gravitate towards a hazy centre ground. Antonio Bassolino was the one figure who stood out. Unassuming but captivating at the same time, he came, I was told, from the 'workerist' tradition of the Communist Party and in the right habitat was known to still use the word '*compagno*' (comrade).

By the time I first arrived in Naples in October 1996, Bassolino had achieved near cult status. As a sign of reverence, artisans had sculpted him into a figurine for the traditional Neapolitan Christmas crib, while his thick provincial accent was frequently lampooned by local comedians. Above and beyond this personal acclaim, the city's revival had become a prominent subject of public and private conversation. Everyone, it seemed, had a firm, clear-cut opinion about what was happening. A common refrain was that the historic centre had finally emerged from decades of abandonment, and this had been accompanied by a renewed sense of civic pride. However, there appeared to be a discrepancy between such pronouncements and what was occurring on the city's streets. A day would not pass without some part of Naples being brought to a standstill by groups of people protesting for jobs or housing. Restored spaces and monuments, which had been inserted into new tourist trails, typically served more prosaic purposes. Church doors were converted by teams of children into goalposts while the bollards protecting the new pedestrianized zones became slalom posts for the ubiquitous Vespas. Many people I met insisted that Naples had fundamentally changed, but I had never come across such conspicuous contradictions in a city.

Meanwhile, politicians, media pundits and even some academics would often speak effortlessly about improving 'Naples' for 'Neapolitans' and rehabilitating 'local identity' as if these responded to a set of universally accepted, *positive* criteria. Such formulae served as the reassuringly neutral touchstones around which critical evaluations of more immediately pressing questions were made, for instance the practicality of closing a street to traffic or the delayed inauguration of a new park. And yet, of course, 'Naples', like any other place, had always been constituted by internal differences, and as such its appraisal in the 1990s can be regarded as simply another assault on the discursive battlefield. More significantly, the demographic composition of Naples, like every other city in Italy, had recently become increasingly diversified as a result of foreign immigration, but besides self-congratulatory paeans to a putative tradition of welcoming others, this fact was barely reflected in general descriptions of the city. I was thus deeply intrigued by the ways in which different people, particularly local politicians and the media, articulated ideas about urban change but also what these might mean in practical situations; in other words, how transformations in the built environment were experienced in the everyday and the extent to which these experiences concurred or deviated from the dominant representations of the city during the period.

The decision to concentrate my analysis on three public open spaces in the city's historic centre (from now on *centro storico*) grew out of these specific concerns. The *centro storico* was a fulcrum for urban renewal strategies and narratives during the two Bassolino administrations, while a number of its public spaces stood at the interface between discourse and practice, where ideas about Naples took shape and were challenged. Each selected space encapsulated a set of key themes. Piazza Plebiscito, the city's largest historical piazza and until the early 1990s a giant car park, was an immediate focus of attention. Following its pedestrianization in 1994, the piazza was widely considered the symbol of a new Naples and became a frequent venue for large public events. It offered a fascinating insight into the rescripting of the city's troubled relationship with motorized traffic and the subsequent process of creating a heritage space. At the same time, the piazza's newly acquired status enhanced its role as a scene of political protest, and its closure to vehicles led to unintended consequences (becoming, for instance, the *centro storico*'s most popular football pitch), which suggested a more complex, recalcitrant social domain to the rarefied place imagined in city promotional literature and tourist guidebooks.

Piazza Garibaldi, the second selected site, is the first place that many visitors (myself included) see when arriving in Naples. Situated in front of the main railway station, the piazza has been the economic and social arena for a significant section of Naples's immigrant population for over a quarter of a century.[7] During the 1990s, the Bassolino administration and local media sought to conceive the same space as the 'gateway' to the *centro storico*. But whereas Piazza Plebsicito was cast as the ideal image of urban renewal, Piazza Garibaldi was instead represented as its problematic opposite, and attempts to reshape the space came to be framed by security concerns and exclusive definitions of the public realm. The piazza was thus chosen for study in this book to explore the different relationships between immigrant groups and urban space and to examine how and why their presence became a source of conflict.

The third site is DAMM (Diego Armando Maradona Montesanto), a *centro sociale* (social centre) located next to a small park built after the 1980 earthquake in the popular neighbourhood of Montesanto. As self-managed social, cultural and political spaces based in and around squatted properties and offshoots of the radical urban movements of the 1970s, *centri sociali* were particularly active in Italian cities during the 1990s. In contrast to other examples in Naples, DAMM's occupation sought to involve local residents in creating a multipurpose public place. The site was also chosen for this study in order to analyze political and media representations of the *centro storico*'s popular quarters, traditionally seen as the 'anomalous' localities of the city, and to examine how such images were contested by DAMM through its reuse and redefinition of urban space.

This book, therefore, makes no claim to be a definitive history of Naples during the Bassolino administrations. It does not, for instance, consider in depth the proposed redevelopment of former industrial sites such as the Bagnoli steelworks or the planning instruments that were established during the period. But by shrinking the arena of investigation, it is able to adopt a more ambitious conceptual and methodological understanding of the city and to pay greater attention to the messiness of detail normally lost in global accounts. Naples, of course, does not coincide with its *centro storico* nor does it stop at its administrative boundaries; indeed some would argue that the city is better understood as an 'unending, amorphous sprawl' that stretches from the provincial capitals of Caserta in the north to Salerno in the east (Pace 2004: 19). Neither, as Doreen Massey would argue, can the *place* of Naples be conceived

---

7. I choose to use the terms immigration/immigrant rather than migration/migrant aware of the problematic nature of both sets of categories. While migration captures the cultural, social, economic as well as the more positive libertarian-utopian aspects of transnational movement, immigration underlines political and legal limits in which this movement takes place as well as its categorization in public discourse – and is therefore more appropriate in the context of this study. Certainly, immigration implies a unidirectional experience, while it is often the case that the (im)migrant will often make (or hope to make) onward or homeward journeys.

simply as the sum of its internal component parts, for it is also the product of human, capital and information flows that make it interdependent with *other places* (Massey 2007). This said, cities in Italy are commonly perceived and portrayed in terms of a 'centre' and a 'periphery', whereby the former is an unequivocal, reconciled and privileged site, and the latter is typically boundless, abandoned and possesses all the 'real' problems, such as poverty and social exclusion. Regardless of whether it captures some element of reality, this powerful-yet-contrived dichotomy inevitably reifies the spatial relations that are continually produced and contended within cities (Lefebvre 1991). In fact, the *centro storico* in Naples (which in any case had its own fair share of poverty and social exclusion) was not the undisputed arbiter of a dominant identity but a battleground of competing claims and interests.

The focus on individual public spaces purposely aims at subverting smooth narratives about the 'centre'. Each of the three micro-studies adopts a two-pronged approach. First, in-depth histories of place will provide a sort of *longue durée* of the relationship between public space and urban representations, excavating the buried layers of significance that have been forgotten or deemed irrelevant with the passing of time and bringing to the fore breaks and continuities that occurred during the 1990s. Second, a synchronic analysis of the meanings and uses of each space during the Bassolino era, contrasting value-laden public debates with the dispassionate commentaries of everyday users, will form the basis of a critique of urban renewal. Each study can hence be read as the intimate biography of a small segment of Naples, replete with curious disclosures and the disentanglement of contradictory threads. The ultimate goal, however, is to move beyond a nonessentialist reading of place in order to understand how conflicts *in* and *over* space were themselves a fundamental element of urban change that ultimately played a part in the production of the new Naples.

Deciphering the new city: methods and structure

This book adopts a multi-method approach to studying the city and draws upon empirical and theoretical insights from across a range of disciplines, including geography, planning, political and social history, anthropology, and cultural studies. There exists a copious academic literature in Italian on the myriad changes that occurred in Naples during the 1990s in terms of urban policy and planning (Allum 2003; Palestino 2003; Corona 2007; Belli 2007), the political-administrative apparatus (Cappelli 1998; Brancaccio 2000; Cappelli 2003a) and elites and their networks (Amaturo

2003; Savonardo 2003). Such developments have also attracted interest from foreign-based researchers over the last decade (Pasotti 2004; Bull 2005). But while general accounts have been penned about the changing face of the city (e.g. Lepore and Ceci 1997; F. Amato 2006), there have been very few detailed analyses of the social impact of urban renewal strategies in the *centro storico* (although see Rossi 2004b).

Besides engaging with the local literature, this study takes a close interest in the role of language in the making of the new Naples. This interest arose partially in reaction to a distinct lack of concern on the part of local scholars to ponder upon the discursive foundations of urban renewal, such as 'civic pride' and 'historic identity' (although for a brief review of the euphemistic jargon in urban policy, see Lepore and Ceci 1997: 100–102). On the contrary, many assessments of the 1990s have been framed around the assumed views of an imaginary (Neapolitan) public or the opinions of the authors themselves (see, for instance, P. Amato et al. 2006). In the spirit of Raymond Williams (1983), I reflect upon the genealogies of key ideas such as '*centro storico*' and '*cittadinanza*' (citizenship), in order to explore how certain familiar terms acquired new connotations in the 1990s and why these were often a source of fierce contention.

The study also draws on critical work about urban space and place. Following the so-called 'spatial turn' in Anglophonic human geography and social sciences more generally (Soja 1989), largely through the popularization of French Marxist and post-structuralist theorists such as Henri Lefebvre and Michel Foucault but also via a rereading of classic urban thinkers such as Georg Simmel, space has no longer been perceived as an abstract container (and place as simply its subjective adjunct) but a dynamic, constituent element of social life and a key sphere for exploring power relations and material and symbolic boundaries in societies (see, for example, Sibley 1995). A lot of the empirical and theoretical work, especially in the field of geography, has been characterized by a heavy Anglo-American bias, and, despite taken-for-granted claims to a universal understanding of spatial relations, will need to be rescaled and treated with due care in relation to Naples (Berg 2004). Moreover, the assertion made by Donald Moore over a decade ago that geography tended to be 'ethnographically thin, resulting in impoverished representations of the cultural meanings of spatial practices' (Moore 1998: 347) in the main still holds true, at least in the case of Italy.

The sociocultural dimensions of urban space and place have likewise become established concerns within anthropology. Key monographs include Michael Herzfeld's classic study of contested experiences of historic conservation in a Cretan town (Herzfeld 1991) and Setha Low's fascinating work on two central plazas in San José, Costa Rica (Low

2000).[8] Such questions have been less of a focus of inquiry in Naples, where the field site has often been conceived as little more than the ready-made stage set for observing the lives of local people. Important exceptions are the research by Amalia Signorelli (1996) and Angela Giglia (1997), who both explore the interface between planned and lived space in the neighbouring port city of Pozzuoli and whose work will be discussed in Chapter 4.

Since its origins in the 1970s, anthropological research in Naples has considered a range of questions, such as popular religion (Provitera, Ranisio and Giliberti 1978; Niola 2003), family and poverty (Belmonte 1989), gender and outwork (Goddard 1996), morality and entrepreneurship (Pardo 1996), as well as literary representations of the city (De Matteis 1991; Ranisio 2003). Over and above the theoretical and interpretative differences, this body of work has together made a significant contribution to comprehending social and symbolic systems in Naples and, ergo, to redressing popular and scientific commonplaces about local society. However, at the risk of generalization and without wanting to diminish its salience for this book, I also think that the anthropological literature on Naples presents some methodological limitations for an analysis of urban change.

First, the idea of Naples as a 'city' is frequently an ambivalent one and rarely at the centre of theoretical reflection. Its distinguishing characteristics as a Mediterranean metropolis are invariably underlined, but connections and cross-references are more likely to be drawn on the basis of the specific subject matter or to rural and small urban settlements in the Italian South, than to large cities elsewhere in Italy and abroad or to the urban literature of other disciplines. Moreover, research has prevalently concentrated on the city's *centro storico* and not on its postwar residential suburbs or industrial districts. As the former has often been deemed to be disconnected in some way from the dominant, assimilating trajectory of urban modernity, it has provided the anthropologist with the opportunity to holistically represent a particular aspect of everyday life that is less likely to be discernible in other European cities. The prior task, therefore, is to oust the *centro storico* of Naples from anthropology's pantheon of privileged field sites and to revisit it as one part of an *ordinary* city.

Second, until the 1990s, studies focused almost exclusively on the lower classes of the *centro storico,* or at least those seen to share the same values and cultural practices. Certainly, this section of the population had been misunderstood and negatively represented by social science, but the

---

8. For a fine collection of anthropological studies of place and space, see Low and Lawrence-Zúñiga 2003.

near total disregard for other social groups and city users would appear to suggest that these did not require investigation or were simply not anthropologically interesting. More recently, the situation has changed, with, for instance, growing ethnographic research on new immigrants in the city (Harney 2006, 2007; Nare 2009; Pardo 2009). What remains missing, however, is a serious reflection on the interactions and conflicts between different social groups and how these shape meanings about the built environment. A case in point is the emotive issue of cultural heritage. As Berardino Palumbo has pointed out, very few ethnographic accounts in Italy have sought to unpack the links between power, ideology and heritage (Palumbo 2003: 38–40), while in Naples itself, scant attention has been paid to the correlation between people's disparate notions of monumentality and their affective attachments to place and whether or not these percolate into bureaucratic homilies about conservation and tradition.[9]

Lastly, much of the pioneering anthropological work on Naples was characterized by a superficial treatment of historical change, partly due to the city's perceived isolation from the macro-processes of capitalism. Belmonte's study of poverty in the mid-1970s, for example, coincided with a national upsurge in political activism that also involved many inhabitants of the *centro storico* in Naples, yet none of this gets a mention in his original write-up and is little more than a passing detail in the book's second expanded edition.[10] While greater heed has since been paid to the intricacies of local history, there is still a sense that the principal endeavour is to identify endemic and enduring reasons for social and cultural behaviour rather than to grasp the shifting, multiscalar and less immediately tangible layers of context in which fieldwork and subjects are embedded. The challenge, as Marcus and Fischer have argued 'is not to do away with the synchronic ethnographic frame, but to exploit fully the historical within it' (1999: 96). The fact that there are no major eth-

---

9. Various anthropologists have deliberated upon the reuse and resignification of historical monuments in Naples, especially during exceptional moments such as football-related street festivities (Signorelli 1996: 182–84; Massa 2002), but this has not been, to my knowledge, a focus of theoretical or empirical research. Michael Herzfeld has reflected at length on the concept of monumentality, and this is one of a number of issues explored in his ethnography of urban restructuring in the Monti neighbourhood in central Rome (Herzfeld 2006, 2009).

10. Of course, as I have shown above, this does not mean that as a temporally and spatially traceable portrait of poverty, *The Broken Fountain* cannot also be read as a historical text. Italo Pardo, in contrast, conducts a diachronic study of the political motivations and choices of 'ordinary' Neapolitans between the 1970s and early 1990s (Pardo 1993). However, while seeking to illuminate how (two) people's views of the Left in Naples changed over this period, he simultaneously reifies the PCI's class-based ideology as monolithic, immutable and alien. The representation of time in anthropological discourse is instead an established theme in North American disciplinary debates. See, for example, Fabian 1983; Cohn 1987; Marcus and Fischer 1999.

nographies conducted either *in* or *on* the Bassolino era is especially surprising given that this period saw fundamental anthropological concepts like 'culture' and 'identity' enter forcibly into public lexicons about the city. Indeed, it is my firm belief that the sorts of probing questions posed by anthropologists in Naples can and need to be historically recontextualized so as to elicit a richer understanding of the processes that were taking place in the 1990s. In other words, the premise of an 'interdisciplinary' approach is not about synthesizing various fragments of theory and analysis to attain a more complete picture, but about honing them together into an incisive critique.

The bulk of my empirical data for the three micro-studies was collected over a three-year period after I returned to Naples in autumn 1998. This research sought to integrate two spheres that tend to be separated in studies of public space: the 'official' realm of physical alterations and historically significant episodes that are potentially seen to disclose important clues about the city at large and the 'vernacular' world of unpredictable, everyday human experience that, while offering insights into local forms of public culture or the affordances of urban design, is otherwise considered irrelevant to the greater scheme of things. In order to analyze these two dimensions and the interconnections that existed between them, different methodological strategies were adopted.

First, each micro-study examined a range of visual and textual sources, including city and district council documents, urban plans, photographic images and secondary material such as architectural monographs. Extensive use was made of the postwar press collections in the city's two newspaper libraries. Newspapers were used not simply to sift information about daily events or to collect the sound bites of politicians, but to explore representations of the three spaces before and after the election of Bassolino and to examine the forging of public narratives about Naples during the course of the 1990s. I specifically chose to concentrate on the local mainstream press: *Il Mattino,* the city's principal broadsheet; the Naples edition of *La Repubblica*; and *Corriere del Mezzogiorno,* the Neapolitan insert of *Corriere della Sera* (although this was not launched until June 1997).[11] This selection was not only made for practical reasons (media analysis is exceedingly time consuming) but because these newspapers were most concerned with charting the transformation of the *centro storico.* They played an instrumental role in elaborating and transmitting

---

11. *Il Mattino,* founded in 1892, had a regional circulation of 166,000 in 1992 (Lumley 1996). The centrist Milan-based *Corriere della Sera* and left-leaning Rome-based *La Repubblica* have long been Italy's main dailies. The former had a national distribution of 900,000 in 1994, the latter 699,000 in 1990 (ibid.). Both local editions regularly published opinion pieces by Neapolitan intellectuals and academics.

ideas about the city and, although generally supportive of the Bassolino administration, were the main forums for often heated debates.[12]

Second, ethnographic fieldwork was conducted in each of the three spaces in order to develop an understanding of the diverse and dynamic relationships between people and urban space. During this period (as well as my subsequent three-year 'overstay') I lived in the Montesanto neighbourhood, which meant that each site was easily reachable on foot or, more often in the case of Piazza Garibaldi, by public transport. The fieldwork consisted in extended periods of participant observation (which included involvement in a series of place-specific activities, from organized events in Piazza Plebiscito and weekly self-management meetings at DAMM to sitting in on council negotiations for the establishment of a 'multi-ethnic' market next to Piazza Garibaldi), as well as semi-structured interviews with a range of users. In each case, the approach necessarily responded to local circumstances and is therefore discussed at greater length in the relevant chapter. My intention from the start was not to arrive at a definitive account of the three sites or to provide the final word on the experience of public space in central Naples, but to confront people's multiple meanings and uses of urban space with political and media representations of the *centro storico*. This also meant drawing out inconsistencies within the interview and observation data themselves. The challenge of writing ethnography from the 'partial truths' (Clifford 1986) offered by the field is not just about being alert to the incomplete and at times impenetrable nature of public space or, more generally, to the narrative devices that scholars use to construct a meaningful text. Rather, it is integral to this book's overall objective of scrutinizing the seamless, coherent recitals about urban change in Naples during the 1990s.

The book is structured in four parts, each of which is divided into separate chapters. Part 1 sets out the historical and theoretical framework and introduces keywords. Chapter 1 unpicks the concept of the *centro storico* and examines its evolution and place in urban renewal schemes in Naples following Italian Unification. Chapter 2 critically discusses some of the pivotal themes surrounding urban regeneration in Western European cities and asks whether these accurately reflect the experiences in Naples during the 1990s. It is argued that if the idea of 'regeneration'

---

12. A focus on the (less-read) right-wing press such as *Il Giornale di Napoli* or minor publications such as *La Verità* would have offered a different slant. However, the former usually snubbed or ignored the administration's initiatives in the *centro storico*, while the latter were more concerned with news about crime and local celebrities rather than urban-related issues. As such, they proved less useful for examining debates about urban renewal. Nevertheless, these and nonlocal dailies such as *Corriere della Sera* and *Il Manifesto* were consulted in the case of particularly controversial matters or where events received national coverage.

is contextualized, it can be useful to account for the official urban strategies and discourses that emerged in the period. Chapter 3 examines the political design of the Left that underpinned regeneration and, in particular, the importance attributed to a reinvigorated sense of citizenship. It starts by interrogating the recurrent idea of Naples as a civically deficient, 'anti-modern' city, before exploring the historically problematic relationship between the Communist Party and Naples, and ends by analyzing Bassolino's formulation of a new vision of municipal politics in the 1990s. Chapter 4 focuses on the question of public space. Reviewing late twentieth-century debates from North America and Europe, it contemplates arguments about the decline and revival of the public realm and what these might mean in the case of Naples. It proceeds to build a working theory of 'contested space' that can also serve the empirical analysis and finally discusses the piazza as an emblematic urban form and metonym for public space and how Naples fits into this prevalently northern-central Italian model.

Part 2 presents the study of Piazza Plebiscito.[13] Chapter 6 investigates the history of the piazza, from its status as the physical and symbolic heart of royal power to its use as a massive car park. Chapter 7 charts the metamorphosis of the car-free piazza into a synecdoche for a culturally rehabilitated *centro storico*. It traces the attempts to prescribe the space with a set of functions and connotations and reflects upon two key moments when these were challenged. Chapter 8 makes use of systematic observation to unearth the everyday piazza unrepresented in media and political discussions and, through selected interviews, it analyzes different situated experiences of the space and how these force a rethinking of the high-minded assumptions that underlay the piazza's transformation.

Part 3 investigates how the Left's ambitions for Naples were translated in the socially complex space of Piazza Garibaldi. In a similar way to the study of Piazza Plebiscito, chapter 11 explores the history of Piazza Garibaldi and its immediate surrounding area, from the development of the railway station after the Unification of Italy to the piazza's ambivalent identity following its modernization in the 1960s. Chapter 12 analyzes how the politics of tourism, security and immigration during the 1990s shifted the piazza's significance, before looking at public debates and disputes over its design, management and control. Chapter 13 examines immigrant experiences of the piazza, drawing on observation, interviews and guided visits to the area with documented and undocumented immi-

---

13. Note that parts 2, 3 and 4 are each accompanied by brief introductory and concluding chapters that are also numbered but are not discussed here, hence the non-consecutive sequence of numbered chapters in this following section.

grants and considers how these illuminated and contested ethnocentric definitions about public space in Naples.

Part 4 on DAMM is set out slightly differently to the other two micro-studies. Chapter 16 analyzes the place of the central 'popular' quarters in ideas about the city during the late twentieth century, reflecting in partic-ular on the PCI's political rapport with their inhabitants, before looking at how their position changed under the Bassolino administration. While the question of 'popular' Naples will be introduced in Part 1, the decision to concentrate most of the analysis here is precisely to avoid the all-too-common error of treating 'popular neighbourhood' and '*centro storico*' as interchangeable concepts. The last section of the chapter reconstructs a history of the small residential area in the Montesanto neighbourhood that was demolished after the 1980 earthquake and rebuilt as a series of paved and green spaces, and which from 1995 was partly self-managed by DAMM. Chapter 17 provides a historical overview of the *centri sociali* in Italy, before examining the occupation of DAMM and the attempts by activists to create a public space that offered an alternative to the domi-nant trajectory of urban change in the *centro storico*.

A final, concluding chapter draws together the key arguments from the three sites and reflects upon the implications of integrating a more com-plex and provocative understanding of public space and urban change into the history of Naples. It also interrogates the legacy of the Bassolino era and the Left's agenda of creating a 'good city' (Amin 2006).

Rubbishing the Renaissance: new narratives of decline

A large part of this research was originally presented in a Ph.D. thesis in Autumn 2001 (Dines 2001), a few months after Rosa Russo Iervolino, a former Christian Democrat and member of the Olive Tree centre-left alliance, became the first female mayor of Naples. Iervolino was able to benefit from the solid support that the administration had built over the previous eight years, although she would assume a lower profile approach to running the city than her predecessor. Antonio Bassolino, meanwhile, had resigned as mayor in 2000 (to be briefly replaced by vice-mayor Ric-cardo Marone), in order to stand for president of the Campania regional government, an election he duly won with 54.4 per cent of the vote, albeit with the crucial support of the old Christian Democrat fiefdoms in the provinces of Benevento and Avellino. As capital of the region, Naples effectively remained his seat of power, and in fact the former mayor con-tinued to play a prominent role in local affairs, from overseeing the ex-pansion of the metro system to promoting public art commissions. At the end of 2003, the Italian media commemorated the tenth anniversary of the Left's victory in Naples. Despite mounting criticism over unsolved structural problems and the personalization of politics, the general consensus was that the last ten years had changed Naples for good.

Shortly afterwards, however, the city's fortunes took a decisive turn for the worse. Having taken a backseat in urban representations during the 1990s, the eruption in late 2004 of a bloody war between the Di Lauro clan and a breakaway faction in the northern suburbs of Naples hurled the Camorra back into the national and international limelight.[14] The spate of killings would be the centrepiece of Roberto Saviano's international bestseller *Gomorra,* a powerful depiction of the criminal system in Campania that mixed journalistic reportage and judicial archive material with semi-fictionalized memoirs (Saviano 2006). As a result of the book's rapid nationwide success and the author's reckless courage in denouncing the names of bosses in public, Saviano received a series of death threats and was subsequently placed under permanent police protection. Meanwhile, a long-running refuse crisis in the region culminated in late 2007, with piles of uncollected rubbish lining the streets of Naples and people protesting against the (re)opening of landfills. At the root of the crisis was the failure of the regional government to implement a sustainable waste management system, and the cost-cutting practices of contracted firms that had led to the proliferation of untreated (and thus unrecyclable) domestic refuse and which opened the door to organized crime. As special commissioner for rubbish between 2000 and 2004, Bassolino was among those held responsible for the fiasco, and on 28 February 2008 was charged, along with twenty-seven others, of abuse of office.[15]

Images of festering garbage and bullet-peppered corpses circumnavigated the globe. During the preparation of the manuscript for this book, Naples had returned to being portrayed as the aberrant city of old, while the popularity of Bassolino, the former darling of the Italian Left, had nosedived. In October 2008, Matteo Garrone's film adaptation of *Gomorra* was released in the United Kingdom. The titles of the British

---

14. Although organized crime rarely impinged on discussions about urban renewal in the *centro storico* during the Bassolino administrations, it controlled a large part of the city's informal and illegal economies, and while most murders were confined to the city's outskirts or beyond, during the late 1990s there were still armed conflicts in central neighbourhoods such as Sanità, Forcella and the Spanish Quarters (Barbagallo 1999; Gribaudi 1999).

15. Among the eight charges, Bassolino was accused of signing a modified contract for the region's refuse management that effectively allowed the winning tenderer to avoid separating household waste, which led to the saturation of existing landfills and millions of bales of untreated rubbish being piled up on agricultural land. For in-depth analyses of the refuse crisis, see Gribaudi 2008; Iacuelli 2008; Rabitti 2008.

trailer were unambiguous: 'Imagine a city built by crime. Imagine its people ruled by fear. Imagine a system poisoned by corruption. Naples, Italy 2008.'[16] Naples was once again beguiling to an international audience as an urban outcast, in this case as a real place that indulged a global predilection for mob movies. It reconfirmed the limits of a 'normal' Europe, as Garrone himself intimated in an interview with a British newspaper: 'I'm from Rome – just two hours from Naples – but I didn't expect to find a place at war in 2008' (Film Weekly Podcast, *The Guardian,* 8 October 2008). Over and above the important public impact of both the book and the film and their best intentions (including the former's insistence upon the Camorra's symbiotic relationship with a deregulated globalized economy), there lies a real danger that the city and its problems come to be filtered exclusively through a criminal lens. Anything out of the ordinary or formally illegal is hastily explained away as 'Camorra'. Moreover, where it becomes unhinged from its contingent complexity and turned into an ontological key or a moral dictum, 'Camorra' risks numbing critical reasoning altogether and with it the possibility of a deeper analysis of the city. Nowhere was this more evident than in the national and international media coverage of the rubbish crisis, which often summarily pointed the blame at organized crime, conflated the illegal dumping of toxic waste with the breakdown of the refuse disposal system and overlooked administrative ineptness and the profiteering of big business. That the Camorra should also be used to affirm the otherworldliness of the crisis says much about how Naples is perceived in relation to the West. Indeed, it is interesting that the recurring garbage problem in New York, another city cinematically associated with the mafia, should instead compel onlookers to reflect whether such a situation might happen closer to home.[17]

Organized crime is not a direct focus of this book, although it frequently enters obliquely into discussion. In the current post-*Gomorra* era, this statement might sound like an apologia, and would probably not have been written had this study been published earlier. The question of the Camorra is neither avoided nor underestimated: it simply had little to do with the three spaces under analysis or the wider question of redefining Naples during the 1990s.[18] This perhaps says as much about the shifting

---

16. The British trailer can be viewed at www.youtube.com/watch?v=hky53gXyjX0, last accessed 1 September 2011.

17. A refuse crisis had in fact arisen following the closure in 2001 of Fresh Kills, the city's main dump on Staten Island. See O. Burkeman, 'A walk on the whiffy side', *The Guardian,* 22 March 2002.

18. I would therefore argue that Naples was markedly different from Palermo, where the contemporaneous process of urban renewal was symbolically and politically bound up with the (predominantly middle-class) antimafia struggle, even if some of the main dilemmas, such as the social and cultural

significance of the Camorra as a political and public discourse as it does about its actual presence in the city.

Most important, recent events have had a huge impact on discussions about the city's not-too-distant past. The optimism of the 1990s appears a distant memory. The term 'Neapolitan Renaissance', already used somewhat sceptically at the time, has been ridiculed across the political spectrum, especially by the Right, which was extremely weak and near absent from public debates about the city during the previous decade, but also by the Left and among former sympathetic commentators. Giorgio Bocca once again sparked controversy with a new damning account of a moribund Naples, victim of yet another failed revolution and en route back to hell (Bocca 2006). The eagerness of the media to disparage the rhetoric of the past has paradoxically (but not surprisingly) introduced new ideological axioms about the transformation of the city. There has been next to no historiographical reflection about how Naples was debated during the 1990s, little connection with the wider political processes that were taking place and no interest in the complex interplay of different subjective encounters with the city. Within this recent climate, which I will have a chance to return to in the final chapter, a critical ethnographic history of Naples during the two Bassolino administrations – one that deciphers representations of place, examines the urban vision of the post-Communist Left and seeks to understand grounded experiences in the *centro storico* and how these reshaped urban space – is all the more timely. As such, even though it was born out of the particular field of Italian studies, this book also aspires to contribute to a more general meta-methodological critique of how we *write* about the contemporary city.

---

consequences of historic conservation for the *centro storico*'s poorer inhabitants, were quite similar. On the mafia and antimafia in Palermo, see Schneider and Schneider 2003, especially the chapter 'Recuperating the Built Environment' (pages 235–59).

Part 1

Urban Change in an *Ordinary* City

Naples during the 1990s

Chapter 1

The *Centro Storico*
History of a Concept and Place

Beyond the commonplace of the *centro storico*

Like the North American 'downtown' area with its skyscrapers towering over low-rise sprawl or the English 'town centre' with its motley mix of Victorian brick, reinforced concrete and postmodern bric-a-brac, the *centro storico* is often a taken-for-granted feature of the Italian city. For many people it evokes instant images of ancient churches, palaces, piazzas and cobbled streets. Yet, in actual fact, '*centro storico*' is a relatively recent term. Its first systematic use can be traced to the 'Charter of Gubbio', a manifesto for the 'protection and renewal of *centri storici*', drawn up by a group of administrators, planners and environmental campaigners in September 1960 (Cervellati 1991; Dainotto 2003; Corona 2007).[1] The document highlighted contemporary concerns about the disruptive impact of the postwar building boom upon the preexisting fabric of Italian cities. It also mirrored a broader notion of urban heritage that had already been elaborated during the 1950s by cultural elites such as the conservation association Italia Nostra.[2] Heritage was no longer seen to be exclusively embodied in a few individual monuments but now encompassed an entire urban area corresponding to the city's limits at a certain historical point in time (Corona 2007). Among its various proposals, the Charter of Gubbio called for the formal demarcation of the *centro storico,* the classification of all historical buildings within it, a stop to the

---

1. The Charter of Gubbio can be viewed in Italian at: http://www.ancsa.org/it/files/ANCSA%20-%20STATUTO.pdf.

2. Italia Nostra (Our Italy) was founded in 1955 originally to oppose the proposed demolition of historic buildings in central Rome to make way for a new road system. Early members included Elena Croce, daughter of the Neapolitan liberal philosopher Benedetto Croce, the novelist Giorgio Bassani, and Antonio Cederna, author of the seminal text *I Vandali in Casa* (*The Vandals at Home*), first published in 1956, which denounced the destruction of Italy's urban and natural environment.

demolition of even the most modest edifices, and a guarantee that any restoration work would not affect the social composition of residents.

From the outset, the *centro storico* was not simply a descriptive label but relayed a particular idea about the city and its development. As well as simply protecting a city's architectural patrimony, its conservation was underpinned by an environmentalist logic. The restoration and reuse of existing buildings was considered a means to maintain social cohesion and stem the lava-like spread of concrete and asphalt over the surrounding landscape. The ideas that lay behind the *centro storico* resonated with Jane Jacobs's coeval polemic against the excesses of modern planning in American cities (Jacobs 1961), and in their own way, both the Charter of Gubbio and Jacobs's classic *The Death and Life of Great American Cities* can be considered forerunners, by some three to four decades, of debates about sustainable urban development. In the immediate term, however, the charter's idealistic demands seemed out of kilter with the pressures of modern life and the rampant economic growth of the early 1960s. As urban expansion continued unabated, the centres of many Italian cities were reshaped with the construction of office blocks and trunk roads, while some quarters were left to crumble as former residents moved out to new suburbs. Nevertheless, a few significant initiatives went against the tide and provided counter-narratives for an urban planning literature otherwise characterized by despair and pessimism (De Lucia 1989; Cederna 1991); none more so than the internationally acclaimed *centro storico* plan for Bologna, adopted by the PCI-led administration in the early 1970s, which restored and converted old buildings into social housing (Jäggi, Müller and Schmid 1977; De Lucia 1989).

At one level, urban conservationism in Italy pursued a clearly radical agenda. It sought to provide an antidote to urban sprawl and counter real estate speculation both inside and outside the old city (the Bologna plan had in fact proposed expropriating privately owned buildings but had to eventually opt for the less controversial method of buying up vacant property). It also insisted on safeguarding the demographic and economic makeup, as well as the physical fabric, of the *centri storici* and was at least alert to the risk of their 'museumification' (Cervellati 1991). Most of the key figures associated with this 'urban environmental' approach, including Pier Luigi Cervellati (author of the Bologna plan) and Vezio De Lucia (chief planner during the first Bassolino administration), were close to the Italian Communist Party, even if they were often in open dispute with the party's limp defence of the public ownership of land and its reticence to stand up to the interests of private construction firms (De Lucia 1989). At the same time, however, debates about the *centro storico* tended to be marked by a moral paternalism. First, they often betrayed a distaste for the modern city. The postwar periphery represented a sort of rootless 'anti-city' that encroached on the 'authentic' urban life of the *centro storico*.[3] Second, the idea of the *centro storico* itself was infused with essentialist discourses about 'historical identity' and 'civic memory' which, when not fixed in some golden era, were blind to questions of agency and conflict. What the past meant for different people and who had the power to define it were questions rarely posed by partisans of the *centro storico* lobby.[4]

The theme of the *centro storico* would in fact soon extend beyond the realm of specialists, enlightened administrations and cultural elites to become a grassroots issue. During the 1970s the *centro storico* was a key setting for collective struggles against, for instance, substandard housing and rising rents (Ramondino 1998; Corona 2007). Urban social movements in major Italian cities, including Naples, organized mass occupations of buildings and the self-reduction of utility bills and public transport tickets. They also opposed redevelopment schemes in city centres, not on the grounds of preserving heritage, but in order to resist evictions and, very often, to assert subaltern attachments to place (Belli 1986). Indeed, over the same period, the threat did not simply come from demolition and modernization, but also from restoration projects in traditionally poorer neighbourhoods (coupled with the purchase of property and termination of protected tenancies) set in action by urban elites increasingly attracted to the *centro storico* as a place to live and work (Fazio 1977).

The *centro storico* was therefore never just the product of a particular idea about the city, but it was a lived space that comprised diverse and, at times, discordant social, economic and cultural dimensions. This observation, however self-evident, is a crucial starting point for a more dynamic understanding of the *centro storico* that recognizes preconceived value judgements about its presumed attributes and cross-examines arguments both for and against its protection. Furthermore, any generalized account of the Italian *centro storico* runs the risk of forsaking geographical differences for a coherent narrative. While it is possible to identify common trends in their development during the postwar era, the *centri storici* in Italy actually vary greatly, not only in terms of their physical transformation, local economy and demographic composition, but also with regards to their reputations as places of 'historical identity'

---

3. For an incisive critique of public discourses about the urban periphery in Italy, see Foot 2001b: 135–55.

4. For instance, Gabriella Corona's otherwise excellent reconstruction of the intellectual history of urban environmentalism in Naples and Italy (Corona 2007) uses the term 'historical identity' without a hint of critical reflection.

and 'civic memory'. Thus, while the *centri storici* of Rome, Venice and Florence have experienced the impact of mass tourism and gentrification in former popular quarters, those of Naples and Palermo in the South – and to a certain extent, Genoa in the North – continue to possess a large lower-class residential population, as well as local artisan and informal economies, and have more recently seen the settlement of new immigrant communities. At the same time, each *centro storico* is itself marked by refractory and contradictory elements. As such, the frequent contention that its genesis merely represents the commodification of space or the inevitable ascendancy of the museum city (Dainotto 2003) is both theoretically vacuous and empirically unfounded, even when directed at Italy's principal tourist cities (as exemplified by the protracted altercation between residents and storekeepers in the *centro storico* of Florence regarding the latter's decision to board up their premises during the 2002 European Social Forum).

Vestiges of a swollen city: the *centro storico* of Naples

Naples possesses one of the largest *centri storici* in Europe. In 1500 the city already had a population of over 100,000 people. Under the Spanish viceroys, it enjoyed numerous fiscal privileges and became a pole of inward migration from the impoverished and oppressed countryside. By the eve of the 1656 plague, which wiped out more than half the city's inhabitants, the population of Naples stood at around 450,000, making it roughly the same size as Paris and second only to Istanbul in the Mediterranean.[5] During this period, the city's economy was unable to absorb the influx of people which instead swelled the ranks of an urban poor that survived by its wits and through a subsistence 'slum economy' (Allum 1973; Galasso 1978). Moreover, the city did not grow sufficiently in size to accommodate the rising population. As a result, every available space was converted into living quarters, from stables to caves in the tuff escarpments. Extra storeys were added above buildings to compensate for the lack of territorial expansion. These developments compounded a peculiar pattern of residential stratification whereby different social classes lived on top of each other: the populace at street level, the aris-

---

5. During the first half of the eighteenth century, following a few decades of stagnation, Naples once again experienced rapid demographic growth and by 1765 its population had reached pre-plague levels (De Seta 1981: 167). Naples remained one of Europe's major metropolises until the early nineteenth century and was Italy's largest city until the First World War, by which time it had a population of 670,000. According to the 1921 census, this had risen to almost 760,000, but the city had by now been surpassed by Milan and was only slightly more populous than Rome.

tocracy on the *piano nobile* (usually the first floor), and the professional and merchant classes on the upper floors. Present-day features such as narrow alleyways, ancient high-rise tenement blocks and ground-floor single-room dwellings (locally known as *bassi*) represent the physical legacy of this intense urbanization.

The layout of the *centro storico* of Naples, if not all of the city's buildings, today remains largely intact and, despite a fall in population after the Second World War, is still one of the most densely populated urban areas in Europe.[6] The *centro storico* comprises a rectangular ancient core (the *centro antico*) which conserves the street plan of the Greco-Roman settlement and is where many of the city's architectural monuments are situated. Surrounding the *centro antico* and climbing up the adjacent hills are a number of *quartieri popolari* (popular neighbourhoods) which developed between the sixteenth and eighteenth centuries. Perhaps the most (in)famous of these neighbourhoods are the Spanish Quarters, an extremely tight grid of blocks and alleyways punctured by a number of tiny piazzas that rise to the west of the city's principal commercial street, Via Toledo (popularly known by its former name, Via Roma). Originally designed in the mid-sixteenth century during the reign of the viceroys as a garrison for Spanish troops – hence the name – the area swiftly came to be associated with the urban poor, prostitution (both male and female) and, on occasions during the twentieth century but particularly during the 1980s, organized crime. To this day it is still considered the quintessence of 'low' or 'popular' Naples. Contrary to a tendency which conceives the various *quartieri popolari* and *centro antico* as a uniform entity, there are notable social and urban differences between areas and different relationships with the rest of the city.

Between the south-west corner of the *centro antico* and the sea lies the second monumental district of the *centro storico*. This area is characterized by a series of wide streets and large piazzas and comprises the city's major public and administrative buildings. These include the former Royal Palace, now a museum and national library; the Maschio Angioino, a castle

---

6. According to the 2001 census (Comune di Napoli 2007), the *centro storico* had a density of 13,525 inhabitants per square kilometre, which rose to over 30,000/km² in the most crowded central districts of San Lorenzo (34,701/km²) and Montecalvario (30,292/km²). The overall density for Naples (8,565/km²) was the highest among Italy's main cities and was followed by Milan (6,887/km²), Turin (6,643/km²) and Palermo (4,318/km²). Statistics for the *centro storico* are here based on the twelve districts containing the pre-twentieth century core of the city: San Ferdinando, Chiaia, San Giuseppe, Montecalvario, Avvocata, Stella, San Carlo all'Arena, San Lorenzo, Mercato, Pendino, Porto and Posillipo. These districts cover an area of 24.3 square kilometres and in 2001 had a total population of 328,511. The overall density is skewed downwards by the fact that five of the outer larger districts (Chiaia, Posillipo, Avvocata, Stella and San Carlo all'Arena) include swathes of twentieth-century housing, agricultural land and green spaces.

keep that houses a museum and the city council chambers; Palazzo San Giacomo, the city hall; Teatro San Carlo, the city's opera house; and the Galleria Umberto I, a late nineteenth-century shopping arcade. A few hundred metres along the coast is the Castel dell'Ovo, perched on a rock linked to the mainland by a short causeway, which is used for temporary exhibitions and, like the Palazzo Reale, as a venue for international conferences and political summits. Stretching west from the Castel dell'Ovo are the relatively airy and more salubrious middle- and upper-class quarters of Chiaia (which includes the city centre's principal park, Villa Comunale), Mergellina and Posillipo. Although a variety of fishing hamlets, religious buildings and villas had existed here since at least medieval times, these three areas did not fully urbanize and become an integrated part of the city until the eighteenth century (De Seta 1981). They are physically cut off from the rest of the *centro storico* by the Monte Echia promontory and Vomero Hill, and they are often considered distinct from the older core of the city.[7]

During the last 150 years, the *centro storico* has been torn between calls for conservation and demolition and has passed through alternating periods of neglect and attention. The incorporation of the South into the Italian state in 1861 had immense repercussions on the city whose principal economic base had been linked to its status as capital of the Kingdom of the Two Sicilies (Macry 1997). The city's overcrowded and filthy slums became a thorn in the side of the new state, and their renovation a common theme of national debate. In particular, two somatic terms came to be associated with attempts to modernize the city's ancient 'body': '*risanamento*' (which means 'building improvements' but also 'healing') and '*sventramento*' (which implies 'clearance' but literally means 'disembowelment'). The Risanamento, when written with a capital 'R', also specifically refers to the extensive building programme which followed the cholera epidemic of 1884. Special legislation was passed to fund slum clearances in the Mercato and Pendino districts near the port. In his masterly study, *Naples in the Time of Cholera,* Frank Snowden argues that this epidemic was the first national emergency for which the new nation-state could be held morally responsible, and thus the government's intervention 'carried the powerful subliminal message that Liberal Italy was at last fully committed to

---

7. For the sake of orientation, the rest of Naples can be roughly divided into the following areas: the middle-class residential districts, including Vomero and Arenella, which are located on the hills overlooking the *centro storico;* the western lower-middle-class neighbourhoods of Soccavo and Fuorigrotta; the former heavy industry district and seaside resort of Bagnoli, on the city's western edge; the eastern industrial and working-class suburbs of Ponticelli, Barra and San Giovanni a Teduccio; and, finally, the lower-income residential and social housing districts in the north and north-west of the city, including Scampia, Secondigliano and Pianura. Most of these outer suburbs were separate communes before they were incorporated into the administrative territory of Naples between 1925 and 1927, as part of Fascism's urbanization programme.

answering the grievances of the Mezzogiorno' (Snowden 1995: 363). The wide boulevards lined with sober buildings served to replace the uncomfortable images of urban blight with a vision of order and modernity. This Haussmann-inspired 'urban cleansing' programme, however, did little to alleviate the city's most pressing problems, namely the dire poverty and hazardous sanitary conditions. In her impassioned attack on the Risanamento's failings, *Il Ventre di Napoli* (*The Bowels of Naples*), published at the turn of the twentieth century, the journalist Matilde Serao famously described the principal new thoroughfare, Corso Umberto I, as a '*paravento*' (a windshield), because, she claimed, it had merely protected the middle classes and visitors from ungainly sights (Serao 1994).

Under the Fascist regime, the Monteoliveto market area and the Rione Carità, located between the *centro antico* and the Spanish Quarters, were demolished to make way for a new administrative centre consisting of public offices, a central post office and government buildings. As with the Risanamento, the Fascist '*sventramento*' – the disembowelling of popular Naples – was justified as a modernizing, sanitary measure, but the underlying pretext was to reinforce both the regime's physical presence and raise the city's national status.

Following the Second World War, the city experienced a massive and unplanned expansion. Thousands of middle-class residents moved out to the new, more comfortable suburbs which were mushrooming around the old city. They were later followed by a sizeable number of poorer inhabitants who moved out to the public housing estates that were built from the late fifties onwards, such as Rione Traiano in the western district of Soccavo. The population of the *centro storico* subsequently fell from 621,000 in 1951 to 495,000 in 1971, while the city's total population over the same period rose from 1,011,000 to 1,227,000 (Comune di Napoli 2007). The urban landscape was totally transformed. The surrounding hills that had been farmed for centuries were suddenly covered in high-rise blocks of flats. The unplanned building developments during the Monarchist and Christian Democrat administrations of the 1950s and 1960s were officially sanctioned as a social and economic palliative and often involved collusion between local politicians and speculators, as was famously denounced in Francesco Rosi's 1963 film *Le Mani sulla Città* (*Hands Over the City*).[8]

---

8. In *Le Mani sulla Città* the headquarters of the chief planner were symbolically located in the city's tallest building, the thirty-storey Società Cattolica Assicurazioni skyscraper, erected during the expansion of the Rione Carità in the mid-1950s. Its construction was made possible by a 1935 decree that granted the mayor (in this case Achille Lauro) the faculty of choosing the height of buildings considered to be of monumental character. The building epitomizes the anti-planning attitudes and disregard of urban landscape during the early postwar period.

Serao's *Il Ventre di Napoli* was now eclipsed by the *città abusiva:* the unplanned, illegal city.

The rapid and unregulated expansion of Naples led to a de facto demarcation of the *centro storico*. In comparison to its outskirts, there was
relatively little construction work in the heart of the city. New buildings
were erected on sites damaged by bombs during the Second World War,
but, with the notable exception of the redevelopment of Via Marina by the
port and the extension of the Rione Carità by the Monarchist administration under Mayor Achille Lauro during the 1950s, these barely altered the
overall morphology of the *centro storico*. While the massive expansion of
the periphery ultimately spared the *centro storico* from the bulldozers, the
political inability or disinterest to implement urban improvements meant
that large tracts of it were left in a state of decay. The area was afflicted by
a series of crises which reinforced the external image of a 'backward' city.
Rotting edifices collapsed, often with tragic consequences, and by the late
1970s, between 250 and 300 families were being made homeless every
year (Belli 1986: 79). An outbreak of cholera in 1973 suggested that sanitary conditions had improved little since the time of the Risanamento. The
whole city lacked basic services: a local education commission in 1973,
for instance, concluded that 4,000 extra classrooms were needed to solve
the problem of school sharing (Cederna 1991). Nevertheless, the *centro
storico* remained the fulcrum of commercial, tertiary and administrative
activities and was thus burdened with ever-increasing levels of traffic. Indeed, during the 1960s and 1970s, planning agendas were consumed by the
need to modernize the city centre's road system and relocate activities to a
new administrative and business district (known as the Centro Direzionale),
which after over two decades of discussions was eventually commenced in
1985 to the immediate north of the railway tracks of the central station.[9]

On 23 November 1980 a violent earthquake struck Campania and Basilicata, causing over 2,700 deaths and destroying whole villages. While
the loss of life in Naples was relatively low compared with the epicentre in
the mountainous region of Irpinia, the earthquake had a devastating impact
on the city.[10] Almost 10,000 buildings were declared unsafe for habita-
tion, and by the end of January 1981, 112,000 people (approximately 10
per cent of the city's population) had had to abandon their homes (Belli

---

9. The high-rise Centro Direzionale, described as a 'hypertrophied Neapolitan version of La
Défense' (De Lucia 1998: 65), has had very little impact on the city's traffic problems and social
conditions in the surrounding neighbourhoods, and a limited effect on the city's economy (Cavola and
Vicari 2000).

10. Just over seventy people died in Naples during and immediately after the earthquake, including
fifty-six inhabitants of a jerry-built council block that collapsed in the eastern suburb of Poggioreale,
a handful of people crushed by falling masonry, a dozen people who died of heart attacks and three
prisoners killed by fellow inmates in the city's main prison.

1986). The *centro storico* bore the brunt of the disaster: in the poorest neighbourhoods, such as Montecalvario and Mercato, between 30 and 60 per cent of inhabitants were evacuated. The homeless were temporarily housed in hotels and makeshift caravan parks around the city and on ferries in the port. Many were later moved to empty holiday homes along the Domitian coast, to the north of Naples, and into 2,500 prefabricated huts on the edges of the city. The compounding effect of the tremor upon existent social and economic problems led to an upsurge in unrest: schools and other public buildings were squatted, the unemployed intensified their fight for regular employment, while social movements mobilized against the transferral of residents from the *centro storico*.

Despite the damage to buildings and disruption to everyday life, there was no major plan to restore or rebuild the old city. Although the '219' law for the reconstruction of Campania and Basilicata, passed by central government in May 1981, earmarked funds for the structural renovation of damaged buildings (Belli 1986: 119–23), most of the main projects for Naples were located in the rundown suburbs in the north and east of the city and in satellite towns where 20,000 new apartments, leisure facilities and schools were planned. Repairs to damaged housing stock and minor monuments were often held up by bureaucracy, and many buildings in the centre remained clad in giant scaffolding frames until the mid-1990s. In the decade after the earthquake, the population of the old city dropped from 441,000 in 1981 to 355,000 in 1991, although after reaching an all time peak in 1971, the overall population of Naples also fell from 1,212,000 in 1981 to 1,067,000 in 1991 (Comune di Napoli 2007). While the initial phase of reconstruction in the city's suburbs was widely considered one of the few positive planning achievements in the postwar history of Naples (De Lucia 1998), the later period instead came to be associated with the unfinished white elephants such as new motorways, the vast sums of money that flowed into the hands of corrupt politicians and criminal organizations, and the general deterioration of Naples's image (Barbagallo 1997).

Amidst a climate of general neglect, there had nevertheless long been an interest in the *centro storico*'s heritage, both in terms of its relation to notions of local identity and its importance for the tourist industry. This was very much an elite tradition which singled out a number of monuments as mnemonics of a distant, more noble past in contradistinction to the mass of vernacular buildings considered to be of no architectural value.[11] For instance, the restoration of the Maschio Angioino in the 1920s involved the

---

11. The early flag bearer of this tradition was the journal *Napoli Nobilissima*, set up in 1892 by a group including the liberal philosopher Benedetto Croce and the poet and playwright Salvatore Di Giacomo, with the declared aim of contributing 'to the conservation, respect and improvement of

destruction of the eighteenth-century houses and workshops that had been built around its base. There was little change in approach during the post-war period. Many minor monuments such as small churches were either permanently closed, remained in a state of disrepair or, more often, were converted to meet more pressing needs (housing, workshops or car parks). Attention focused on a few symbolic restoration programmes, in particular the Santa Chiara monastery, which had been badly damaged during the war. The idea of conserving whole areas rather than single monuments did not arise until the 1970s, and this initially focused on the *centro antico* (Fratta 1986). The *centro storico* was officially delineated for the first time in the 1972 master plan, with the supposed purpose of safeguarding the city's architectural heritage from the threat of demolition. The protected zone eventually encompassed a total area of 720 hectares which corresponded to the pre-twentieth century core of the city. However, the risk of major restructuring remained, especially in the popular neighbourhoods, because the general restrictions could still be overturned by proposing individual alterations known as *varianti* (Cederna 1991). With the election of the left-wing administration in 1975, this threat was put temporarily on hold only to resurface after the 1980 earthquake.

During the 1980s, the *centri storici* of cities across Italy, which had been reclaimed by social movements and the cultural programmes organized by left-wing administrations in the previous decade, became increasingly desirable places in which to live and work. In 1985, 30 per cent of investment in building in Italy was in restoration work, and by 1989 this had risen to 50 per cent, although the percentage was markedly higher in the North.[12] After the earthquake, concern about the fate of Naples's *centro storico* grew. A small number of publicly visible cultural associations, heritage groups, intellectuals and historians campaigned for the protection and restoration of the whole centre (although the focus was initially on salvaging derelict monuments rather than saving the crumbling housing stock). The emphasis on revaluing the city's heritage was in sharp contrast to the economic interests of private businesses and local authorities, for whom redevelopment in the old city promised huge profits. Symptomatic of the opposing interests was the clash over the Regno del Possibile (Realm of the Possible) project in 1986, which proposed wholesale demolition and new building in the popular neighbourhoods. The protests organized by intellectuals and associations were partly instrumental in defeating the project.[13] Despite

---

everything that represents our ancient patrimony' (from 'Note to Readers' in *Napoli Nobilissima*, No. 1, 1892).

12. In 1985 the proportion of investment in restoration in the building industry stood at 55 per cent in the North but only 13 per cent in the South (*La Repubblica*, 10 February 1989).

13. This episode will be examined in greater depth in Chapter 16.

such proposals, there were no major interventions in the city centre. Under the Christian Democrat- and Socialist-dominated administrations between 1984 and 1993, building schemes were dependent on vast sums of public investment which were instead channelled into the post-earthquake reconstruction programme in the Campania region and the building of the new Centro Direzionale.[14]

At the beginning of the 1990s a few highly publicized restorations of buildings and pedestrianizations of public spaces were carried out for the most part by cultural associations with little or no public funding. The Monumenti Porte Aperte (Monuments Open their Doors) and La Scuola Adotta un Monumento (The School Adopts a Monument) programmes, annually organized by the Napoli 99 Foundation from 1992, opened up 'forgotten' historic buildings to the public and represented a symbolic moment for the amount of people they managed to mobilize (Barracco 1999; Palestino 2003). During the same period, a campaign was initiated by heritage groups to obtain UNESCO recognition of the *centro storico* as a world heritage site, which was eventually accorded in 1995. Also, from the beginning of the decade, and largely on the wave of the Pantera student movement in early 1990 which occupied various university departments in the city centre, parts of the *centro storico* became popular among young people as sites of leisure and cultural consumption, which in turn led to the consolidation of a small but vibrant night-time economy.

The growing consensus around the importance of the *centro storico* in public life was politically endorsed with the direct election of Antonio Bassolino in December 1993. Not only did the new administration expand the borders of the protected zone to include all buildings constructed before the Second World War (in other words, prior to the city's uncontrolled expansion), it now considered the *centro storico* to be a fundamental resource for the city's economic and cultural revival. The subtext of social justice contained in the Charter of Gubbio and the Bologna plan was now superseded by a grand narrative about urban renewal, while (unproblematized) ideas about memory and identity became increasingly prominent. Certainly, the southern metropolis presented a very different situation to a small Umbrian hill town or the capital of Emilia-Romagna, but it was also true that the political and economic climate had changed radically over the course of a quarter of a century.

---

14. Despite some significant pieces of national legislation, such as the 1985 Galasso Law that formally protected areas of environmental interest, the 1980s were generally an era of counter-reform, during which restraints on building were lifted and progressive reforms, such as the expropriation of land for public use, were overruled. Even within the PCI there were those who thought that *abusivismo* (unauthorized building) was largely a symptom of excessive regulations, and in fact many in the party supported a 1985 amnesty for illegally built constructions because they believed it directly benefited low-income households (see De Lucia 1992: 171–90; Corona 2007: 112–13).

Chapter 2

Between the General and the Particular

A Neapolitan Version of 'Urban Regeneration'

Urban regeneration in a European context: definitions and problems

> Personally, I've never used such extravagant terms, nor do I think we've created
> a situation in Naples that can only get better. As for the term 'renaissance',
> all I'd say is that we've embarked on a path, we face a series of important
> innovations and find ourselves at an indisputable turning point, and so
> we need to try to reason as best we can. (Bassolino 1996a: 57)

The Bassolino era coincided with renewed international interest in the plight of cities. Urban development had returned to the top of social science and policy agendas and had migrated from specialist journals onto the front pages of the mass media (Amin and Graham 1997). It is commonly argued that a new kind of city emerged during the last quarter of the twentieth century which was forced to adapt itself to the effects of deindustrialization and a parallel shift towards a 'post-Fordist' political economy characterized by flexible capital accumulation and production processes (Harvey 1989b, 1990; Amin 1994). According to such accounts, cities were faced with the difficult task of transforming their economic and fiscal base by developing service-, information-, tourist-, cultural- and knowledge-based industries. At the same time, cities were seen to regain economic importance and leverage and thus had to compete amongst themselves to attract inward investment, jobs, skilled workforces and visitors.

Many of the keywords used to label the vast range of policies and schemes accessory to these changes contain a common prefix ('ri-' in Italian and 're-' in English) and convey the sense of a new beginning and, by inference, the end of a period of decline or crisis. So far I have mainly opted for the more generic-sounding term 'urban renewal', but even this is loaded with historical references and ambivalent connotations. In the United States, for instance, the term is closely associated with the controversial clearance of inner-city slums after the Second World War and their replacement with high-rise housing projects and expressways. The label '*Rinascimento Napoletano*' (Neapolitan Renaissance) has often been applied to the Bassolino period but, at the time, was rarely more than a parochial media slogan through which commentators either applauded or derided the achievements of the administration.[1] Here I want to propose a broad definition of 'urban regeneration' as a possible means of reading the institutional agendas and public narratives about Naples during the 1990s. Regeneration is by no means a neutral concept. It is rooted in religious, socio-biological and medical traditions that are shot through with conservative and liberal political ideologies – from the hope of individual spiritual salvation to the moral rehabilitation of the poor through education and work (Furbey 1999). In the contemporary British context it is used normatively to refer to urban policies that seek 'to bring about a lasting improvement in the economic, physical, social and environmental condition of an area that has been subject to change' (Roberts 2000: 17). At the same time, it tends to be inflected in everyday language with conceptual slippages, such as the idea that it constitutes a specific stage in history that is both inevitable and incontrovertibly positive. The term '*rigenerazione*' has recently started to be employed by Neapolitan scholars to describe what occurred during the Bassolino era,[2] but it is unlikely that it will ever become the shibboleth that it has been in British public discourse.[3] The intention is not to foist this connotative baggage onto Naples, but to set up an appropriate frame for analysis

---

1. The term *Rinascimento Napoletano* was previously used in the early 1990s to refer to a new generation of Neapolitan film directors including Antonio Capuano, Pappi Corsicato and Mario Martone. One of the first occasions in which it was publicly discussed in relation to the Bassolino administration was at a round table at the Galassia Gutenberg book fair in February 1996 (Bassolino et al. 1996). The mayor himself was a discussant and, as this chapter's opening quote demonstrates, was reticent to embrace the idea. The use of 'renaissance' in connection with Naples should not be conflated with the British idea of 'urban renaissance', promoted by the 1999 Urban Task Force report chaired by Richard Rogers, which focuses primarily on improvements to the design and vitality of the public realm in British cities (Imrie and Raco 2003).

2. See Palestino 2004; Iaccarino 2005; Belli 2007. It should be noted that these authors directly draw on English-language texts when discussing regeneration or have, like Iaccarino, conducted their research in the context of a comparative analysis with a British city.

3. The hegemonic position that the term 'regeneration' enjoyed in New Labour's urban policy appears to be on the wane since the formation of the Conservative-Liberal Democrat coalition government in May 2010, not because of any significant change in political direction but because such a term jars somewhat in the face of massive cuts in the public sector and the current global crisis of capitalism.

that also encourages cross-references with other urban situations. Hence, here I sketch some of the themes that are typically associated with the regeneration of cities in Western Europe[4] before critically considering their relevance to the case of Naples.

First, urban regeneration is connected to a transition in the running of cities. From the late 1970s onwards, the traditional role of local government as provider of public services and welfare began to be undermined by major spending cuts and increasing pressure for 'entrepreneurial' forms of action aimed at urban economic growth (Harvey 1989b; 1990; Amin and Graham 1997; Hall and Hubbard 1998). This was accompanied by a move away from centralized and party-based structures of government towards a greater emphasis on collaborative partnership with other urban actors, principally the private business sector but also educational and cultural institutions, voluntary associations, social movements and labour organizations. These actors, however, often possessed quite different goals and a varying degree of capacity to steer policy. Indeed, urban regeneration has been typically marked by a tension between, on the one hand, entrepreneurial governance which prioritized and advanced particular (usually private) interests and, on the other, a simultaneous promotion, at least at a formal level, of the democratization of decision-making processes (Imrie and Raco 2003). Paradoxically, as David Harvey has noted, the difficulty of forming effective alliances has been such that it has opened the way for an individual such as a charismatic mayor or a wealthy business leader to influence the nature and direction of urban entrepreneurialism (Harvey 1989b: 7). Moreover, given the speculative design of many urban policies, city governments often sought to build public consensus around a regeneration 'vision' of a shared urban future, expounded through public pronouncements, architectural images and enticing slogans, that legitimized priorities (and cuts) as both inevitable and commonsensical and precluded alternative paths of development (Furbey 1999; Dines 2009). Significantly, urban entrepreneurial strategies were equally pursued by right- and left-wing local governments. Although these varied from a politically conservative focus on property development and enterprise culture, as epitomized by London's Docklands during the 1980s, to a greater stress on community resources and collective identity among social democratic administrations, as exemplified by Barcelona under the mayorship of Pasqual Maragall between 1982 and 1997 (McNeill 1999, 2003), the central objective

---

4. Processes that typically fall under the banner of 'regeneration' are by no means exclusive to the West. See, for example, work on the restructuring of heritage spaces in Bangkok (Herzfeld 2006); urban renovation programmes aimed at recuperating cosmopolitan pasts in Alexandria, Egypt (Starr 2005) and the long-term redevelopment vision for a globalized Johannesburg (Robinson 2006).

of modifying the city to the demands of an increasingly flexible economy would remain the same.

Second, 'culture' rapidly became a key ingredient and buzzword in urban regeneration. It would be harnessed in multifarious ways: from the construction of new museums, public art commissions and the establishment of 'cultural quarters' to ephemeral events such as film festivals and street carnivals or simply the promotion of customs and practices seen to comprise a local urban culture. At a general level, the emergence of a more fluid and open understanding of culture during the latter decades of the twentieth century and its rise to universal prominence in urban-policy agendas has been seen to correspond to a concomitant erosion of traditional class-based hierarchies and the decline in dominance of a few metropolitan centres such as Paris and New York over artistic and intellectual life (Featherstone 1991: 95–111). Although age-old exclusionary distinctions persisted or were recoded by new elites, culture was no longer conceptualized exclusively on the basis of aesthetic taste or erudition, but interconnected with everyday ways of life and mass consumerism. It thus had as much to do with popular entertainment, youth subculture or multicultural cosmopolitanism as it did with fine art or theatre.

Nevertheless, the formulation and role of culture in urban policy varied across different historical and national contexts. It was accorded greater collective significance in continental Western Europe than in Great Britain (Bianchini 1993). In the 1970s and early 1980s, the cultural policies of many European cities had clear social and political concerns, perhaps best illustrated by Renato Nicolini's programme of cultural events in public spaces under the left-wing administration of Rome, which sought to reassert the social function of the city centre and combat atomization during the summer months (Gundle 2000). With greater curbs on public spending, cultural policies in the 1980s became increasingly oriented towards economic growth and were targeted as much at city users and tourists as the local population. It was during this period, according to Bianchini (1993), that 'culture' became directly associated with 'regeneration'. By the 1990s, the idea that culture could enhance a city's competitiveness and contribute to social cohesion had become an orthodoxy among local governments, especially in Britain, where this approach was captured by terms such as 'culture-led regeneration' (Miles and Paddison 2005) and the 'creative city' (Landry and Bianchini 1995). However, as many observers have underlined, while cultural investment perhaps resurrected a city's reputation or led to a rise in visitors and consumers, its long-term ameliorative impact upon the urban economy and society in general was frequently exaggerated (Lovering 1995; Gómez 1998; Stevenson 2004). It tended, rather, to generate limited numbers of low-skilled service jobs or highly paid managerial positions, which exacer-bated disparities in wealth and often accelerated uneven development in and between neighbourhoods. Moreover, definitions of what constituted a vibrant urban culture and how this benefited a local sense of identity, even when this implied celebrating popular or multiethnic cultural forms, would often be a source of contestation and, where this directly involved urban-restructuring schemes, could lead to outright social conflict (Dines 2009). Despite the customary rhetoric about revitalizing cities, certain urban areas were perceived to be *too lively* and their sociocultural com-position incompatible with a regeneration vision. No matter how fluid and open its definition, the harnessing of culture often chimed with more inflexible issues such as security, social control and decorum.

A third central element of urban regeneration is place promotion. This typically consists in a dual process of remoulding the external reputation of a city and rehabilitating its self-image so as to, on the one hand, attract investors and the 'right people', such as well-educated, skilled work-forces and up-market tourists, and, on the other, bolster local confidence and build consensus around urban growth policies (Philo and Kearns 1993). The strategy of selling places is not new: civic boosterism has a particularly long tradition in North American cities (Ward 1998), while the phenomenon can be traced back as far as the Hanseatic League and the Italian city-states (Harvey 1989b). However, during the late twentieth century, it became an increasingly common tactic for cities to regrade themselves upon national and international urban scales and to exalt the memory of past glories, such as industrial prowess, as the foundation for a new sense of civic or entrepreneurial spirit (Hall 1997; Gómez 1998). Place promotion has been pursued through various forms and often ac-companied by sophisticated advertising campaigns, from highly vis-ible 'mega-projects', like the Guggenheim Museum in Bilbao (McNeill 2000) and the marketing of industrial heritage to the construction of new retail districts, the reuse of historic buildings and the pedestrianization of public spaces. Special occasions, such as major political, sporting or cultural events, as well as anniversaries (for example the bicentennial of the French Revolution in Paris in 1989) or temporary awards such as the European City of Culture have also been considered highly important for reorienting images and discourses about cities. Not only have one-off occasions served to raise a city's international profile, but they have often been considered an opportunity to permanently transform the shape of a city and to trigger longer-term renewal. This was the case in Barce-lona, where preparations for the 1992 Olympics became the premise for a massive programme of urban improvements which included peripheral areas not directly linked to the games (McNeill 1999).

Place promotion is at the same time a highly precarious process. The ubiquitous celebration of the uniqueness of cities has ironically resulted in the emulation of events and the serial reproduction of urban forms. Beyond the immediate attribution of status, the economic impact of the umpteenth art festival or waterfront development has a limited life span and can work to reinstate traditional hierarchies between cities. The trouble with pursuing regeneration through a quick-fix remedy or the creation of a feel-good factor is not simply that it might produce ephemeral results, but that these have the habit of consuming public and political debate, thus deflecting attention and resources away from broader problems and can, in the long run, have the counterproductive effect of raising cynicism and disgruntlement among local people (Harvey 1989b; Miles and Paddison 2005).

Finally, city centres have usually played a pivotal role in urban regeneration in Europe, irrespective of the degree to which increased urban mobility or sprawl has dislocated experiences and perceptions of the city. Flagship architectural schemes, adjustments to the design of the public realm and the restoration of historic zones have all been seen as expedients for showcasing the centre as the fulcrum of local identity and enhancing a city's desirability. During the 1980s and 1990s, industrial cities like Birmingham, Frankfurt and Glasgow began to devise ways of improving what were widely regarded as dull, ugly and anonymous city centres by opening new cultural facilities and establishing pleasant pedestrian environments (Bianchini 1993; Hall 1997). Historic cities also sought to upgrade their centres, both to maximize the economic benefits of cultural tourism and to render the areas consonant with overall development goals. Approaches ranged from selective demolition to create new public spaces in central neighbourhoods of Barcelona to the 'hands-off' conservationist approach typical of many Italian cities during the 1990s. The regeneration of working-class or run-down areas in city centres often intensified processes of gentrification, with increasing numbers of young, high-income professionals attracted by relatively cheap property and more stimulating urban lifestyles.[5]

This short and by no means exhaustive summary of the overlapping themes of urban regeneration helps to frame the transformations which occurred in Naples during the 1990s. It would be possible to trace some

---

5. It is important not to conflate regeneration with gentrification even though they may often be interdependent processes. Gentrification, which is constituted by a particular socioeconomic and cultural dynamic, usually (but not always) anticipates regeneration. Zukin (1988) and Smith (1992) have both outlined how gentrification occurs during urban decline, in other words, when rents and prices are at their cheapest, and is set in motion by 'pioneers', often cultural or intellectual workers, who move into districts with ailing economies.

immediate analogies, such as the role of the *centro storico* in marketing a new image for the city. However problems soon arise when the central arguments are applied too mechanically. Presupposing an epochal shift not only risks overlooking lines of continuity but also divergent paths of urbanization and capitalist development. For instance, an understanding of the emergence of a 'post-industrial' society in Italy should not just focus on the rise of small and specialized business districts, particularly in the north-east of the country also known as 'Third Italy' (Bagnasco 1977), but must take into account a number of fundamental factors, including the rapid modernization and economic growth of the postwar period, the symbiotic relationship between a developed North and an underdeveloped South and the crucial role of internal migration, and the impact of a decade of intense labour and social struggles during the late 1960s and 1970s which precipitated the crisis of the Italian Fordist model (Vercellone 1996). Naples itself cannot be neatly bracketed into conventional categories such as the 'industrial' or 'post-industrial' city. The city's manufacturing-based economy, as shall be shown, existed largely as a result of state intervention, was often controlled by clientelistic networks and, although it was central to developmental discourses during the 1960s and 1970s, had a limited impact on reshaping local urban culture.

In other words, caution must be taken when drawing on theoretical discussions about regeneration that have been generalized from a singular historical tradition or a few paradigmatic cases (Wacquant and Bourdieu 1999). For example, Donald McNeill argues that applying uncritically the idea of the 'entrepreneurial city' to the case of Barcelona (itself cast as an exemplar of urban regeneration) underestimates the impact of Spain's transition to democracy: 'The concept seems to have emerged from some sort of mid-Atlantic theoretical and empirical convergence. Applying it to Barcelona would miss one pretty hefty local narrative: the fact that the city had thrown itself forward with such haste was closely related to its delayed or halted development under dictatorship' (McNeill 1998: 242). In the case of Naples, 'regeneration' refers as much to a relegitimization of the local state following a period of political degeneracy as it does to an idea of interurban competition, while the very notion of 'entrepreneurial politics' was associated locally with the collusion between politicians, businessmen and organized crime during the 1980s. Indeed, one could see this nefarious alliance itself as a sort of 'illicit governance'!

Some scholars have sought to highlight and challenge the geographical bias inherent within much urban theory. The Greek geographer Lila Leontidou argues that the Mediterranean metropolis represents an alternative urban tradition to northern European cities, which have long been both a focus of theory and the locus of its production: 'The political economy of societies where Fordism seldom took root has been based on late industrialization, a feeble bourgeoisie, and informal labourers rather than a proletariat. The culture of such societies flowers in constellations of cities developed in the South, where modernism has never been a hegemonic culture' (Leontidou 1996: 180). The problem is that Leontidou's argument appears to deconstruct one meta-narrative ('the northern city'), only to replace it with another ('the southern city'). Indeed, the fact that Naples does not easily fit into her alternative paradigm further underlines the risk of simplification when adopting preconceived models, be they 'northern' or 'southern'.[6] The task is not to overhaul urban theory but to decentre its dominant parochialism and its dependency on privileged sites. For it to be a meaningful concept, regeneration, along with its interconnected themes of governance, culture and place promotion, must be premised on the recognition that all cities are distinctive and contingent and yet part of the same field of analysis (Robinson 2006).

A Neapolitan history of regeneration

The emergence of a regeneration agenda in Naples during the 1990s needs to be understood in the light of a number of contributing factors. First, at the beginning of the decade, the city's economy was beset by a severe national recession and chronic unemployment.[7] The closure or restructuring of large and medium-sized factories during previous years had led to a heavy reduction of the industrial workforce. The Bagnoli steelworks, the symbol of the city's heavy industry for almost a century, was finally shut down in 1992 in order to comply with European directives on production, despite huge investment in the plant's modernization during the course of the 1980s. The economic downturn in Naples was not simply a familiar story about industrial decline. Under the Giuliano Amato government (June 1992 to April 1993) drastic cuts to public expenditure were introduced to reduce the country's massive budget deficit so as to bring Italy into line with the strict fiscal constraints imposed by

---

6. Consider, for example, Leontidou's following diagnosis in the context of Naples: 'Upgrading of derelict inner cities is very rare in southern urban complexes where high-class neighbourhoods have prevented the core from decaying' (Leontidou 1996: 191).

7. In 1993, national consumption dropped for the first time since the Second World War by 2.5 per cent, and the GNP fell by 1.2 per cent (Ginsborg 2001: 272). According to the 1991 census, the total official unemployment in Naples stood at 42.7 per cent of the active population (a rise from 36.1 per cent in 1981). Of the 179,366 Neapolitans out of work, over three-quarters were in search of their first employment. The equivalent national rate of unemployment in 1991 was 17.8 per cent, while it stood at 18.9 per cent in Rome; 9.5 per cent in Milan; 14.1 per cent in Turin and 34.8 per cent in Palermo (Comune di Napoli 2005).

European economic and monetary union (Ginsborg 2001: 264–65). This culminated with the termination in late 1992 of the '*Intervento Straordinario*' (Extraordinary Intervention) in the Italian South. Already in the late 1970s it had become clear that the system of state economic policy, which since 1950 had served to close the gap between the North and South by funding infrastructural projects and industrial districts, had failed to stimulate wider economic development (Dunford and Greco 2006). The various success stories in Abruzzo, Molise and parts of Puglia and Basilicata pointed as much to endogenous circumstances, such as the high concentration of self-employed agricultural workers and pre-existing commercial activities, as to the helping hand of the state, while elsewhere, economic growth was slow and the private sector remained generally weak (Trigilia 1992; Bodo and Viesti 1997). Instead, state interventionism had raised income and consumption levels (although these officially remained below the national average[8]) and had maintained social consensus through the redistribution of contracts, jobs and welfare. This had subsequently encouraged the development of political rather than economic entrepreneurship, and dependency upon political connections rather than economic efficiency (Trigilia 1992). However, as Bari-based sociologist Franco Cassano (2009) and others have argued, this massive dose of public expenditure was also fundamental to the industrial development of the Italian North (precisely because it opened up new markets) and far from being anomalous, needs to be viewed in the context of the compromise between capitalism and democracy that existed throughout the West during the first three decades of the postwar period.

The end of the *Intervento Straordinario* and its eventual replacement with a European-approved 'ordinary administration' that now limited spending to the most depressed areas, not just in the South but across the country, appeared to symbolize the final death knell of an era, even if various forms of state subsidy directed prevalently at the South remained, such as the 'Socially Useful Jobs' scheme for the unemployed. In its wake, greater importance would be attached to promoting small businesses, cultural industries and tourism, to establishing partnership-led forms of local development (known as 'negotiated planning') and to bidding for supranational (i.e. European) resources (Rossi 2004a; Dunford and Greco 2006). The underlying idea was that local-tier institutions

---

8. In 1991, per-capita annual incomes in the South were between 50 and 80 per cent lower than the national average (*Corrier Economia del Mezzogiorno*, 26 February 2001). These figures help as an indicator of the economic divide between the North and the South but cannot be considered very reliable given the proliferation of shadow and illegal economies in the South, which maintained levels of disposable income comparable to those of northern regions (Vercellone 1996: 88).

were in a better position to determine economic priorities and outcomes than their central counterparts, even though this situation had arisen not out of autonomous change but from political decisions taken from above (Lovering 1995). These new circumstances also created the sense that the city was now an active agent rather than a passive recipient of economic change, a potentially powerful ideological tool that worked to obfuscate the complex multi-scalar processes and social relations structuring urbanization (Harvey 1989b: 5).

The termination of southern industrial policy was interwoven with a political crisis triggered in early 1992 by the start of judicial inquests into the system of political kickbacks dubbed *Tangentopoli* (or 'Bribesville'). While the extraordinary upheaval instigated by the *Mani Pulite* (Clean Hands) trials was swift and sudden, it essentially signalled the epilogue to the peculiar and unsustainable combination of monetarist policies, spiralling public expenditure and rampant corruption of the 1980s. But in the process it also stigmatized and, at least in the short term, emasculated a long-established way of doing politics in Italy. Since the 1960s, clientelism had been an important basis around which the Christian Democrats first seized and then maintained political control in Naples (Allum 1973). Major segments of the local economy, from construction to commerce, were dependent on the political ruling class. While there was a temporary reprieve under the left-wing Valenzi administration (between 1975 and 1983), during the *Pentapartito* governments[9] of the 1980s the clientelistic machine became more intense as the flow of funds for the post-earthquake reconstruction grew (Barbagallo 1997). *Tangentopoli* did not begin in Naples until March 1993 (over a year after it began in Milan[10]), but it would have a devastating impact on the city. A whole political generation was practically decapitated by the swipe of the judicial sword. The principal political bosses and brokers were arrested, while many publicly funded or politically sponsored urban projects were blocked or abandoned.[11] In a matter of months, the five parties – the Christian Democrats (DC), Socialists (PSI), Democratic Socialists (PSDI), Liberals (PLI) and Republicans (PRI) – that had run local

---

9. '*Pentapartito*' refers to the alliance of five parties – the Christian Democrat (DC), Socialist (PSI), Democratic Socialist (PSDI), Liberal (PLI) and Republican (PRI) Parties – that governed Italy between 1981 and 1991 (and Naples between 1984 and 1993) and which marginalized the Communist Party after its de facto sharing of power during the late 1970s.

10. The fact that *Tangentopoli* erupted in Milan (and that the neologism in the beginning referred specifically to this city) demonstrated that corruption was by no means confined to the Italian South (Foot 2001b).

11. On 29 March 1993 the Christian Democrat Antonio Gava, who had dominated Neapolitan politics since the late 1960s, was officially accused of possessing contacts with the Camorra (Ginsborg 2001: 276).

government for almost ten years had either become defunct or were a mere shadow of their former strength. The political forces that had been marginal in Naples during the previous decade – notably the PCI/PDS on the left and the MSI on the right – would find themselves propelled to the centre stage.

The destructive impact of *Tangentopoli* was shortly followed by local institutional reform. City administrations were very often instable and short-lived. This was largely because the '*giunta*' or cabinet, consisting of the mayor and *assessori* (executive members), was selected by councillors from cross-party alliances that were subordinate, especially in large cities, to the fickle dynamics of national government politics (Koff and Koff 2000; Baldini 2002). Between January 1984 and August 1993 (when the city council was dissolved on account of bankruptcy), there were no less than ten different administrations. Law No.81, passed in March 1993, radically changed matters. The mayor was now directly elected by voters and could personally appoint the assessors of the *giunta* from outside the city council. Key decisions still had to be debated and passed by city council (on which the coalition supporting the mayor was guaranteed a majority), but the reform effectively increased the autonomy and power of the mayor, shifted (at least theoretically) decision making away from the intrigue of party politics, and assured greater stability and visibility for the administration. The new situation also lowered the profile of the opposition on city council, as debates were increasingly conducted in the local media and direct influence was seen to be increasingly exerted by the citizenry.

The triumph of left and centre-left mayoral candidates in the local elections of 1993 appeared to signal a change in fortunes for many Italian cities, as well as for progressive politics in general. The victories recalled the PCI's astonishing advances in the mid-seventies. In the cases of Naples and Rome, the showdown with the extreme Right created a highly politically charged atmosphere that had not existed for years.[12] Parallels with the past were purely formalistic, however. While the left-wing administrations elected in 1975 responded to a radical groundswell within Italian society, the ushering in of a new 'mayoral season' in 1993 represented the consummation of the collapse of a discredited political

12. The anti-Fascist vote against Alessandra Mussolini and Gianfranco Fini played a decisive part in the victories of Antonio Bassolino and Francesco Rutelli. Despite the MSI's traditional strength in Naples and Rome (although in the former city its vote had dropped to 9.2 per cent in the 1992 local elections), there still existed, at least formally, an anti-Fascist consensus in public life. It was the crumbling of this consensus over the following years, coupled with the post-*Tangentopoli* political vacuum and a steady shift to the right in Italian political culture, that enabled the 'post-Fascists' of National Alliance (AN), the party founded following the dissolution of the MSI in early 1995, to move into the political fold.

system and a popular desire for a general but decisive change in direction. Indeed, it was the promise of a break from the old regime and the restoration of legality and order – and not a defined programme of urban reform – that lay at the centre of Antonio Bassolino's election campaign.[13] Bassolino sought to build support around a broad-sweeping, cross-class vision of a morally rehabilitated Naples. Pledges were often vague and somewhat populist. They included a commitment to the fight against the Camorra, the establishment of a neighbourhood police force and the construction of a new school funded by recouped kickback money. More concrete proposals were contained in a plan for Bassolino's first hundred days of office, which focused on immediately feasible and symbolically significant interventions, such as sorting out the city council's finances and opening post-earthquake projects to the public. Generic allusions were made to the importance of art and culture for the city's future. The *centro storico* was accorded a prominent role in the campaign: press conferences were often conducted from a bar located in the recently pedestrianized Piazza Bellini, while the campaign headquarters was a rented apartment overlooking Piazza San Domenico, in the heart of the *centro antico*. There was no clear indication, however, that this part of the city would later become the focal point of urban regeneration.

The election of Antonio Bassolino at the head of a left-wing coalition, unimaginable only a few months earlier, generated a great deal of enthusiasm and expectation in Naples. Although the close-run battle against Alessandra Mussolini had rekindled the Communist identity of the new mayor, his election campaign was actually marked by a renunciation of a conflict-laden view of the city and a move away from the realm of party politics. In fact, Bassolino made the significant decision of appointing academics and professionals rather that party officials to his cabinet. Some of the executive posts were given elaborate new titles such as 'Liveability' (planning), 'Normality' (commerce and environment) and 'Dignity' (social policy).[14] At the end of 1994, the post of 'Identity' – with responsibility for cultural policy and tourism – was also added. In spite of their Orwellian undertones and fuzzy boundaries, these titles were

---

13. For inside accounts of the election campaign, see Leonetti and Napoli 1996 and Marone 2002. For a political analysis, see Pasotti 2004.

14. The original lineup of eight assessors was: Scipione Bobbio (professor of engineering at Naples University) at Human Resources and Decentralization; Riccardo Marone (administrative lawyer) at Transparency; Roberto Barbieri (financial manager) at Strategic Resources and Budget; Vezio De Lucia (architect and former chief official of public works in the Italian government) at Liveability; Ada Becchi (economist in the department of town planning at Venice University) at Mobility; Lucio Pirillo (president of Acli, a Catholic labour organization) at Dignity; Guido D'Agostino (historian at Naples University) at Education, School and Sport; and Amato Lamberti (sociologist at Naples University and founder of a Camorra-monitoring group) at Normality.

supposed to capture a more public-friendly and imaginative idea about local politics (Lepore and Ceci 1997: 101). The implementation of 'the first hundred days' programme on a restricted financial budget was instrumental in projecting a sense of change and acquiring public and media approval. Parks, sport centres and schools which had been built in the suburbs with post-earthquake reconstruction funds but which had been subsequently abandoned were swiftly inaugurated. The city's busy coastal boulevard, Via Caracciolo, was turned into a traffic-free promenade on Sunday mornings. The administration's fleet of official cars was donated to the municipal police force, while in turn public officials who flouted codes of practice were brought to account. And in an ironic anticipation of future events, heaps of rubbish were cleared from the city's streets. The interventions and gestures were clearly limited in the face of the city's deep-set problems, but, as members of the administration themselves admitted, even the slightest signs of change in the aftermath of *Tangentopoli* acquired great significance (Marone 2002: 20).

As was the case with many cities, the launching pad for a clear narrative about urban regeneration came with a specific event. In July 1994 the city hosted the G7 summit, the annual meeting of the leaders of the world's main industrial powers. While the choice of Naples the previous summer had seemed absurd amidst the city's various crises,[15] the event was to become the ideological cornerstone for the city's revival and a fortuitous springboard for the new administration. The government released 55 billion lire (28 million euros) to fund hasty adjustments to the *centro storico*. Over one hundred interventions were carried out, ranging from the restoration of buildings and fountains and the repaving of streets and piazzas to the removal of almost a thousand wrecked vehicles from the roadside. The fact that the work was completed in the allotted time and that 5 billion lire was left over was in itself highly symbolic. Comparisons were made with the 850 billion lire spent on the city's preparations for the 1990 World Cup football tournament held in Italy, much of which was squandered on unfinished or ineffective projects. The summit itself also involved an unprecedented security operation which transformed Naples into a '*città blindata*' (literally a 'fortress city'). Eight thousand soldiers were drafted from across Italy to patrol streets, large parts of the centre were blocked off to the general public, demonstrations and street trading were temporarily banned and 'Operation Tramp' transferred the homeless to makeshift hostels on the outskirts of the city. During the three-day summit, Naples enjoyed an intense moment of international

---

15. During mid-1993, municipal police went on strike and there were daily protests over contaminated mains water. To make matters worse, the city council declared itself insolvent at the beginning of the summer and was subsequently dissolved by the interior ministry in early August.

publicity which, thanks to the injection of public funds and draconian security measures, played a pivotal role in transforming the city's dismal reputation. In the following weeks, Bassolino paid a visit to business leaders in America and to Gianni Agnelli, the head of Fiat, in Turin, in order to encourage private investment in the city, while in the autumn, figures were released showing a sharp rise in the number of Italian and foreign tourists in the city.

Bassolino insisted that Naples's route to economic recovery would be slow and arduous but that the city was back on track (Bassolino 1996b: 53). Following the G7, great emphasis continued to be placed on small-scale, low-cost interventions with an immediate impact, such as open-air spectacles, pedestrianization schemes and the reopening of monuments and public buildings.[16] The administration also pursued long-term objectives, such as the construction of a comprehensive underground rail network and the redevelopment of the Bagnoli steelworks and its surrounding waterfront location as a new tourist, cultural and service district.[17] The plethora of initiatives received wide publicity across Italy and abroad (Cappelli 2001). In its first few years the administration enjoyed a privileged relationship with the national and local press, in particular *Il Mattino,* which had traditionally been DC-orientated and fervently anti-Communist. The popularity of the mayor was confirmed by his landslide reelection victory in November 1997. Bassolino's second term was characterized by less furore than in previous years, while an upsurge in organized crime and the frustration at not seeing structural improvements dampened the initial enthusiasm.[18] With the entry of the Italian Popular Party (PPI)[19] into the supporting coalition, the second Bassolino administration also lost its original compactness and radical spirit (it now technically became 'centre-left', and the number of cabinet posts rose to sixteen to accommodate the various party affiliations). Even so, cultural

---

16. Some buildings had been shut for decades, as in the case of the eighteenth-century Teatro Mercadante, which had closed its doors in 1963 only to resume regular performances in 1995.

17. There is an extensive literature on the redevelopment of Bagnoli. For inside accounts, see Bassolino 1996b: 31–37; De Lucia 1998: 114–32. For critical analyses, see Bull 2005; Iaccarino 2005; Lepore 2007.

18. Clear signs of the limits and fragility of urban renewal were already apparent before Bassolino's reelection. In January 1996 a street collapsed in the northern district of Secondigliano, killing eleven people (for a reconstruction of the event, see Rossomando 2002). In July 1997 the Prodi government sent soldiers to patrol the streets of Naples following a spate of Camorra killings.

19. The PPI was founded in 1994 by former Christian Democrats. It later allied itself with the PDS and smaller parties to form the centre-left Ulivo (Olive Tree) coalition, which won the 1996 general election. In 2001 the PPI formed the principal component of a new centrist party, La Margherita (The Daisy). In 2007 La Margherita and the Democrats of the Left (DS, formed in 1998 out of the fusion between the PDS and a number of reformist left groups) formed the Democratic Party (PD), Italy's main centre-left party of which both Antonio Bassolino and his successor, Rosa Russo Iervolino, are members.

heritage, tourism and the promotion of the *centro storico* all remained key areas of urban policy.

Naples during the 1990s thus bore many similarities with what was occurring elsewhere. The Bassolino administration's achievements were acknowledged in international treatises about the 'creative city' (Landry and Bianchini 1995: 36), as well as in new studies of the European city (Le Galès 2002: 88–89, 222, 252). Naples was now comparable with former industrial cities such as Liverpool and Glasgow that it was once seen to lag behind (Savitch and Kantor 2002). This said, there were aspects that flew against standard regeneration models. Most important, the new planning agenda adopted by the Bassolino administration stood in stark contrast to the public-private partnerships or 'negotiated planning' schemes commonly pursued by centre-left and centre-right administrations in Italy and further afield (Berdini 2000; Rossi 2004a; Belli 2007). The Bagnoli master plan reasserted public control of the planning process and proposed a grand environmental design that consisted primarily in a huge park and public beach, as well as a small marina, conference centre, museums and new housing. It thus prioritized procedural transparency and accountability over a pro-growth strategy, although its rejection of a participatory governance approach not only sidelined private economic interests but also local community associations and social movements (Bull 2005).[20] On the other hand, the promotion of the *centro storico* (which was itself now subject to rigid planning restrictions) often sought the collaboration and approval of noninstitutional actors, such as heritage groups, and appeared to reflect more readily the cultural regeneration policies of other European cities.

These divergent approaches were personified by executive members of the first Bassolino administration: Vezio De Lucia, the head of 'Liveability' and mastermind behind the Bagnoli plan, was one of the historic figures of urban environmentalism in Italy and a fierce opponent of negotiated planning and building amnesties (and was variously labelled by his critics as a 'Bolshevik' and 'Jacobin'); Roberto Barbieri, responsible for the council budget, was a 'creative' financial economist who coordinated the investment of council bonds on the New York Stock Exchange to raise much-needed capital; while Renato Nicolini, the asses-

---

20. The planning process was criticized both from the Left as hierarchical and undemocratic and from the Right as rigidly dated and economically unproductive (Corona 2007: 189–92). In reality, the Bagnoli plan was forced from the start to reach compromises with independent enterprises that already existed in the designated area. Later in 2003 the administration was ready to overrule the plan in order to accommodate a bid for the America's Cup. Although the hosting of the sailing regatta was eventually awarded to Valencia, the bid was a clear attempt to placate public criticism at the lack of the plan's progress and to reconcile its environmental vision with a more explicitly entrepreneurial approach (Bull 2005: 404–6).

sor of 'Identity', was the nationally reputed 'king of ephemera' who had made his name coordinating the 'Roman Summer' programme in the late 1970s but who now viewed cultural heritage as a key urban economic resource.[21] All three had been close allies, if not members, of the PCI. Together they now represented the contradictory facets of a municipal left in transition.

The singular mixture of traditional top-down managerialism and urban entrepreneurialism was nonetheless underscored by the common objective of redefining the city's economic role and enhancing its prestige on the international stage. Irrespective of its deviation from the norm, the hybrid model of urban regeneration pursued in Naples during the 1990s coincided with the end of an era. The industrial vocation that had lay at the core of leftist developmental discourse for nearly a century had finally been surpassed by its traditional adversary – the tourist city – historically regarded in Naples as the economic design of conservative elites (Becchi 1984). Images of open green spaces and sandy beaches replaced the pollution that had once billowed out of the chimneys of Bagnoli, while questions of cultural and tourist consumption in the *centro storico* overshadowed more traditional concerns about social and economic marginalization.[22] In their own ways, the planning and cultural policies of the Bassolino administration espoused the similar idea of the city as a collective entity in contradistinction to the mega-projects and corrupt practices of the 1980s and the unbridled speculation of the postwar period. In other words, while the master plan for Bagnoli and the revaluing of neglected monuments in the old city indicated distinct strategies, they were both construed as signs of democratic and political renewal.

Some closing words on 'regeneration'

In conclusion, I want to spell out how the idea of regeneration is used in this book. First, regeneration is understood as a set of institutional strategies and public discourses that constituted and responded to a broad vision of a new city. In political terms, it refers to the attempts to restore democratic accountability and trust in local government. In terms

---

21. When Nicolini was appointed assessor of Identity in October 1994, he declared that Naples was second only to Paris in Europe in terms of its cultural heritage: 'The city must become a big open-air museum for twelve months a year and must recover its role as an international tourist attraction. The unusable factories need to removed and the space given over to hotels and marinas' (*La Repubblica*, 28 October 1994).

22. Bassolino was no longer reluctant to embrace a tourist vocation for Bagnoli. Indeed, he declared that the steelworks had been important for the city's history but had been built in the wrong place (Bassolino 1996b: 33).

of planning it was largely about reinstating public controls, while at an economic level it denoted the belief that local resources and creative solutions could steer Naples to urban recovery and growth. It meant long-term future designs, such as the redevelopment of Bagnoli, but also an ongoing commitment to rehabilitating a sense of civic pride. Regeneration is therefore not to be conflated with a particular historical epoch (like the label 'Neapolitan Renaissance', which tends to refer to a period running from the mid- to late 1990s), nor should it be deployed as a surrogate term for urban change in general. A serious analysis, rather, must consider how ideas and manifestations of a new Naples were produced within particular historical circumstances and how they connected with other contemporaneous processes, such as immigration and socio-demographic change in the *centro storico*.

A second important consideration is how we assess regeneration. It takes little stretch of the imagination to mock the hubristic claims inherent within words such as 'renaissance' and 'regeneration'. But should we be concerned with measuring their 'success'? And if so, how should this be done? On the regenerators' terms? According to a set of ideal criteria that correspond to our own notions of urban justice? Or perhaps upon some quasi-scientific 'quality-of-life' or 'creative-city' scale? I would instead argue that a preoccupation with ascertaining success actually endorses the visionary rhetoric in regeneration agendas. Of course, it is important for a city that urban policies create 'jobs rather than discourses' (to invert the terms of one serial regeneration basher (Lovering 1995)), but even if the types and conditions of work created are put to scrutiny, this approach prioritizes outcome over process.

During the 1990s in Naples, there were two dominant interpretations about regeneration in the *centro storico*: on the one hand was a polemic that saw it amounting to little more than an ephemeral 'image politics' (Ragone 1997), and on the other a more sympathetic critique that viewed it as a necessary strategy for raising public confidence and laying the basis for long-term improvements (Coppola, Sommella and Viganoni 1997). However, in both cases, regeneration tended to be conceived as an *end result,* which thus solicited evaluations of what had or had not changed. Instead, in this work, regeneration is viewed as an *entry point* from which to explore how new ideas about the *centro storico* and public space materialized during the Bassolino mayorship and as a lens through which to examine the evolution of the Left's relationship with Naples.

Chapter 3

The Left, the Politics of Citizenship and Shifting Ideas about Naples

Citizenship as a new organizing discourse

The regeneration of the *centro storico* coincided with a political and ideological transition of the Italian institutional Left. The traditional class analysis, which had always faced major stumbling blocks in central Naples, and the talk, rhetorical or otherwise, of imminent socioeconomic justice faded into the background.[1] To the forefront arose a liberal-inspired anthem about citizenship, which in turn provided the foundation for a range of interlinking concepts such as 'democratic renewal', 'civility', 'civic pride' and 'urban identity' that together informed narratives about progress and a new Naples.

The idea of citizenship, at least in the West, is routinely associated historically and etymologically with the city and its public life, from its origins in the ancient Greek agora and Roman forum to the civic traditions of the medieval city-state (Isin and Turner 2002). This link was severed with the rise of the nation-state and, later in the twentieth century, with the development of national welfare systems (Bauböck 2003). The modern 'Marshallian' formulation of citizenship denotes the series of political, civil and social rights, and duties assigned by membership of a sovereign state and which enables full participation in the social, economic and

---

1. A class discourse in Naples during the 1990s was pursued by Communist Refoundation, the Left component of the alliance supporting Bassolino, but this rarely encroached on debates about the *centro storico*. Its critical positions rather tended to be articulated through a 'privileged centre' versus 'excluded periphery' perspective or around the city-wide issue of employment, but did not dwell on the social cleavages in the *centro storico* itself. Indeed, for the most part and at least at an official level, Communist Refoundation during the 1990s countenanced the administration's discourse of a reinvigorated citizenship vis-à-vis a revived *centro storico*.

political life of society (Marshall 1950; Zolo 1994). As such, and indeed throughout history, citizenship has represented a mechanism that defines not only inclusion, but also exclusion from a political community.

Since the 1980s there has been renewed interest in citizenship as a political category, largely in response to the impact of globalization, state restructuring and the emergence of multileveled forms of governance, but also in light of the demands for rights and recognition made by groups mobilizing around different identities, from sexuality and gender to ethnicity and ecology (Kymlicka and Norman 1994; Smith 1995; Isin and Turner 2002). Citizenship is not simply considered a formal legal status but also a contested space of struggle where social actors and groups actively engage in redefining its meanings and boundaries (Isin and Siemiatycki 1999). Debates have also focused on the increased role and significance of the city (see, for example, Isin 2000). At one level, urban citizenship is understood as the rescaling of governance and the dislocation of local citizenship from national conceptions of membership which has led, for instance, to arguments for a residence-based 'denizenship' (Bauböck 2003).[2] In broader sociological terms, the city is more than merely the place where status and rights are conferred: it is conceived as the key site 'where the concentration of different groups and their identities are intertwined with the articulation of new claims and citizenship rights' (Isin and Siemiatycki 1999: 8). Although national citizenship continues to be relevant in the production of noncitizens, particularly in the case of immigrants, it is the city where these same groups nonetheless mobilize to demand their inclusion (ibid.).

In this chapter I want to consider how the term itself was deployed by the Bassolino administration to mould political meaning around its regeneration strategy for Naples. As such, I break from the common dichotomy between 'citizenship as status' and 'citizenship as activity' (Kymlicka and Norman 1994: 354) to consider citizenship as a particular 'organizing discourse' at a specific historical juncture.

It is important to note that besides its normative and sociological dimensions, the term '*cittadinanza*' in everyday Italian also refers to the aggregate population of a city. The fact that these various meanings frequently overlap suggests an underlying ambiguity: not only does citizenship denote the rules of membership, but also the members themselves. In public discourse it tends to evoke essentialist notions of 'identity' and 'community' and emphasizes commonality over diversity. Furthermore, the idea of *cittadinanza,* especially at the urban level, is often articulated in terms of a civilizing process and is subsequently infused with ideas

---

2. This term indicates residents who enjoy a status between alien and citizen.

about conduct and virtue. During the 1990s in Naples, the adjectives '*civico*' and '*civile*' stood out in public discussions about urban change. Although the precise meanings of the two words sometimes appeared blurred, generally speaking, the former implied public-mindedness while the latter was used to describe appropriate citizen behaviour.[3]

Citizenship, in other words, is much more than an abstract political category. Its terms are at the same time generated and embedded in a specific context, in this case Naples and its *centro storico*. Moreover, if it is true that the concept can mean opposite things to different people, from a politically progressive emphasis on the language of rights to a conservative insistence on obligations (Smith 1995: 190), it is also true that it can encapsulate many things at the same time. Hence, the semantically elastic idea of a reinvigorated citizenship advanced by the Left during the 1990s requires being disassembled into its various constituent parts if one is to fully comprehend how urban regeneration was politically interpreted and presented. Before this can be done, two crucial questions need to be explored. First, what are the implications of a discourse about citizenship in the history of a city so often seen to represent the polar opposite to stereotypes about Italian civic culture and urban propriety? Second, what was the relationship between the Left (specifically the PCI) and Naples prior to Bassolino, and why did it come to employ a term in the 1990s that it had never previously used in connection with the city?

Naples: a city with a civic deficit?

Prior to the 1990s, Naples had long appeared, like the rest of the South, to lack an active citizenship and public life. According to a famous study coordinated by Robert Putnam of the functioning of regional administrations in Italy, Campania was one of the least civic regions in the country (Putnam, Leonardi and Nanetti 1993: 97). Putnam's notion of 'civic community' was defined in terms of participation in public affairs, political equality, solidarity, trust and tolerance. The South's 'uncivicness' was indicated by a scarce number of associations, a low newspaper readership, a low turnout in referenda and a high incidence of preference voting (ibid.: 86–91).[4] Putnam argued that the failure to develop democratically

---

3. For a lively discussion of the implications of the terms 'civil' and 'civic' in the everyday life of a central neighbourhood in Rome undergoing gentrification, see Herzfeld 2009, especially 75–84.

4. According to Putnam, associations instilled in their members habits of cooperation, solidarity and public spiritedness. Newspaper readership was a mark of citizen interest in community affairs. The primary motivation for referendum voters was concern for public issues (whereas electoral turnout was theoretically enforced by law and conditioned by private interests), while preference voting was considered a reliable indicator of personalism, factionalism and patron-client networks.

and economically had been determined back in the Middle Ages when, in contrast to the city republics of northern and central Italy, the South was subject to highly centralized monarchical rule. The Unification of Italy had merely annexed the region into a foreign modern state without changing the structure of society (ibid.: 121–48).

Putnam's research was extremely influential, especially within the international Centre-Left, because it provided, for the first time, systematic empirical insights into the impact of 'social capital' upon democratic government. But it also generated intense debates and much controversy. The deluge of criticisms included accusations of historical inaccuracy and cultural determinism (Sabetti 1996; Ginsborg 2001: 106–7), a disregard for the role of political economy, state building and institutional actors upon political and economic performance (Tarrow 1996; Dunford and Greco 2006), a failure to apprehend the different socioeconomic situations in the South (Trigilia 1994) and a romanticized, conflict-free image of community (Levi 1996; Delanty 2000).

It is not my intention to dwell on Putnam's work or on the debate that surrounded it. I am not interested in a causational analysis about 'what makes democracy work' but in examining and challenging the power relations underlining the language of civics that shaped ideas about urban space in Naples during the 1990s. I want to consider how the city has fitted into the entrenched image of a 'civically inferior' Italian South in order to contextualize some of the key issues at stake during the Bassolino era.[5]

Naples's particular relationship with modernity has often been seen, à la Putnam, to possess distant historical roots. According to Percy Allum (1973), whose milestone study of postwar Neapolitan politics and society remains a point of reference in scholarly debates about the city, the residual hallmarks of a feudal-monarchical social system and the persistence of familist relations blocked the emergence of a modern society based around collective interests and organized action. 'This *Gemeinschaft* system ... was built on the notion that it was the ruler's business to provide a livelihood for the people. ... Today the state and the deputy have replaced the prince, and the clientela has replaced royal patronage' (ibid.: 55). Although modern, class-differentiated (middle-class and

---

5. By doing so, I do not wish either to endorse a diametrically opposed approach to Putnam that exalts a putative 'southern thought' (Cassano 1996) or a 'southern public spirit' (Piperno 1997) as alternative emancipatory narratives to alienating, unsustainable models of development. Although these might be considered local examples of what Jenny Robinson terms 'cosmopolitan' understandings of modernity (2006), such perspectives tend to hinge on an essentialist vision of 'southern Italian identity', which not only inverts negative stereotypes into positive generalizations but also removes traces of tension and oppression within the South (Palumbo 2001; Zinn 2007).

proletarian) residential districts arose on the city's outskirts after 1945, Naples remained isolated 'from the most dynamic economic and social changes of the postwar period' (ibid.: 28). The economy, social practices and ideals of the inhabitants of the 'casbahs' in the *centro storico* reflected a static, premodern world. Here the boundary between the public and private was blurred, and collective, impersonal ties were practically nonexistent. Instead, life was dominated by the closed, communal structure of the 'slum economy' (ibid.: 40) in which everyday survival revolved around a few steady incomes, minor remunerations and social allegiances.

Besides the inadequate, piecemeal nature of industrial development and the pervasive presence of clientelism in economic and political affairs, Allum argued that Naples's problems lay in the absence of a true bourgeoisie capable of modernizing local urban society and installing the principles of public life. The gap between the gentry and the populace was instead historically occupied by an intermediate class of bureaucrats, professionals and tradesmen sustained by the city's status as capital and later as privileged recipient of state funds, which after the Second World War was swelled by a more modern (but still largely dependent) class of public managers and civil servants.

This inherently conservative class stood in sharp contrast to the progressive tradition of an elite minority which traced its roots to the eighteenth-century enlightenment and the short-lived Parthenopaean Republic of 1799, when a small ensemble of idealistic aristocrats attempted to install a bourgeois state drawing directly on the principles of the French Revolution (Cuoco 1995). During the Republic's five-month existence, the term '*citoyen*' (citizen) was used publicly in the city for the first time. Its protagonists sought to install in the masses the moral virtues of citizenship and encouraged popular participation in a series of new public debating halls:

> [The formation of public opinion] could no longer be done through aristocratic salons, academies, lodges, colleges and libraries, but had to be widened to include the churches, theatres, public squares and streets, popular societies and instruction halls, because the welfare of the state itself now depended on this new 'public spirit'. Culture and politics in 1799 had to be shifted from the elites to the people. (Rao 1999: 360)

As Allum argues, the Parthenopaean Republic ultimately failed because it lacked a solid social basis and made no attempts to carry out the necessary economic reforms in order to gain mass support. For the urban poor, it offered little more than revolutionary catechism. The emphasis on the '*incivilmento*' (civilizing) of the masses was imposed from above with foreign (French) concepts that had scant regard for local cultural values or social practices. The Republic quickly fell in June 1799, after the withdrawal of the French troops and the arrival of the Royalist army, and its leaders were executed or forced into exile.

The episode left an enormous symbolic legacy on the history of the city. A century later, Benedetto Croce saw the 1799 Republic as a critical turning point in the history of the South and considered its moral virtues a founding myth of the new Italy (Davis 1999). However, the Republic also confirmed the gulf in interests between a '*borghesia illuminata*' (enlightened bourgeoisie) and a predominantly Royalist populace. In the face of a rich but abstract and hermetic intellectual tradition (Allum 1973: 81), Naples found itself during the twentieth century bound to the idea of a premodern 'uncivic' South (Gribaudi 1997), only instead of the isolated village in Basilicata at the focus of Edward Banfield's famous theory of 'amoral familism' (1958), there stood the image of an insubordinate and seething metropolis.

The idea of Neapolitan society as immutable and inchoate, individualistic but also hierarchical, has never entirely disappeared from representations of the city. Nevertheless, from the 1970s onwards, it would be severely questioned by critical scholars and disproved by events. The *Gemeinschaft-Gesellschaft* distinction, applied as a heuristic for the social and economic polarities in Naples, was deemed inadequate for explaining the complexities of the city. The argument of a persistent *Gemeinschaft* was itself disputed. Empirical evidence demonstrated that the significance accorded to a self-sustaining 'slum economy', the central lifeline for the inhabitants in the old city in Allum's 1973 thesis and a backbone of the vertical set of relations, was exaggerated and, with the onset of the economic crisis in the mid-seventies, was overshadowed by a vast informal economy based around outwork in the clothing industry – either at home or in small family-run firms – and low-level service jobs (Laino 1984; Pinnarò and Pugliese 1985; Goddard 1997). More important, Allum's research did not contemplate the political and social upheavals that were taking place during the 1970s. In the wake of the student and workers' movements of 1968 and 1969, large swathes of Neapolitan society, as in many other parts of Italy, became radicalized. For example, the organized unemployed groups, many of whose members hailed from the *centro storico,* not only demanded socially useful work for their ranks but also proposed the replacement of arbitrary forms of assistance with a universal guaranteed minimum income (Lay 1981; Vercellone 1996; Ramondino 1998). The intense struggles of the 1970s (discussed at greater length in the next chapter) provided a set of organizational models and political repertoires – including, significantly, the language of social rights – that would be drawn upon and reworked over the following years.

Traditional stereotypes and categories pertaining to the city's lower classes also began to be interrogated. During the 1970s, terms such as '*sottoproletariato*' (subproletariat or lumpenproletariat) and '*popolo*' (common people) were either rejected or invested with positive connotations.[6] Renewed interest in the 'lumpenproletariat' at the beginning of the decade, partly influenced by the anti-colonial work of Frantz Fanon, no longer perceived this group to be the dregs of society and inimical to revolutionary change, but a catalyzing, insurgent force that could and needed to be incorporated into the struggle for working-class hegemony (Salierno 1972: 99–121). The New Left, such as Lotta Continua, began using the term 'precarious' (or 'marginal') proletariat (Esposito 1973: 166–206; Fofi 2009: 108), so as to underline its strategic role within modern capitalist relations of production. Anthropologists, meanwhile, singled out more culturally sensitive, 'native' expressions that departed from a class perspective, such as '*popolino*' (little people) (Belmonte 1989: 132; Pardo 1996: 2–5), although sometimes at the risk of extrapolating from limited empirical evidence.[7] The flexible idea of '*classi popolari*' (popular classes) would be commonly adopted in the plural form by local and foreign researchers to purposely account for the different socioeconomic relations of neighbourhood residents who might otherwise appear to comprise a cohesive group.[8] (This is also the term that I choose to employ and which I discuss in greater depth in Part 4.) Certainly, attentiveness to a more engaged, critical vocabulary did not mean that negative representations of lower-class Neapolitans were finally laid to rest. On the contrary, the old pejorative images retained their currency in public and political debates, especially during critical moments such as local and national crime scares, and, as I will show, would become

---

6. For an in-depth analysis of the array of stereotypes associated with Neapolitan popular culture and society in the twentieth century, see Signorelli 2002.

7. Italo Pardo, for one, appears to overstate the everyday application of '*popolino*' as an expression of collective self-identity. From the personal experience of living in the *centro storico* for seven years, although at a later historical date (Pardo's research was mainly conducted in the 1980s), I would contend that this term is certainly not articulated by all those who might be seen to fall under its label, and even when it is, it is rarely used exclusively but is bound up with other forms of local, national and class identification.

8. Jane and Peter Schneider choose to describe the 'less privileged groups' of central Palermo as 'popular classes' so as to convey 'a more open-ended and varied understanding of work' (Schneider and Schneider 2003: 233). It must be noted that the term '*popolare*' has different connotations in different parts of Italy. In Rome, for instance, it is used to refer to a neighbourhood with a majority of artisan and industrial working-class residents, while in the Italian South it is generally employed in distinction to the blue-collar working class.

more discreet and nuanced as political and cultural frames of reference shifted.

Another disputed issue was the purported lack of associations. Allum had claimed that there were no cultural associations in Naples and that attempts to organize and maintain them after the Second World War had failed either due to general indifference or because they fell under the control of individuals who saw them as platforms for extending personal prestige and influence (Allum 1973: 61). A significantly different picture was provided by research conducted during the early 1990s, which discovered that associative activity across the Italian South was unexpectedly vibrant and that 70 per cent of the 6,400 registered organizations had been created after 1980 (Trigilia 1995: 15–22). Some of this growth developed out of the experiences of collective action of the previous decade but was also attributable to a rise in education levels and the expansion of the mass media. Associations tended to operate in the third sector, in the area of cultural consumption or around matters relating to the urban or natural environment (although a significant minority also mobilized against organized crime), and very often focused on single issues, such as the rehabilitation of heroin addicts, the running of cinema clubs or campaigns to save historic buildings (ibid.: 167–68). However, especially in the second and third cases, these activities involved mainly a restricted sphere of intellectuals, students and salaried middle classes, and few managed to engage the lower echelons of southern society (ibid.: 194). It was these 'virtuous minorities' that were commonly seen to constitute the germs of a modern civil society in the South. In mainstream Italian political and media debates, the idea of '*società civile*' not only indicated the intermediate area between the family, the market and the state (such as the activities of the church and political parties), but was used to specifically refer to those networks which stimulated democracy, equal rights and public debate in opposition to an 'uncivil' society characterized by vertical subordination, conformism and obedience (Ginsborg 2001: 94–96).[9]

---

9. Antonio Gramsci's famous reworking of 'civil society' as the non-state arena where the struggle for political hegemony takes place would be put into practice by the Italian Communist Party's postwar strategy of challenging the social and cultural primacy of the Catholic Church (see next section), although the term itself was never a key organizing category during this period. The rise in popularity and shift in significance of the term 'civil society' in Italy during the 1980s can instead be considered coeval with, and in part influenced by, its resurgence at a global level in reference to the resistance of dissidents and social movements to authoritarian regimes, especially in Latin America and Eastern Europe, and, later and more generally, to the actions of nongovernmental groups that aimed to revitalize democracy (Cohen and Arato 1992: 29–82). However, 'civil society' has also always been a notoriously polysemous idea (Fine 1997), while public debates have tended to be infused with ethical preconceptions about its role and standing in society. For this reason, and because it is not a concep-

This value-laden image of civil society was particularly pronounced in Naples during the 1980s and 1990s, where a number of heritage groups and cultural associations self-represented themselves and were singled out by the local press to be the principal progressive force in public debates amidst a general degeneration or decline of party political activity (Dini, Esposito and Nicolaus 1993: 30). Significantly, two of the most publicly visible expressions of this local 'civil society' drew directly on the liberal values of the Parthenopaean Republic. The internationally renowned Istituto Italiano di Studi Filosofici, which was set up by the flamboyant lawyer Gerardo Marotta in 1975 'in defence [in his own words] of an enlightened and European image of what was once a cultural capital' (*La Repubblica,* 10 March 1985), moved in 1984 to Palazzo Serra di Cassano, which had famously once belonged to a family of Jacobin martyrs and whose front gates had not been opened since the Bourbon Restoration.[10] During the 1980s and early 1990s, Marotta and other intellectuals were instrumental in coordinating opposition to urban restructuring programmes. For example, in 1991, the 'Assizes of Palazzo Marigliano' (named after the historic palace in the *centro antico* where meetings took place) brought together the city's cultural elite and members of opposition parties in protest at a government plan for a spate of new building in the city (De Lucia 1998: 85–86). This assembly was not only successful in identifying and blocking irregularities but in managing to create and sustain the semblance of a public sphere in the face of growing disillusionment with local democratic institutions.

A group at the forefront of cultural heritage debates during the same period was the Napoli 99 Foundation, set up in 1984, which coordinated restorations of monuments and, during the early 1990s, organized the Monumenti Porte Aperte programme. It, too, took its inspiration directly from the 1799 Revolution. The memory of the values of the failed bourgeois republic converged with the desire to salvage the city's threatened heritage. In contrast to the negative images of 'slums' and 'casbahs', the *centro storico* was considered testimony of the city's rich cultural traditions through which a positive sense of Neapolitan identity could be rebuilt (Governa 1997: 154). By restoring and opening monuments to the public, Napoli 99 hoped to involve Neapolitans from all social backgrounds in the formation of a common 'civic consciousness' (ibid.). Its president, Mirella Barracco, declared in 1999: 'The key to the success

---

tual focus of this book, I have decided not to employ 'civil society' as a descriptive label and only to consider it when it is used by others.

10. These gates would be temporarily opened for the first time by Marotta in 1995 on the fiftieth anniversary of the liberation of Italy from Fascism, thanks also to the climate of change introduced by the Bassolino administration, although Marotta later publicly admitted that this had been a mistake.

of our initiatives was the recovery of the city's memory. ... Our project seemed a bit utopian and Jacobin, tied as it was to 1799' (Barracco 1999: 77).

The idea of the *centro storico* as the repository of an illustrious history and the site of collective identity would become a central theme of urban regeneration during the 1990s. The experiences of groups such as Napoli 99 and individuals like Marotta were mobilized by the Bassolino administration. The council initially sponsored and later coordinated the Monumenti Porte Aperte programme, which after 1994 was renamed Maggio dei Monumenti (May of Monuments), while the mayor regularly participated in public debates at the Istituto Italiano di Studi Filosofici. This local elite represented a more enlightened Naples to the rampant corrupt city of the 1980s, as Bassolino exclaimed: 'We must be grateful to all those intellectuals who, during the politically dark years, did some extraordinary things and opened the way to political change' (Bassolino 1996a: 58). The memory of the 1799 Revolution resonated with the administration's attempts to 'ennoble' the *centro storico,* while its associations with liberal democracy and civicness were particularly pertinent to the Left's political project of the 1990s.

However, 1799 was by no means an exclusive historical point of reference,[11] and as much as there were close rhetorical affinities and forms of collaboration, the enlightened elite ultimately had limited impact on the administration's overall agenda for Naples. Arguably, accentuating the influence of individuals such as Marotta and Barracco during the Bassolino era, as has become popular among recent journalistic critiques (Scotto di Luzio 2008), overlooks the transformations that took place both in the city and in the institutional Left and its social base during the last three decades of the twentieth century (and, in particular, underestimates the emergence, from the 1970s onwards, of a highly educated, cosmopolitan and politically progressive middle class). Rather, the symbolic and cultural role attributed to the *borghesia illuminata* indicates the complexity of Naples as an arena for thinking about citizenship. If the city had long been seen to represent a deviant model that disturbed the archetypal topography of modernity, then the 1799 Revolution and its bicentennial legacy can be understood as an alternative internal narrative:

---

11. The bicentennial celebrations of the Neapolitan Revolution, in 1999, in part organized by the Bassolino administration, included theatrical reenactments in piazzas and palace courtyards of events connected with the Republic. Although these initiatives specifically aimed to connect with the more general revaluing of the *centro storico,* the bicentenary primarily revolved around a plethora of conferences organized by the Istituto Italiano di Studi Filosofici. Moreover, it was just one of many grand commemorative events held after 1993 and was indeed overshadowed the following year by a massive series of exhibitions dedicated to the memory of the Bourbon kingdom. Therefore, to highlight the bicentenary would be to attribute it a central significance that it never really had.

a top-down, idealistic project that sought to raise civic consciousness and nurture virtuous citizens. This coexisted alongside the upsurge in militancy after 1968, which likewise challenged the city's 'underdeveloped' citizenship – but through a groundswell demand for social rights and services. The overlapping and incongruous facets of this local genealogy would unravel during the Bassolino administration.

The Italian Communist Party and the enigma of Naples

Many commentators have rightly underlined the impact of the 1993 local electoral reform upon a new style of politics in Italian cities (Vandelli 1997; Baldini and Legnante 2000). Research has also focused on the central commanding role of mayor Antonio Bassolino in Naples (Pasotti 2000; Allum and Cilento 2001). Underlying these various studies is the premise that local politics during the 1990s became more personalized and less ideological: municipal programmes were seen to respond to contingent circumstances, while political parties, which had become increasingly detached from society, receded into the background. The problem with this reasoning is that, by extension, regeneration is invested with an air of inevitability and inherently ideological processes (such as the redefinition of public space) are reduced to merely technical matters. The Bassolino administration's idea of local government and its urban vision cannot be solely considered the obligatory responses to a change in rules, but rather evidence of deeper, long-term transformations on the Left that accelerated and materialized with the direct election of mayors. Thus, in order to (re)situate the 1990s in a broader political and historical context, we must first cast our eyes backwards and examine the relationship between the Italian Communist Party and Naples.

The Italian Communist Party played a major part in shaping the social, cultural and political landscape of postwar Italy. After its emergence from clandestinity in 1944, the PCI turned its back on Leninist vanguardism in favour of building a mass parliamentary party and, notwithstanding its allegiance to the Soviet Union that remained more or less unquestioned until the end of the 1960s, committed itself to an 'Italian Road to Socialism' based on reforms through existing institutions. At the peak of its electoral success, in the 1976 general election, the party polled 34.4 per cent of the total vote and had 1.8 million members.[12] While it never participated directly in national government, it ran numerous cities, particu-

---

12. The PCI's membership peaked at 2,145,317 in 1954 but dropped by over a quarter during the next decade, reaching 1,576,000 in 1966, only to rise again during the first half of the 1970s (Ginsborg 1990).

larly in the 'Red Belt' regions of Emilia-Romagna, Tuscany and Umbria. It also developed a formidable network of parapolitical structures, organizations and events, such as the *Case del Popolo* (Houses of the People) and the *Feste dell'Unità* (fund-raisers for the party's daily newspaper), which united its membership and challenged the traditional hegemony of the Catholic Church (Kerzer 1980; Ginsborg 1990: 195–99). But at the same time as creating what Stephen Gundle has described as 'the last great left-wing subculture in Western Europe' (Gundle 2000: 7), the PCI's diagnosis of the deep changes in Italian society was frequently marked by social conservatism and ideological rigidity. This was particularly pronounced in its negative response to the rise of a mass consumer culture during the 1950s and 1960s. The party was also dismissive, at least initially, of the 1968 student protests and over the following decade enjoyed a stormy relationship with the New Left and the myriad of social and cultural movements. If Bologna represented the international showpiece of Communist local government with its innovative planning and social policies (Jäggi et al. 1977), it was also the place where tanks were brought onto the streets in 1977 to quell the student 'plague-bearers' (as the then national leader Enrico Berlinguer described them) who had deigned to challenge the status quo in the PCI's backyard (Ginsborg 1990: 381–83).

The situation in Naples was a far cry from that of the Emilian capital, which had been run by the Left since the end of the Second World War and possessed strong anti-clerical and cooperative traditions. The PCI became the largest party in Naples for the first time in 1975 when it won 32.3 per cent in the municipal elections, and in the following year it went on to reap 40.9 per cent in the general election. These results were considered extraordinary given the city's age-old associations with the political Right and clientelism. Almost 80 per cent of Neapolitans had voted for the monarchy in the 1946 referendum, and thereafter local government was dominated firstly by the Monarchists and, from 1962, by the Christian Democrats. In reality, the PCI had steadily grown since its measly 8.2 per cent showing in the Constituent Assembly of 1946 (Cappelli 2003b). In the 1953 general election the party polled 21.3 per cent in Naples, and from 1958 onwards it either equalled or surpassed its national share of the vote and consistently fared better in Naples than in Milan or Rome (Comune di Napoli 2000). As the mass party took shape, the PCI rooted itself in working-class neighbourhoods such as Ponticelli, Barra and San Giovanni a Teduccio, in the east of the city, where throughout the postwar period it regularly polled over 40 per cent of the vote (and exceeded 60 per cent in the 1976 general election), but also became a significant presence in poor central districts such as Mercato and Stella, where it regularly exceeded its city average in both municipal and general elections (ibid.).[13]

During the 1960s, 'urban workers' (a classification which included both industrial workers and the urban poor) accounted for over half the party's rank and file in Naples and a sizeable proportion of the party's intermediate leadership, although they provided only 10 per cent of local members of parliament. Intellectuals, professionals and students, on the other hand, represented less than 5 per cent of membership (which was relatively high compared to the federations of other cities) but held over half of the local leadership posts and represented the overwhelming majority of PCI deputies in parliament (Allum 1973: 233–34). The disproportionate representation of the intelligentsia in the party's hierarchy reflected the disparate aspirations of a social and cultural elite, which viewed the PCI as a political instrument and career path, and the rank and file, which instead considered it as a way of life (ibid.: 235). Furthermore, the local federation was characterized by internal political differences between the reformist right-wing leadership, which placed emphasis on building alliances with the middle class and the Socialist Party, and a vocal leftist opposition, especially among students and industrial workers, which instead prioritized class struggle and pressed for greater internal democracy.[14] Such tensions were nevertheless kept in check by a common sense of loyalty and the party's rigid structure of democratic centralism or else were resolved by expulsions or defections.

It is crucial to understand that Naples presented Communists with political and organizational quandaries that they did not face elsewhere. The national strategy of the PCI had originally rested on building an alliance between the urban industrial working classes of the North and the peasants of the South, with the former assuming hegemonic leadership (Gramsci 1982). For Antonio Gramsci, the 'mystery' of Naples – a city that on paper was the fourth industrial centre after Milan, Turin and

---

13. While the PCI's electoral results steadily improved from the 1950s onwards, local party membership actually dropped by half in just over a decade, from 76,000 in 1954 to 34,000 in 1967. This was partly due to the establishment of the DC's new historic bloc in the South and the centre-left national government in the early 1960s, which drew away middle- and lower-class members, but also because many original recruits became disenchanted by the lack of grassroots militancy and did not renew their membership (Allum 1973: 230–39; Amyot 1981: 95–96).

14. The Communist Party in postwar Naples was dominated by the figure of Giorgio Amendola (1907–1980), who was also considered national leader of the pro-government wing that pressed for industrialization in the South on the premise that local society suffered from the absence of capitalist development. During the 1960s, a Left opposition, nationally led by Pietro Ingrao, called for a broad alliance with left-wing Catholics against the idea of a pact with lay and bourgeois left-wing parties. Political strategy in the South had to be explicitly anti-capitalist and not the 'two-stage' struggle envisaged by the Communist Right – first capitalist industrialization and then socialism (Amyot 1981: 87–102; Ginsborg 1990: 293–95).

Genoa but where local society remained unproductive and parasitic – was explained by its economic dependence on the circulation of the capital of large southern landowners (Gramsci 1978).[15] Also writing in the 1930s – but from exile in France – Emilio Sereni argued that while the demographic growth and urban life of Milan and Turin had been determined by industrial and commercial development, 'the large human agglomerate of Naples and its social structure ha[d] far more distant origins that [we]re the product of *other* economic conditions and *other* forms of life' (Sereni 1938, italics added). These early Communist attempts at deciphering Naples only further exacerbated its anomalous position both in relation to other cities and to the rest of the country, the South included.

After the Second World War, the party in Naples set about mobilizing campaigns in the popular neighbourhoods over housing shortages and poverty in order to keep the right-wing offensive at bay (Cappelli 2003b: 190).[16] The industrial proletariat played a political and symbolic role, not only as the motor of change, but as the 'civilizing force' for the entire city. The idea of a modern, collective-minded working class was contrasted to an individualistic and consumerist bourgeoisie[17] and shone as a guiding light for an undisciplined and politically fickle '*sottoproletariato*'. Industrial plants such as the Bagnoli steelworks, with their highly unionized and combative workforce, became beacons of political organization. The problem was that the party's working-class heartlands never represented more than 20 per cent of the city's population. In other parts of the city the industrial working class was dismembered and isolated, especially in the *centro storico,* where it was surrounded by 'the vast sea of artisan workshops and the seemingly endless waves of the unemployed' (Chubb 1980: 58). Here the proletariat was seen to live in perpetual risk of 'contagion' from the life of the alley. In her journeys around Naples and its province in 1968 as PCI parliamentary candidate, Maria Antonietta Macciocchi frequently recorded the mutual hostility between workers and their 'lumpen' neighbours or family members. At one point she visits Arturo, a party comrade and manual worker who

15. It should be noted that Naples is never mentioned in Gramsci's writings on the Italian South (penned between 1916 and 1926 and collected in *The Southern Question* (1982)) but is rather discussed in his article on 'Americanism and Fordism', which was written in prison in 1934.

16. During the immediate postwar period, for example, the PCI sent poor Neapolitan children on holidays to Emilia-Romagna, where they stayed with the families of comrades. For firsthand accounts of the Communist Party in Naples during the early postwar period by leading local members, see Cacciapuoti 1972; Palermo 1975. For a fictional reconstruction of the lives of *l'Unità* journalists in the city during the 1950s, see Rea 1995.

17. Throughout his life, Giorgio Amendola held firm the idea of a morally upright working class willing to make sacrifices for the collective good. In justifying the PCI's support for wage restraints in 1978 he claimed that '[the working class] does not want to imitate the bourgeoisie but ... wants to acquire a new, more collective and more fraternal way of living' (Forgacs 1990: 103–4).

lives at home with his parents. Like his father, Arturo used to work as a *magliaro,* a travelling salesman of poor-quality fabrics, which was a common trade among the Neapolitan 'sub-proletariat'. Macciocchi finds herself fascinated with the father's stories of foreign travels and ingenious selling techniques.

> Arturo looks on with shame and embarrassment. This *magliaro*-father of his obviously upsets him very much, for it is written all over his face. He keeps his head down and refuses to take part in the discussion. He acts as if the two of us were being in some way contaminated by certain stories, or challenged in our 'pure' choice of a communist life. ... I try to question Arturo about the alliance between proletariat and sub-proletariat in Naples, for example, given that it represents such an essential political problem in the struggle for socialism here. But Arturo I. looks at me from very far away, as if I were ingenuous, a romantic, *one who does not know.* (Macciocchi 1973: 233, original italics)

Whether perceived as a threat to class consciousness or the source of libertarian energies, the urban lower classes represented a particular psycho-political trope for the Neapolitan Left, one which, as will be examined in Part 4, would acquire new significance during the Bassolino era.

The glorious seventies

During the early 1970s, political attitudes among sectors of the city's population began to change. The broad swing to the left that swept Italy would also resonate deeply in Naples. First, there was a discernible shift in outlook among the bourgeoisie, in particular professionals and university-educated youths who had become disaffected with the corruption and inefficiency of DC-dominated administrations. Moreover, the 1974 referendum on the new divorce law, in which over 60 per cent of Neapolitans voted against the repeal of existing legislation, demonstrated the increasing autonomy of the middle-class Catholic electorate (Chubb 1980: 58–62). Second, the exponential growth and success of workers' struggles from 1969 onwards signalled the reverse of the timeworn idea of 'contagion', for it was now the sub-proletarian mass that became 'infected' by external models of political organization and action. This situation was accelerated by the numbers of former factory workers and young graduates who, with the looming economic crisis, began to swell the traditionally 'lumpen' ranks of the unemployed (ibid.).

A key turning point came with the cholera crisis in 1973.[18] At the end of August an outbreak of the deathly virus – which the authorities

---

18. The post-1968/69 swing to the left was not immediate: in the 1972 national election the neo-Fascist MSI made major gains in Naples, arriving at a postwar high of 26.2 per cent, just ten thousand votes short of the PCI.

blamed on contaminated mussels farmed in the polluted waters of the Gulf of Naples but which spread fundamentally as a result of the city's substandard sanitary conditions – caused several deaths and put over two hundred people in hospital. At the time, the prospect of an outright epidemic in a city already registering levels of child mortality and infectious disease double the national average laid bare the consequences of decades of mismanagement and clientelism.[19] A huge city-wide vaccination programme, the largest seen in Europe since the Second World War, was hastily organized. Of all the local political forces, the PCI played a leading role in setting up inoculation centres across the city and, in doing so, was able to project itself as a party of government. The crisis had an adverse affect on the informal economy. The countless farmers and street vendors of mussels suddenly found themselves out of work, and many would subsequently join forces with New Left groups to form the Organized Unemployed Movement. But cholera also put the whole city on alert, including those residents of wealthier districts, who had previously been little affected or concerned by the inadequate sanitation or dilapidation of the urban fabric in the *centro storico* (Chubb 1980). The cholera crisis thus represented a sort of political epiphany for the urban poor and middle classes. The two social groups which had been viewed as the central pillars of Christian Democrat power now began to see in the Left an alternative project for Naples.

The Communist Party's major gains in the 1975 municipal elections opened the doors to the first left-wing government in the city's history. Under veteran anti-Fascist Maurizio Valenzi, the PCI led a series of minority administrations until 1983, in alliance with the Socialist, Democratic Socialist and Republican Parties.[20] Naples was considered the jewel in the crown of the party's advances across Italy. The elections revealed the underlying democratic spirit of Neapolitans. In September 1976, the national *Festa dell'Unità* was held in Naples for the first time ever. The occasion offered local Communists the chance to demonstrate their organizational discipline to the rest of the country: the overgrown grounds of the Mostra d'Oltremare trade fair were hastily tidied by volunteers, an exhibition entitled 'Naples Produces' became a central attraction, while

---

19. For a reconstruction of the cholera crisis, see Esposito 1973. In 1970, Naples registered 58.9/1,000 deaths in the first year of a child's life, in contrast to the national average of 29.2, while infectious diseases reached a level of 33.8/1,000, in contrast to a national average of 8.3/1,000 (Chubb 1980: 77).

20. For firsthand accounts of the Valenzi administrations, see Geremicca 1977; Valenzi 1978; Wanderlingh 1988. For critical analyses, see Cappelli 1978; Chubb 1980, 1982; Ginsborg 1990: 398–99; Minolfi and Soverina 1993: 229–40.

the final rally with Enrico Berlinguer was attended by over one million people.

The record of the first left-wing government in Naples was a mixed one. There were some notable achievements. The administration was relatively successful in eliminating corruption and, at least in the beginning, absenteeism within the city council. During its eight years in power, it carried out around four hundred demolitions of illegally built structures and confiscated a further ten thousand housing units. Much of its scarce finances were channelled into social services. For instance, between 1975 and 1980, 333 new nursery classrooms were opened, compared to the 210 during the previous 30 years (Chubb 1980: 78). From 1979, echoing the initiatives already experimented in Rome, the administration coordinated a series of cultural events in public spaces, such as open-air cinema, aimed at enlivening the city centre during the summer months and establishing a new collective spirit. Over this period, the international reputation of Naples improved: a major exhibition on eighteenth-century Neapolitan culture travelled to Paris, London and Washington, while between 1979 and 1980 Jacques Chirac (the then-mayor of Paris), Pope John Paul II and Queen Elizabeth II all paid the city an official visit. As Valenzi would recall in the late 1980s: 'People in Europe started to talk about Naples no longer as the city of spaghetti with the revolver in place of the tomato topping, as it had been represented by a well-known German magazine [nb *Der Spiegel* in 1977], but as a great cultural capital' (Wanderlingh 1988: 30). Indeed, by the end of the 1970s some people had even started to venture the term 'Neapolitan Renaissance' (ibid.), although without the reverberations that this same expression would later provoke during (and after) the Bassolino era.

However, although the administration's good intentions and emphasis on honest government brought it wide respect, the initial popular enthusiasm was dampened by the Left's inability to meet expectations, particularly around job creation and infrastructural improvements. The administration immediately found its hands tied. It inherited a bankrupt, malfunctioning public sector riddled with clientelism, while the absence of an overall majority in the city council excluded the possibility of long-term projects. Moreover, the city council was unable to levy its own taxes, which meant it was dependent upon central state funds that, like the key command posts of the local economy, were firmly under the control of the Christian Democrats. At the same time, the PCI lacked an outright radical agenda. In response to the onset of the international economic crisis and the toppling of the Allende government in Chile in 1973, the PCI had renounced a left-wing political alternative in favour of economic austerity and a 'historic compromise' with its traditional DC rivals.[21] As Judith Chubb points out, 'In the eyes of the masses, the Communist Party had become a full participant in government, yet many … increasingly came to feel that nothing had changed but the political formulas' (Chubb 1980: 69–70). To top matters, the administration soon faced a growth in social protest in the city, not just from new unemployed lists organized by the DC and the extreme Right, but also from the very movements that had contributed to its victory. Indeed, contrary to the PCI's ideal of a productive economy based around technologically advanced industries, the Left eventually had to resort to the tried-and-tested tactic of using city government as a means of absorbing the jobless and, thanks to national legislation for youth employment passed in 1979, was able to create over six thousand posts in a range of areas, from rubbish collection to the restoration of monuments. Although the PCI experienced an upturn in support in 1979, thanks in part to the end of the historic compromise and the party's renewed grassroots activity,[22] the earthquake on 23 November 1980 practically spelt the beginning of the end of the Valenzi experience. Engrossed by the emergency, the administration's room for manoeuvre was greatly reduced, and while its handling of the aftermath compared favourably with later city governments, it finally fell in July 1983, after the PSI and the other minor parties switched allegiances to the Christian Democrats.

Crisis and transformation

The 1980s were a period of deep crisis for the Italian Communist Party both nationally and locally. The upsurge in collective action of the previous decade which had bolstered the PCI's electoral success and rejuvenated its ranks had abated in the face of defeat, disillusionment, increasing violence and state repression. From 1980, both the party's proportion of the vote and membership steadily dwindled. Even though it still managed to obtain over a quarter of the nation's votes in the 1987 general election, it lost the advances that it had made during the mid-1970s. Politically isolated but locked into the machinery of power through *lottizzazione* (the division of spoils, for instance in state television), the party often found

---

21. Austerity measures in Italy included a hike in fuel prices, a reduction of street lighting, early closures of shops and entertainment venues, and the suspension of private traffic on Sundays. The PCI's emphasis on workers' sacrifices did little to ameliorate its relations with social movements. The historic compromise was enacted nationally following the PCI's advances in the 1976 general election which saw the PCI supply external support to the government (Ginsborg 1990: 351–60).

22. The 1979 general election saw the PCI's vote in Naples drop by over ten points in the space of three years, from 40.8 to 30.7 per cent. However, it managed to limit its losses in the local elections the following year, polling 31.7 per cent, which was only 0.6 per cent less than its 1975 result.

itself unable to formulate meaningful responses to changes in Italian society without falling back on ideological certainties and could no longer presume to wield hegemony over anti-systemic opposition (especially following the rise of the regionalist 'leagues' in northern Italy during the late 1980s). While PCI-led city administrations had revolutionized cultural policy and some of its own events continued to draw huge crowds – the *Festa dell'Unità* in Correggio near Reggio Emilia, for instance, became famous during the period for its international music festival that staged acts as diverse as Jethro Tull, King Sunny Adé and Siouxsie and the Banshees (Pelliciardi 2008) – beneath the spectacle, the party hierarchy 'struggled to make sense of the waning appeal of an orthodox political language' (Gundle 2000: 3). For Communists in Naples, the industrial working class continued to represent a bastion of democracy (Ranieri 1994), but in the face of factory closures and restructuring, political campaigns increasingly turned their attention to defending existing jobs.

All this said, one cannot overlook some important changes that nevertheless took place during the 1980s. First, there was a major generational turnover in the national party leadership with the arrival of younger people, such as Massimo D'Alema, Piero Fassino and later Walter Veltroni, who were less immersed in Communist ideology, if not the party's organizational methods, and who would mastermind the metamorphosis of the Left over the following two decades. Second, with the demise of the mass party and its roots in working-class neighbourhoods, the social makeup of the PCI's electorate in Naples became more heterogeneous. Significantly, it consolidated its vote in middle-class residential districts such as Vomero and Arenella. In 1987, the PCI's overall result in Naples was similar to 1968, but its vote was now more evenly spread across the city (Cappelli 2003b: 201).[23] Third, the party began to revise some of the fundamental tenets of its economic thought, assuming unabashedly pro-market positions, which included support for private enterprise and even privatization of state companies. Despite its steadfast defence of the role of heavy industry in the city's development, especially the Bagnoli steelworks, the PCI in Naples acknowledged the need to develop a mixed economy that included services and tourism (PCI 1986). Finally, in response to its ideological predicament and the new demands posed by its increasingly cross-class electorate, the party seriously took on board themes that had traditionally been alien to its political culture, such as civil rights, feminism and the environment. After the electoral defeat of

---

23. It is worth noting here that the New Left party Proletarian Democracy (DP) (between 1975 and 1987) and the Green Party (from 1987 onwards) both received some of their highest share of the vote in Vomero and Arenella, as well as in the lower-middle-class suburbs of Fuorigrotta and Soccavo and the mixed middle-class and popular central district of Avvocata (Comune di Napoli 2000).

1987 and under the leadership of Achille Occhetto, the review of the party's core doctrine intensified amidst growing awareness of the need for a break with the past (Ignazi 1992; Hellman 1996). It was during this period that some began to openly propose the broad theme of citizenship – and with it the intertwined triumvirate of democracy, liberty and rights – as the central guiding value for a renewed Communist Party.[24]

The PCI had therefore already begun to confront its political and organizational impasse long before its dissolution was triggered by the fall of the Berlin Wall in November 1989. The drawn-out and acrimonious period of transition culminated in February 1991 with the foundation of the Democratic Party of the Left (PDS) and a sizeable dissenting group, Communist Refoundation.[25] This outcome has been conventionally read as the straightforward split between moderate reformists and nostalgic hardliners. In reality, both parties sought a change in direction to arrest the general decline of the Left, and, with the end of democratic centralism, each came to be characterized by internal factions. Communist Refoundation, which accommodated the die-hard (and traditionally pro-Soviet) wing of the PCI but also remnants of the New Left (following the merger of Proletarian Democracy in June 1991), aimed at rekindling a radical, anti-capitalist opposition that was seen to have withered during the latter years of the PCI. The PDS incarnated the reformist and 'party of government' ambitions that had existed in the PCI but from the outset was divided between radical liberals and social democrats as well as a 'movementist' left wing, which, although less politically influential, symbolized the 'depository of the old anti-systemic tradition' (Ignazi 1992: 176). The PDS leadership intensified the revisionist process that had begun in the late 1980s and was now propelled by the removal of traditional mores and taboos. It wholeheartedly embraced the tenets of liberal democracy and civil rights alongside a generalized discourse about social solidarity as it steadily moved away from a class-based vision of politics. It became an enthusiastic advocate of institutional reforms and, later, economic liberalization (Cioffi and Höpner 2006) and in the arena of foreign policy was an unquestioning supporter of European Union integration and Italy's participation in NATO. But if it had officially relinquished its traditional alter ego of 'party of struggle', the PDS continued

---

24. The terms 'citizen' and 'citizenship' were first officially pronounced and discussed by delegates during the PCI's XVIII Congress in 1989 but had been raised during previous years in debates about the party's renewal. One of the first reflections was in the PCI journal *Rinascita*, in July 1986, where Luigi Berlinguer argued that the citizen rather than class should become the privileged category in Communist politics: 'Moving to the side of the citizen would represent a great cultural revolution' (quoted in Ignazi 1992: 56).

25. For an analysis of the dissolution of the PCI, see Ignazi 1992; Ginsborg 1998: 297–304. For firsthand accounts from both the PDS and PRC perspective, see Fassino and Garavini 1992.

to tap into what it perceived to be the moral legacy and unique status of Italian Communism. Hence, even though a number of PDS functionaries were indicted in *Tangentopoli,* the party portrayed itself as historically immune to the systematic corruption that existed in the DC and PSI (Bull 1996).[26]

The transformation of the PCI did not pay immediate dividends. On the contrary, in their first major electoral tests in the local and national elections of 1992, the two new left-wing parties did particularly badly. In Naples, the combined PDS and Communist Refoundation vote in the municipal elections of 16.9 per cent was lower than any of the PCI's previous results in the city since 1946, and for the first (and last) time was overtaken by the Socialists. Significantly, the only areas where the PDS vote held firm were the middle-class districts, which confirmed its ongoing metamorphosis from a traditional mass party into a cross-cleavage electoral party.[27] Between the trail of destruction left by *Tangentopoli* and the entry of Silvio Berlusconi into national politics at the head of a new centre-right alliance, the mayoral victories of late 1993 provided the Left with a momentary respite from its long-term political crisis and electoral freefall. As noted in the previous chapter, these elections were played out amidst general aversion for the old-party system. There was no mass demand for major socioeconomic changes as there had been in 1975, but rather a popular expectation of moral palingenesis. Temporarily relieved of the pressures of addressing structural issues such as unemployment, the Bassolino administration found itself – and the mayor *in prima persona* – in the singular position of commandeering this 'new beginning', not only in terms of developing an agenda of urban renewal but also in elaborating a new political imaginary for the Left. In fact, the publicity accorded to municipal agendas after 1993 would provide the Left with a strategic foothold in national politics over the following years. Although the Alliance of Progressives (the same alliance that had backed Bassolino in December 1993) would lose to Berlusconi in the national general election of March 1994, the widespread popularity of the left-wing mayors, and especially Antonio Bassolino, would play an influential part in the Olive Tree Alliance's success in the 1996 elections, which saw the PDS enter into national government for the first time.

---

26. For an in-depth analysis of the party identity, organizational structure and strategy of the PDS/DS during the 1990s, see Bellucci, Maraffi and Segatti 2000; Giannetti and Mulé 2006.

27. Following the passage from the PCI to the PDS, national membership dropped by half from 1,417,000 in 1989 to 682,000 in 1995 (Giannetti and Mulé 2006: 464), with an immediate exodus of 129,000 members to Communist Refoundation (Foot 1996: 174). In 1995, the provincial federation of the PDS in Naples had 16,500 members, of which only 6,776 were in the city itself (Cappelli 2003b: 211). Numerous party sections closed or were sometimes substituted by 'thematic structures' that dealt with specific issues such as women, social solidarity, the environment and the *centro storico* (ibid.).

The post-Communist imaginary: reclaiming urban citizenship

> During the frantic and extraordinary changes of recent years we have all had ... a guid-
> ing principle: to reconstruct the rights of citizenship, the elementary foundations of
> freedom and democratic participation which, during the final phase of the Pentapartito
> regime, had seriously and dangerously deteriorated. (Bassolino 1996b: 85)

In the wake of *Tangentopoli,* and with the direct election of mayors, a
new overarching discourse about citizenship entered the centre stage of
local politics. This underlined a more interactive relationship between
voters and the administration, encompassed an emphasis on a series of
rights and obligations and alluded to a rebuilding of affective ties between the city and its inhabitants. Across Western Europe during the
1990s, citizenship became a new privileged category in the urban politics of the reformist Left. The changing social structures and decline of
class-based voting meant that social democratic urban regimes looked
for broad support for their policies to remain in power. The city, rather
than class, was cast as the basis of collective identity and the site of mutual interests (McNeill 1999). At a wider level, citizenship responded to
a general ideological crisis and the 'need for a radical but realistic revi-
sion of Western political grammar' (Zolo 1994: ix), which reflected the
influence of liberal thought on Western European socialism during the
1980s and which became more pronounced following the collapse of
Communist regimes after 1989.

The 'conversion' to citizenship was particularly conspicuous in the
writings of Antonio Bassolino.[28] During the 1970s and 1980s, as a leading exponent of the PCI's Left, Bassolino had been at the forefront of
political campaigns to defend workers' rights and prevent the dismantlement of industrial plants across the South (Leonetti and Napoli 1996). He
disputed those in the Communist Party who continued to view southern
Italy – and Naples in particular – as socially and economically backward.
In his 1980 book *Mezzogiorno alla Prova* (*The Italian South on Trial*),
Bassolino highlighted the city's modernity: '[Naples] is not just destruction and degradation, but also a great civil, productive and democratic
reality. ... It is a city with a strong sense of its own autonomy. It does not
want more centralism but the chance to count' (Bassolino 1980: 24). The
PCI needed to build its political strategy around 'a new historic block
consisting of a plurality of protagonists' (ibid.: 139), namely women,
youths and mass intellectuals, but also progressive Catholic organiza-

---

28. The focus here is on Bassolino not simply because he was mayor but because, more than others,
he reflected upon the changes in left-wing politics. For testimonies by other executive members of the
administration, see in particular: Becchi 1994; Nicolini 1996; De Lucia 1998; and Marone 2002.

tions: 'Today "Southern city" means many things: housing, work, free time etc. … but it's also about [for instance] the new needs of youths with whom Communist organizations are unable to establish positive and creative relationships' (ibid.: 34). Nevertheless, the working class would remain the principal 'agent of transformation', both as a democratic and productive force and as the backbone of the PCI's electoral support (ibid.: 134). Working-class hegemony needed to expand to incorporate the new demands of other subjects in order to build a new road to socialism (ibid.: 147).

After 1993, the central role attributed to the working class in transforming the city would disappear from Bassolino's political analysis. In his 1996 book *La Repubblica delle Città* (*The Republic of Cities*), based on a series of interviews with the editors of the journal *Meridiana*, issues of class identity and conflict intermittently enter discussion only as (positive) memories of a closed chapter in the city's recent history. As a mayor who no longer considered himself a Communist but a 'leftist' who had shed his 'ideological straitjacket' (Marrone 1996: 26), Bassolino now increasingly spoke in terms of *'cittadini'*. The post of mayor demanded a nonpartisan relationship with the city, which meant acquiring the trust of all citizens and bypassing the traditional practices of parties and unions to 'deal directly with the problems of common people' (Bassolino 1996b: 79). But the language of citizenship was more than just a pragmatic adjustment to a new system of local governance. Bassolino located its rediscovery in a broader social and cultural movement that had arisen in response to the crisis of welfare systems and traditional political organizations (ibid.: 85–86). It also reflected the consequences of the 'undisputed hegemony' of neoliberalism during the 1980s, which from its origins as a right-wing economic philosophy had permeated the entire social arena (ibid.: 86–87). According to Bassolino, this ideological shift had swept the Left up in its tracks:

> By appropriating and assimilating the key values of liberalism, it was inevitable and sacrosanct that the Left finally placed the concept of citizenship at the centre of its action. … This meant accepting the liberal tenet that there can be no form of political democracy which does not protect the rights of the individual citizen (Bassolino 1996b: 87).

Nevertheless, the idea of citizenship ran the risk of becoming an abstraction (Bassolino 1996b: 87). During the referendum season on institutional and electoral reforms of the early 1990s, a great emphasis was placed on the role of citizens in seizing back sovereignty from the clutches of a corrupt regime (ibid.: 88), but while producing important changes, this euphoria had tended to reduce 'the complexity of politics to the liberating moment of the vote' (ibid.: 89). Instead, citizenship needed to be understood as the arduous, ongoing process of reconstructing a political community. The starting point for Bassolino was 'the idea and the reality of the city' (ibid.: 91).

The notion of a reinvigorated urban citizenship operated at three general levels. First, it was conceived in terms of a closer relationship between the city and its political institutions, which meant 'finding the instrumental means for involving as many people as possible in administrative decisions' (Bassolino 1996b: 81). The PCI had always placed great importance on mass political participation, but this was typically encouraged through party or trade union membership. In order to enrich and broaden local democracy, Bassolino instead sought to mobilize and involve '*la società civile*', not only the nationally renowned cultural associations such as Napoli 99, but less prestigious organizations such as Catholic voluntary groups working in the third sector (ibid.: 55). Groups which had previously operated independently or had reverted to direct action in the face of political indifference now enjoyed a symbiotic relationship with the local administration. For instance, members of the environmental organization Neapolis 2000 who had once chained themselves to city council gates in 1987 to prevent an ancient cemetery being turned into a car park, now collaborated with the Bassolino administration in organizing guided visits and public events in the *centro antico*. Like Bassolino, the group's president extolled the virtues of an active citizenship:

> The association's project not only strives for a cleaner and more organized city with efficient transport, more green space and less pollution, but also aims to contribute to the realization of a civil city – the citizens' city – which is able to face and overcome hardship and solitude and create a sense of belonging and a desire to participate. (Maturo 1999: 14–15)

At the same time, Bassolino frequently spoke of the need to build a new *classe dirigente* (ruling elite) to inspire and guide the transformation of Naples. As mentioned, his own executive initially drew on the experiences of experts from outside party politics. Furthermore, public opinion assumed a greater political influence compared to its more subordinate role in the past. The local media became a significant forum of debates as well as a line of communication between the mayor and intellectuals, cultural and tourist operators and business people. This sense of increased accountability, whereby the mayor was 'subjugated to daily, even obsessive, controls by the press and organized groups of citizens' (Bassolino 1996b: 79), represented a decisive break from the previous situation when parties and political alliances masterminded the direction of administrative affairs. Maurizio Valenzi complained that as mayor of

Naples he had to answer to his party every fifteen days. Ironically, one of his habitual inquisitors was Bassolino, then regional secretary of the PCI (Vandelli 1997: 26).

Second, citizenship encapsulated a series of individual and collective rights and duties. These were integral to a political strategy of constructing consensus around the administration and its new municipal vision (Pasotti 2000). Bassolino argued that employment remained a central pillar of citizenship: 'It is the daily relationship with work which transforms every individual into a citizen and a conscious and participating member of a community' (Bassolino 1996b: 67). However, in the face of the crisis of welfare provisions, rights were no longer simply linked with traditional economic and social concerns but increasingly encompassed wider issues such as the quality of, and respect for, the environment (which translated into measures such as traffic restriction and pedestrianization schemes and the provision of public parks), mobility (improved public transport), the recuperation of the city's cultural heritage for public fruition, and guaranteeing the personal security of residents. This last commitment, in particular, was seen as a priority for a responsive administration:

> Just as in the past the right to jobs, healthcare and housing were the stable conquests of a civil existence, now we need to guarantee the right to security as one of the fundamental rights of citizenship. ... Concepts such as security, public order and legality must enter fully into the language of the Left. ... They are not right-wing matters. They are matters of democracy. (Bassolino 1996b: 60, 63)

At a third level, the idea of citizenship was used to denote the strengthening of bonds between Neapolitans and their city. Citizenship, according to Bassolino, was first and foremost a local phenomenon that was bound to a sense of belonging and a set of social relations. The identity of a city was not an invention of the new mayors but something they had nevertheless been able to rediscover and revitalize (Bassolino 1996b: 73). The project of harnessing civic pride through the recuperation and valuing of the city's cultural heritage was more plausible in Naples because, Bassolino argued, it possessed a much more homogenous population than other large Italian cities. While 95 per cent of Neapolitans were born locally, only 35 per cent of inhabitants in Rome were 'Romans'.

> [Naples] has continued, especially in recent decades, to sustain itself demographically. So while there was a negative sense of belonging in the past when the city was on the brink of disaster, so there was a strong, positive sense of a new identity when it was clear that we could pull ourselves out of this situation on our own. (Bassolino 1996b: 15)

The notion of 'napoletanità' (Neapolitanness) had been treated with suspicion by the Left. Maurizio Valenzi had considered traditional ideas about Neapolitan identity as reactionary in the way they tended to exult the city's weaknesses and social and cultural anomalies and resort to folklore that was indelibly linked to subaltern and nonworking-class cultures (Valenzi 1978: 172–74). According to Valenzi, a more politically progressive *napoletanità* needed to assimilate an enlightened, intellectual tradition represented by the likes of Vico and Croce and celebrate the city's past as 'a great capital', when it had attracted illustrious visitors from across Europe (ibid.: 173–74). In a not entirely different way, but now incorporated into a more specific idea about urban change, Bassolino spoke out against what he termed the 'ideology of ugliness' (Bassolino 1996b: 55), which referred to what he considered a masochistic attachment to the dirt and disorder of the 'old' Naples. In order for the city and its citizens to flourish, this perverse sensibility would have to be wiped out. Regeneration narratives about Naples sought to remove the negative images of urban neglect, political indifference and a general disdain for the public realm and construct in their place more unequivocal images about the city based around positive notions of heritage and decorum.

These three principal elements of urban citizenship – greater participation, an expanded set of rights and obligations and a rehabilitated sense of local identity – traced out a course for a new left-wing urban politics and provided the ideological ballast upon which the Bassolino administration developed its vision for a new, all-inclusive city. Neapolitans were no longer considered in terms of social class but as individuals who constituted a common community. They were made to feel part of a shared project that would improve Naples for Neapolitans. According to some commentators, this sense of collaboration was instrumental to the initial growth in the mayor's support (Pasotti 2000). The *centro storico* played a fundamental role in constructing a more tangible and expansive idea of citizenship. This was the physical and symbolic heart of Naples, which all its citizens were now able to retrieve as part of their 'collective identity' (Bassolino 1996a: 59).

The limits of a reinvigorated citizenship

If the category of class had often been problematic in relation to Naples, where alignments were not always clear cut, so too was the broad idea of citizenship in a city of deep divisions. While class was an inherently conflictual discourse, this element tended to be neutralized in citizenship. The PCI's class-based politics had implied, at least at an idealistic level, the struggle against inequality. In contrast, Bassolino's conception of citizenship suggested a design to reconcile social cleavages for the overall good of the city. As a political corrective, however, this vision possessed numerous blind spots. If the mayor had once advanced the idea of a working-class hegemony that incorporated the demands of women, young people and others, the new grand narrative of urban citizenship – as Bassolino expressed it – did not directly address particularistic interests.[29] Similarly, it could be argued that the PCI's class discourse, in spite of everything, had been forced, over the years, to confront the city's complexities. In comparison, the universalist posturing of citizenship sounded extrinsic and often implausibly grandiloquent.

Beneath the rhetoric of inclusion, there were tensions and dilemmas. First, the possibilities of direct participation in administrative affairs were, in reality, limited. The vast majority of Neapolitans had very little say in the reordering of the city. The discourse about democratization referred more immediately to putting right the abuses of the previous decade than a serious programme of participatory governance. While the new electoral reform provided for greater stability and autonomy, it had also delegated more power in the hands of the mayor and the executive which led to decisions and policies being made 'in the interests of the city' that circumvented public and political debate (Allum and Cilento 2001; Brancaccio 2003). Moreover, the insistence on an efficient and functional administration sat uncomfortably with the prospect of active citizen involvement in public affairs which was a typically slow, nonlinear and conflict-laden process.

At the same time as paying lip service to greater cooperation in urban affairs, the administration was actually distrustful of certain sectors of Neapolitan 'civil society', which in part recalled the PCI's aloofness towards associative activity (Ginsborg 2001: 158–59). It reputed some middle-class organizations to be self-interested and to have been em-

---

29. With this I do not want to suggest that Bassolino suddenly became indifferent to questions of age or gender (indeed, his long-term partner Anna Maria Carloni was, in 1998, one of the founding members of the Emily Association, which supported women in centre-left politics). Rather, it is to provocatively argue that such issues were accorded greater significance in his concept of class in the early 1980s (that had been forced to take on board the social and cultural upheavals of the previous decade) than in the post-Communist regeneration narrative of the 1990s. As mayor, Bassolino continued to place great emphasis on young people and children, but these were now seen less as the bearers of particular claims than as individuals to be cultivated as the city's future citizens (Bassolino 1996b: 67). Such observations stand in contradiction to the commonly held view that a key reason for the flourishing of debates on citizenship in the 1990s was because this was precisely a category that could embrace the cultural, gender and generational differences previously eclipsed by class readings of social conflict. But at the same time, they ultimately underline the Centre-Left's ambivalent appropriation of citizenship as the frame for a politics of conciliation.

broiled in the clientelistic system of the previous regime.[30] But it also appeared reticent to involve popular and social movements now that an organized working class no longer provided leadership (Bull 2005: 404). This was clearly demonstrated with the Bagnoli plan, which was drawn up according to a preset agenda of public-planning controls and environmental sustainability and only afterwards consulted local associations (Bull 2005; Corona 2007). In key urban interventions, the administration was more inclined to command from above or to collaborate with consultants and their entrusted networks (Amaturo 2003), although this latter point could also been seen as a reflection of the fragmented nature of local elites and their inability to influence political decisions in a durable way (Savonardo 2003).

It was not always enough that people played by the rules. Access to decision-making processes was contingent upon skewed distributions of power, resources and status. The idea of democratization through the local media – structured as it was around editorial agendas, privileged voices and assumed audiences – was ambivalent to the say the least and indeed contributed greatly to the personalization of politics (Cappelli 2001). On the other hand, some people were simply not able to contribute to Bassolino's project of a new Naples, and the mantra of an active citizenship merely accentuated rather than mitigated their exclusion. This was most blatant in the case of immigrants. Although many were city dwellers (and therefore *cittadini* in the everyday Italian sense), they were not entitled to the political rights of citizenship (which above all meant they could not vote in local elections), and, as shall be examined in the case of Piazza Garibaldi, had a very limited voice in debates about the city.

Similar contradictions stood out in the discourse about a new set of urban-based rights and duties. It was not always clear who was able to enjoy entitlements and who instead was more subject to obligations. The right of access to the city's cultural heritage appeared to privilege visitors more than local residents, who were expected to appropriately adapt their use of the public realm, while immigrants in certain areas of the *centro storico* were at times considered more a source of 'insecurity' than

---

30. Amidst accusations made prior to the 1993 election by Democratic Alliance (AD, a small liberal reformist party that backed Bassolino in the second round) that civic associations were underrepresented in the Left alliance's campaign, Bassolino retorted that not all of civil society was pure and immaculate (presentation of electoral programme, 4 October 1993, http://www.radioradicale.it/scheda/57869?format=32), while PDS leader Achille Occhetto sarcastically reminded AD that working-class organizations also represented an important element of civil society (press conference in Naples, 22 October 1993, http://www.radioradicale.it/scheda/59314?format=32).

the beneficiaries of greater public order. As long as issues of heritage and security were fluid and contextual, these could not be understood as equally distributable like modern forms of welfare. The administration's strategy of a rights discourse thus served less to broaden a notion of urban justice than to lay down a set of values and prerequisites for a more cohesive city. What these rights meant in concrete situations was often open to dispute, as will be demonstrated in the case of DAMM, where activists' attempts to encourage a mixed use of a neighbourhood park sharply contrasted with official pronouncements about the purpose of public space.

Finally, the notion of rebuilding people's affective ties with the city was problematic in the way it generated and sanctioned rarefied ideas about local identity. Following its exponential rise in popularity as an explanatory category during the 1980s, '*identità*' has consistently been conceived in Italian public discourse as a sort of inner truth and only very rarely as something socially constructed and relational (Fabietti 1995; Remotti 1996). According to Stuart Hall's evocative formulation, the main function of such an idea of identity is that it provides *a good night's rest*: 'Because what [it] tell[s] us is that there is a kind of stable, only very slowly changing ground inside the hectic upsets, discontinuities and ruptures of history. Around us history is constantly breaking in unpredictable ways but we, somehow, go on being the same' (Hall 1991: 43). The situation in Naples was somewhat more complex in that the search here was for a place to have this rest. Most of the city's pundits concurred that Neapolitan life during the 1980s had been caught up in a living nightmare of illegality, disorder and poverty. The city's identity had literally been lost beneath these 'hectic upsets' and now needed to be retrieved, not as a defensive strategy against the outside world but through an internal surgical operation. As Iris Marion Young argues, the most serious political consequence of the urge for a mutual sense of belonging is that 'It often operates to exclude or oppress those experienced as different' (Young 1990: 234). I would argue that this was particularly pronounced with the regeneration of the *centro storico* during the 1990s, where the conception of a rehabilitated Neapolitan identity as the common denominator and basis of collective identification did not only automatically exclude immigrants (who could not make any 'authentic' claims to being Neapolitan) but also marginalized those 'natives' whose social, cultural or economic practices stood in opposition to official ideals about civic pride or urban decorum. Local identity was not simply read off according to a list of telling traits but exalted the behaviour of responsible citizens and restrained (at least discursively) that of a recalcitrant populace.

Good citizens for a regenerated city

The Bassolino administration was certainly not intent on projecting a rosy image of Naples. On the contrary, the mayor openly spoke about the huge difficulties and challenges facing the city. The desire for a cohesive citizenship was not simply a tactic aimed at making Naples and its *centro storico* more attractive to economic investment or tourism (Amin and Graham 1997: 426). Citizenship met Bassolino's need for a progressive register and a new approach to thinking about the city that could transcend the Left's traditional class-based worldview and critique of the structural inequities of capitalism. This 'new realism' did not signal a post-ideological pragmatism, as some have intimated, but rather the reframing of meanings about democracy, rights and identity in view to remedying the 'uncivic' failings of the city in the past.

The reinvigorated sense of citizenship that permeated the urban project of the Bassolino administration was articulated as a noble and benign objective and therefore smoothed over its underlying discriminatory and contradictory logic. A helpful analogy here is provided by Yasemin Soysal's work on recent shifts in European school history curricula. Over the last two decades a common trend has occurred in different countries whereby the representation of national identity has been redefined according to the principles of human rights, liberal democracy and transnationality (Soysal 2007). With the end of the Soviet bloc, Europe has no longer had any internal ideological rivalries. The only principle 'other' remains the Holocaust as a source of collective guilt, while the continent's colonial past has been eclipsed and reframed by current intercultural experiences with the rest of the world. Otherwise, the portrayal of European national histories has been rendered coherent and freed of conflict. Soysal sees these changes in history curricula as recodifying what it means to be a 'good citizen' in a globalizing world.[31] Likewise, the narrative of a regenerated Naples was closely bound to the idea of nurturing 'good citizens', each of whom ideally contributed to the bolstering of local identity, aspired to participate (even if this was not possible) in a collective project and adhered to a common set of values and norms of conduct (Rose 2000). It was around such figures that a new city could be rebuilt and secured. But beneath the 'noble' pursuit of reinvigorating citizenship lay 'a process of recruitment that [was] calculative, cultural and disciplinary' (Newman and Clarke 2009: 172).

---

31. Soysal and her research team focused on the cases of the United Kingdom, France, Germany, Greece and Turkey. An analysis of Italy would have identified an intensification over recent years of an ideological battle waged by the (mainly ex-MSI) Right to 'depoliticize' history textbooks and, in particular, to play down references to the anti-Fascist resistance in the founding of the Italian Republic.

My interest will be to examine how this dominant version of citizen-ship played out in the public domain of the city. The implications of citizenship vis-à-vis regeneration raise a series of questions that have been rarely addressed in Naples. For example, how did prescribed ideas about the *centro storico* as the site of cultural heritage and civic pride clash with the acts and experiences of its various users? How far was dif-ference acknowledged? When was it labelled deviant? How, by challeng-ing official formulations of citizenship, did difference become political? (And here it should be remembered that citizenship claims could also be reactionary, especially regarding the question of security.) The issue of citizenship therefore contextualizes political debates about regeneration during the 1990s, but by producing tensions and contradictions, it also provides a useful framework through which to examine conflicts in and over the city: from the problematic presence of immigrants in Piazza Garibaldi and the divergent interpretations of Piazza Plebiscito as a new urban symbol to the alternative urban project of DAMM based on the ideals of direct participation and the self-management of a public park. The idea of local citizenship henceforth needs to be considered not just as a fixed dimension that circumscribes political action, but also as a field of struggle through which people's differentiated claims to the city are continually made and given meaning.

Chapter 4

Public Space and Urban Change

The 'fall' and 'rise' of public space

On returning to the city in early 1993, after almost ten years spent in Rome, Bassolino claimed to be struck above all by the sorrowful state of the city's public realm: 'What shocked me more than anything else was that nobody protested about the level of ungovernability and *degrado* [degradation] which the city had reached. Piazza Plebiscito, which had become a gigantic car park, was unrecognizable. ... This and many other historic collective spaces no longer existed' (Bassolino 1996b: 16). An immediate goal of the new administration was to eradicate the sense of disorder that had befallen the city. Following the opening of the post-earthquake parks and facilities on the outskirts of Naples in early 1994, the focus of attention soon converged on the *centro storico,* where, during the preceding years, local judges, cultural associations and young people had begun to reclaim pockets of space from traffic and illegal activities and to establish new social and recreational activities. These different initiatives were enthusiastically endorsed by the cash-strapped administration as it sought ways to recuperate what the mayor himself described as the city's 'places of collective identity' (Bassolino 1996a: 59). Over the ensuing years, streets and piazzas were refurbished and pedestrianized in order to turn them into places where citizens could feel comfortable to gather and where visitors could safely experience the city's vibrant life. According to Vezio De Lucia, head of planning during Bassolino's first term, the possibility of 'using the *centro storico* without feeling condemned to *degrado*' was one of the hallmarks of 'finally living in "ordinary conditions of normality"' (De Lucia 1998: 89). Herein, however, lies a pressing question: exactly what would a *normal* public space mean and entail in Naples?

The idea of public space is interrelated with the concept of citizenship. As the domain in which actions and opinions assume political and social significance, public space has occupied an important ideological position in democratic societies (Mitchell 1995: 116). The term 'public sphere' is used to indicate a communicative arena where private individuals come together as a public, the historical origins of which are located, according to Jürgen Habermas, in the rise of a modern bourgeoisie during the eighteenth century (Habermas 1989). At a commonsensical level, 'public space' instead denotes the physical realm of symbolic display and sociability outside of the private domain. Often used to measure the quality of urban life, it ideally represents the place where the diversity of a city is experienced and negotiated. As Iris Marion Young has pointed out: 'Because by definition a public space is a place accessible to anyone, where anyone can participate and witness, in entering the public one always risks encounter with those who are different, those who identify with different groups and have different opinions or different forms of life' (Young 1990: 240).[1] Ideas about 'public' and 'public space' are obviously far more complex and shift according to different theoretical and disciplinary approaches. Besides the notion of sociability, the 'public' might also be read in 'liberal-economistic' terms as being located within the administrative functions of the state as opposed to the market economy. From a 'republican-virtue' perspective it is understood as a political community and therefore distinct from both the market *and* the administrative state; while according to feminist scholars in particular, the public is often reformulated around the market economy or civil society in contraposition to the private world of the family.[2] In this book, a multilayered idea of public space emerges from the specific empirical settings of the three selected urban spaces in the *centro storico* (which in the case of DAMM also includes a closed space in the form of an occupied building). I am not only interested to trace the social and political life of these three sites but also to explore how material and immaterial (or nonspatial) elements are entwined in debates about the city at large. In short, public space here provides the bedrock for compiling a historical ethnography of urban change in Naples.

As with citizenship, the notion of public space has always been framed by tensions. Although theoretically open to all and sundry, public spaces

---

1. It should be remembered that public space can also be experienced and appreciated by individuals as a 'nonrelational' space which provides the opportunity to be *alone,* for instance as a place of refuge from the social pressures of the domestic environment (Dines et al. 2006).

2. These correspond to the four general distinctions between public and private in social analysis, identified by Jeff Weintraub (1995). Staeheli and Mitchell (2007) have recently drawn on Weintraub's taxonomy to explore the different ways in which the public is defined both by academic researchers and actors involved in public-space controversies.

have just as often been places of segregation. In the ancient Greek polis, the *agorà* was the physical domain of public debate where citizenship was constructed in opposition to foreigners and 'non-persons' (women and slaves). In other words, it was a 'community of the unexcluded' (Viale 1996: 172). Over history, people have been refused entry or restricted in their use of public space on the basis of, among other things, gender, class and race. Feminist urban historians, for instance, have examined the patriarchal structuring of the grand social spaces of nineteenth-century cities, such as the shopping arcades, where mobile, independent public women were typically viewed as prostitutes and a threat to propriety, while 'respectable' women were confined to the controlled private sphere of the home (Wilson 1991; Rendell 2002). In the modern city, public space increasingly became a site of social control. Bourgeois values about social life and appropriate behaviour were projected onto urban places, both in reaction to the corrupt extravagance of the aristocracy and in order to put subordinate classes 'in their place' (Philo and Kearns 1993: 12). City plans and architecture were therefore not only manifestations of power but the expression of a distinct 'bourgeois urban culture' which sought to discipline in creative as well as restrictive ways (ibid.). For example, the rebuilding of Paris after the 1848 Revolution took into account the needs for counter-insurgency (Cohen 1985) and at the same time constructed impressive 'corridors of homage to the power of money and commodities' in the form of new boulevards lined with cafés and dazzling window displays (Harvey 1985: 204).

The delineation of 'proper' and 'improper' places by dominant powers was, however, never entirely straightforward. Stallybrass and White (1986) argue that urban carnivals, once the symbolic crucibles of absolute power and moments of popular release, were increasingly disowned by the middle classes but that elements of the 'low' were nevertheless internalized by the urban bourgeoisie as marginal (but desired) 'others'. This ambivalent bond between the socially peripheral and the symbolically central was manifest in the reports on poverty by Victorian urban reformers. The likes of Sir Edwin Chadwick and Charles Booth in London (but also Matilde Serao in Naples) were simultaneously repelled by and attracted to the squalor of the lower-class slum: the wish to eradicate what they saw as moral and social degradation was accompanied by an urge to write effusively about the unregulated body of its inhabitants (ibid.).

During the latter decades of the twentieth century, numerous urban critics, primarily in North America (Jacobs 1961; Sennett 1974; Walzer 1986; Davis 1990; Sorkin 1992) but also in Europe (Augé 1995) and in Italy itself (Desideri 1995; Desideri and Ilardi 1997; Agustoni 2000;

Forni 2002), pointed to an erosion and constriction of public spaces in Western cities.[3] Various overlapping reasons were given: the legacy of modernist planning and the ascendency of motorized traffic; suburbanization and the growing dominance of the private sphere over social life; capitalist restructuring of the city which privileged the needs of select groups of people such as professionals and tourists; and the intensification of socioeconomic inequalities which saw the proliferation of conspicuous poverty on the streets (especially in the form of homelessness) and its subsequent implication in the deterioration of the public realm. Developments in architectural design and surveillance technologies aimed at protecting private interests and reducing crime effectively prevented the possibility of meaningful public interaction. Rather, their ultimate expression was found in the 'gated communities' (Davis 1990) or the politics of 'zero tolerance' (Wacquant 1999) that were premised on the suppression of all forms of public disorder. At the same time, many cities saw the spread of privatized or 'pseudo-public' spaces (Goss 1997), such as shopping malls and leisure complexes, which were geared to consumerism and where social and cultural diversity was encouraged within carefully planned and controlled environments. The French anthropologist Marc Augé spoke instead of the multiplication of 'non-places': mono-functional spaces of consumption and transit such as supermarkets, airports and motorways that were devoid of history, identity and organic social life and which characterized the experience of late-capitalist 'supermodernity' (Augé 1995).

While this critical literature forcefully highlighted the different processes that were reshaping (often in a detrimental way) the form and function of cities, narratives about the subsequent decline or, worse still, the *end* of public spaces were less persuasive. They reflected, rather, some general misconceptions and lacunae in scholarly and popular debates about urban public space that are worth spelling out here.

First, such a diagnosis was by no means new but had been recurrent throughout the modern history of the city. At the end of the nineteenth century, for example, the Austrian planning theoretician Camillo Sitte famously lamented the disappearance of intimate, irregular spaces from northern European cities and their replacement by sterile schemes of oversized squares and streets that prioritized traffic flows (Sitte 1965). In the case of the United States, Peter C. Baldwin's study of Hartford, Connecticut, between 1850 and 1930 demonstrates how the demise of a

---

3. Such debates in Italy emerged during the 1990s and initially drew heavily on foreign texts, especially Mike Davis's *City of Quartz* and Marc Augé's *Non-Places* (both first translated into Italian in 1993). The concern about the transformation of the urban realm was by no means confined to the West. See, for instance, Caldeira's (2000) work on fortified enclaves in São Paulo, Brazil.

diverse street life had not only begun long before Jane Jacobs wrote her famous attack in the early 1960s on modernist planning, but also pre-dated the advent of mass motorization (Baldwin 1999). Instead, Baldwin identifies its origins in the nineteenth-century urban-reform movement and its limited capacity for protecting vested class interests. The phil-anthropic urge to cleanse and domesticate the city centre's public realm through the creation of multi-purpose parks eventually capitulated with the realization that it was far more effective to separate social and com-mercial activities according to zoning laws and municipal regulations. Hence, by the 1920s, forms of peddling had been banned or moved to side streets, property values in upmarket residential districts had been safeguarded, while the main thoroughfares had been cleared and adapted to serve their function as transport arteries.

Second, and as a number of contemporary observers were swift to underline, discourses about the end of public space simply did not square with empirical reality (Lees 1994; Crawford 1995; Merrifield 1996). They tended to extrapolate from iconic central spaces in North American cities, which often reflected the more extreme consequences of neolib-eral restructuring. Peripheral and nondescript spaces, on the other hand, were generally ignored. As Paddison and Sharp have asserted in their study of two inner-city districts of Glasgow, 'much public space func-tions in a more banal way, integrated with the routines in which everyday life is conducted in the local neighbourhoods making up the city' (2007: 88). Moreover, it could be argued that the restructuring of city centres did not so much represent the end as the emergence of a new kind of urban space, which, even if it had become increasingly segregated, privatized and controlled, nonetheless remained the object of competing meanings and uses of the public realm. Similarly, the use of 'non-place' as a term of critique, common in Italian intellectual debates during the 1990s, was decidedly ethnocentric in the way it presupposed an unvarying confor-mity in people's spatial behaviour.[4]

Third, general concerns about the dwindling opportunities for social interaction and unfettered assembly tended to hinge on unproblematized assumptions about a 'good' public space rooted in a bygone era. In her study of children and open spaces in Turin, the sociologist Elisabetta

---

4. For instance, the idea of the airport as the archetypal 'non-place' through which passengers un-reflectively move and consume (Augé 1995: 2–3) might in some way capture an aspect of time-space compression or express what we dislike about such places. But how then do we interpret moments such as the spontaneous or organized resistance to the deportation of undocumented migrants or the occu-pation of runways by environmental activists? Isolated glitches in an otherwise smooth (and secured) system or an alternative sense of place in the making? And what about the more stable population of ground staff, retail workers and cleaners? Was not the airport for them a place of everyday social rela-tions and, on occasions, the site of labour struggles?

Forni, for instance, claimed that 'parks and piazzas, before their tragic physical, semantic and sociocultural metamorphosis in recent years, were … places planned for different uses, accessible to everyone, and where tolerance was a fundamental ingredient' (Forni 2002: 44). But, as feminists such as Nancy Fraser have admonished, this sort of representation idealized a golden age of free access that never actually existed (Fraser 1992). At no point in history had public space been stable or guaranteed. On the contrary, by its very nature it had always been produced through struggle and debate (Mitchell 1995). The understanding of public space as an ongoing, messy process was therefore somewhat lost on those keen to identify model types in distinctive urban forms and civic traditions. For numerous North American architects (Carr et al. 1992; Rowe 1997), the ultimate example of public space was provided by the Italian piazza, and none more so than Siena's Piazza del Campo, where 'civic life, … aspirations and … responsibilities' were seen to 'have been inscribed indelibly' since medieval times (Rowe 1997: 6). As we shall see however, the public aura surrounding the piazza was as much an ideological construction as the reflection of a particular collective sensibility and was far more dissonant than was typically acknowledged.

Finally, if proponents of the 'end-of-public-space' theorem were emphatic in their analyses, details as to what a meaningful alternative might look like and how this would be brought about were, in comparison, vague and inconsistent. It was one thing to chart the decline of public space and the consequences this had on democracy, but another to plot its revival. In fact, some observers appeared far more eager to critically dwell on doom-laden scenarios than to formulate escape routes (Sorkin 1992). Otherwise, progressive visions of a resurgent public space were often divergent and, for all the radical intent in exposing its crisis, politically ambivalent. This is well illustrated by a debate from 1986 that appeared in the left-leaning US journal *Dissent* under the title 'Public Space: A Discussion on the Shape of our Cities'. In the opening contribution, communitarian-liberal philosopher Michael Walzer introduces the idea of 'open-minded' space, that is, space designed for a variety of uses where citizens are prepared to loiter and 'to tolerate, even take an interest in, things they don't do' (Walzer 1986: 470). Despite the predominance of 'single-minded' spaces such as zoned business and residential areas, Walzer believed that there remained a deep-rooted desire for open-minded space, a fact discernible in the increasing popularity of hybrid retail spaces such as waterfront developments that accommodated (within certain limits) different activities. For these places to operate in 'ordinary neighbourhoods' (ibid.: 475), there needed to be a broad political and cultural consensus. Walzer re-evoked Jane Jacobs's famous idea of the self-policing street as the most plausible means of attracting diverse kinds of people back to the open spaces of cities: 'Without regular and confident users, they become settings for social, sexual, and political deviance: derelicts, criminals, "hippies", political and religious sectarians, adolescent gangs. All these belong, no doubt, to the urban mix, but if they are too prominent within it, ordinary men and women will flee as soon as they can into private and controlled worlds' (ibid.: 474).

Although the distinction between single-minded and open-minded space might offer an entry point to thinking about public space, it is at the same time naïvely deterministic in the way it assigns characteristics to particular places and leaves little room for human agency. How far is a shopping centre truly single-minded? Are the forms of self-discipline and consumer stimulation so effective that no other use is possible? And is the central square always 'the epitome of open-mindedness' (Walzer 1986: 471)? William H. Whyte's famous study of the life of small urban spaces in central New York (Whyte 1980) discovered that most plazas were privately controlled and rarely predisposed to 'mutual respect, political solidarity and civil discourse' (Walzer 1986: 472). But more problematic still is Walzer's uncritical differentiation between 'deviant' and 'ordinary', which ignores how these two categories are socially constructed. One is left wondering exactly whose interests are represented in open-minded space and what lofty appeals to 'tolerance' and 'diversity' actually imply.

In a rejoinder, the Marxist humanist philosopher and urban historian Marshall Berman complained that Walzer's concept of open-minded space was not open enough (Berman 1986). Because public space, by definition, accommodated difference it should be open to precisely what Walzer mistrusted: expressions of modern individualism and the urban poor (ibid.: 480). According to Berman, true social interaction and greater solidarity can only occur when 'a city's loose ends can hang out' and policing remains in the background (ibid.: 484). However, this libertarian view raises another, not dissimilar, dilemma: namely that 'letting it all hang out' would in practice privilege certain groups, such as middle-class males 'searching for that authentically gritty dystopian pleasure' (Merrifield 1996: 62), while displacing or deterring weaker others. And what about racism, sexism and other forms of discrimination? Would these be left to hang out or would they naturally fade into insignificance as 'society's inner contradictions … express and unfold themselves' (Berman 1986: 484)?

Of course, public space was not something that could be *settled* through the enlightened imagination but was, as already noted, continuously produced through power relations and conflict. Nor was it just about committing public money to pay the police, gardeners and others to make public space work (Walzer 1986: 474) or establishing commercial rent controls to prevent gentrification (Berman 1986: 484), but about confronting the structural and political dynamics that force people apart and create the conditions that might preclude social interactions taking place (Merrifield 1996). What Walzer and Berman were really expressing, besides a North American perspective on the question,[5] were their own voluntaristic ideals about urban society and politics. Yet like many other contributions to scholarly and popular debates about public space during the 1980s and 1990s, theirs were not timeless reflections on the 'good' or 'just' city but positions firmly embedded in the historical and geographical context of a burgeoning neo-conservative hegemony and a political Left in crisis.[6]

More significant, the revival of public space was by no means confined to the deliberations of concerned intellectuals but crucially often lay at the heart of urban regeneration programmes, particularly those of centre-left administrations, which were less bothered with the subtleties of what constituted 'open-mindedness' and were certainly not interested in 'letting it all hang out'. For instance, after 1997 under the Labour government, public space gained unprecedented attention in British urban policy (Imrie and Raco 2003). The implications were twofold. On the one hand, great emphasis was placed on the influence of brand new and refurbished open spaces in connecting local communities in deprived urban areas and, as the focal point of crime prevention and anti-social behaviour measures, in simultaneously disciplining and remoralizing some of their members (DETR 2000; Lees 2003). On the other hand, a quite different image of public space that exalted high-quality design, cultural diversity and 'continental' models of consumption (such as 'café culture') instead articulated new middle-class attitudes to urban life and was often directly implicated in the gentrification of formerly down-at-heel or unsung parts of cities (DETR 1999, Atkinson 2003). These two apparently irreconcilable versions of public space were in reality interdependent. They reflected what Stuart Hall has termed the 'double-shuffle' of the New Labour project (Hall 2003), whereby a neo-communitarian

---

5. The final contribution to the *Dissent* debate is made by the British sociologist Michael Rustin who, unlike Walzer and Berman, does not argue for a particular ideal of public space but rather offers a longer historical perspective on the transformation of public space and also notes a different situation in England, 'where precapitalist architectural and spatial forms have retained a more pervasive role' (Rustin 1986: 486).

6. In fact, at the beginning of his article, Walzer argues that the US Left urgently needed to reconsider the question of public space which it had for too long overlooked: 'Thinking about freeways, shopping malls, and suburban homes', he posited, 'might have led us to anticipate Reaganist politics' (1986: 470).

approach to social policy and poverty management was accessory to an overarching neoliberal agenda that sought to further reconfigure British society according to the demands of an increasingly globalized and de-regulated capitalist economy. By simply being ameliorated, the physical realm of public space could play host to economic growth and social cohesion (Cooper 1998).[7]

The question is how Naples fits into this wider picture. As noted, the city was traditionally seen to lack public space in the 'civic', northern-central Italian sense. It had always been, in many ways, a promiscuous city, where aristocratic residences backed onto slums and where private life, especially that of the ground floor *bassi,* spilled onto the street. There had also long existed a stereotype of Naples as a permissive city where everything did indeed 'hang out' or was, as Benjamin and Lacis put it, 'porous and commingled' (Benjamin 1978: 171). It has been argued that, as in many southern European cities, bourgeois urban culture in Naples was never hegemonic (Leontidou 1996), while the maladies of anomie and impersonality that afflicted the industrial city were seemingly absent. As such, modern Naples did not appear to possess the rigid social and spatial controls of the great bourgeois metropolises of London or Paris.

Visitors over the centuries have invariably been appalled and enthralled by the city's 'anarchic' urban life and lenience on the part of its authori-ties. The French writer Louise Colet, in Naples at the time of Garibaldi's arrival, expressed her shock at seeing so many ungainly sights on the city centre's crowded streets. The greatest scandal of all, according to Colet, was not that beggars and cripples existed in such quantities but that they were at liberty to 'infect' the public realm (Ramondino and Müller 1992: 53). Pier Paolo Pasolini, writing over a century later, instead declared his admiration for the spontaneity of Neapolitan urban life and Neapolitans' defiance in the face of a normalizing Italian modernity and mass cul-ture. He compared this Neapolitan 'tribe' with the Tuareg Bedouins of the Sahara Desert for their ability to hold out against outside pressures (Ghirelli 1976: 15–16). This mixed response of outsiders to the city has persisted. During the 1980s, as tourist operators blacklisted Naples, in-trepid travellers were drawn by the city's unbridled vitality. Reminiscing about the pre-Bassolino Naples, the erstwhile resident Peter Robb sighed that 'the absurd comedy was gone [but] Naples, I consoled myself with

---

7. All this, of course, did not unfold smoothly. The question of public space in the United Kingdom under New Labour was often a focus of oppositional politics, from the direct actions of the anti-capitalist Reclaim the Streets movement that challenged, among other things, the dominance of motor traffic, to local-based campaigns that resisted the redevelopment of existing social spaces such as street markets (Dines 2009).

thinking, would always be more *interesting* than other places. Naples would never bore' (Robb 1998: 169, original italics).

While these historical maxims and literary representations could be deemed to capture something distinct about Naples, the corollary that public space in the city is undeveloped, marginal or extrinsic rests on the false premise that 'real' public space is the product of a 'complete' modern project and that anything less than complete is in some ways disengaged from the processes that lead to its formation.[8] In fact, one particularity of Naples is that it would seem to present a paradox: if not endowed with the exemplary public spaces of northern and central Italian cities, it was nevertheless renowned for its vibrant social life.[9] Moreover, much of this vibrancy, imaginary or otherwise, had historically been the upshot of the spatial hegemony exerted by subaltern classes at the city's core. Irrespective of whether this might exhilarate or disturb the observer accustomed to the traditions of other Western cities, such a situation calls for a high degree of critical sobriety. Just as it is important to refrain from making facile generalizations about the imprint of organized crime upon urban space (Leonardi and Nanetti 2008: 65), it would be equally dangerous to consider the city as more accommodating of difference simply on what appeared to be an unrestrained diversity in contrast to more 'sedate' situations of elsewhere. Need it be said, urban life in Naples is just as mediated by social codes and rules and is subject to exclusionary mechanisms on the basis of, for instance, gender, mental and physical ability and, increasingly during the 1990s, perceived ethnic, national and legal status. Moreover, it is important to comprehend how different boundaries between acceptable and deviant behaviour in public space are constructed and internalized by different social groups and how these may change from space to space and evolve over time (Sibley 1995), rather than taking for granted the impressions of Walter Benjamin and others that Naples was eternally open to the flurry of the city.

---

8. This line of reasoning has often been uncritically endorsed by social scientists who are keener on investigating the city's idiosyncrasies than pondering more mundane issues about the public realm. Indeed, the image of an extraneous public space can serve as a rhetorical device to reiterate the self-contained world of neighbourhood life. This is exemplified in Belmonte's opening description of Naples: 'The boulevard was modern and bustling, lined with drab turn-of-the-century office and residential buildings. But the side streets, the narrow, winding *vicoli*, appeared shadowy and broken, far older in architecture and somehow removed from the activity of the street' (Belmonte 1989: 1). Later, he comments: 'A bottle of brandy sold for five hundred lire less at a bar inside the quarter than at an establishment serving the *general, anonymous public*' (ibid.: 119, italics added).

9. This reputation has also been affirmed by nonspecialist academics outside Italy. For instance, the British geographers Ash Amin and Stephen Graham cite both Naples and Bombay as 'vibrant theatres of active public life' (Amin and Graham 1997: 423).

All this is particularly important to consider when examining the urban transformations of the 1990s. Much of the late twentieth-century debate about the 'end of public space' is clearly not very pertinent to the case of Naples. And yet, as we have seen, Bassolino himself commented that before being elected in 1993, many 'historic collective spaces *no longer existed*' (Bassolino 1996b: 16, italics added). Such a claim will always be disputable, but it alerts us to how ideals about public space and sociability are by no means universal but are recodified locally. Likewise, the need to revive public space stood at the top of the mayor's urban agenda. Yet, for the most part, this did not mean enticing people back to the city's streets and piazzas but, on the contrary, redefining and heading off the existing flow. Like Walzer, Bassolino stressed the importance of creating a general consensus around the value of public space; however, he appeared to doubt the capacity of many Neapolitans to respect the public realm and therefore placed great emphasis on encouraging a 'culture of rules': 'There is no doubt that left to its own devices, the city tends not to adhere to many of the rules of good communal life. But if involved … the people of Naples participate' (ibid.: 66). Hence, in contrast to Walzer's notion of 'open-mindedness', it might be said that Bassolino envisaged 'civic-minded' spaces where citizens were not only sociable and orderly but were inculcated with new values about the public realm.

Towards a working idea of 'contested space'

Not since the slum clearance schemes of the late nineteenth century had there been such a strong link between public space in central Naples and the politics of urban change. While the latter, during the postwar period, had been mainly connected with the city's unchecked expansion and imperfect industrialization, most attention now focused on readjusting what already existed. Tracing the transformations to the spatial environment during the 1990s through the actions and words of administrators and their entourage, however, can only provide us with a partial picture. Prescriptive terms such as open-mindedness and assertions about the deterioration or resurgence of public life might plot out a terrain for debate, but they are not useful to derive a methodological strategy for grappling with the everyday dynamics of public space (Low 2000).

Public space is part of a dialogical and relational process and is therefore never univocal, complete or predictable. Social controls within it, however insidious or repressive, are never totalizing. This is not to deny that various technologies, such as architectural design, policing or legal mechanisms, play an important part in determining the spatial order or that the *publicness* of space may also be shaped through the internalization of such technologies (Foucault 1979). It is rather to stress that people are not 'passive pieces on a chessboard' (Merrifield 1996: 67) that dominant powers can move around at their will but that people are players who are actively engaged in creating their own realities and symbolic meanings (Low 2000).

This key point lies at the heart of Henri Lefebvre's theory of space (Lefebvre 1991). For Lefebvre, space is not neutral geometry but is constantly produced through a relationship between *representations of space* (the conceived space of technocrats, planners and social engineers), *representational space* (the lived space which is invested with symbolism) and *spatial practice* (which denotes the way people generate, use and perceive space) (ibid.: 38–39). Lefebvre argues that dominant *representations of space* that drive urbanization are tied to a specific mode of production and to the 'order' that its relations impose (ibid.: 33). *Representational spaces*, contingent on time and place and based on less formal and more local forms of knowledge, offer 'counter spaces' (ibid.: 381–83) which contain 'the seeds of a new kind of space' (ibid.: 53). *Spatial practices* secrete a society's space through the daily 'routes and networks which link up the places set aside for work, "private" life and leisure' (ibid.: 38), ensuring that conceived and lived spaces are held in a dialectical tension. These basic tenets of Lefebvre's theory of social space have been immensely popular, especially among Anglo-American geographers, in laying out a general framework for interpreting urban spatial conflict.[10] They are also useful for thinking about how the regeneration of urban space does not simply seek to impose a particular vision of the city but can act as a marshalling point for collective resistance to change and the elaboration of new, alternative meanings about place.

Even though Lefebvre is concerned with the everyday and the centrality of the body in appropriating and producing space, he sees social and class struggle as the prime agent in the creation of 'counter spaces' (Lefebvre 1991: 55). However, the constant renegotiation of prevailing ideas about space does not necessarily involve a consciously political project. Much of our 'contestation' is mundane, fleeting and low key, consisting in minor infractions and altercations. While public space is the site where individuals and groups struggle to be included in the pub-

---

10. Nicholas R. Fyfe (1996), for instance, juxtaposes the postwar master plans for the modernization of Glasgow with the reading of subsequent changes in the works of local poets in order to map the urban landscape of the modern city. It should be noted that few scholars have actually reflected on how the at-times cryptic idea of the 'spatial triad' can be effectively applied to empirical analysis. For a critical discussion of the appropriation of Lefebvre's work in Anglo-American geography, see Elden (2001).

lic sphere, it is at the same time the arena in which counter-hegemonic everyday meanings and uses of the urban environment unfold. A myriad of relationships exist between different people and urban spaces. Where these cross official boundaries and discursive limits, they may be conceived as transgressive, deviant and 'out of place'.

The notion of 'contested space' is therefore deployed to refer to those practices and representations that are either purposely in opposition or find themselves at odds with dominant visions of space but which, at the same time and in different ways, are also constitutive of that very same space. It can comprise a diverse set of characteristics: symbolic and material; discursive and nondiscursive; embodied and cognitive; reflexive and intuitive; premeditated and spontaneous; proactive and reactive. The adjective 'contested' contains the dual meaning of the verb *to contest*: on the one hand *to challenge or dispute,* suggesting a purposive action involving controversy, and on the other hand, *to contend or compete in,* implying a rival striving for the achievement of objectives but which does not necessarily entail discord.

For it to be meaningful and not theoretically abstruse or politically aphoristic, the idea of public space as 'contested space' is here anchored to an ethnographic inquiry into the daily life and experience of individuals in the *centro storico* of Naples. It is not employed as a fixed model but as a protean concept which has value in empirical settings and specifically offers a critical perspective on urban regeneration. Here I want to introduce three facets that will be examined in depth in the case studies: urban collective action; spatial habitus (as the everyday sense of place that structures action and generates meaning); and transgression. These are not distinct realms and can coexist in a space at any given moment, but for the sake of clarity they are treated separately.

'Collective action' can be broadly understood as action taken by a group in pursuit of shared interests. The specific notion of 'urban collective action' is that which consciously aims to transform the city in some way, regardless of its actual success in doing so (Melucci 1984; Castells 1997). This may involve direct demands for material improvements or transformations to the political system but also encompasses the promotion of alternative ideas about collective identity, democracy and, importantly, urban space.

In the wake of the student and worker uprisings of the late 1960s, there was a prolonged period of intense political struggles in Italian cities (Balestrini and Moroni 1997). Urban problems that had been accentuated by the postwar economic boom, such as the lack of affordable, decent accommodation and basic social services, became a focus of mobilization alongside traditional labour issues (Marcelloni 1979). Protest groups were often socially diverse and increasingly locality – rather than workplace – based. Nevertheless, as Lumley argues, these social movements could only 'struggle into existence' by confronting previous traditions: 'The worker and student movements provided the models which other movements attempted to replicate, revise or break away from' (Lumley 1990: 273). Naples became, like other large cities, a centre of militancy. After the cholera epidemic of 1973, various *'comitati di quartiere'* (neighbourhood committees), consisting of New Left groups and local residents, were formed in the popular neighbourhoods of the *centro storico* to demand clean water and acceptable sanitary conditions, as well as to push for grassroots participation in decision making (Esposito 1973; Marcelloni 1979; Ginsborg 1990). Out of these experiences emerged the Organized Unemployed Movement, the first movement of its kind in the Western world, that amassed almost fifteen thousand active members at its peak in 1975 and which strove for the provision of regular jobs on the basis of need and commitment to struggle rather than along political or clientelistic lines. The main streets and piazzas and public buildings in the *centro storico* became the arenas of continual direct action, as one of their activists explained: 'As we can't strike or close a factory, for the moment the streets are our factory, and as the workers stop production, so we stop the traffic' (quoted in Ginsborg 1990: 365). There were also less conflict-laden initiatives, such as the pedestrian campaigns at the end of the 1970s, which reclaimed the historic flights of steps linking the *centro storico* with the Vomero district and elaborated for the first time a critical public discourse about the relationship between the city and traffic (Capasso, Niego and Vittoria 1982).

Collective action was not only concerned with material issues but also (and often contemporaneously) pursued more immeasurable goals, such as practising direct democracy, cultivating group autonomy and solidarity, and creating alternative cultural codes – issues that had existed only marginally, if at all, in traditional organizations such as political parties and trade unions (Melucci 1984; Lumley 1990). The development of different lifestyles and cultural identities often involved the search for alternative spaces. For instance, groups of self-named 'proletarian youths' occupied empty buildings in and around cities not only to meet immediate material needs, but as a means of establishing autonomous spheres through which to carry forwards political and cultural agendas.

Although the upheavals of the 1970s would dissipate during the following decade, spurred by a growing disillusionment with collective action that coincided with the so-called *'riflusso'* (the mass retreat into private life) (Ginsborg 1990; Lumley 1990), urban protests did not suddenly disappear or become redundant. While labour struggles would become increasingly defensive as they sought to counteract the consequences of deindustrialization and the organized unemployed groups would proceed in their battle for jobs albeit factionalized and, in some cases, capitulating to clientelism (Cerase, Morlicchio and Spanò 1991), new concerns arose such as the protection of buildings and spaces threatened by redevelopment schemes. These often drew on preexisting political repertoires and involved former militants while at the same time devising new forms of direct action or 'media event creation' (Castells 1997) to amplify publicity.

The emergence of the *centri sociali* as a nationwide phenomenon during the early 1990s reflected most acutely the series of breaks and continuities with the past. Political traditions were reworked within new contexts and were at times superseded, while new modes of cultural production (such as rap music) were experimented and alternative ideas about the 'post-industrial' city were promoted through the self-management of occupied buildings and open spaces. DAMM, which refuted the 'ideological' positions of other *centri sociali,* constructed an alternative urban project around the reutilization of an abandoned park in the Montesanto neighbourhood. Even though it was not born in direct opposition to Bassolino, its activities would frequently challenge the administration's urban policies. The reimaging of the *centro storico* under Bassolino would also transform certain 'new' spaces, in particular the pedestrianized Piazza Plebiscito, into places of protest over 'old' problems such as unemployment and housing, as well as emergent issues such as immigrant rights. The three case studies will therefore explore how the city was both the *site* and *object* of organized action and how the various experiments and protests related to collective experiences of the past.

It should be remembered that collective action is not always politically progressive and that that which is might well foster narrow or socially conservative views about the public and how it should conduct itself. A more probing and challenging idea of 'contested space' therefore also needs to address the multiple and sometimes conflicting relationships between different people and urban space. Pierre Bourdieu's reworking of the concept 'habitus' provides a theoretical starting point from which to consider why individuals and groups act and think in the ways they do. For the French sociologist, habitus indicates the socially structured, embodied sense of place that in turn generates and conditions meaningful practice and experience (Bourdieu 1977). It consists of a system of mental and physical dispositions (Bourdieu 2005: 43) imbued with various forms of economic, social, cultural and symbolic capital with which people manoeuvre through and make sense of the range of 'fields' of practice and struggle that exist in society – from employment to politics, housing to planning, and education to cultural consumption (Hillier and Rooksby 2005). For instance, Bourdieu's own famous analysis of the tastes and aesthetics of the French bourgeoisie and their reproduction through class-based distinctions (Bourdieu 1984) is suggestive for thinking about how particular ideas of urban heritage and decorum were formulated in Naples during the 1990s. It is important to underline that habitus is understood here as a dynamic rather than a durable and repetitive dimension.[11] In other words, people's behaviour is not necessarily routine and predictable but operates through repertoires that are remoulded by historic circumstances and new social experiences. In fact, the transformation of streets and piazzas during the Bassolino era elicited situated responses both to the physical changes and to the discursive shifts in representations of the built environment. Moreover, the *centro storico* over the same period became an increasingly heterogeneous place where new users and residents, such as immigrants and tourists, made different claims to space, which consequently impacted upon other people's encounters with the city.

The Italian urban anthropologist Amalia Signorelli, who has worked extensively in and around Naples, offers a stimulating and locally sensitive methodological framework which recalls both Lefebvre's spatial triad and the idea of habitus. She sees three basic processes as constituting people's sociocultural relationships with urban space: *assegnazione* (ascription), *appropriazione* (appropriation) and *appaesemento* (symbolization).[12] *Assegnazione* refers to spaces assigned to a subject as a result of history, birth, social position or through urban transformations planned from above. *Appropriazione* denotes the adapted uses of space which satisfy needs and desires and tend to improve the relationship between people and places. Angela Giglia (1997), a former student of Signorelli, examined how residents reorganized the social spaces of a new housing project built following the evacuation of the *centro storico* of Pozzuoli (to the immediate west of Naples) due to bradyseismic activity in the local area in 1983. The various unintended (although not entirely unforeseen) appropriations of the planned space were structured around gender relations. Hence, while the open patches of land and road junctions transformed respectively into football pitches and meeting places were used predominantly by males, the principal spaces of interaction for many women were created on landings inside the tower blocks or

---

11. For a critical discussion of the question of durability in relation to Bourdieu's idea of habitus, see Hillier and Rooksby 2005.

12. This material derives from a series of combined urban anthropology and town planning seminars held in the Department of Sociology at Naples University between 1999 and 2000. See also Signorelli 1996: 57–66.

immediately outside the buildings. Finally, *appaesemento* refers to the meanings conferred to a space which serve for individuals and groups to make sense of their environment. Even those so-called 'non-places' (Augé 1995) considered to be devoid of any identity are invested with significance by its users. Giglia examines how the same housing project was 'symbolized' with self-constructed shrines and decorative adjustments to the interiors and exteriors of buildings. Therefore, a space that was considered by outside observers to be lacking in any aesthetic or human value became for some (but not all) residents the subject of positive feelings and a sense of belonging (Giglia 1997: 199). This anthropological approach can also be employed to examine the public spaces in the *centro storico* of Naples. For example, the pedestrianized Piazza Plebiscito was appropriated by users as, *inter alia,* a giant playground and a place for the unlicensed vending of refreshments. Built features not only assumed new roles (such as the equestrian statues that were turned into goalposts) but became symbols that mapped out alternative ideas about the piazza.

Signorelli points out that space is always a finite resource and there are various limits (legal, cultural, environmental and so on) that condition its appropriation and symbolization (Signorelli 1996: 59). Social space is replete with boundaries that differentiate between the core and the marginal, order and disorder, 'us' and 'them'. As David Sibley argues in his compelling analysis of spatial exclusion, at the basis of the boundary-making process in Western culture lies an underlying urge to purify space from the presence of the 'abject', materially and metaphorically conceived as pollution and filth (Sibley 1995). Boundaries are not simply traced out by dominant powers but are also constructed and enforced from below. Individuals learn in childhood to understand the world as a series of self-other relationships and from there on seek (but without ever completely succeeding) to reject dirt and its equivalents (ibid.: 8). For Sibley, the systems of boundaries that structure space shift according to time and place. The weaker the system, the less interest there is in maintaining divisions and the more likely that difference is accommodated. A stronger system instead tends to be governed by inflexible rules and equates difference with deviance. It hence repels aberrant elements only to experience more profoundly the encroachment of the abject on its borders (ibid.: 72–89). As the boundaries of public space are modified over the course of history, perceptions of deviance either intensify or decline, while notions about appropriate behaviour are reframed.

It is when boundaries are trespassed or exposed that one can talk in terms of 'spatial transgression'. People and things only transgress if they are conceived to be in the 'wrong place': if there is no 'wrong place', then there is no transgression (Cresswell 1996). In contrast to politically significant forms of collective action, spatial transgression can appear ephemeral and inconsequential. But it is through the contradiction or inversion of urban codes, values and norms that 'disobedient' spatial behaviour may tell us something about the ordering of the city and the role of space in social control (Sibley 1995: xiii). According to the British geographer Alastair Bonnett, the city is 'alive with errant geographical manoeuvres' (Bonnett 1998: 35). This he exemplifies by describing two observed cases of routine spatial transgression: young jaywalkers who perform provocative pirouettes on an inner-city motorway and elderly women who visit their friends working at the tills in Tesco, bringing their own food into the store. Bonnett stresses that these acts of spatial contestation are politically contradictory. Their radical potential – the boys' refusal of alienating planning and the women's rejection of the supermarket as solely a place of consumption – is at the same time structured and enabled by 'conservative identities': 'The lads running across the traffic and the elderly women in the supermarket are both disobeying on terrains in which they feel comfortable. ... The refusal of Tesco's spatial discipline is carried out by these women both as something spontaneous and challenging and as something that accepts and accommodates itself to the limitations placed on women's spatial activities' (ibid.: 29).

Transgression must not be considered a priori as progressive. The carnivalesque, as White and Stallybrass argue, momentarily overturns notions of power but at the same time 'violently abuses and demonizes weaker, not stronger, social groups – women, ethnic and religious minorities, those who "don't belong" in a process of *displaced abjection*' (Stallybrass and White 1986: 18, original italics). Transgression may effectively reveal 'topographies of power' (Cresswell 1996: 176), but disruptions to the spatial status quo do not in themselves lead to social transformations. Bonnett laconically points out that the 'till talkers' were eventually moved along after the store manager was changed.

Bonnett's discussion also raises another problem. The process of identifying spatial practices needs to be foregrounded so as to avoid reifying transgression into 'counter spaces'. What the observer describes as transgressive is not necessarily perceived as such by the agents involved. Moreover, what is deemed aberrant in one locality may not be so in another. This needs to be especially considered in the case of Naples. The city has been regularly dubbed by outsiders as 'the capital of transgression' on account of an apparent widespread disregard for rules and public order.[13] This persistent image of a timelessly recalcitrant Naples does not

13. This accolade was for instance endowed on the city in spring 2001 by the RAI current affairs television programme *L'Elmo di Scipio* in reference to many Neapolitan motorcyclists' refusal to wear crash helmets.

attempt to situate practices within local frames of meaning that are themselves shifting and subject to dispute. For instance, during the 1990s the
selling of contraband cigarettes was locally regarded by some as a vital
and acceptable source of income, by others as an illegal act controlled
by the Camorra. While this vocation would take place openly in certain
areas and at certain times, the conspicuous presence of the *contrabbandiere* in the 'reclaimed' spaces of the *centro storico* would lead to public
outrage (although this rarely occurred, because the vendor assumed more
covert and mobile selling methods).

Collective political action, the various appropriations and symboliza-
tions of space, as well as instances of transgression, together constitute
the contested spaces of Piazza Plebiscito, Piazza Garibaldi and DAMM.
Through an examination of these three interconnecting issues, it is possible to analyse the (re)making of public space during regeneration and,
in doing so, interrogate the contemporary official discourses about a new,
socially inclusive Naples. Moreover, the idea of contested space allows
us to move beyond the simplistic vision of a binary clash between the
dominant and dominated, just as thinking seriously about public space
in Naples also precludes any notion of a singular, enduring cultural relationship between Neapolitans and their urban environment.

The piazza: a preeminent public space
and its place in central Naples

Part 1 has reflected theoretically and methodologically on four themes
that are central to this study: the *centro storico,* regeneration, citizenship
and public space. As a final piece to this puzzle – and as a prelude to the
case studies – I want to dedicate some final thoughts to that most eminent
of public spaces: the Italian piazza. In fact, two of the spaces explored in
this book are, nominally at least, 'piazzas'. As with other concepts previously discussed, it is vital to think about what this particular spatial form
means in the context of Naples. The piazza is one of the most distinctive
and emblematic features of the Italian city. Its genesis can either derive from a single architectural project, for example Piazza San Pietro in
Rome, or, more commonly, from the gradual accumulation of buildings,
signs, monuments and spatial modifications over time, as in the case of
Piazza San Marco in Venice (Locatelli 1989). Across the centuries these
'organized voids' (Isnenghi 1994: 4) have stood as measures of urban
beauty, order and harmony. Judging by the selected examples that grace
the many architectural monographs on the subject, *ugly* historical piazzas do not exist or are, presumably, simply not worth writing about.

As an arena of social interaction, the piazza has traditionally been perceived as the quintessential 'theatre of public life' (Burke 1986: 10): a place of assemblies, debates, proclamations, rituals and exchanges. Ever since the time of the medieval city-states, the Italian piazza has stood as the embodiment of citizenship and the public sphere (Berman 1986), an exemplary 'good' place transmitting the values of individual freedom, civic engagement and cultural memory. But, of course, piazzas were also places where power was displayed and controls were exerted. Patricians in seventeenth-century Venice, for example, would take over Piazza San Marco every evening to conduct their public affairs while keeping commoners at bay (Burke 1986: 8). As a space of dominion, the piazza was therefore a stage of challenges to power and internecine feuds. Furthermore, the piazza possessed a darker history that was as much linked with death as it was with life. It is easily forgotten that some of today's most popular tourist spots, such as Piazza della Signoria in Florence or Campo dei Fiori in Rome, were once places where rebels and heretics were publicly executed (Basson 2006).[14] Additionally, it is important to note that the urban culture of the piazza was never exclusively fixed to a particular locality but was simultaneously conceived as a deterritorialized space of flows and circulation. If the religious festival was a means to reinforce a sense of local identity, the travelling fair of itinerant musicians, storytellers and pedlars of new scientific discoveries was instead a rare opportunity for the general population to acquire knowledge of the world that lay beyond the city walls (and it is no coincidence that this use of the piazza was often suppressed by authorities during revolutionary periods). Norberto Bobbio has pointed to the imprint of the piazza's political and social import upon the Italian language. While it bears explicit democratic, populist or authoritarian connotations in Italian, as in the examples 'to resort to the piazza' (to search for popular consensus) or 'to place in the piazza' (to put into the public eye), equivalent expressions in English, French and German instead use the words '*street*', '*rue*' and '*strasse*' (Dardi 1992: 54).[15]

Mario Isnenghi (1994) identifies three basic types of historical piazza: the religious space where processions and festivals were enacted, the political piazza where governing institutions were located, and the marketplace where commercial exchange was carried out. Although these often

---

14. It was in Piazza della Signoria in 1498 that the Domenican priest Girolamo Savonarola was first hanged and then burned, on the same spot where a year earlier he had ordered the Bonfire of Vanities to destroy objects deemed to symbolize moral permissiveness. In Campo dei Fiori, in 1600, the philosopher Giordano Bruno was burned at the stake by the Roman Inquisition.

15. The word '*piazza*' first came into use around 1250. Its etymology is not connected with the public spaces of Roman and Greek antiquity (the forum and polis) but with the Latin and Greek adjectives '*platea*' and '*plateia*', meaning 'wide' or 'broad' (De Mauro and Mancini 2000).

corresponded to precise locations in the city – Piazza Duomo, Piazza Castello and Piazza Mercato – their functions overlapped. Hence the central piazza of the independent city-state which represented the physical and symbolic heart of political and religious authority may also have served as a marketplace on certain days of the week (Canniffe 2008). This said, any attempt to construct a universal typology of piazzas faces a number of practical problems. First, it implies a set of spatial criteria that distinguishes the piazza from open, shapeless spaces. These are typically defined as '*spiazzi*' or '*larghi*' (Guidoni 1989) despite the fact that 'piazza' may be their official toponym and that they may be perceived as such by their users. Second, there exists a complex hierarchy that ranks the piazza in terms of its functional and symbolic properties vis-à-vis its location within the city. At the top of this hierarchy resides the central piazza or a series of spaces which share a city's spatial supremacy, while towards the bottom one would find the smaller and peripheral spaces that might not immediately possess any of Isnenghi's three elements and may appear little more than empty pockets in built space or intersections at the confluence of streets. The positioning within this hierarchy is never fixed over time and may fluctuate according to a city's development. Third, there exists a sort of geographical discrimination that has traditionally excluded the piazzas of southern Italy from national accounts. They barely feature in Isnenghi's social and political history of piazzas in modern Italy, while some writers specifically equate the piazza with the public spaces of central Italian cities (Aymard 1999: 140). This can be partly explained by an absence of historic piazzas of the iconic status of Piazza del Campo in Siena or Piazza San Marco in Venice in southern Italy, but it can also reflect the traditional image of the South as lacking both civic space and a rich urban culture.[16]

Although numerous guidebooks have used Neapolitan piazzas to talk about the city (Delli 1994; Ruggiero 1996), Italy's third city has, at times in the past, been considered to lack true piazzas (Capasso 1993). The case of Naples, however, is useful precisely because it problematizes the rigid typology based on northern and central Italian cities. Naples certainly does not possess a central emblematic piazza characteristic of other cities, such as Piazza Duomo in Milan or Piazza Maggiore in Bologna. The city peculiarly possesses no equivalent of a Piazza Duomo (the cathedral is instead set slightly back from the street), although there are countless spaces which owe their existence and names to adjacent churches. While there existed a Largo Castello (present-day Piazza Mu-

---

16. The state-funded *Agorà* project at the end of the 1980s set out to resolve this imbalance by analysing and documenting 168 piazzas across the *Mezzogiorno,* at the same time as drawing up proposals for their restoration and conservation (Barbiani 1992).

nicipio), there also existed a nearby Largo di Palazzo (Piazza Plebiscito), yet, significantly, neither of these were originally called 'piazzas'. Indeed in many cases, the word 'piazza' was imported after the Unification of Italy. Before 1860, the term '*largo*' (or '*lario*' in Neapolitan dialect), meaning 'open space', was more commonly used. This did not carry the array of connotations of the piazza. It was this apparent absence of architectural types and languages – particularly those of Tuscany and the Florence of the Medici – which acted to further marginalize the city from the cultural foundations of the new Italian state (Gribaudi 1997: 85). There did exist, however, a Piazza Mercato (known by this name from the early seventeenth century onwards) located on the south-east corner of the *centro storico* (Gambardella 1990). This was a space of intense commercial exchange and very much the symbolic heart of popular Naples. It also historically possessed a religious component (in the Church of Santa Maria di Carmine) and a political component (in the form of the government tax office). These elements were all present in the famous uprising of Masaniello in 1647: the mock battle enacted during the Feast of the Virgin Mary became the pretext for market traders and local poor to burn down the government building in revolt over rising bread prices (Burke 1986).[17]

The *centro storico* also possesses a range of other open places that reflect various stages in the city's history. The numerous piazzas in the *centro antico* are mostly little more than tiny cleavages in the dense urban fabric. They are invariably dominated by one or more churches and are characterized by a rich mix of architectural periods, from the Graeco-Roman foundations often visible at the base of buildings through to the baroque churches and *palazzi* of the seventeenth and eighteenth centuries. Some of the piazzas in the adjacent popular neighbourhoods are similar in appearance but belong to a more historically recent era, although others are either crossroads or open spaces that were never built on. Similarly, some of the busiest piazzas in between these neighbourhoods and the *centro antico* are essentially large road junctions (Piazza Trieste and Trento, Piazza VII Settembre) or wide streets (Piazza Museo).

Naples does not possess the grand planned Baroque piazzas of Rome or Turin. However, some of the city's larger piazzas are partially or entirely the result of urban projects. Under the Bourbons, during the late eighteenth century and early nineteenth century, neoclassical semicircular 'forums' were built to impose order onto three of the city's principal open areas (present-day Piazzas Plebiscito, Mercato and Dante). The

---

17. Piazza Mercato was also the city's historic execution ground where, for instance, numerous leaders of the 1799 Revolution were put to death.

post-cholera Risanamento programme contributed a series of airy but sombre piazzas (Nicola Amore, Bovio and Garibaldi), which stood in stark contrast to the tiny spaces of the cleared slums. The demolition of the ramparts of the Maschio Angioino during the early twentieth century led to the present-day layout of Piazza Municipio, while the Fascist administrative district of Rione Carità gave the *centro storico* its last major piazza: the imposing Piazza Matteotti.

All these aforementioned piazzas, with the exception of Piazza Mercato, have served as important nodes in the city's transport system. While such piazzas came to be associated with this particular function, others were often characterized by their dominant social makeup. The piazzas in the *centro antico* and the surrounding neighbourhoods have been considered 'popular' spaces in terms of the activities carried out in them, from hawking to religious parades, and the local groups that frequent them. Meanwhile, a select number of piazzas in the more affluent areas have been traditionally dubbed '*salotti*' (exclusive meeting places), in particular Piazza dei Martiri in Chiaia and Piazza Vanvitelli in the late nineteenth-century heart of Vomero. These were the 'islands' of upper-class and bourgeois urban life and café society. Hence, as this swift summary demonstrates, by avoiding a narrow historical typology, a much more multiform image of the piazza emerges. Furthermore, not all of the types of spaces cited above are peculiar to Naples but are commonly present in northern Italian cities as well.

It is frequently argued that with the advent of the modern city, the piazza's role as a crucible of public life began to decline (Nuvolari 1989; Isnenghi 1994). Its ideological properties were re-evoked on certain occasions, for instance during Unification and under Fascism, while it would remain a rallying point for political protest. However, with industrialization and the rapid expansion of cities, the street rapidly acquired a more central position in urban design and thought. The connotations of movement, progress and modernity associated with the street sharply contrasted to the closed confines of the historical piazza. Hence, while De Chirico paid homage to the timeless quality of the piazza in his metaphysical paintings, the piazza's very sedateness was hated by the Futurists as a symbol of small-town life.[18] In Naples, the late nineteenth-century Risanamento provided the city with new piazzas, but these essentially served as decorative accoutrements for the programme's principal intervention: the new boulevard which linked the railway station with the

---

18. In his manifesto of 1913 'The Death of Syntax: Imagination without Strings – Words in Freedom', Filippo Tommaso Marinetti declared: 'An ordinary man can in a day's time travel from a little dead town of empty squares … to a great capital city bristling with lights, gestures and street cries' (Fisdall and Bozzolla 1977: 8).

commercial and administrative heart of the city. During the same period, a 'covered' piazza in the form of the Galleria Umberto I was constructed in front of the city's opera house. As in other major Italian cities, the concept of the piazza as a site of face-to-face interaction was transplanted into a shopping arcade: the new bourgeois monument to consumption.

Over the course of the twentieth century the public role of the piazza in cities is said to have diminished further or disappeared altogether (Isnenghi 1994; Desideri 1995). Forms of entertainment which previously centred on the piazza – the travelling fairs and musicians – gave way to an emergent leisure industry of dance halls and cinemas. New technologies such as radio, television and the Internet gradually led to the rise of surrogate 'electronic' or 'cyber' piazzas, which no longer demanded a physical public space (Mitchell 1995). The boom in road traffic had perhaps the greatest impact of all, turning some piazzas into car parks or bus stations. The automobile, in particular, has long been conceived by theorists of the city and the public sphere as 'a fiendish interloper that destroyed earlier patterns of urban life' (Sheller and Urry 2000: 738). Jürgen Habermas, for example, has argued that:

> A meaningful ordering of the city as a whole … has been overtaken, to mention just one factor, by changes in the function of streets and squares due to the technical requirements of traffic flow. The resulting configuration does not afford a spatially protected private sphere, nor does it create free space for public contacts and communications that could bring private people together to form a public. (Habermas 1989: 158)

This drawn-out eulogy to the piazza would appear premature in the case of Naples. The car certainly had a major impact on the city's public spaces, as exemplified by Piazza Plebiscito's use as a giant car park from the early 1960s onwards. However, certain changes that were construed as signs of the piazza's demise elsewhere in Italy – for instance the replacement of open-air markets by superstores (Isnenghi 1994) – had not occurred in the *centro storico* of Naples.

Over the last two to three decades and in what appears to be a turnaround in fortunes, the piazza has become a popular leitmotif in European programmes of urban regeneration. The restoration, redesign and pedestrianization of the piazza was seen as a means of retrieving a sense of place and memory, of creating people-friendly spaces and of linking up detached parts of the city (Nuvolari 1989; Locatelli 1989). Moreover, it was relatively cheap to transform, it bore immediate results and it connected with the growing political emphasis on citizenship. In Naples the reclamation of the piazza was initially seen as a means of clawing back 'collective identity' from the grip of traffic, illegal activities and pollution. At the beginning of the 1990s, environmental and heritage groups successfully campaigned to eliminate a car park in Piazza Bellini, located on the western edge of the *centro antico,* which was subsequently transformed into a symbol of an enlightened public's fight against the city's neglect. This would be followed by the retrieval of other small piazzas in the heart of the city by the interventions of judges, again against car parks. Therefore, prior to the election of Bassolino at the end of 1993, the piazza was already considered a crucial element to urban renewal.

However, the regeneration of piazzas is not such a straightforward process. The piazza finds itself in a contradictory position in the contemporary city. As Isnenghi observes: 'If you do not exclude [cars] from historic piazzas these are reduced to foul-smelling, glistening car parks. If you remove them, you risk cutting piazzas off from the present, of embalming and reducing them to a simulacra of what they once were but where life has since dispersed' (Isnenghi 1994: 8). Although (auto)mobility has been construed as inimical to civic life, which was instead seen to be *located* in fixed places, the right to movement has also stood as a basic objective of urban democracies. As much as it might be a cause for despair, car ownership has reshaped citizenship and the public sphere (Sheller and Urry 2000: 740, 742). The conflicts surrounding the eviction of traffic and the subsequent invention of a cultural sense of place would be central issues in Piazza Plebiscito after its restoration in 1994. It is to this space that I now turn.

Part 2

The Making of a Regeneration Symbol

Heritage, Decorum and the Incursions of the Everyday in Piazza Plebiscito

Chapter 5

Enter the Historic Piazza

One of the largest piazzas in Naples, Piazza Plebiscito[1] is situated between the city's main commercial and administrative district to the north-east, the crowded popular neighbourhoods of the Pallonetto to the south-west, and the Spanish Quarters to the north. It is enclosed by four buildings: the seventeenth-century Royal Palace, which presently houses a museum, the city's main library and the *Soprintendenza per i Beni Ambientali e Architettonici* (the government body responsible for environmental and architectural heritage in Naples and its surrounding region); the Church of San Francesco di Paola, built in the first half of the nineteenth century at the centre of a semicircular colonnade; and two near identical neoclassical palaces, Palazzo Salerno, the southern headquarters of the Italian army, and Palazzo della Prefettura, the seat of the prefect for the province of Naples (see illustration 5.1).

In her 2001 election brochure, Rosa Russo Iervolino, the Centre-Left's successor to Antonio Bassolino, described Piazza Plebiscito as 'Europe's most beautiful piazza' (Napoli con Iervolino 2001: 15). A few years earlier, the use of such a superlative would have sounded odd. Until the beginning of the 1990s Piazza Plebiscito had been used as a car park and had long held a peripheral place in the popular iconography of Naples. Moreover, it was rarely considered a masterpiece of urban design. As the Neapolitan architectural historian Renato De Fusco declared in 1989, 'It does not compare to Piazza del Campo in Siena or Piazza San Pietro in Rome. It's an honest neoclassical work whose main value is its spaciousness' (De Fusco 1996: 102). The proclamation of the piazza's incomparable beauty in 2001 rather underlined the space's privileged position in public narratives about a resurgent Naples, following its restoration and closure to traffic for the G7 summit in 1994 and the political capital that this had afforded the Bassolino administration. During the second

---

1. Officially 'Piazza *del* Plebiscito' (Piazza of the Plebiscite), the space is here referred to as simply 'Piazza Plebiscito', which is the name usually used both at local and national level.

half of the 1990s, the piazza's image was to be found everywhere: on posters, book covers, tourist paraphernalia, even in a national television advertisement for a brand of biscuits.[2] As the city's ceremonial centre stage, it was now also frequently used for major public events. Such was the piazza's power as a metaphor for political and urban renewal that on occasions it was deployed to convey a virtuous trajectory in the nascent Second Italian Republic.[3]

There exists an extensive literature that explores the pivotal role that places and buildings play in urban regeneration strategies (Harvey 1990; Kearns and Philo 1993; Hubbard 1996; Ward 1998; Julier 2005). Some have been interpreted as emblematic of wider cultural and socioeconomic processes shaping cities. The redevelopment of Times Square in New York, for instance, has often been considered in a North American context as paradigmatic of contemporary conflicts around issues of public morality, security and gentrification (Reichl 1999; Makagon 2004), while the Guggenheim Museum in Bilbao has come to internationally epitomize the boosterist logic underpinning flagship architectural projects and highbrow cultural policies (McNeill 2000). The post-G7 Piazza Plebiscito has also been regarded, at least in Italy, as exemplary of a cultural and civic reawakening of Naples. However, unlike Times Square or the Guggenheim Museum, scholarly debate about Piazza Plebiscito has remained conspicuously cursory and has tended to be marked by value judgements about the new space rather than any serious critical engagement with the processes and discourses that its transformation generated. For its promoters, the piazza became an almost sacred site that had redirected the course of history and projected the image of a brighter future (De Lucia 1998). For its detractors and critics, it represented a façade that masked the unresolved problems of the city (Ragone 1997), as well as the 'museumification' of public space (P. Amato 2006).

The premise for a detailed ethno-historical analysis of Piazza Plebiscito is not simply to address the paucity of academic inquiry or to move

---

2. In 1995 the biscuit maker Mulino Bianco used television trickery to metamorphose Piazza Plebiscito into a cornfield. This was one of a series of commercials in which famous Italian urban settings were transformed into rural idylls.

3. For example, the combined Italian edition of Paul Ginsborg's two-volume history of contemporary Italy (1998) includes a colour plate of the post-G7 piazza. In the short presentation of the book's illustrations, Ginsborg concludes: 'To end, a ray of hope: Piazza Plebiscito in Naples, restored and saved' (no page number). Piazza Plebiscito is in fact the final image of a series of 97 photographs spanning the postwar period and immediately follows a picture of the *Mani Pulite* team of prosecutors in Milan. It is worth noting that the main text itself does not mention the piazza once and makes only a passing reference to Bassolino's electoral victory in 1993. A short discussion of both Bassolino's mayorship and the piazza (minus the illustration) appears in the updated British edition of Ginsborg's second volume *Italy and its Discontents: Family, Civil Society, State, 1980–2001* (2001: 315–16).

beyond the conceptual and narrative structures ascribed to the piazza by local cultural and political elites. Rather, it is based on the conviction that the space provides crucial insights into particular dynamics of urban change that are otherwise indiscernible in general overviews of the city. To fully comprehend the significance of the regenerated Piazza Plebiscito, it is first necessary to reconstruct the multi-layered history of the 'old' piazza, from its distant royal past to the car-dominated space of the postwar decades, in order to examine the space's shifting position in representations about Naples and to scrutinize the selective readings of its past after 1994.

Illustration 5.1. Piazza Plebiscito from the air, 1994. *Courtesy of Archivio Fotografico Parisio.*

Map 5.1. Piazza Plebiscito and surrounding area. *Designed by Nick Dines.*

Chapter 6

From Royal Courtyard to Car Park

Between ceremony and excrement: the historical role of the piazza

An open space known as Borgo Santo Spirito had existed on the same spot as Piazza Plebiscito since the thirteenth century. The term '*borgo*' (literally 'village') denoted its location outside the city walls, while Santo Spirito referred to one of four surrounding ecclesiastical buildings which were all demolished as the present piazza took shape. With the completion of the Royal Palace in 1602, the name of the space was changed to Largo di Palazzo. As the symbolic and physical centre of monarchical power, Largo di Palazzo provided the stage for royal pageants, weddings and funerals, papal visits and, above all, military parades. It was also the setting for annual festivals that directly involved the lower ranks of Neapolitan society. One such event was the assault of the *Cuccagna,* the main Carnival attraction under the Bourbons during the second half of the eighteenth century. The *Cuccagna* was a mountainous fabrication of wood, papier mâché and cloth adorned with food and livestock that was erected in the centre of the piazza. On the four Sundays before Lent, as the king and his entourage assisted from the balcony of the Royal Palace, the *Cuccagna*'s guards would withdraw from their posts, leaving groups of men free to scale the structure and plunder its booty. This would result in violent brawls and acts of unrestrained lawlessness as neighbourhoods competed to hoard the most spoils. Any signs of conflict were, however, integral to the spectacle, and participation was considered a sign of allegiance to the Bourbon regime (Barletta 1997).

Unsurprisingly, Largo di Palazzo also became a focus for challenges to royal authority. In 1799, the Neapolitan Jacobins, some of whom had already campaigned for the abolition of the *Cuccagna* as a sign of the

Bourbon regime's backwardness, read 'The Declaration of the Republic' from the balcony of the renamed National Palace before erecting a 'liberty tree', the emblem of the Revolution, in the middle of the piazza. A decade later, the city's Napoleonic governor, Gioacchino Murat, planned to transform Largo di Palazzo into a lay and bourgeois piazza by demolishing the adjacent churches in front of the Royal Palace and building in their place a neoclassical civic forum and semicircular colonnade. Work was cut short with the return to the throne in 1815 of Ferdinando IV, who immediately commissioned, as an ex-voto, a basilica in honour of San Francesco di Paola to replace the assembly rooms of Murat's project. This building, which reestablished the alliance between Catholicism and the monarchy, has been described as Europe's principal monument to the post-1815 Restoration (Villari 1995: 137).[1] However, the fact that the colonnade was kept in the final design reflected the king's pragmatic approach to the legacy of the French occupation, a sharp contrast to the indiscriminate, bloody vendetta of 1799 (Petrusewicz 1998). Certainly, the new spatial layout gave the piazza a more sombre aspect. Popular festivities and carnivals were abolished or relocated to other, less formal parts of the city (Nuvolari 1989), while the military, royal and papal ceremonies became predominant. Moreover, following the insurrections of 1830 and 1848, travelling musicians, deemed by the Bourbon police to be susceptible to revolutionary ideals, were banned from the piazza and the surrounding area (Genoino 1989).

With the fall of the Bourbon monarchy, Largo di Palazzo was rebaptized Piazza del Plebiscito in commemoration of the plebiscite of 21 October 1860, announced from the piazza itself, which formally sanctioned the South's incorporation into the new Italian kingdom. The piazza's symbolic centrality in Naples and southern Italy diminished, as political power shifted to the North. The main monuments to the new nation were raised elsewhere, such as the giant statue of Vittorio Emanuele on horseback that was erected, significantly, in front of the city hall in nearby Piazza Municipio.[2] Besides the change in title, no real attempt

---

1. A parallel can be drawn with the construction at the end of the nineteenth century of the Basilica of Sacré Coeur in Montmartre, which reinforced clerical authority in the wake of the Paris Commune of 1871 and sought to eradicate the neighbourhood's close connection with the uprising (Harvey 1989a).

2. Piazza Municipio became a key symbolic space after Unification. In addition to being the municipal heart of Naples, the piazza's eastern edge bordered one of the most important ports in Italy which served as the point of departure for millions of southern Italian emigrants, as well as the disembarkation for returnees, such as the Italians expelled from Libya in 1968. Unlike Piazza Plebiscito, Piazza Municipio underwent a series of structural changes after 1860. The workshops and small factories surrounding the ramparts of the Maschio Angioino were removed in the 1920s in order to enhance the monument's presence. During the mid-1930s a new passenger terminal, the Stazione Marittima, was built as part of the Fascist regime's grand design to transform Naples into the 'port of the empire'

was made to eradicate the vestiges of the Bourbon regime. During the fervour of Unification, the equestrian statues of Ferdinando I and Carlo III in the centre of Piazza Plebiscito risked destruction at the hands of an angry mob. A Garibaldian priest reputedly intervened to calm the situation and reassured the crowds that the heads would be replaced with those of Garibaldi and Vittorio Emanuele, but this proposal died as anti-Bourbon resentment withered (Gleijeses 1968). The piazza certainly retained close associations with authority, but these reflected Naples's new provincial status. The Italian army set up its regional headquarters in Palazzo Salerno, the former home of a Bourbon prince, while the prefecture, the national government's representative in the city, occupied the Palazzo della Foresteria. The Royal Palace became a Savoy residence, and although it was assigned over to the state as a national monument in 1919, a wing of the building was kept for the Italian royal family until it went into exile in 1946.

Given its size and design, Piazza Plebiscito nevertheless remained the city's principal setting for ceremonial and civic events, such as opera concerts, society weddings and military parades. Under Fascism, the piazza was exploited as an arena for mass meetings and propaganda stunts, such as during the 'Battle for Grain', when threshing machines were set up in the piazza. In the postwar period it was used by political parties for election rallies that often attracted crowds of up to a hundred thousand people. In a series of letters to the French philosopher Louis Althusser written during her campaign trail as a local PCI parliamentary candidate in 1968, Maria Antonietta Macciocchi's reminisces about Communist leader Palmiro Togliatti's appearances in Piazza Plebiscito:

> Togliatti used to give the concluding speech of the [national] campaign here in Naples. And he used to give the speech here in the vast semi-elliptical harmony of Piazza Plebiscito, in front of the former Bourbon Palace. … Can you imagine a speech in the Place de la Concorde, with a red platform ten metres high, complete with a red curtained backdrop, and the square absolutely jammed with people? That is the way you have to imagine this speech at Naples, and the success of the undertaking was a sort of 'sign' as to how the whole election had gone. (Macciocchi 1973: 240)

However, following the massive gatherings for Communist, Christian Democrat and Monarchist leaders during the 1950s and 1960s, and apart from the odd occasion, notably Enrico Berlinguer's visit to Naples in 1976 at the height of the PCI's electoral support, these rallies became

---

(Belfiore and Gravagnuolo 1994), which provided the piazza with a new seaward backdrop. In 1956, the Monarchist mayor Achille Lauro sought to reshape Piazza Municipio in his image after ordering, contra council and public opinion, the felling of rows of 120-year-old holm oaks in front of the city hall.

less spectacular and the stage was gradually brought closer to the Royal Palace to conceal the dwindling crowds (Corsi 1994). A depleted audience was as politically damaging as a full piazza was uplifting. By the 1980s, parties switched the majority of their campaigning to smaller and more tactically viable places. Piazza Plebiscito was also a regular place for demonstrations, although this was chiefly due to the presence of the prefecture, and protests were confined to single issues in which the prefect played an arbitrating role. Political marches, unless they were particularly large and required a suitably sized arena, would begin and end in other locations of the city.

Piazza Plebiscito did not evoke the archetypal image of the busy Italian piazza. Although incorporated into a number of popular processions such as the Piedigrotta music festival (Mancini and Gargano 1991) and the parade of the Nzegna (Broccolini 1998),[3] the piazza was generally a peripheral place in the everyday collective experience of the city. Organized events would sometimes pull huge crowds, but otherwise there was little in the piazza to attract people. Caffè Gambrinus, one of two literary cafés located on its corners (the other being Gran Caffè Turco, which closed in 1932), was for many years an exclusive microcosm of the bourgeois public sphere. After it reopened its doors in 1890 following the cholera epidemic, it became the haunt of a Neapolitan intelligentsia and cultural elite and was temporarily shut down by the neighbouring prefect in 1936 as a threat to the Fascist regime. However, despite having windows that overlooked the piazza and apart from the fact that it always was (and indeed remains) an exclusive meeting place, Gambrinus was more closely bound to the adjacent, much smaller and busier Piazza Trieste and Trento. Instead, the buildings facing Piazza Plebiscito were either officially off-limits (as in the case of Palazzo Salerno), had entry restrictions (such as the prefecture and the Royal Palace) or were rarely open to the public, as in the case of San Francesco di Paola, which, until it became a parish church in 1990, was used solely for state ceremonies. The colonnade, which housed a number of artisans' workshops, was the only space that encouraged interaction. As one of the few public places in Naples to offer shelter from the elements, it was popularly associated with the city's more destitute inhabitants. There existed a saying '*Vàje*

---

3. Until its demise in 1953, the annual parade of the Nzegna, a costume reenactment of the rapport between the Bourbons and the *popolino* organized by locals from the Pallonetto and Santa Lucia neighbourhoods, would cross Piazza Plebiscito in front of the Royal Palace as it wound its way down through alleyways towards the sea. This route, together with the ritualized reversal of roles and participants' mocking disregard for authority, created a spatial symbiosis between the poor, dark, cramped neighbourhood of the Pallonetto, physically screened behind the buildings surrounding San Francesco di Paola, and the open, palatial setting of Piazza Plebiscito.

a fernì sotto 'e culonne 'e san Francisco 'e Paola' (You'll end up living under the colonnades of San Francesco di Paola), which was a warning to those who wasted their time and squandered their money. In her depiction of late nineteenth-century Naples, Matilde Serao mentioned the colonnade's function as a public dormitory and also noted that the street immediately behind San Francesco di Paola served as a latrine (Serao 1994). A public urinal was later installed at one end of the colonnade, and although this was removed during the 1950s, it remained a customary place for males to urinate. This liminal, 'low', everyday space directly adjoined the ceremonial, regal arena of Piazza Plebiscito.

Piazza Plebiscito in the era of mass motorization

During the postwar period, the daily encounter with Piazza Plebiscito for the majority of people was mediated through transport. From the 1950s onwards, 'circulation' became a key word of urban policy as the city's inadequate and essentially nineteenth-century road system struggled to cope with the rise in traffic. The strip of paving stones in front of the Royal Palace constituted a crucial road link along the city's east-west corridor. For almost three decades, up to 1990, a section of the piazza next to this busy street was used as a terminus for urban and regional bus services. The piazza was a point of arrival and departure for thousands of Neapolitans and city users. Piazza Plebiscito was thus engrained on a mental map of access to, and movement across, the city.

In January 1963, in order to relieve the strain on the *centro storico*'s increasingly congested streets, the city council permanently transformed the remaining space of Piazza Plebiscito into a public car park. The year 1963 coincided with the culmination of Italy's so-called 'economic miracle'. The general rise in living standards of the preceding period had been characterized by an increase in private car ownership, particularly following the introduction onto the market of cheap models such as the Fiat 600, in 1955.[4] In Naples, as in the rest of the South, increasing prosperity was restricted to a middle-class minority.[5] For many of those who had moved out to the new residential districts such as Vomero and Via Manzoni but who worked in offices and public institutions in the *cen-*

---

4. Between 1950 and 1964 the number of registered private cars in Italy increased from 342,000 to 4.67 million, and motorcycles from 700,000 to 4.3 million (Ginsborg 1990).

5. In 1963, the Neapolitan daily *Il Mattino* calculated that one in fifteen Neapolitans now owned a car, claiming that this figure had more than tripled in the space of a few years (*Il Mattino*, 1 December 1963). Nevertheless, during the 1960s, Naples continued to have the lowest number of registered vehicles among the country's major cities (Mastrostefano 1969).

tro storico, the car increasingly became the favoured mode of transport. During the same week that Piazza Plebiscito became a car park, the local Monarchist newspaper, *Roma,* ran an article comparing the motor car to a *salotto,* the Italian word for parlour and equivalent term for salon: 'Whereas life once revolved around the family and home, out of which arose the demand for the *salotto,* today we spend less time indoors. We live in the age of the day-trip and the "weekend". The automobile is needed so as not to cut a poor figure in front of friends, colleagues and clients' (*Roma,* 6 January 1963). More than in northern Italian cities such as Milan (Foot 2001b), the automobile in Naples continued to possess the aura of novelty. Its purchase was equated with a desire to display personal prosperity and one's participation in modernity. As the new bourgeois *salotto,* it represented both an intimate private space and a public status symbol. For local newspapers such as *Il Mattino* and *Roma,* the suburban car-owning family was increasingly imagined as a new audience and articles would often address their particular experience of the city and its traffic.

In contrast, the Communist press held a far more ambivalent attitude about the growth in private car ownership, reflecting the PCI's hesitant and often negative response to the societal changes brought about by the economic boom. The automobile was seen as the harbinger of an emergent consumer society, spurred by the national monopolies, which threatened the collective dimension of urban life. In her correspondence with Althusser, Macciocchi described the impact of mass motorization upon Naples's beleaguered and increasingly underused public transport: 'Buses in traffic are completely immobilized, surrounded and attacked by the little cars, like rhinoceri by clouds of insects' (Macciocchi 1973: 88). She also sardonically noted that a giant portrait of the local Christian Democrat leader had been mounted in the window of the main Fiat dealer in Naples (ibid.: 89). Nonetheless, at the same time the PCI acknowledged a mass desire for private mobility. Cars were offered as prizes to the best newspaper sellers at the party's *Feste dell'Unità.* During the 1960s, as Stephen Gundle points out, apart from hardened old activists and some young idealists, the majority of militants 'acquired electrical appliances and cars as soon as they could afford them' (Gundle 2000: 91). Indeed, throughout her 1968 election campaign in Naples, Macciocchi was chauffeured between meetings by comrades with cars. The commiseration she felt for the lone bus passengers remained entirely vicarious as she peered at them from the passenger seat of a Fiat.

Everyone, however, was in agreement that the narrow streets and alleyways of the *centro storico* could not cope with a continual growth in traffic and that major infrastructural changes would have to be made if it were to ever function effectively at the heart of a modern, motorized city. A series of projects were first mooted during the early 1960s that would dominate planning agendas over the next thirty years: from new trunk roads through the old city neighbourhoods (which would never be realized) and an orbital motorway, the Tangenziale, to the north of the centre (which would be built in the 1970s) to the relocation of services and administrative offices outside the *centro storico* (which would occur with the partial completion of the Centro Direzionale in the early 1990s) and a new metro linking the hillside suburbs and the city centre (which would finally reach Piazza Dante in the city centre in 2002). In the short term, a more urgent matter was the hundreds of parked vehicles on the sides of streets that clogged the flow of traffic on a daily basis. Preventative measures, such as increased fines and municipal tow trucks – the infamous *carri gru* in fact made their first appearance on the streets of Naples in 1963 – had little impact and ultimately kindled the war of attrition between the authorities and the city's drivers that continues to this day.

The decision to turn the historic Piazza Plebiscito into a giant car park caused little fuss in the local press (see illustration 6.1). As the only low note on the historic day, *Il Mattino* printed a photograph of the piazza's resident pigeons and lamented that most would now have to search for new 'pastures' (*Il Mattino,* 3 January 1963). Rather, arguments were

Illustration 6.1. Car park in Piazza Plebiscito, 1967. *Courtesy of Archivio Fotografico Parisio.*

raised over the effectiveness of the new arrangements. *Roma* complained that car club members would lose their parking privileges (*Roma,* 3 January 1963); *Il Mattino* argued that while the available spaces were large, they would probably not be sufficient to meet the demands of drivers (*Il Mattino,* 26 January 1963); while both agreed that *parcheggiatori abusivi* (unauthorized parking attendants) were likely to proliferate outside the designated areas and offer a cheaper service. There was no mention at all of the new car park in the Neapolitan pages of *L'Unità.* Instead, in a report on new parking restrictions a few weeks later, the Communist newspaper accused the recently installed DC administration of doing nothing to reopen the hundred or so streets in the city centre that had been closed due to road cavities or unsafe buildings, and, like the DC-leaning *Il Mattino,* it called for a more holistic vision to the city's traffic problem (*L'Unità,* 26 January 1963).[6]

At the same time, the local press was not indifferent to the issue of urban heritage. On the contrary, throughout the beginning of 1963, *Il Mattino* published a series of articles highlighting the pitiful state of the *centro storico* and called for urgent repairs to buildings and improvements to street signs and lighting. However, the car was not considered incompatible with the city's architectural patrimony. In the preceding years, new models had often been advertised to the public in emblematic spaces such as the Galleria Umberto I and Piazza Plebiscito itself. Instead, the car park played a crucial role in ordering the increasingly chaotic traffic of Naples and projecting a modern, *civilized* image of the city. Moreover, at the outset, Piazza Plebiscito was conceived above all as a sanctuary to the disciplined, non–*centro storico* middle-class driver. It was the uneducated motorist and not the car which was a cause for concern. For instance, *Il Mattino* claimed that certain Neapolitans were, by temperament, uncontrollably prone to speed and road violence: 'Recent clamorous episodes … continue to convince us that many people are not mature enough to benefit from the fruits of technical progress' (*Il Mattino,* 12 March 1963). Such views were echoed by the administration. The DC assessor for traffic argued that Neapolitans were as much to blame for congestion as the city's topographical dilemmas and infrastructural inadequacies (*Istituto Luce* newsreel, 1 March 1963). In addition to certain drivers, pedestrians were also singled out for attack. On the very same day it reported the new measures for Piazza Plebiscito, *Il Mattino* started a month-long campaign against jaywalking. If pedestrians were to share the city with motorists, it argued, they should be sub-

---

6. During the 1960s *L'Unità* was certainly not averse to parking matters. For instance, in the newspaper's Rome edition in 1964, it defended the rights of residents against a city-council plan to abolish hourly parking spaces in the centre of the capital (*L'Unità,* 21 August 1964).

ject to equally severe penalties to curb their wayward habits (*Il Mattino*, 3 January 1963). Debates around discipline and control were certainly not unique to Naples during this period. For example, prior to the opening of the M1 motorway in Britain in November 1959, there was widespread concern that many people were ill prepared for the psychological rigours of motorway driving (Merriman 2006). However, in Naples more than elsewhere, it was the behaviour behind the steering wheel rather than the possession of a particular model that was publicly identified as a sign of sociocultural distinction.[7]

Piazza Plebiscito's traffic-regulating function went largely unquestioned over the following three decades, although as the car became a mass commodity, the prestige that came with ownership began to fade (Viale 1996). During the same period, traffic jams were a daily, chronic problem (Allum 1973; Wanderlingh and Corsi 1987). By 1990, the city possessed the highest level of respiratory disease, the dustiest streets and the slowest public transport in Italy. It was calculated that it took less time to travel from Milan to Tunis in plane than it did to take the Number 140 bus from the seafront district of Posillipo to Piazza Gesù Nuovo in the *centro antico* (*La Repubblica*, 27 January 1990). Piazza Plebiscito's various roles as a car park, bus station and through route all remained fundamental in a city centre that had not reconfigured itself around motorized traffic. It was inconceivable that such a large open space in the *centro storico*'s dense urban fabric be used for anything else. Certainly, by the 1980s, the original pristine image of the neatly arranged, well-kept vehicles of middle-class commuters had been overrun by all and sundry. A disorderly medley of jalopies sat side by side with the dented saloons of public employees, as municipal attendants were forced to compete with the *parcheggiatori abusivi*.

While Piazza Plebiscito's traffic function predominated over everything else, this did not prevent the space from being used for other purposes. Demonstrations in the piazza, in fact, had the added incentive of obstructing traffic to draw attention to particular demands. In 1989, for instance, a protest by construction workers blocked the piazza with bulldozers, lorries and cement mixers, bringing the city to a 'total standstill' (*La Repubblica*, 4 March 1989). The piazza was also occasionally used for organized public events, such as Pope John Paul II's visits to Naples in 1979 and 1990, although some requests, such as the planned two-hundredth anniversary celebrations of the city's military academy in 1987, were turned down by local authorities on the grounds that they

---

7. For a discussion of the link between motorization and the idea of the civilizing process, see Elias 1995. On the topic of car ownership and distinction, see Gartman 2004.

would cause too much disruption (*La Repubblica,* 11 October 1987). On occasions, the piazza's mundane traffic function was supplanted by spontaneous mass gatherings. After the 1980 earthquake, thousands of Neapolitans spent a number of days and nights in Piazza Plebiscito in fear of aftershocks. The piazza was described in the local press as 'a gigantic open-air garage' that served as 'a spy hole on the city's anguish' (*Il Mattino,* 25 November 1980). Seven years later, Neapolitans flocked through the piazza during the citywide celebrations after the local football team won its first ever *Serie A* title. Television specials dedicated to the national champions were projected onto a giant screen mounted in front of San Francesco di Paola, while banners were draped over the scaffolding surrounding the Royal Palace. *Il Mattino* interpreted the jubilant scenes as 'the desire for a piazza in a city without identity' (*Il Mattino,* 12 May 1987). Yet the piazza has played a very minor role in collective memories of both events. In the case of the earthquake, the piazza was connected with the immediate aftermath of the tremor, but this was soon overshadowed as the extent of the devastation in the popular neighbourhoods emerged. During the 1987 *Scudetto* celebrations the piazza was used for its functional advantages, while its location along the route of the main motorcade and its proximity to some of the main street parties in the Spanish Quarters and the Pallonetto turned it into a crossroads of festivities. However, public memory has since focused on emblematic instances of jovial deviance (the swim in the 'Artichoke' fountain in the adjacent Piazza Trieste e Trento), the 'rediscovery' of monuments (such as the daubing of the statue of Dante in the colours of Napoli), as well as the Maradona-themed murals that appeared on walls across the city (Signorelli 1996: 179–94). Indeed, retrospective accounts of these two unforgettable moments only further reiterate the marginal status of Piazza Plebiscito in narratives about Naples before 1994.

By the late 1980s, a small but vocal alliance of environmental and cultural associations began to call for the eviction of sedentary vehicles from parts of the *centro storico*. Attention focused on the small piazzas of the *centro antico* and the city's principal monuments, such as the Palazzo Reale, whose courtyards were used as parking space by shopkeepers, office workers and local councillors. The pressure sometimes bore the desired results, although closures were often carried out by the police on legal grounds, for instance during action against illegal car-park attendants, and not by the city council. The state of the city's traffic was a priority issue, but vote-losing anti-car measures were not at the top of the political agenda of any of the main parties. This said, at the end of 1989 campaigners managed to persuade the city council to pedestrianize the centre of Piazza Plebiscito (albeit leaving a small car park for prefecture employees and military officials). The closure was considered successful for the debate it provoked and an important sign that things could be done (Caniglia 1993; Ferrari 1993), but its promoters were not particularly enthusiastic about the piazza's new arrangement. The space, cordoned off from the surrounding gridlock with rows of tyres, was described by one journalist as 'Fort Alamo' (*La Repubblica,* 27 January 1990). The aim had not been to reclaim the regal space of Piazza Plebiscito, which had limited social and cultural benefits (Caniglia 1993); rather, it was concluded that effective traffic control would have to encompass a wider area and target places frequently used by Neapolitans, such as market areas (Capasso 1993).

While the bus terminal was permanently removed after this experiment, the car park swiftly returned. This had already been reduced in size in 1986 after a segment of the piazza in front of the colonnade was turned into a construction site for the underground 'Rapid Tram Line' (popularly known by its acronym LTR) between the *centro storico* and the football stadium in the western suburb of Fuorigrotta. Incorporated into the preparations for the 1990 World Cup championships, the project was not completed on time due to building delays and safety defects. The benefits offered by the LTR, which would have served what was already the best connected part of the city, appeared a secondary concern. The public resources that were poured into the scheme instead served primarily to create jobs and sustain a clientelistic system (Macry 1994). Indeed, construction was suspended indefinitely after investigations into financial irregularities commenced in early 1993.

In June 1993, several small piazzas in the *centro antico* that had become illegal car parks were confiscated by local judges and hastily pedestrianized with cement flower boxes. Piazza Plebiscito, whose remaining section of car park was public, did not feature in this legal blitz. Ironically, in the same year, the local media was still debating the practicalities of building a multi-storey car park beneath the piazza, which, since its official approval back in 1986, continued to be considered an ideal, if unrealistic, solution to traffic congestion in the *centro storico*. The total closure of the piazza to vehicles would require entirely different (and extraordinary) circumstances.

Chapter 7

The Regeneration of Piazza Plebiscito

The G7 summit and the eradication of signs of neglect

A key turning point in Piazza Plebiscito's history was July 1993, when Italian Prime Minister Carlo Azeglio Ciampi chose Naples as the nation's host city for the 1994 G7 summit. Ciampi's choice took many people by surprise: the city's administration had only recently declared the city bankrupt and would shortly be replaced by a government commissioner, while the Royal Palace – the designated venue for the summit – overlooked a car park and an impounded building site. In the meantime, however, Antonio Bassolino would be elected mayor, and with him a new climate of cautious optimism would emerge. In February 1994, a commission comprised of representatives from the local administration, the cultural superintendencies and national government was set up to delegate state funds and oversee the hasty preparations for the summit. Suddenly Piazza Plebiscito, hitherto unobtrusive in its traffic guise, found itself at the centre stage. Its concrete slabs crisscrossed with tyre marks were replaced with volcanic tiles from a local quarry, surrounding buildings were cleaned and the abandoned LTR construction site was removed. The whole operation was completed in just eighty days, a week ahead of schedule, at the relatively low cost of three billion lire (1.5 million euros). The successful race against time, with workers literally toiling around the clock, was itself seen as a sign of effective institutional collaboration and organizational competence. Vezio De Lucia, the administration's representative on the G7 commission, declared that the piazza represented 'a starting point and indicator of a new direction' for the city after fifty years of speculation (De Lucia 1998: 10).

The empty, resplendent and military-guarded piazza was very much the emblem of the G7 summit of July 1994. Its image was beamed around the world, offering an alternative vision of the city to the traditional stereotypes of dirt and chaos. Locally, the piazza was instantly catapulted to the top of the city's spatial hierarchy and attributed a set of new characteristics. Commentators insisted on calling it the '*salotto di Napoli*'. The term that had been used to describe the car in 1963 was now employed to conceive the piazza as an exclusive, well-kept meeting place. Other common descriptions in newspapers included '*biglietto di visita*' (visiting card) and '*fiore all'occhiello*' (showpiece), which implied that the piazza had been conferred honorary status over the rest of the city. By the end of the year, *Il Mattino* had even started to use the title '*Piazza Grande*', as if to suggest that Naples had earned itself a quintessentially (northern) Italian civic arena.

The new arrangement not only purged signs of urban neglect but also sought to restore the piazza's monumental status. The work had initially assumed the form of an archaeological dig, as the architect responsible for the new design searched in vain for traces of the original nineteenth-century surface beneath the concrete. Bassolino saw the restoration as invoking 'the era of the great monarchies [when Naples] was for a long time the capital of European culture' (Improta et al. 1994: 29), while *Il Mattino* declared that Neapolitans were able to 'rediscover' the piazza's 'forgotten ornamental decorum' (3 June 1994). The general enthusiasm surrounding the retrieval of the royal piazza resonated with the reevaluation of Naples's pre-1860 heritage, which had begun to be a focus in the early 1980s with major exhibitions dedicated to the cultural and civic traditions of the seventeenth and eighteenth centuries. This was not to say that the piazza was suddenly reinterpreted by the city's politicians and media as belonging to a more enlightened tradition. Rather, the patchwork of solemn events, popular festivities and bloody revolts that embellished narratives about the new piazza was part of a historical package which the city was now able to promote (Improta et al. 1994; De Lucia 1998).

In spite of this apparent success story, the transformation of Piazza Plebiscito had to endure a series of hitches and was the subject of heated debates that threatened to jeopardize the city's carefully crafted appearance and which would continue to afflict the piazza after the G7 summit. The start of the work was delayed by a month after the company that had originally been awarded the contract withdrew under accusations that it was not in line with antimafia regulations. Controversy also lingered over the removal of the piazza's principal eyesore, the LTR building site. The government, the administration, the local public transport company and the LTR's constructors all firmly refused to fund its dismantlement, and it was only after several weeks of stalemate that the prefect Umberto Improta was forced to allocate a billion lire for an additional contract. The matter was compounded by construction workers who chained themselves to the machinery to demand assurances that they would be reemployed. Until the last minute, the very symbol of past mismanagement and inefficiency threatened to tarnish the city's rehabilitation. Indeed, during a critical period between March and April, the city's main broadsheet referred to Piazza Plebiscito as 'the piazza of discord' (*Il Mattino*, 26 March 1994), 'the thorn in the side of prefect Improta' (*Il Mattino*, 31 March 1994) and 'the piazza of controversies and delays' (*Il Mattino*, 6 April 1994).

As work on the piazza commenced, a different dispute arose over the proposed paving. The prefect and government representative wanted to replace the dirty cracked concrete in the centre of the piazza with identical new slabs. This was considered the most viable solution given the time and money available. Their priority was the preparation for the G7 and not the resurrection of a piazza. However, the administration, along with the superintendents and heritage groups, pressed for the entire space to be laid with local basalt paving stones. New concrete slabs, it was argued, would be a travesty of the piazza's historical physiognomy and would ultimately signal a return to the car park after the summit. Although the surface of the piazza had in fact changed over time – during the eighteenth and nineteenth centuries its centre had even consisted of beaten earth to accommodate regular cavalry displays – by insisting on aesthetic criteria the connoisseurs and direct inheritors of the piazza (the administration) stressed the value that an appropriately repaved piazza would have for posterity. In the face of mounting opposition (*Il Mattino* claimed to have received many phone calls from 'ordinary citizens ... rooting for the Vesuvian stone' (*Il Mattino*, 10 April 1994)), the prefect eventually acquiesced to the demands of the 'aesthetes', and a compromise was reached after a quarry at the foot of Vesuvius offered to extract the rock in the time available and cut costs by producing thinner tiles. The revamped physical aspect would indeed be fundamental for deploying the space in a new urban narrative. However, the incident demonstrated that, from the outset, the reconceived piazza was not a unanimous project but a terrain of conflicting interests.

The decision to maintain the piazza as a traffic-free zone after the end of the G7 summit led to the Bassolino administration's first major public confrontation. In reality, the removal of the last remnants of the car park next to the colonnade caused little commotion. Rather, it was the proposed permanent closure of the street in front of the Royal Palace which provoked the most controversy. Shopkeepers in the Santa Lucia district (to the immediate south of Piazza Plebiscito) protested that they would be cut off from the rest of the city. Their call for the immediate reopening of the street was backed by business leaders as well as the fledgling right-wing opposition, which used the incident to attack the administration. Geppy Rippa of Forza Italia, for instance, declared: 'This incident is further evidence that the so-called progressive alliance suffers from a serious form of ignorance in urban affairs which will damage the entire city' (*Il Tempo*, 14 July 1994). Numerous left-wing councillors were also wary of the impact the measure would have on the city and recommended a balance be found between the new piazza and its old traffic function (Villone 2000). Various compromises were suggested, including Sunday closures and restricted access to public transport and taxis.

The administration, however, refused to change its plans. Its intransigent position was supported by the city's superintendents, art and architectural experts, cultural and environmental groups and a significant section of the local press (*La Repubblica* and *Il Mattino*). In an interview with *La Repubblica,* the vice-mayor and assessor for Mobility, Ada Becchi, declared:

> Those who want to reopen Piazza del Plebiscito to traffic can carry on shouting, but they won't intimidate me. The piazza is closed to cars and it's going to remain that way. … Do we want to resign ourselves to the preponderance of the car which for decades denied the city of one of its most evocative settings? (*La Repubblica*, 14 July 1994)

The proposal of a partial closure was rejected as naïve, because this, it was argued, would inevitably be violated. The new piazza was presented as a democratic gesture: what had initially been the exclusive privilege for a handful of G7 delegates would now be consigned to all Neapolitans. During a press conference to justify the administration's position, Bassolino was confident that if there were a local referendum, the vast majority of citizens would vote in favour of the restyled piazza, adding that 'the protection of the monumental and artistic values of Piazza Plebiscito is more important than many other problems' and that its closure to traffic was 'one of the most significant investments for tourism' (*Il Mattino*, 19 July 1994). To back this last claim, the mayor revealed figures that indicated a rise in tourism in Naples during the few days following the summit. The precipitous recourse to statistics suggested the piazza's transformation was also premised on an economic growth logic, while speculations about values and consensus simultaneously sought to establish moral and political legitimacy, not only to face down the self-interested shopkeepers, but also to suture the divergent positions that had existed during the G7 preparations.

The permanent closure of Piazza Plebiscito was emblematic of a style of decision making that would characterize the first Bassolino administration (Brancaccio 2000). There was no debate among the ruling political forces nor any prior consultation with the public, as the urban planner Daniela Lepore recalls:

> The whole cleanup was never discussed in the city. You are always informed after things have been decided. ... Buses cannot pass because we are in Naples and it would mean that cars and motorbikes would follow suit. Beneath it all is this idea that you lot are uncivil, you're incapable of managing a space so we have to impose a total closure. (Interview with author, 8 June 1999)

The operation was conducted with an almost evangelical conviction that the piazza's new arrangement benefited the whole of the city. This 'enlightened despotism', reminiscent of the self-assured vanguardist approach to urban renewal in other left-run European cities such as Barcelona (McNeill 1999), had to begin within the administration itself. Vezio De Lucia recollects how he needed to convince his colleagues in the *giunta* that the closure of the piazza was in the city's general interests: 'We explained to the hesitant ones that, apart from salvaging the piazza and preserving the results obtained with the G7, the closure was an important symbolic gesture which was incompatible with half measures. ... When the *giunta* was convinced, the war began' (De Lucia 1998: 17). From now on, the administration's decisions were increasingly announced directly through the media. Debates would assume a routine format: a number of public individuals and associations would rally in support, while those interest groups adversely affected – in this case shopkeepers – would organize protests, through which political opposition (here the Right) would make itself publicly heard. The ensuing confrontations would often be fought out in abrupt, spectacular fashion. Indeed, after the shopkeepers lowered their shutters in protest during the UN summit on crime in November 1994, and apart from the odd letter of complaint to the local press, there was no more public dissent over the closure of Piazza Plebiscito. While successfully repelling the protests, the administration had to nevertheless defend its decision by committing itself to solving the city's traffic crisis, which included pledging money for buses in order to dissuade the use of private transport.[1] And in order to prevent imminent congestion in the surrounding streets, it had to reroute traffic along the coastal road next to the piazza.

---

1. This would indeed become a central aspect of its policy for the *centro storico* over the next two terms: council bonds were sold on the New York Stock Exchange in 1996, and the financial return was used to pay for three hundred new buses. In addition, in June 1999 a limit was placed on traffic entering the *centro antico*, while new *isole pedonali* (pedestrian islands) were set up in Via Roma, the shopping street to the immediate north of Piazza Plebiscito, in 1998 and in Santa Lucia in 2000.

To describe the final outcome as simply the 'pedestrianization' of a large central piazza would be inaccurate (also because the narrow one-way streets in front of the prefecture and Palazzo Salerno were never actually closed to traffic). Certainly, the administration's anti-car sentiment was well known. At the beginning of 1994, Ada Becchi mused that 'without cars, this city would be beautiful' (*La Repubblica*, 4 January 1994). Bassolino himself had never possessed a driving licence, which was somewhat peculiar in a car-ridden city like Naples. Just as many on the Left had reacted negatively to the individualism and consumerism that had accompanied the rise in car ownership during the 1950s and 1960s, there was now a common and, at times, equally peremptory critique about the car's nefarious impact upon the built environment (Viale 1996). In Naples the car was more than just an ecological hazard: it was cast as a negative trope that was synonymous with the neglect that had spiralled under previous administrations and which now represented an obstacle to urban renewal. Pedestrian areas enriched the quality of urban life in the *centro storico* by reclaiming pockets of public space where civic engagement might unfold. But ultimately, the piazza's new arrangement was not the response to a popular demand for a car-free zone. Ada Becchi herself admitted, 'It is not a traffic measure but a way of protecting art and monuments' (*La Repubblica*, 16 July 1994). In the wake of the G7's symbolic success, the removal of traffic was a means of permanently eradicating a stage in the piazza's history in order to re-capture a more glorious, distant past. It is interesting that most narratives about the new piazza paid little attention to the closure of the street in front of the Royal Palace but focused instead on the removal of the car park, which was never really a contentious issue. The sea of stationary vehicles was a far more powerful negative image against which to build an alternative representation of the city than a passing line of cars and buses. On the eve of the G7, the Neapolitan historian Giuseppe Galasso had indignantly commented: 'In no way does the public car park or the bus terminal render justice to the piazza, because this use … not only offends the piazza's name but its whole spatial and historical character' (Galasso 1994: 19).

As a car park, trunk road and bus terminal, Piazza Plebiscito provided a window onto the very imperfect and tormented relationship between Naples and one of urban modernity's key accessories – the motor vehicle. By the early 1990s, it had become like an ailing heart, collecting cars and pumping them back into the city's clogged arteries. After 1994, nothing so suggestive would be said about the piazza's affair with traffic. Rather, the car-park period was generally interpreted as a hiatus in the life story of the piazza. In the reams of press coverage that followed the G7

summit, not a single commentator seemed to remember when the piazza
became a car park or, for that matter, the debates surrounding its experimental closure in 1989. This sudden forgetfulness and the substitution of
historically contingent enquiry with the moral dictum that 'the car park
was bad' were instrumental to reframing definitions about Piazza Plebiscito. The new piazza provided a clean slate from which to construct
alternative narratives about heritage and urban memory and to nurture,
in the words of Dipesh Chakrabarty (2002), a 'citizen culture'.

The construction of a new symbolic space for Naples

After the G7 summit, the administration and official promoters of Piazza
Plebiscito were faced with a dilemma: now that the cars were gone, the
space had to be given some form of practical role to safeguard and exploit its new arrangement. The problems of managing such an enormous
arena, which had frightened off political parties during election campaigns in the past, remained. Empty spaces are associated with the abstract drawings of planners, with abandonment and urban decline or the
restricted zones of global summits, but not usually with regenerated parts
of a city centre.[2] Bassolino had stated early on that the piazza needed to
be made appealing: 'A desolately empty piazza, in the long run, will not
be very useful' (*Il Mattino*, 19 July 1994), although he would also recognize its importance as a site for people who 'want to be alone and reflect
on life' (Bassolino 1996a: 60). The usual panel of experts made their
proposals public, while the local press gathered the thoughts of readers in
straw polls. The ensuing debate was marked by an apparently irreconcilable conflict between aesthetic concerns on the one hand and social con-
siderations on the other, although this was, for the time being, subsumed
by an overarching desire to affix a virtuous identity to the piazza. Some
suggested ways to 'refill' the space to attract more people. The Superintendent for Environmental and Architectural Heritage, Mario De Cunzo,
envisioned Piazza Plebiscito as 'an island reserved for art, music, culture,
performances, a sort of *agora*' comprising galleries and cafés that would
be the centrepiece of a great pedestrian *salotto* stretching from San Francesco di Paola to the Maschio Angioino in Piazza Municipio (Improta et
al. 1994: 61). Others who had been among the more fervent advocates of
the car-free piazza considered the question of its *rianimazione* (revitalization) a trivial matter. For instance, the chief planner, Vezio De Lucia,

---

2. Jane Jacobs had offered words of warning back in the early 1960s: 'Where pedestrian separation
is undertaken as some sort of abstract nicety ... the arrangement goes unappreciated. ... Unmanageable city vacuums are by no means preferable to unmanageable city traffic' (Jacobs 1961: 362).

recalling his debate with the *giunta,* exclaimed: 'The piazza had to remain empty and silent. So that meant no traffic, but no flowers boxes or benches either. There should be nothing at all' (De Lucia 1998: 17).

Such views appear to have held sway. To this day the piazza does not possess any of the usual facilities or street furniture: there are no benches, litter bins or public toilets. Indeed the rubbish carts were removed by the superintendency after the G7 in order to respect the piazza's 'integrity' as a monument.[3] Rather, it was agreed that the suitable launch pad for the space's *rianimazione* was not in the piazza itself but under the colonnade. This, it should be remembered, had long been considered a marginal place. Mario De Cunzo, for instance, observed that 'Before work for the G7 started, the colonnade was a latrine' (Improta et al. 1994: 62). At the same time, this was the one area of the piazza that had always been a gathering place, and after the G7 it would attract a range of users, from teenage couples and unlicensed street traders to groups of mothers and toddlers from the surrounding popular neighbourhoods. In July 1994 a committee was set up consisting of prefecture officials, the superintendents and members of the administration to draw up plans for compatible activities such as craft and antique shops, exhibition spaces and cafés, which would be established in the small state-owned spaces under the colonnade.[4] The declared aim was to encourage certain uses, such as tourism and the *passeggiata,* and to deter undesirables such as adolescent lingerers and marijuana smokers. The Communist Refoundation assessor for 'Normality', Raffaele Tecce, insisted: 'Only when there are bars and art galleries under the colonnade will it be possible to keep the drug addicts and *ragazzacci* [bad lads] away' (*La Repubblica,* 23 December 1995). It was not until 2000 that a new lighting system was inaugurated and the first new activities – a tourist research office and an exhibition space of the local planning department – were opened, although these would rarely lure large numbers of new people to the colonnade.

Piazza Plebiscito was far more effectively deployed as a venue for organized events than a permanent public attraction. A variety of happenings, from military parades and state celebrations to pop concerts and fundraising galas, exploited the open space and legitimated the piazza's newly elevated status. This was by no means a novel role. Indeed, as we have seen, this was very much an integral aspect of the space's history, but it now became an increasingly frequent and spectacular one. Certain

---

3. This was confirmed in interview with the architect at the Superintendency for Environmental and Architectural Heritage, 7 July 1999.

4. A number of these spaces had once housed workshops. In 1999 only a tailor remained (although its entrance was on a street behind the colonnade). An architect's office in a former foundry and a photographic studio were both opened independently during the 1990s.

occasions turned into annual fixtures, such as the 'New Year's Eve in Piazza', which sought to forge a meaningful link between the piazza and Neapolitans. Attempts were also made to evoke the piazza's historical function. In 1997 a giant papier-mâché replica of a *Macchina di Festa* (an elaborate pagoda-like construction which was the main Carnival attraction during the reign of the viceroys) was mounted in the centre of the piazza by the superintendency. The presentation catalogue declared that the initiative 'arises from the wish of a number of Neapolitan academics to retrieve the social role of this great urban space for the sake of public memory and custom' (Lattuada 1997: 135). Many of these organized events were very successful and attracted people from across the city and region. The New Year's Eve celebrations were particularly massive occasions. The 1995–96 edition, featuring fireworks, concerts, recitals and high-wire acrobats, drew over half a million people and was shown live on national television to an estimated audience of ten million.

The success of Piazza Plebiscito led to a plethora of requests. After the last-minute cancellation in June 1995 of a planned variety show in the piazza, which was accused of amateurish organization, unsuitable decor and tasteless commercialism, a special commission was set up by the cultural superintendencies and administration to lay down strict regulations regarding the use of public space in the *centro storico*. As a result, a proposal by a local sports club at the beginning of 1996 for a beach volleyball tournament, which would have seen the piazza covered in sand, was immediately rejected. In a written statement to the media, the new Superintendent for Environmental and Architectural Heritage, Giuseppe Zampino, spelt out his reasons:

> This superintendency considers the idea of covering the space with sand for a sporting event absolutely incompatible with the decorum of the piazza. Such an event is supposed to be carried out in a natural environment and cannot be artificially recreated in a site of enormous historical and cultural interest to satisfy needs which have no cultural import. (*La Repubblica,* 3 January 1996)

His counterpart at the Superintendency for Artistic and Historical Heritage, Nicola Spinosa, added: 'A beach volleyball tournament in Piazza del Plebiscito would be a scandal; it would be like organizing a football match in Piazza del Campo in Siena' (*La Repubblica,* 3 January 1996). The intransigent superintendents' prime objectives were to resist the vulgarization of the piazza and prevent the official sanctioning of any relapse into the past. Football may not be played in Piazza del Campo (although horse racing is welcome), but a historical antecedent is annually disputed in Piazza della Signoria in Florence. Such events are ritually reenacted, in part, to maintain a cultural tradition of place. In the case of Piazza Plebiscito, a sense of heritage needed to be invented, and this included determining which 'popular' uses were historically and culturally significant.[5]

Issues about decorum, heritage and status were closely bound to the symbolic attributes that were ascribed to Piazza Plebiscito. As a symbol, it worked at different levels. First, the piazza was deployed as a new urban emblem. The cultural repositioning of the restored piazza at the heart of the city simultaneously relocated Naples in national and international geography. For instance, television news items on tourism now included images of Piazza Plebiscito alongside the more traditional shots of Piazza San Marco in Venice and the Coliseum in Rome. Vezio De Lucia was unequivocal: 'Naples did not have a centre before the Bassolino administration, a "zero point" from which to measure distances and which could be proudly displayed to the world. Or rather it had lost it, just as it had lost a great deal in identity and confidence in its own resources' (De Lucia 1998: 13). The piazza was reproduced to such an extent in the first few years that it inevitably began to be considered as trite as the more traditional, 'folkloric' images of Naples. For instance the *Corriere della Sera*'s presentation of the 2001 Pirelli Calendar, which used Neapolitan villas as locations, remarked: 'Here is a Naples far removed from the usual scenes of alleyways, Piazza Plebiscito and the unmistakable profile of Vesuvius' (*Corriere della Sera* (*Sette* magazine), 16 November 2000).

Second, Piazza Plebiscito functioned as a metaphor for urban renewal. The piazza stood as a beachhead for the restoration and urban revival of the rest of the *centro storico,* offering, as the mayor put it, 'an idea of development for the city' (Bassolino 1996a: 60), where order and cleanliness replaced the chaos and dirt of yesteryear and cultural heritage provided an alternative economic resource to state-funded development. It was also, as Bassolino claimed, a tourist investment. Its attraction was both as a safe, manageable place for tour groups and independent visitors and as a new monument which would be incorporated into '*Le Vie dell'Arte*' (The Streets of Art), the city's official tourist trails. The image of an empty or sparsely populated piazza became an increasingly common subject for picture postcards, although it never became as popular

---

5. It should be noted that Renato Nicolini, assessor of 'Identity' during the first Bassolino administration, entertained less rigid ideas about urban cultural identity. As the coordinator of the Roman Summer programme in the late 1970s he had in fact been publicly accused of misusing historical monuments and wasting money on ephemeral pursuits (Gundle 2000: 185). In Naples, Nicolini enthusiastically backed, for instance, a proposal to bake the world's largest pizza in Piazza Plebiscito as a way of promoting the local culinary tradition (Nicolini 1996: 118). However, his presence in public debates about appropriate uses of the piazza was somewhat marginal and in any case was usually overshadowed by the interventions of Bassolino and the superintendents.

as the classic vista of the Gulf of Naples. Most important, the piazza was a means of promoting a new Naples on a national and international stage. After the success of the G7, as noted, Bassolino went to Turin to encourage Gianni Agnelli and fellow businessmen to reconsider Naples's credentials, while at the end of 1995 he returned to America to entice potential investors after the financial agency Moody's increased the city's credit rating (Marrone 1996). The effect of Piazza Plebiscito did not directly lead to a rise in capital investment in the city, but, as a symbol of urban renewal, it certainly represented one of the city's selling points. In fact, Piazza Plebiscito was frequently used as a backdrop for advertising campaigns. Local businesses and national companies were quick to exploit the refashioned (empty) piazza as a sort of exclusive showroom. For instance, to publicize its new domestic flight service, the airline Meridiana inserted the image of a jumbo jet in the centre of the piazza, with San Francesco di Paola in the background mutated into an airport terminal.

At a third level, Piazza Plebiscito was an explicitly political symbol. The transformation of the space, at minimal cost and with consequences which went far beyond its practical implications, exemplified the administration's strategy of 'symbolic politics'. Percy Allum described this strategy as 'the creation of a political and cultural climate in which Neapolitans believe that change is possible even though the economic and social situation has not radically changed' (Geremicca 1997: 160). Public attention on the piazza conferred visibility upon the Bassolino administration and projected its achievements in reversing the city's fortunes. Two images of the piazza before and after its G7 facelift (the first showing the car park, the second showing a woman on stilts performing in front of a group of children) were used on the cover of the Centre-Left's reelection brochure in 2001. The slogan 'Una Città in Cammino' (A City on the Move) had a double meaning in Italian: it referred to the increased provisions for pedestrians while suggesting that the city was now moving in the right direction. The piazza's political connotations, in particular its close association with the figure of the mayor, was a continual source of irritation for local opposition parties. In 2000 the post–Fascist party National Alliance promised to reopen the road in front of the Royal Palace if the Centre-Right were elected into power. In doing so, it directly acknowledged the piazza's position within local political narratives: the plan was devised less as a traffic solution than as a means of removing the legacy of Bassolino.[6]

---

6. The national leader of the Centre-Right, Silvio Berlusconi, even tried to claim Piazza Plebiscito as a personal achievement on the grounds that prior to the G7 summit he had ordered the removal of 'ugly' television aerials from the tops of buildings surrounding San Francesco di Paola (somewhat ironic given the fact that he owned three private channels).

Finally, the new Piazza Plebiscito was conceived as a forum for an inclusive citizenship and a site for rebuilding a sense of collective identity which would reinforce the psychological and cultural bond between Neapolitans and their city. Bassolino believed the piazza held a special significance for those who lived in the periphery: 'The sense of identity which the symbol of Piazza del Plebiscito has aroused over the last years … is less important for those citizens who live in the "high" districts, who enjoy a spectacular view every day, than it is for those who come from difficult suburbs such as Secondigliano or San Giovanni' (Bassolino 1996b: 54). Even among those reticent to extol the virtues of the piazza, the idea of the space as a communal asset was defended with conviction. For example, Communist Refoundation, which criticized the privileged position that Piazza Plebiscito enjoyed over more pressing social and economic issues, protested after an entry fee was levied for a pop concert: 'Give the piazza back to the city! … The piazza snatched from the clutches of urban neglect and returned to the city cannot fall back into the hands of speculators and wheeler-dealers' (*Corriere del Mezzogiorno,* 1 July 1997).

The notion of Piazza Plebiscito as the ideal fulcrum of Neapolitan citizenship would pervade public debates about the space during the second half of the 1990s. The rules of conduct that the administration and the cultural superintendencies were keen to establish were couched in the language of 'civicness' and often carried prescriptions about suitable and improper expressions of local identity. Organized events were expected to respect the piazza's monumental status, identify with the city's history and cultural traditions and encourage a sense of collective spirit. These lofty, institutional appeals to *civicness,* however, sometimes appeared to translate into attempts to *civilize.* Just as certain Neapolitans were deemed ill-prepared for the advent of motorization back in the 1960s, some were now seen as unable to fully appreciate the city's rediscovered heritage.

Challenges to the consensus: cultural barbarians and the organized unemployed

The new Piazza Plebiscito was very successful as a material and symbolic resource, whether as the site for massive public events that had been sporadic only a few years previously or as a positive break with the past. However, the closure of the piazza also led to unintended (although not entirely unforeseen) consequences. The giant open space was turned into a football pitch by local children and was continually crossed by motorcyclists.[7] The official promoters of the piazza regarded the young footballers an inevitable upshot, which underlined the severe lack of recreational areas in the *centro storico*. The *motorino* (small-engine motorcycle), on the other hand, was considered the piazza's principal adversary. The new vice-mayor, Riccardo Marone, blamed the 'shameful spectacle' of local residents' 'races' on the 'the indiscipline of Neapolitans' and inadequate policing (*La Repubblica,* 8 August 1995), while the assessor for tourism, Giulia Parente, considered the motorized incursions as 'the eternal threat to the revival of the piazza' (*La Repubblica,* 23 December 1995). The *motorino* was a particularly ambivalent urban accessory. During the early 1990s it had been touted as the answer to traffic problems. The centre-left mayor of Rome, Francesco Rutelli, had championed its use as an environmentally friendly alternative to the car, while in 1997, the centre-left Prodi government introduced incentives to boost the ailing Italian motorcycle industry. However, during the same decade, and especially in Naples, *motorini* were increasingly construed as an ill of urban life: there were too many of them; they were noisy and they got everywhere – which included slipping between bollards and crossing Piazza Plebiscito. It was the return of the abject, only without a roof and doors, much more difficult to control and, in certain hands, a trope for anti-social behaviour and general incivility.

The contradictions between the ideal and lived spaces of Piazza Plebiscito would emerge in the divergent responses to *La Montagna del Sale* (*The Mountain of Salt*). This huge installation by the Italian artist Mimmo Paladino, consisting of a giant mound of salt perforated with wooden horses, was erected in Piazza Plebiscito in December 1995 (see illustration 7.1). It was the centrepiece of New Year celebrations held in the piazza and was shown live on national television. More than any other subsequent installation,[8] the work became a symbol within the symbol, and its image would be used on conference posters and covers of books dealing with contemporary Naples. The presence of 'blue-chip' art (Miles 1997) in the piazza acted to promote a sophisticated, modern and adventurous city. Bassolino, an enthusiastic convert to public art, read

---

7. Back in 1990, after the temporary closure of Piazza Plebiscito, Aldo Capasso had predicted: 'The emptying [of the piazza] cannot offer moments of aggregation due to its enormous dimensions, but only football pitches and racetracks for *motorini*' (Capasso 1993: 48).

8. *La Montagna del Sale* was the first of Piazza Plebiscito's annual end-of-year encounters with public art that would last until 2009. Subsequent artists were: Jannis Kounellis in 1996, Mario Merz in 1997, Gilberto Zorio in 1998, Giulio Paolini in 1999, Anish Kapoor in 2000, Joseph Kosuth in 2001, Rebecca Horn in 2002, Richard Serra in 2003, Luciano Fabro in 2004, Sol Lewitt in 2005, Jenny Holzer in 2006, Michelangelo Pistoletto in 2007, Jan Fabre in 2008 and Carsten Nicolai in 2009 (although this last installation was removed for safety reasons a few days after its inauguration). All of these installations can be viewed at http://www.museomadre.it/plebiscito.cfm.

Illustration 7.1. *La Montagna del Sale,* December 1995. *Photograph by Gianni Fiorito.*

the installation as a clear metaphor of the city's renaissance: the wooden horses symbolized the people of Naples, while the summit represented the challenge of regeneration (*Il Mattino,* 24 December 1995).

However, to the dismay of its organizers and the local press, numerous Neapolitans did indeed climb to the mountain's summit. The structure had to be regularly repaired, and lorries were needed to deliver extra salt to cover up the areas where the wooden framework had become exposed. Some of those who pilfered salt justified their disobedience as an act of devotion to the city's mayor: 'because the salt of Bassolino brings good luck' (*Il Mattino,* 28 December 1995). The installation was transformed into a playground by local children, who were instantly identified by the press as '*scugnizzi*' (street urchins) from the surrounding neighbourhoods (*La Repubblica,* 28 December 1995). While the children's transgression was considered unfortunate but inevitable (for a few it even added local flavour to the piece), the intrusions of adults, or worse, whole families, were deemed totally unacceptable. Paladino himself complained: 'The *scugnizzi* are one thing, but I cannot understand families who have their photos taken on the backs of horses. This represents a lack of knowledge: it is not a toy' (*La Repubblica,* 3 January 1996). In response, measures were taken to increase controls and encourage public awareness. Volunteers were mobilized to patrol *La Montagna del Sale,* while *Il Mattino* organized, with the help of the superintendents and the artist himself, guided tours of both the installation and the piazza. The uneducable children were to be restrained; the ignorant were to be enlightened.

Those who remained behind the railings or were critical in word alone were referred to in the press as 'Neapolitans', whereas those who insisted on physical contact were stripped of their civic status and described as 'vandals' (*Il Mattino,* 2 January 1996) or 'the terrible children from the Pallonetto and Spanish Quarters' (*La Repubblica,* 28 December 1995). In other words, a tautology was constructed whereby all 'Neapolitans' were well behaved and civic-minded. But while there had initially been debate over the legitimacy of publicly financing Paladino's piece, nobody had questioned the practical significance of placing a giant installation in the middle of Piazza Plebiscito. The piazza was reconceived as an exhibition space for the whole of the city, and this meant policing the boundaries of appropriate behaviour. Because the post-G7 piazza was conceived as a *tabula rasa,* the idea that there might be other long-standing local ties with the space was never taken into consideration. Alternative uses which disturbed the dominant vision were therefore labelled as deviant. This did not mean that *La Montagna del Sale* was unappreciated by its 'transgressors'. As one teenager who had previously lived in the Pallonetto neighbourhood recalled: 'The salt statue [*sic*] was *sfizioso* [cool] because children could play on top of it. It was a clever idea because it never snows in Naples. That's what it was supposed to represent: snow' (interview with author, 31 May 1999). The 'vandals' did not intentionally contest the symbolism of the piazza, but by their continual de(con)struction of *La Montagna del Sale* they exposed the bounded nature of cultural policy and undermined official definitions about the piazza.

As the key symbol in regeneration narratives about Naples, Piazza Plebiscito became a natural target for those who challenged the terms of urban change in the city. The publicity surrounding the piazza was criticized as deflecting attention further away from the city's unsolved problems such as housing shortages and chronic unemployment. Protests became increasingly frequent in the post-G7 piazza, as groups explicitly sought to contest the political significance of the space. This was particularly the case with the various organized unemployed 'lists'.[9] For example, in December 1995 a picket line was organized in front of *La Montagna del Sale,* while in February 1997 over two hundred '*corsisti*'

---

9. The unemployed were traditionally organized into lists of a set number of people whose political sympathies ranged from the far left to the far right. Demonstrations tended to follow a set itinerary between different ports of call: the prefecture in Piazza Plebiscito, the city hall in Piazza Municipio and the seat of the regional government in Via Santa Lucia. Usually never numbering more than a few hundred, demonstrators' tactics often involved causing maximum disruption in the city. In January 1997 a group occupied Via Acton on the seafront (the city centre's main east-west axis), forcing the city council to temporarily reopen Piazza Plebiscito to vehicles in order to unblock traffic jams elsewhere.

(unemployed enrolled in job-training schemes) occupied the roof of San Francesco di Paola to demand the release of government money for promised jobs. The quotes in the press were inevitable. In an interview one occupant declared: 'We wanted to draw attention to the drama of the unemployed from the city's *salotto buono*' (*Il Mattino,* 19 February 1997).

Three days later, a trade union march of fifteen thousand people ended in clashes between police and demonstrators in Piazza Plebiscito. Police in riot gear let off tear gas and baton-charged the crowd, while protesters responded by hurling stones and other makeshift missiles. By the end of the half-hour violent conflict, the piazza had assumed the appearance of a battlefield: shattered glass and debris were strewn everywhere, and blood stains were visible on the new paving. The scenes – described by the local press as 'warfare in the *salotto* of Naples' (*La Repubblica,* 22 September 1997) – provoked a range of heated local and national reactions. While the organizers and the centre-left government accused trouble-makers from the unemployed groups who had 'infiltrated' the demonstration as being responsible, protesters blamed the rash actions of the police. Bassolino and the national leader of Communist Refoundation, Fausto Bertinotti, urged the government to seriously address the issue of unemployment. The local right-wing opposition exploited the symbolic connotations of the event to attack the Bassolino administration. Antonio Martusciello, regional coordinator of Forza Italia, proclaimed: 'We are all paying the price of three years during which an entire administration, and the mayor in particular, has dedicated itself to the worship of image' (*Il Mattino,* 24 February 1997). Meanwhile, allies of Bassolino retracted on the rhetorical metaphors. Mirella Barracco, president of the Napoli 99 Foundation, bemoaned the superficiality of the 'renaissance' thesis:

> It was wrong to talk about a renaissance. The revival was only a beginning from which to build upon. What I cannot stand is this categorical image of Naples where either everything is negative, as in the past, or positive, as has been the case during the last few years. The government needs to intervene. Bassolino cannot resolve everything. (*Il Mattino,* 24 February 1997)

It is unlikely there would have been the same public reaction if the disturbances had taken place elsewhere. The success of Piazza Plebiscito as a symbol of urban renewal was a mixed blessing. The demonstration reflected how this could easily backfire and become a gauge for social tensions in the city.

La Montagna del Sale and the unemployed demonstration were two emblematic episodes in which official meanings and prescribed uses of the piazza were challenged. They underlined the problems involved, on the one hand, by trying to impose a sense of decorum, and, on the other hand, by deploying the space as a symbol of urban change. Such events would be forgotten or reinterpreted with hindsight. Instances of conflict were incorporated into an unequivocal narrative about urban improvement. The regular and usually uneventful protests in Piazza Plebiscito would be considered a democratic feature that had been made possible by the piazza's transformation (Viviani 1998).[10] Indeed, within a week of the violent clashes of February 1997, *Il Mattino* felt it apt to print an aerial photograph of the piazza accompanied with the caption: 'Piazza del Plebiscito, the symbol of the Neapolitan renaissance' (*Il Mattino,* 28 February 1997). The scandal provoked by *La Montagna del Sale* was retrospectively read as a triumph of democratic public art. Eduardo Cicelyn, who as organizer of the initiative had originally objected to the misuse of the installation, reminisced in 1998:

> The mountain of salt was climbed day and night. … In this way, everyone created their own game. The artists created according to necessity, but the people continued to live, for better or worse, as they had always done. For one who seriously loves contemporary art perhaps the real pleasures of these works are their transiency, their fleetingness, the way that they are there without a precise need to dominate the space, but almost abandoned to the metropolitan destiny of the piazza; ready for anything and without shame. (Cicelyn 1998: 27. Translation in text.)

Dominant representations of Piazza Plebiscito distanced themselves from any potentially radical or subversive meanings through a process of 're-semanticization' (Hall 1997: 216). The reconceived piazza was made to 'disclose' certain positive aspects of Naples, such as art, tourism or civicness, and to 'enclose' others considered negative: dirt, disorder and uncivilized behaviour. However, this decontextualized 'representation of space' (Lefebvre 1991) was continually laid bare and renegotiated. By acknowledging the hegemonic interpretations of Piazza Plebiscito, images of the space entered into an alternative vocabulary about the city. A photograph of the police baton charge and retreating protesters by local photographer Luciano Ferrara, which was published in the national media at the time of the events, would be adopted as a counter-testimony to the 'Neapolitan Renaissance' (see illustration 7.2). In 2000, for instance, it was used as an album cover by the local rap group 99 Posse. Meanwhile, the reappropriation of *La Montagna del Sale* would be reenacted out at a less spectacular, more prosaic level in the everyday lived space of Piazza Plebiscito.

---

10. For example, Umberto Zoccoli, Bassolino's press secretary, insisted that unemployed protesters were as much a part of the public life of the piazza as anyone else (interview with author, 27 July 1999).

Illustration 7.2. Unemployed protesters clash with police, February 1997. *Photograph by Luciano Ferrara.*

Chapter 8

Sous les Pavés, la Place!
An Ethnography of the New Piazza Plebiscito

___

Exhuming the everyday piazza from the regeneration symbol

The various sources used thus far, from local press reports to accounts by members of the administration, indicate how Piazza Plebiscito was re-imaged as a place of culture, tourism and civicness. The media's portrayal of the piazza was largely framed by the definitions espoused by local politicians and recognized experts such as superintendents and architectural historians. Voices of dissent or alternative opinions were occasionally reported to enhance the newsworthiness of certain events – as in the case of the protesting shopkeepers during the closure of the piazza after the G7 summit – but these counter-arguments inserted themselves into a preestablished debate which acknowledged the symbolic and material importance of the piazza.

There was surprisingly little interest in the everyday piazza in these regeneration narratives. One would have expected a surge in media interest to chronicle the life of the city's new asset. Instead, when it was not filled with concert goers or Sunday crowds, concerns were voiced that the piazza was 'empty'. For some, this was a means to criticize the rationale of the operation. Local planner Daniela Lepore compared the piazza to the eerie architectural scenes of Giorgio De Chirico's metaphysical paintings: 'The construction of voids', she argued, 'continues to strike me as a miserable, uninteresting goal which would be dangerous if it were turned into a *model*' (Lepore 1995: 31, original italics). For the press, allegations about the piazza's emptiness were usually accompanied by a call for its '*rianimazione*'. For instance, in 1999, a *La Repubblica* journalist bemoaned that without the services under the colonnade the piazza was destined to remain 'just a showcase and a piazza for official ceremonies [as well as] a place for tourist pilgrimages and the evening and Sunday strolls of Neapolitans' (*La Repubblica,* 17 March 1999). Claims that the piazza was only used in specific moments and by certain people were commonly made, despite the daily presence of local children playing football. They hence conveyed a sense of disappointment that the piazza had not been 'properly' appropriated by the public.

The prior task for an ethnographic study of Piazza Plebiscito is to attempt a more meticulous, dispassionate picture of the space that moves beyond the judgements of privileged commentators. The following description of the piazza draws on observation conducted between October 1998 and November 1999.[1] Thanks to its arena-like dimensions and uncluttered space, the piazza lent itself particularly well to the monitoring of its different activities (see map 8.1). At times the experience was compelling, as I began to identify routines and recognize the same figures. On other occasions, especially when sitting on the colonnade steps in the pouring rain and with few people around, it all seemed a bit pointless, but as the first phase of fieldwork, it felt like a mission. Places are always full of banal manoeuvres, but together these begin to make more sense and assume an almost epiphanic quality once they are considered alongside public representations of the same place.

As noted above, Piazza Plebiscito possesses none of the basic amenities – benches, toilets, litter bins – that are often considered necessary prerequisites for 'successful' public space (Whyte 1980; Hass-Klau et al. 1999). The only permanent objects in the piazza itself are two early nineteenth-century equestrian statues. Sitting space is coincidental and located at its edges: the steps of the colonnade, the stone ledges along the façade of the Royal Palace and the bollards and chains which close the sides of the piazza off from passing traffic. The middle of the piazza and the pedestrianized street in front of the Royal Palace were generally clean and tidy. The colonnade and the adjacent area were more unkempt, although this was not visible to anyone standing on the Royal Palace side of the piazza (which was, significantly, the principal viewpoint for public images of the piazza after 1994). During the summer, tufts of grass appeared on the steps and on the area in front of the colonnade. The ground was often strewn with litter, and in certain parts, particularly on the steps and under the colonnade itself, there were traces of human urine and pigeon and dog excrement. This area of the piazza was at its cleanest in the early morning, after the street cleaners had passed. A number of

---

1. In total, thirty-seven observation sessions were carried out in all weathers and at different times of the day. These lasted usually between twenty minutes and one hour (although on one occasion a whole day was spent in the piazza) and were all recorded on site maps. For a detailed discussion of the methods used in the study of Piazza Plebiscito, see Dines 2001. For other examples of the mapping of social activities in public spaces, see Whyte 1980 and Low 2000.

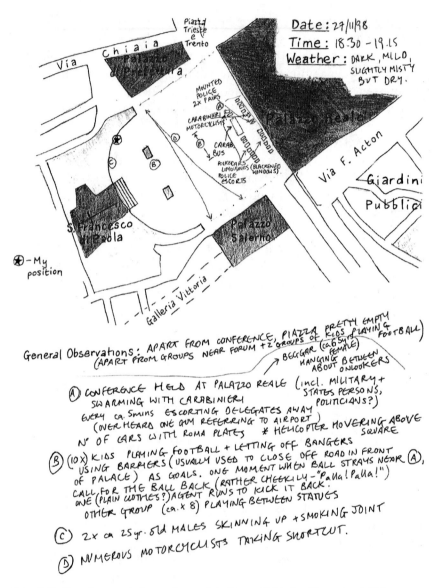

Map 8.1. Sample map of observation work in Piazza Plebiscito, November 1998. *Designed by Nick Dines.*

the vacant spaces under the colonnade appeared in a state of disrepair, with broken doors and boarded-up windows. On two occasions during the morning, abandoned mattresses and blankets were spotted in their door wells. The columns of the colonnade and plinths of the equestrian statues were covered in graffiti. This consisted mainly of football-related matter, swollen genitalia and amorous declarations, although there were a few hammer and sickles and the odd Celtic cross. Two points can here be inferred: first, that tarrying was more likely to occur on the piazza's perimeter, where it was possible to sit, and second, that the colonnade appeared more 'used' than other parts.

The human presence in the piazza was dependent on the time of day and year, as well as on the weather. Many people crossed the piazza without stopping, usually in front of the Royal Palace, their numbers increasing during peak periods (early morning, lunchtime and at the end of work) and decreasing during rain and the summer months. This pedestrian route between the city centre and Santa Lucia was also used by police cars (which, without flashing lights or sirens, did not appear to be in an emergency), despite the official ban on all vehicles (De Lucia 1998). Motorcycles crossed the piazza, primarily in front of the colonnade, at all times of the day, with a peak during the late afternoon.[2]

The piazza was at its busiest on special occasions, such as Epiphany and Carnival, and during organized events, such as the inauguration of art installations and the annual street marathon, which finished in front of the Royal Palace. Unless these events were large enough to fill up the entire space, crowds were confined to certain areas. Otherwise, the piazza was used most regularly as a recreational or meeting place. By far the most frequent and visible recreational activity was football. This would be played daily, particularly from the afternoon through to early evening and during weekends and school holidays. Players were predominantly male, of primary- or secondary-school age, although in the evening young men would sometimes organize a game. Nearly every player spoke in Neapolitan dialect, and most would enter and leave the piazza by the colonnade, in other words from the side of the Spanish Quarters and the Pallonetto. Matches would be played in all parts of the piazza, but in particular around the statues in the piazza or under the colonnade in front of the entrance to San Francesco di Paola. Often, three or four matches would take place contemporaneously. The few objects in and around the piazza – the chains, the bollards, the church door, the statues – would be turned into goal posts or would mark out pitch boundaries, while non-participating children often perched on the railings surrounding the two equestrian statues or on the plinths themselves in order to spectate. Other forms of recreation were far less frequent and conspicuous. One notable exception was during the evening of Epiphany, when young children descended on the piazza to play with their new toys. Many were accompanied by parents and entered the piazza from Piazza Trieste e Trento.

---

2. For example, on 11 June 1999, between 3:45 p.m. and 4:15 p.m., thirty-three motorcycles were counted crossing the piazza, including one policeman and one *falco* (member of a plainclothes anti-crime squad).

Generally, two distinguishable types of children were identifiable: on the one hand, regularly present, unaccompanied, dialect-speaking locals, and on the other, Italian-speaking nonlocals escorted by adults who generally visited the piazza on special occasions or on Sunday afternoons.

The main meeting places were in areas adjacent to Piazza Plebiscito: Piazza Carolina, where young people would regularly congregate in the evening, and Piazza Trieste e Trento, where tourists and shoppers gathered outside bars throughout the day. However some groups of people would meet on the steps of the colonnade. From the spring onwards, local mothers with small children met every afternoon in the same spot on the unshaded side of the colonnade, close to Piazza Carolina. Smaller groups of teenagers, some smoking hashish, and young couples would meet on both sides of the basilica from the midafternoon through the middle of the night, in all weather conditions, unless it was particularly cold. In all cases, many would arrive in the piazza on *motorini.*

Tourists were a minor presence and were usually spotted during the morning when the piazza was much quieter. All Italian and foreign visitors entered the piazza from Piazza Trieste e Trento, but less than half actually crossed it to visit the basilica, and almost all would spend no more than fifteen minutes in the piazza. The majority would come in small groups of two to four people. Large groups of school students and pensioners were observed on only three occasions. Of the few people who looked at Robert Rauschenberg's *Banners,* which were hung between the columns of the colonnade between April and September 1999, most were tourists. Overall, though, the piazza did not appear to be a popular tourist attraction.

The largest groups most frequently present in the piazza were protesters who assembled during the day in front of the prefecture. These included organized unemployed groups, evicted occupants of council houses from Neapolitan suburbs and undocumented immigrants. Demonstrations, which rarely numbered more than a hundred individuals, would last between one and two hours and would then move on to other destinations: either the city hall in Piazza Municipio or the seat of the regional government in Via Santa Lucia. On each occasion there was a large police presence, and the road in front of the prefecture was temporarily closed to traffic. However, the protests would never arouse the attention of other users (the mothers and footballers), which suggests that they were accustomed to their presence in the piazza. After protesters moved on, the ground would be littered with picnic material, such as plastic cups and sandwich wrappers, but very few political leaflets.

Itinerant vendors of drinks, balloons and tourist prints and two immigrant traders selling baseball caps and sunglasses were observed during the spring and summer. Apart from a *granita* (crushed-ice drink) seller who was permanently positioned on the Piazza Carolina edge of the colonnade, the others did not remain in the piazza for more than ten minutes. Given the lack of people in its centre and in front of the Royal Palace, one can assume that the piazza was not a particularly lucrative pitch. Other common activities included people walking their dogs, wedding ceremonies in the basilica (on which occasion a red carpet was laid on the main steps) and photographers taking pictures of newly wedded couples in various parts of the piazza.

Finally, there was little visible evidence of effective policing in the piazza apart from during the demonstrations, in which case the clear aim was to maintain public order and protect the prefecture. A mobile *Carabinieri* (military police) unit was often parked in the adjacent Piazza Trieste e Trento and carried out spot checks on motorists and motorcyclists. The gap between the bollards near the colonnade used by *motorini* to enter the piazza was blocked just twice by *vigili urbani* (municipal police). On three other occasions police crossing the piazza on large motorcycles made detours to evict offenders, but as soon as they left the scene, the *motorini* reappeared.

As the above detailed description suggests, Piazza Plebiscito was certainly not 'empty'. Admittedly, it did look rather barren on first inspection and at certain points of the day was literally deserted, but it was nevertheless crisscrossed by various routines and uses that were generally omitted from public accounts about the space.

The multi-layered experiences of the new Piazza Plebiscito

In order to elaborate upon the preliminary insights provided by the observational data, semi-structured interviews were conducted with a range of users of the new piazza.[3] The majority of informants can be divided into three broad groups: individuals who had a public link with the new piazza as a result of their employment, for instance in the city council and superintendency, but who did not use it on an everyday basis; nonlocals whose workplaces were situated under the colonnade and who therefore had a daily connection with the piazza; and local users of the piazza who

---

3. A total of thirty-two individual and group interviews were conducted between December 1998 and August 1999. These were all carried out *in situ,* either in the piazza itself or in workplaces nearby. Where possible, interviews were preorganized and taperecorded. These lasted between twenty minutes and two hours. Shorter unrecorded meetings lasting between five and fifteen minutes took place in unforeseen circumstances (protesters), where interaction was limited (*Carabinieri*) or in cases where recording would have been unsuitable (young football players).

lived in the surrounding neighbourhoods.[4] Here I concentrate on four interviews: a joint interview with two city-council employees of the *Osservatorio Turistico Culturale* in the Royal Palace (which in 2000 moved to a workspace under the colonnade), two separate interviews with the custodian and parish priest of San Francesco di Paola, and a *granita* seller from the Spanish Quarters. These interlocutors have not been selected as representative of the three groups, although they do share some common attitudes, and, where useful, comparisons will be drawn with other interviewees. Rather, focusing on a small number of interviews allows me to explore the multifaceted nature of people's relationships with the piazza and to identify similarities and differences that lie between them. The analysis of each interview is organized along the same basic lines. It first examines how the people interpret the new piazza and its past, paying attention to the different registers used to describe urban change before looking at ideas about decorum and social control and how these relate to the experience and/or conception of the piazza as a public space.

Franca Pastore, age fifty, and Gaetano Santucci, age forty (names of all informants have been changed), both worked for the city council–run 'tourist observatory', which monitored cultural activities in the city, although, following an increase in visitors after the G7, their office also doubled as a public-information service. Franca Pastore, who had worked in the tourist sector for ten years, had previously coordinated foreign affairs during the left-wing Valenzi administration, while Gaetano Santucci had been actively involved in a local environmental organization for over fifteen years. They can be considered members of a progressive Neapolitan middle class that emerged during the 1970s and which provided the backbone of support for the Bassolino project during the 1990s. The joint interview was dominated by Santucci. Pastore would often interrupt to express her agreement or add emphasis to Santucci's discussion of the piazza. She did, however, speak at length about the issue of safety and control, which is outlined below.

Santucci was one of the few respondents to speak at any length about the 'old' Piazza Plebiscito. He recounts his personal experiences of the piazza before the car park:

About thirty-five years ago, when I was young, it was the place where mums would bring their children to play and to feed the pigeons, as happens in Venice today. We would buy corn from some old guys and give it to the pigeons. It was a place to bring

4. The first group was primarily comprised of supporters of the new Piazza Plebiscito. The one exception was the former president of the Shopkeepers Association of Santa Lucia, who had organized the protests against the piazza's permanent closure to traffic in 1994. Like others in this first group, his deliberation over the piazza's transformation did not reveal intimate knowledge about the daily life of the space. For a more detailed description of the interviewees, see Dines 2001.

children into close contact with nature. Around 1964, 1965, there weren't many cars. It was before the boom. There was, however, this enormous bus park. Children, the corn sellers and the passing tourist would meet in the empty spaces. There was also the traditional photograph of children on the backs of the lions [sculptures located at the end of the colonnade]. All of us Neapolitan children would have our photo taken there. ... In 1965 the *motorino* and the car didn't pose any danger. Few people had cars. There was more respect for the highway code, and so it wasn't dangerous to play on the streets. I remember as a boy we could play on the streets in any neighbourhood. Today street games no longer exist. Back then mums would take their children to the piazza, the beautiful piazza, perhaps the largest piazza in Europe, certainly after San Pietro [in Rome]. And we'd play. There were the balloon sellers. I'd come here on a Sunday, eat an ice cream and get a coloured balloon on the end of a string. (Interview with author, 24 June 1999)

This extract reveals more than just nostalgia for a traffic-free environment. The piazza had once reflected a more harmonious world where children intermingled with street traders, nature (the pigeons), monuments (the lion statues) and even vehicles (buses). 'Us Neapolitan children' suggests that this was a collective experience. Venice is used as a positive urban trope to link this image with the present, while the purported lower level of traffic and greater respect for the highway code distances it from contemporary Naples. Personal recollections of the piazza are punctuated by dates and 'objective' facts, such as 'the boom' that serve to historify the arrival of cars. Besides a number of inaccuracies (first and foremost the car park already existed in 1965), it is significant that the car (but not the bus) should be disassociated from the subjective realm of memory.[5]

Santucci's subsequent discussion, in fact, abruptly switches from the intimacy of childhood experience to a detached account shaped by the dominant public depiction of the piazza's ignoble past. The LTR fiasco represented the 'many failed promises' and the rampant corruption of the pre-Bassolino era, while the chaos of the car park was believed to have encouraged illicit activities such as the selling of contraband cigarettes. The piazza's restoration and closure to traffic in 1994 is instead read as the combined result of a particular occasion (the G7), a growing awareness about environmental issues and an intelligent administration. The latter's decision to maintain the closure after the G7 summit was considered a radical and courageous gesture:

The administration is far more advanced than its own citizens. When citizens are not on the same wavelength as a city's administrators, it becomes difficult to govern. If a bus were allowed to cross the piazza, a hundred cars would follow it. Just imagine Naples as

---

5. It must be said that none of the thirty-two informants spoke about what it was like to park a car in Piazza Plebiscito, despite the fact that for three decades this was a daily activity for thousands of Neapolitans.

if it were a bit like Venice. Would you ever be able to go down a canal on a *motorino*? No. Well, imagine Piazza Plebiscito as a beautiful canal.

Piazza Plebiscito is interpreted as a metaphor for the city's resurgence. The unwitting 'citizens' need to be nurtured and constrained into recognizing the benefits of this change. Venice not only represents the ultimate car-free city (although submerged in water, the piazza would resemble a lake!), but is deployed to underline the irreversibility of the piazza's new arrangement. The act of clearing the piazza is considered more significant than the raised profile of the surrounding buildings:

> The empty space is part of its beauty. You don't have to necessarily fill something for it to be beautiful or for it to be reappropriated. You might obscure the beauty with something else. ... It can be used as a container which has sometimes happened: you had *La Montagna del Sale,* now you've got the Banners of May, then there's New Year's Eve and so on. But the beauty of the space must remain, also to respect its artistic and historical characteristics. This is a military piazza, in other words an empty space that was occupied by the army or the king for events such as the *Cuccagna.* But these were ephemeral and not fixed moments.

Although the vast, car-free piazza is valued mainly in terms of its rediscovered heritage, it also possesses an implicitly social dimension. Santucci uses the Caffè Gambrinus to elaborate his argument:

> It is a civic piazza, but this is difficult to fathom because it is so big. Perhaps you see it on its edges. When we meet up at Bar Gambrinus, which is a landmark for Neapolitans, we have a coffee and then go for a stroll in Piazza Plebiscito, where we continue to discuss our problems. ... Gambrinus is exclusive for those who frequent it every day, but you get the family who comes every Sunday and sits down all the same. It becomes the treat after a week's work, and perhaps people come only on Sundays because they haven't got the time or because they come from the suburbs or provinces.

A generalized 'we' and the imagined user are combined to form a discourse about the 'civic piazza', but one which is spatially and temporally delimited. Activities are confined to the boundaries of the piazza, whereas its centre is a space principally traversed. Meanwhile, Sunday is the day when the piazza is at its busiest and certain extravagances (such as paying five times the normal price of a coffee to sit at a table) are no longer the reserve of a privileged few. Nevertheless, it is these very aspects which are seen to render the piazza 'Neapolitan' and not simply a tourist attraction:

> A space becomes pleasant and usable especially when it has been reappropriated by its citizens. This has to be the first step before it can become a tourist space. ... Tourism today demands a convivial relationship with citizens. You would never go to a place where people are unfriendly. In Piazza Plebiscito you find the conviviality of Neapolitans because *they are there.* Piazza Plebiscito is not part of an exclusive tourist itinerary. It's an itinerary for Neapolitans where tourists also go to find Neapolitans.

Convivial Neapolitans are on display in the piazza. This suggestion is reminiscent of the media representation of Piazza Pebiscito as a '*biglietto da visita*'. What is usually used as a rhetorical device to promote a new Naples is inserted into a discourse about citizenship. The piazza is not simply an emblem, but a physical place where Neapolitans and tourists can interact.

Those who subscribe to a regeneration narrative of Piazza Plebiscito identify a common set of positive functions as confirmation of collective participation: art, culture and the *passeggiata*. There is less general agreement over what constitutes a threat to the piazza. For instance, the architect at the Superintendency for Environmental and Architectural Heritage (whose offices are located in the Royal Palace) would like to see street traders banned from the piazza, while Santucci considers the traditional Neapolitan *abusivi* (unlicensed vendors) an authentic part of local popular culture: 'They're well liked, they're photographed. Perhaps nobody buys the ice cream because they don't know where it comes from. But they're a part of Naples that still exists and isn't false, and so they're tolerated. This space is surrounded by the Spanish Quarters, where people invent a day's pay'. This is the only moment in the interview when reference is made to the particular socioeconomic composition of the surrounding area. The local street trader in the piazza is tolerated as an acceptable 'other'. Football and the demonstrations are considered inevitable consequences of the pedestrianization. Santucci prefers 'the shouts of children to the noise of cars.' It is understandable that without available space in the *centro storico* the piazza should be used for such recreational activities. The 'invasion of *motorini*', on the other hand, is firmly condemned as an unjustifiable act of deviance which violates the piazza's new cultural status. Both interviewees would be very severe with offenders: 'I'd confiscate the *motorino*' (Santucci); 'I'd put a point on their licence' (Pastore). The present policing in the piazza is considered inadequate, although both interviewees are eager to stress the importance of education. According to Santucci, 'The only problem is the lack of surveillance by the *vigili urbani* and the *motorini* that shoot past. Would you ever cross? What we need are educational projects; a respect of rules starting from the streets. An educated person would never go through a 'No Entry' sign, even if it meant a diversion of an extra kilometre'. Franca Pastore believes that certain people need to 'learn to reappropriate the piazza'. On the only occasion that either of them alludes to personal experience in the new piazza, she recounts the moment she decided to contact the police:

> A few weeks ago I had to personally call the [municipal] police because there were children playing and motorbikes continually passing by. But they were busy elsewhere [sarcastic laugh] due to the Maggio dei Monumenti festival. So I called the *Carabinieri*,

who, I must say, arrived immediately, set up a roadblock and stayed for the whole day. More surveillance is certainly needed, but we have to think about reeducating these people. With the present state of affairs the problems will never be solved because wherever a *vigile* is absent, they'll find a way of doing something illegal.[6]

Neapolitans are no longer conceived as a homogenous public. The positive portrayal of citizens as civic and friendly is pitted against the antisocial behaviour of motorcyclists. The words 'they'll find a way' suggest the presence of a persistent abject element among the piazza's users which will not be eradicated by simply increasing controls.

The priest and custodian of San Francesco di Paola (both in their late sixties) were interviewed on separate occasions inside the basilica. The custodian lived in the middle-class, hilltop district of Vomero and had worked for the church on a voluntary basis for six years. Padre Cozza had been the parish priest for the last five-and-a-half years. In both interviews, discussion about the piazza revolved almost entirely around the basilica and the colonnade. The custodian is ambivalent about the basilica's central position in recent representations of the piazza:

The piazza was cleared of cars and so was made to stand out. After the G7, TV crews came from all over the world. They noticed this jewel. The piazza is more beautiful, people can enjoy it more. When there were cars, you couldn't see it. ... But it is a question of image and little else. There have been no advantages for the church. There has been a greater flow of tourists, but mass hasn't changed: it's still a normal parish. Certainly for me, as a Neapolitan, it's pleasing because I really love this church. This is one of the finest examples of neoclassicism not only in Naples, but in the whole of Italy. It was the last gift which the Bourbons gave to this city. Since then nothing else has been done. (Interview with author, 23 June 1999)

The custodian does not refer in any detail to the public debate about the new piazza. The G7 is mentioned in passing as the turning point in the piazza's fortunes. However, the claim that it is just a 'question of image' suggests an acknowledgement of an official discourse about the piazza's transformation. By alluding to the historical achievements of the Bourbons, he further downplays the significance of the change while intimating his political distance from Bassolino. Nevertheless, he is pleased that the closure to traffic has attracted more visitors to the church, later explaining that he enjoys giving information to visitors (in doing so he is able to use his French and English). His intimate relationship and professed fondness for the church contrasts to Santucci, who considered

---

6. The suggestion that the local municipal *vigili* were inefficient in maintaining order in Piazza Plebiscito was made by a number of respondents and was emphasized during a short interview with the *Carabinieri* in Piazza Trieste e Trento (23 June 1999).

the building more of a backdrop to the new pedestrianized zone.[7] According to the custodian, the piazza itself is not a lively public space: 'It has not been a centre of attraction. It's a passing place. It's not like, say, Piazza Maggiore in Bologna. The life of the city does not take place here. There are other piazzas. In Vomero, people gather in Piazza Vanvitelli'. Bologna is used as an urban frame in a similar way as Santucci's use of Venice, but here this is used to distance the piazza (but not the city) from a particular image of public space: the busy central piazza of a northern Italian city.

Padre Cozza is reticent to acknowledge any meaningful personal relationship with either the church or the piazza: 'I'm here today but could be told to go tomorrow. I must follow what my superiors say. The church isn't important. It's not mine' (interview with author, 16 July 1999). While he welcomes the piazza's closure to traffic, he believes the city council should be more flexible in the event of weddings:

> The bride and groom can't arrive by car. This limits the joy of the happiest day of their lives. Cars sometimes get informal permits. It depends on the *vigile urbano*; some are more lenient than others. The bishop made a special request to the [city] council, but we've been waiting five years for an answer. The council should be more responsible. When a couple has to go to sign a document in Piazza Municipio, they have to walk.

The city council is portrayed as distant and not in tune with people's desires (which here involves the use of the car). The custodian and Padre Cozza are unenthusiastic about the organized events in the piazza. Without ever referring to any particular public figure, they both complain that the church is never involved in the organization and thus can do nothing to prevent the damage which occurs to the building:

> The [city] council is its own boss. They even send lorries and cranes to set up the fireworks, which ruin the asphalt surface [of the roof]. Then it's left to us to go up and clean away the debris. They know that we won't let them come through the church, so they set them up from outside. (The Custodian)

> The [city] council should show more respect for the church and ask its permission. But the colonnade doesn't belong to the church [nb the colonnade is the property of the Italian state and hence is under the jurisdiction of the neighbouring prefecture]. People living in Largo Carolina asked me to complain about the launching of fireworks from the roof, but what can I do? (Padre Cozza)

The works of public art are similarly perceived as foreign artefacts which are erected without any prior consultation. The custodian sees them as

---

7. In reference to San Francesco di Paola, Santucci commented: 'Everyone has used the church as a symbol, even if it isn't beautiful and not much in terms of architecture'.

spoiling the overall effect of the monument: 'I'm no expert and don't want to make a judgement, but I don't like them. I think this mixture of art from two periods leaves a jarring effect. Placing Paladino's horses between the two equestrian statues, which are by Canova, produces an unpleasant effect'.

The custodian and Padre Cozza demonstrate firsthand knowledge of the piazza's daily activities. Both claim that football had always been played around the colonnade and that, with the closure to traffic, this had merely spread across the piazza. Padre Cozza thinks that some children can be a nuisance but do not pose any real problem: 'They play in front of the church and are always kicking the ball against the door. I can't tell them not to play when the church is closed. It's another matter when the church is open. Children are children. You always get a few hotheaded ones'. The occupation of the basilica by unemployed protesters is re-membered as a regrettable moment, but neither attributes any particular significance to the occasion nor do they express any animosity towards the protesters. Padre Cozza recounts:

> It was a sad event. I can't remember exactly when it happened. It must have been winter because they complained about the cold. They damaged the plaster, they smoked, they made lots of noise, a few who had the fear of God kept quiet. I can understand they need to protest. But what's the church got to do with it? We can try to help them. … But I don't think that the symbolic aspect of the piazza played a part. It was a decision taken on the spur of the moment. They came here because the prefecture is over there, but they've never been back.

The priest designifies an event which was publicly interpreted as a con-testation of the piazza's symbolic meaning by distancing the church from the debate about the piazza. The church as an institution can try to help the needy, but the basilica itself is insignificant.

As with other users of the basilica side of the piazza, the priest and custodian elaborate upon the rubbish and excrement in the immediate area. Interestingly, they do not refer at all to the *motorini*. It would appear that the condition of the colonnade is more of a pressing matter than the frequent infractions of motorcyclists. The employees of the tourist ob-servatory, in contrast, barely mentioned the dirt, which not only reflected their physical distance from the colonnade but would suggest that this mundane and circumscribed problem did not encroach on their symbolic reading of the new piazza. In a different way to Santucci and Pastore, the custodian stresses the need for more controls:

> There's no surveillance. People write on the walls and urinate. If there were surveil-lance, the monument would be in a better condition. They come in the morning to clean, but then the tourists are not very disciplined. When there's less traffic, there's less rub-

bish, also because in planning the piazza's new arrangement they did not provide any bins. Without an appropriate place, the tourists leave their rubbish under the colonnade. . . . There's talk about [opening] art workshops. Certainly after six p.m. in the autumn and winter there's no life. And so it becomes the realm of this lot who smoke joints. The workshops would bring a bit of life back.

The discussion about decorum reiterates an apparent indifference towards regeneration narratives about the piazza. Tourists are messier than local users (the custodian claims that 70 per cent of the graffiti is by people from outside Naples). The area needs bins, but these, as the architect at the superintendency responsible for the piazza confirmed, were removed for aesthetic reasons. One can infer that while bins have a practical use for those under the colonnade, they represent an eyesore for those who admire the basilica from the opposite side of the piazza. At the same time, the custodian suggests that new workshops would enliven the colonnade by attracting a different sort of user and hence here concurs with those in the administration keen to revitalize this side of the piazza.

The interview with Salvatore Esposito, a thirty-five-year-old resident of the nearby Spanish Quarters who sold *granita* drinks in Piazza Plebiscito, took place by his pitch at the end of the colonnade by Piazza Carolina. He had conducted this '*mestiere*' (profession) every spring and summer in the same place for the last twelve years. As with other local users, remarks about the car-park period are pithy but not categorically negative. He does not mention the traffic, but he remembers the fountain erected in 1985:[8] 'After the earthquake they built this fountain, which was really nice because it attracted an enormous amount of people. Then they removed it because it was missing original bits and looked shabby' (interview with author, 11 June 1999). No direct reference is made to the public debate over the transformation of the piazza or to the plans for the colonnade (despite the fact that he was interviewed on this side of the piazza). Esposito's initial description of the piazza betrays a disregard for its newly forged reputation. Pointing across the piazza towards a partially visible Vesuvius on the horizon, he explains: 'There are two other *granita* sellers: one on the corner of the road, over there by the postcard, the bit where you can see Naples and the gulf. We call it the "postcard" because in the background you can see the Gulf of Naples'. These natural features are the very same images that the promotion of the post-G7 Piazza Plebiscito as an urban emblem had sought to transcend. Ironically, they remain yardsticks which Esposito uses to gauge the symbolic import of

---

8. This was a replica of a fountain built in the middle of Piazza Plebiscito after the cholera epidemic of 1884 to celebrate the opening of the Serino aqueduct that brought fresh water into the city.

the piazza. Nevertheless, the new arrangement is enthusiastically endorsed and is used to point to some general improvements in the city:

> The piazza has changed enormously; it's gone from rags to riches. I think this piazza
> is beautiful: you've got people about; you're unlikely to see rows or fights; what else
> would you want? Our mayor Bassolino hasn't just stopped in the piazza. He's done other
> things like [pedestrianizing] Santa Lucia. Yes, some wrong things, but ninety per cent
> has been a good job. Politically, I'm neither Communist nor Fascist, but I see that he's
> done some great things. Before the buses never passed, now they come by every five
> minutes. You never hear about robberies here or in Via Roma or Via Chiaia. After all,
> these are controlled areas. That's what I mean: this is the façade and it's beautiful, but if
> you go a hundred metres from here and climb towards Sant'Anna di Palazzo, the whole
> lifestyle changes. In the Spanish Quarters there's the Camorra, but we live well because
> we help each other out: as Neapolitan people that's what we're like.

Where there was once a shabby fountain, there is now a pleasant open
space. As with the fountain, 'beauty' is evaluated in terms of the piazza's
social function rather than its architectural or monumental form. Esposito draws on the common representation of Piazza Plebiscito as a
general signifier of urban change, but this is delimited by underlining its
proximity to the different reality of his own neighbourhood.

Esposito stresses that the car-free piazza has become a recreational
and meeting place for the surrounding neighbourhoods. Through his local roots and daily presence in the piazza, Esposito claims to personally
know most of the children and women who play and sit around the colonnade. Besides offering refreshments, he mentions the services which he
additionally provides: litter collection in the immediate vicinity and first-
aid assistance (during the week he had already attended to two children
who had hurt themselves playing football). When describing the social
dimension of the piazza, he assumes the role of a knowledgeable guide:

> Right, let me explain you something. This is a piazza which is used a lot by the *popo-
> lino* because we've got the Spanish Quarters right next door, and that's almost thirty
> thousand people. Then there's the Pallonetto, Santa Lucia. For the children it's the only
> piazza where they can come and feel a bit freer. Not many *motorini* come past, there
> are no cars. In the mornings during this period, ninety per cent of the mums from the
> [Spanish] Quarters and the Pallonetto go to the Royal Palace gardens, where it's shady
> and fresher. In the afternoon they all come over here.

Esposito maps a different time-space relationship to the one indicated
by Santucci and Pastore. Activity is concentrated around the colonnade,
which builds up in the afternoon. The area is at its busiest in the evening,
but at this point most of the (young) people are concentrated in the adjacent and smaller Piazza Carolina:

> The piazza is much smaller but there's an impact when you enter. Young people go there
> to show off their Dolce Gabbana and other brands. You can't enter on a *motorino*, you

can't stop in the car. Now everybody from the [Spanish] Quarters meets up in Piazza Carolina, including those who aren't football fans. Every Saturday it bursts with people. Sometimes there's been more than two thousand of us in that little piazza.

Esposito describes 'Piazzetta' Carolina – architecturally nondescript and traversed by traffic – as a more vibrant, intimate space. It is also more closely bound to personal memory: this was where he and fellow fans celebrated Napoli's *Scudetto* victory of 1987.

Officially promoted functions of the piazza are reinterpreted or simply not recognized. Esposito never mentions the *passeggiata*. By 'occupying' the piazza, the whole notion of 'strolling' is undermined. As with other local respondents, Esposito only refers to the public art when directly asked for an opinion: 'Yes, very nice. Look, at night the piazza is much more beautiful. At night there are loads of people in the piazza drinking and listening to music. The whole piazza, lit up by these paintings here [Robert Rauschenberg's *Banners*], gives off a special effect'. This response, which cannot be used to infer any particular reading of the piazza's installations, seems to suggest that public art is appreciated as a backdrop to Piazza Plebiscito's function as a social space. Meanwhile, tourists have provided him with a new clientele:

When tourists come with their expensive watches, we tell them: 'Look, remove it, because people are eyeing you up'. Many come to me because apart from doing fresh orange and lemon juice, I'm the only one of the three who speaks a bit of English. I can get by in Spanish too. In Naples we have a lot of imagination when it comes to selling, a desire to live and not to do the same thing three times. So you explain a bit about the piazza. For the *granita* you ask two thousand lire, but they can give you five, ten thousand lire, depending on your imagination. We try to talk.

Esposito renegotiates ideas about conviviality and Neapolitanness into a way of earning money. The acknowledgement of a general discourse about decorum is further reiterated by numerous references to cleanliness. He claims to do his own bit by keeping his patch tidy: 'They've complained a lot. We've changed a lot. Don't throw things on the ground, try to be cleaner'.

What is deemed unacceptable behaviour in the piazza – robbery and violence – is also unacceptable everywhere else. The size and visibility of the space gives certain acts a heightened impact. For instance, he recounts the time he intervened to stop a pensioner stabbing his adulterous wife: 'It was the middle of the day and the two of them were down there in the middle of the piazza, and we were all up here, and nobody would go to help her'. Otherwise, there are no inappropriate uses specific to Piazza Plebiscito. Football is not simply an 'inevitable' consequence of pedestrianization, but the piazza's principal daytime use. 'Some of the children are even good players; they've got talent'. The smoking of hashish in the piazza is also considered 'normal':

> Lots of hashish is smoked in the piazza. I smoke, as well, what's the problem? Now it's become a really normal thing to do. You get children as young as fourteen who stop to smoke. It's a piazza where loads and loads and loads of it is smoked. But dope isn't sold here. Probably someone will come by on a *motorino*. Basically, you roll the joint in the piazza because it is more covered and the police car can't pass by. You can enter only from the sides. You've got enough time to see them. At worst, you leave it on the ground and go back later. … It's like Amsterdam here: normal, as if it were legal. By law it isn't legalized, but the way we smoke, it's as if it were!

What is considered an illicit activity by the custodian is seen by Esposito to be an entirely acceptable social activity, even though it is formally illegal. Once again, an urban trope is used to frame representations of Naples. In this case, Amsterdam signifies the permissive city. (Just as the administration had hoped, Piazza Plebiscito indeed found itself resituated on a national and international map, but this clearly provided for unexpected interpretations!) In the evening Piazza Plebiscito offers a sheltered space to roll and smoke joints. During the day he maintains a good rapport with the *vigili,* many of whom, like himself, are from the Spanish Quarters.

> The *vigili urbani* should be stricter with us because we haven't got licences. We're *abusivi.* But they let us work because they understand our situation. If we don't do this, what would we do? In Naples, sixty per cent of work is illegal. At most they come to us and politely tell us, 'Move on, you can't stay here'. Sometimes you get the *vigile,* who threatens you, but that's rare. They've never taken my cart and I've never had a fine because, as I said, even the *vigili urbani* know me. We're educated: they see that I keep the piazza tidy. There's my litter bin. These *vigili* are nearly all old, the youngest have done at least ten years' service. Four or five of them are from the Spanish Quarters. They're all very agreeable.

Esposito conveys a pragmatic attitude towards the question of control in relation to the piazza. While he argues that the aggressive behaviour of young motorcyclists should be stopped by the police, he still sees how the *motorino* serves a practical purpose: people can arrive at meeting points (as his friend did during the interview), and marijuana can be delivered. The *vigili* are treated with respect. He claims to be repeatedly let off (not for being in Piazza Plebiscito, but for not having a licence), because the municipal police, as locals themselves or through their long-term service in the area, empathize with his socioeconomic situation. The conflation of Piazza Plebiscito with a perceived laxness of rules in Naples thus contravenes the aura of civic discipline that cultural and political elites had sought to inculcate through the new piazza.

Chapter 9

Exit Piazza Plebiscito
Rethinking 'Civic' Space

> It might seem that monumentality remains largely unchallenged and unchal-
> lengeable. To accept this proposition, however, is to accept the self-serving
> ideology of the nation-state or similar institution, and to ignore the agency of
> those bureaucrats who attempt to create, not only 'facts on the ground', but also
> to inculcate into individual bodies those habitual relationships to the built envi-
> ronment that supposedly induce political docility and ideological complaisance.
> It also means ignoring the agency of those who are neither docile nor com-
> plaisant, have little power to affect the planning that displaces them from their
> accustomed lifestyles and abodes, and yet manage to 'muddle through' and to
> change the meanings of those contested spaces. (Herzfeld 2006: 129–30)

The Bassolino administration and its allies promoted the 'new' Piazza
Plebiscito as an unequivocal case of urban improvement (Bassolino
1996b; De Lucia 1998; Marone 2002). Opposition parties such as Forza
Italia and National Alliance, as well as left-wing social movements, accused the operation of producing a superficial '*vetrina*' (showcase) (Ragone 1997; Officina 99-lo Ska 2000). This rather simplistic and ultimately
unsatisfactory interpretative framework tells us little about Piazza Plebiscito as a public space. The ideological taking-of-sides merely added
new and conflict-laden associations to those already accumulated in the
piazza's history. The selected interviews indicate the imbricated but often
discordant ways in which the cultural regeneration of public space was
experienced and understood. Points of view were constructed around discursive and corporeal relationships with Piazza Plebiscito, which were
simultaneously intersected by variables such as age, gender and social
class.[1] Positive readings of its transformation were pronounced by pro-

---

1. Overall, responses did not reveal any specific gender-based relationships with the piazza, although women tended to express more concern about pedestrian safety. This would seem to reflect the
findings of a study on pedestrian behaviour in European city centres, which concluded that males in
Italian cities were less worried about motorized traffic (Hass-Klau et al. 1999: 125). However, while
the mothers from the Pallonetto neighbourhood complained about the young motorcyclists who drove

moters and users alike but through different kinds of interaction with the piazza. For Esposito, Piazza Plebiscito was beautiful at night, because he could meet up with his friends to have a beer with the Gulf of Naples in the background, while for Franca Pastore in the tourist observatory, the space was conceived as a place where Neapolitans could come to stroll: 'Neapolitans like this piazza a lot. They like the idea of being able to stroll from here down to Santa Lucia and the sea. Even the shopkeepers have got used to the idea'.

Allusion to the public debate surrounding Piazza Plebiscito also ap-peared to be linked to the type of rapport with the piazza. While Santucci and Pastore deliberated over the political and historical context in which the piazza was pedestrianized, the local and nonlocal users referred briefly to the principal protagonists of the new Piazza Plebiscito – the G7, Bassolino and tourists – in order to articulate their personal expe-riences of its transformation. The common recognition of the piazza's improvement did not necessarily mean subscribing to official accounts about its change. Discussion of the symbolic significance of the piazza led Esposito to indicate the unchanging situation in his own neighbour-hood. By acknowledging the new status of the piazza, the custodian and Padre Cozza were able to underline the disadvantages for the church.[2] The interviews likewise highlighted the limits of fixing formal defini-tions to urban heritage (Herzfeld 1991; Signorelli 1996). The restoration of Piazza Plebiscito had not simply reinstated the space to its former glory but had also enabled unforeseeable and unintended uses and accen-tuated those that had been less visible (and publicly insignificant) before the G7 summit. The monumental space was selectively consumed and renegotiated through its various functions: as a parish church, a setting for wedding ceremonies, an informal commercial space or as a place for 'skinning up'.

The piazza's transformation was assigned with what Henri Lefebvre (1991) defines a 'sense of transparency'. Pedestrianization was promoted by the administration as a democratic gesture, even though, as the cus-todian and Padre Cozza complained, there had been little consultation with some of the piazza's established users. For Santucci and Pastore, Pi-azza Plebiscito was bound to a wider discourse about urban citizenship. The new piazza represented the reclamation of a public space that ben-

---

past the colonnade close to their children, many nevertheless entered the piazza on *motorini* (interview with author, 11 June 1999).

2. The urban geographer Phil Hubbard makes a similar observation in his study of residents' inter-pretations of the redevelopment of Birmingham's city centre: 'Meanings of entrepreneurial landscapes as promoted by local politicians and the media were not accepted unproblematically by all individuals but were internalized differently according to people's positionality within broader structures of social space' (Hubbard 1996: 1458).

efited Neapolitans. As a generalized, positive construct, the 'Neapolitan' was imagined as a civic-minded, educated, well-behaved (and implicitly middle-class) citizen. Those who did not respect the piazza's traffic-free function went against the collective good. But what emerged most vividly from the period of observation and the interviews was not the image of a hermetically sealed *tabula rasa* from which to construct a hegemonic civil vision of Naples, but a multivalent social space. While the piazza had historically been, as Santucci explained, a ceremonial site, the colonnade had also traditionally been appropriated from below. Indeed, it was evident that the piazza straddled two distinct social environments: the administrative, commercial and monumental heart of the city, which lay beyond Piazza Trieste e Trento, and the *quartieri popolari* located behind San Francesco di Paola and the prefecture. In other words, the restored royal courtyard was at the same time the backyard for the Pallonetto and Spanish Quarters. This juxtaposition, rarely acknowledged in public debates, was perhaps most discernible in the different values expressed about decorum. For instance, promoters of the new piazza considered the entrance of *motorini* into Piazza Plebiscito unacceptable and a clear example of incivility (unlike Santucci and Pastore, other promoters were more explicit in blaming the local '*popolo*' for such acts of recalcitrance). On the other hand, for Esposito and other locals from the surrounding neighbourhoods, including mothers with their children (see footnote 1), the motorized relationship with the piazza was endowed with practical significance and was hence perceived as 'normal', although this was not without its own set of definitions about appropriate behaviour.[3]

The fact that seemingly irreconcilable meanings and uses should unfold in the *salotto* of the 'Neapolitan Renaissance' suggests a certain discrepancy between the discursive realm and social reality of urban change in Naples during the 1990s, as well as a mismatch between the implementation of controls and the maintenance of symbolic boundaries in the piazza itself (Sibley 1995). While the ideal piazza was constructed from firm notions of decorum, culture, history and transgression, the lived space was characterized by openness to difference: divergent presences, from the tourist to the protester and footballer, coexisted. Although the original, pristine image of the piazza had been the upshot of an off-limits security zone, the dystopian vision of the '*città blindata*' (fortress city) during the G7 summit was clearly not possible in ordinary circumstances

---

3. In a similar way, the US anthropologist Setha Low saw 'class-based taste cultures' as underpinning the social and symbolic conflicts over the restoration of a central plaza in San José, Costa Rica – between professional and middle-class Josefinos who yearned for the nostalgic image of an elite strolling park and the daily users who experienced it as a socially heterogeneous gathering place (Low 2000: 134–36).

nor was it on the agenda of the administration. However, the proposed *rianimazione* of the piazza, which had still not taken place when Rosa Russo Iervolino was elected mayor in May 2001, would have inevitably involved 'enclosing' the space with cultural and tourist facilities and increasing the police presence.[4] This process was thwarted by the piazza's immense size, the presence of unusable buildings on its borders and the fact that the only viable space – the colonnade – had already been independently appropriated for different uses. The lived space of Piazza Plebiscito continually disrupted the contrived coherence of public representations of the piazza as a regeneration landscape. This was most blatantly exemplified by the gap between the superintendents' edict against organized sports and the piazza's daily use as a football pitch.

What, then, might be meant by Iervolino's 2001 declaration that the piazza had been 'given back to Neapolitans'? The history of the transformation of Piazza Plebiscito calls into question the claims of an all-inclusive citizenship made in its name. The dominant narrative of the piazza as a heritage site and urban symbol tended to privilege those people who possessed certain levels of cultural capital and who, in any case, were seen to act within the limits of propriety and legality. Those residents and city users whose social, cultural or economic practices were deemed deleterious to a new, positive image of Naples were marginalized or censured. The piazza's transformation assumed a subtle form of urban revanchism (Smith 1992). The 'civilized' car driver from the hilltop districts who parked in Piazza Plebiscito during the mid-1960s was now returning as a pedestrian. The frustrations expressed by some that the new piazza was not always appropriately used revealed less about the recalcitrance of Neapolitans (for, indeed, this had rarely been an issue before 1994) than it did about the construction of an urban imaginary inhabited by 'civil' and 'well-tempered' citizens (Miller 1993), which was often unwilling or unable to comprehend other forms of sociality that had 'historically come into being' in the same space (Chakrabarty 2002). Nevertheless, this 'enlightened' vision, at times crudely articulated in terms of 'cultural identity' and 'civic pride' by the local media and a ruling Left fumbling for ideological ballast, frequently came unstuck in Piazza Plebiscito. For it was here, in the very symbolic heart of the 'new' Naples, that alternative viewpoints about the city were voiced and where other claims to urban space were made.

---

4. In 2006, a bookshop and bar were opened under the colonnade. In March 2007, when the colonnade was closed to the public in order to repair damaged plaster, the city council was still awaiting proposals for a 'literary café', an 'ethnic restaurant' and craft shops (*La Repubblica*, 27 March 2007).

Part 3

Deprovincializing Urban Regeneration

Piazza Garibaldi and Immigration
during the Bassolino Era

Chapter 10

Enter the Station Piazza

Migrant workers, already living in the metropolis, have the habit of visiting the
main railway station. … [I]t is one of the few places where events occur and they
can remain spectators, and outnumber the citizens. The constituents of leisure:
the right to watch and the capacity to be at ease with those of your own choosing.
(Berger and Mohr 1975: 64)

Piazza Garibaldi, located on the eastern edge of the *centro storico,* is
the first place one encounters on emerging from the central railway station of Naples (see illustration 10.1). As well as functioning as a major
road junction, this immense space is the hub of the city's rail and bus
network. Running down its sides are neat rows of late nineteenth-century
buildings and the odd postwar block that houses an assortment of electrical stores, nondescript shops, hotels, bars and restaurants together
with a few local institutions such as Bar Mexico, reputed to serve the
best coffee in Naples, and two four-star hotels, Terminus and Cavour. Its
pavements are lined with the stalls of Neapolitan and immigrant street
vendors who sell an array of goods, from pirate DVDs and secondhand
books to mobile phone cases and fake designer sunglasses. Add to this
the food and clothes markets in the immediate surrounding area, and it
is understandable that for most of the day Piazza Garibaldi heaves with
traffic and people.

For over a quarter of a century, Piazza Garibaldi has been the focal
point for a number of immigrant groups drawn by cheap rents and hotels
and the area's traditional role as a meeting place and centre of commercial exchange. North and West Africans first started to arrive during the
1980s. Many settled in the area, and some would later open retail and
wholesale businesses, particularly in the Vasto neighbourhood to the immediate north of the piazza. From the mid-1990s onwards, with a rise
in immigration from Eastern Europe, the piazza was the rendezvous on
Thursdays and Sundays for hundreds of people, mainly Poles and Ukrainians, most of whom were female and worked in the domestic and care

sectors. Towards the end of the decade, the station area became a point of distribution for the Chinese rag trade located in the towns around Vesuvius and for products imported from the Far East, which coincided with a sharp rise in Chinese-run shops and warehouses around the piazza, as well as an influx of Chinese street vendors.

For many years, Piazza Garibaldi constituted a particular doxa about everyday urban life in central Naples. The hustle and bustle of the station area was as much an inevitable, indeed defining, part of the cityscape as the car park in Piazza Plebiscito. With a renewed emphasis on tourism and a heightened concern for the city's image after 1993, it would instead be conceived as a strategic place in public debates about Naples. But while the revamped Piazza Plebiscito was promoted as the emblem of a 'new' city, Piazza Garibaldi would be regarded an 'unregenerate' space (Furbey 1999) that continued to be overrun by traffic, pollution, social disorder and illicit activities. Above all, the unregulated congregation of immigrants in and around the piazza began to be seen as a hindrance to the area's long-term renewal.

Piazza Garibaldi provides an opportunity to explore the interrelationship between shifting ideas about public space and the impact of immigration in Naples which, although an issue before the Bassolino era, assumed increasing political importance during the course of his administration. There is an abundant literature on immigration in Naples and Campania (Calvanese and Pugliese 1991; Cattedra and Memoli 1992; Amato et al. 1995; Coppola and Memoli 1997; Coppola 1999; Amato 2000; Trani 2004; Russo Krauss 2005). Although useful in providing a general map of the phenomenon and an overview of related questions such as employment and housing, much of this work is premised on a notion of the city as a container and of immigrants as figures of 'integration' or 'assimilation'.[1] The concomitant process of urban regeneration remains, by and large, a separate issue. In fact, if one's grasp of late twentieth-century Naples were merely based on the chronicles of the 'Neapolitan Renaissance', one would be forgiven for being oblivious to the most significant sociocultural and demographic development taking place in the city at the time. For in such accounts, immigrants are almost nowhere to be seen.

This analysis of Piazza Garibaldi instead starts from the assumption that a critical approach to the period must necessarily take into account

---

1. Since my original research on Piazza Garibaldi was conducted, more detailed and critical ethnographic research on immigration in Naples has been completed, notably French researcher Camille Schmoll's excellent study of North African economic networks around Piazza Garibaldi (2004) and Nicholas Demaria Harney's work on migrant bus users and Bangladeshi street vendors in the city (2006, 2007).

how the institutionally determined condition of immigrants (for instance as bearers of restricted and selective rights and subject to mechanisms of control) is reproduced at the level of the city and how the rescaling of the borders of citizenship is at the same time actively contested by immigrants themselves, commencing from their very presence in public space (Isin and Siemiatycki 1999; Mezzadra and Ricciardi 2005). Early studies of urban conflicts over immigration in Italy tended to focus on northern cities such as Florence, Turin and Milan (Masotti 1990; Foot 2001a, 2001b). For the most part, immigration was not considered a source of social tensions in Naples. The city was typically viewed by local politicians, the media, academics and indeed by many immigrants themselves as more predisposed to difference. However, while Piazza Garibaldi was not the setting of major disputes, such as the anti-immigrant torch processions organized by resident committees in Turin (Foot 2001a), it nevertheless came to be almost exclusively associated with a negative discourse about immigration. The fact that this occurred as the *centro storico* was being reimaged as the cohesive core of a city that had retrieved its rightful place on the international stage forces us to interrogate the foundational tenets of a 'new Naples'.

Illustration 10.1. Piazza Garibaldi, late 1960s. *Courtesy of Archivio Ferrovie dello Stato.*

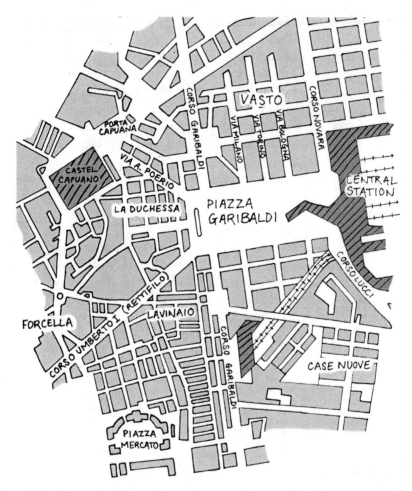

Map 10.1. Piazza Garibaldi and surrounding area. *Designed by Nick Dines.*

Chapter 11

Antechamber to the Southern Italian Capital (1860–1994)

From elegant forecourt to a gaping hole

The origins of Piazza Garibaldi are directly connected with the post-Unification development of the city's railway system. The first central station, completed in 1866, was raised to the immediate east of the city walls on what was then open marshland.[1] This side of the city had historically been the point of departure of the main roads to Rome, Puglia and Calabria. During the nineteenth century, the same area was also a setting for the city's sporadic industrialization and immediately after Unification was envisaged as a site for a major new working-class neighbourhood that was to alleviate the congestion of the city centre. Plans for a comprehensive expansion of Naples to the east were thwarted, however, by the hasty building of a new railway terminus. The neoclassical edifice blocked the principle artery in the area (Via dell'Arenaccia, today divided between Corso Lucci and Corso Novara), while an entanglement of railway lines carved up the open fields. As Lidia Savarese argues in her historical study of the east side of Naples, the station 'totally altered the relationship between the nucleus of the city and this suburban area, and became the fulcrum of all successive development plans' (Savarese 1983: 29). Attention instead switched in the opposite direction, to designing a boulevard link between the station and Piazza Municipio that would allow for swift transit across the medieval city as well as improve the immediate panorama for visitors arriving by train. This proposal was to later materialize with the massive building programme of the Risanamento, following the cholera outbreak

---

1. This was not the first railway station in Naples. The city's first station was built in 1839 as the terminus to the Naples–Portici line (the first railway in the Italian peninsula) and was located directly south of Piazza Garibaldi next to the present-day Circumvesuviana terminal. In 1842 a second station serving Caserta and Capua was opened nearby. Both lines were later incorporated into the new central station.

of 1884. In addition to the new thoroughfare, Corso Umberto I, or as it is popularly known, the '*Rettifilo*' (literally 'straight line'), the space in front of the station was turned into a piazza by the demolition of the city walls, while a new neighbourhood, present-day Vasto, was built to the immediate north of the station. This piazza, roughly a quarter of the size of today's Piazza Garibaldi and originally called Piazza dell'Unità Italiana, was arranged around neat gardens and an ornamental fountain. This fountain was replaced in 1914 by an imposing statue of Giuseppe Garibaldi, and the piazza was given its present name.

The location of the central station left a negative legacy upon the city's subsequent growth which has preoccupied planners to this day. The 1939 master plan for Naples contemplated moving the station two kilometres to the east to clear the way for a grand avenue and a radical tertiary development of the eastern periphery. This proposal, abandoned during the 1950s, would later be considered one of the greatest missed opportunities in Naples's postwar history. Giulio De Luca, one of the authors of the 1939 plan, argued that the station's relocation would have mitigated the destruction of the green belt by concentrating a substantial amount of new building to a single area (De Luca 1987: 30), while Vezio De Lucia claimed that the same plan had influenced the Bassolino administration's

Illustration 11.1. The 'old' Piazza Garibaldi, 1950s. *Courtesy of Archivio Fotografico Parisio.*

choice of location for the city's future high-speed train terminal (De Lucia 1998: 51–52).

The postwar project for a new station (1954–66) and the subsequent enlargement of Piazza Garibaldi was not part of a wider planning agenda but rather stemmed from a series of less ambitious, short-term criteria: to modernize the railway service, to rejuvenate the immediate surrounding area that had been badly damaged by Allied bombs during the Second World War and to deal with road congestion. The old station created a bottleneck for traffic which converged on the miniscule Piazza Garibaldi (see figure 3.2). A number of trains arrived and departed from inside the building on four tracks located below street level, but the majority of platforms were situated three hundred metres to the east of the station, which passengers had to reach by foot. The government-funded competition, organized in 1954 by the Italian State Railways (FS) in agreement with Naples City Council, stipulated that the new terminal be built at the head of these tracks while the other four would be covered over to form a secondary underground station, thus allowing for the increase in the size of Piazza Garibaldi. The final design, which combined the ideas of three entries that included some of Italy's most renowned architects, such as Pier Luigi Nervi and Bruno Zevi, was characterized by a low roof that covered the atrium of the station, ticket hall and various passenger services, as well as a canopied walkway, popularly dubbed the '*proboscide*' (elephant trunk), which linked a row of bus stops in the centre of the piazza. The unusual architectural elements (the *proboscide* and the pyramidal forms on the roof) were counterbalanced by the decision to locate a sixteen-floor tower to one side so as to leave an unimpeded panoramic view of Vesuvius.[2] FS officials stressed the technical improvements to the city's road and rail system. At a promotional conference held in May 1960 during the middle of construction, the local FS chief, Mario Borriello, promised that Naples would have 'the most modern and functional station in Italy and, perhaps, in Europe' (Borriello 1961: 182). The new piazza would feature an efficient rotational traffic system to avoid jams, as well as car parks, green areas and a series of subways for pedestrians. 'From the top of his pedestal, "Garibaldi" will be able to recognize that the hundred years since his entry into Naples have not passed in vain' (ibid.: 179).

The project was enthusiastically supported by the Monarchist-controlled administration of Achille Lauro. During the 1950s it had embarked

---

2. The station's idiosyncratic features were made known to the nation after the singer Mina sang 'Se Telefonando' from its roof for a 1966 episode of *Carosello* (a popular television show that combined commercials with music and entertainment). An abbreviated version of this video can be viewed at: http://www.youtube.com/watch?gl=GB&hl=en-GB&v=qgDq02iPjHE.

on a phase of massive building through which Lauro sought to boost both his personal popularity and local confidence by projecting a vision of Naples as the capital of the South and 'Garden of Europe' (Galasso 1978: 248). Open abuses of planning regulations had opened the way to uncontrolled speculation in new housing on the city outskirts and the construction of various tower blocks in the *centro storico,* one of which at the end of Via Mancini today overlooks Piazza Garibaldi (Dal Piaz 1985). The new station represented a prestigious addition to the modern city (a plastic model of the project went on public display in the Galleria Umberto I) and was interpreted as an official endorsement of local building programmes. The Lauro-owned newspaper, *Roma,* welcomed the imminent transformation with the front page title: 'Another great step towards Naples's revival' (3 March 1956). During the weeks prior to the start of work, the paper repeatedly spoke of the 'resurrection', 'renewal' and 'reconstruction' of Naples and referred to the 'ingenious' features of the future station and layout of the piazza. In his public speech during the inauguration of demolition work (and after having taken the first symbolic swipe with a pickaxe to the old station), Lauro drew comparison between the new Piazza Garibaldi and his administration's alterations to Piazza Municipio.[3] The two resystemized piazzas were heralded as the gateways to the city: 'The new, imposing Piazza della Ferrovia and the renovated Piazza Municipio will be the grand receptions for all those who come, by land or sea, to visit our wonderful, welcoming and hospitable city, which, with gigantic bounds, has set out on the road to a well-deserved future' (*Roma,* 25 March 1956). The collective benefits of the area's modernization were extolled. The assessor for public works, Guido Grimaldi, claimed that by removing the physical barriers posed by the old building and therefore revolutionizing the experience of train travel the new station would enable and encourage interaction between Neapolitans and the 'outside world':

> Every form of control concerning access to the station will be abolished, and the abandonment of this police-like system will demonstrate the level of civility that Naples has reached, because a city which regards tourism as one of its chief interests wants its people to live in continual and cordial contact with its visitors. Our people have the right to a bright future both for their eminent virtues and past sacrifices and as compensation for the city's recent state of abandonment under local and central authorities. (*Roma,* 16 March 1956)

The administration's hyperbole was, to a lesser degree, reproduced in tourist publicity. A promotional brochure in 1961, for instance, declared

---

3. These alterations principally involved the illegal felling of rows of holm oaks in front of the city hall.

that the 'inconvenient neoclassical station' would be replaced by 'one of the most beautiful and vast stations in Italy' that would 'offer the tourist from the moment of arrival a clear example of the extensive urban renewal that has taken place in recent years' (Tornincasa 1961: 25). For a number of years, local guidebooks paid close attention to the station's new facilities. The 1970 guide *TuttoNapoli* spends two pages detailing the various services – which include a luxury bar, a second-class 'tourist' bar, a shoe shiner, a writing room, a barber, a lottery office and a wax museum – before finally commenting: 'So while the station arouses perplexity for its excessively avant-garde architectural style, it does not lack any of the services that exist in the more traditional stations' (Fratta, Volpe and Vajro 1970: 18).

For all the initial fanfare and promotion of its facilities, the new station and layout of the piazza were not greeted by the public with much enthusiasm. Already in 1955, the architectural critic Roberto Musatti noted: 'The winners have distinguished themselves as the most talented contenders and offer functional guarantees for future Neapolitan travellers, but at the end of the day, let's be frank, they haven't spread their wings over the peaks of poetry' (Musatti 1955: 27). As work proceeded, the local press – nonplussed by the station's uncompromising modern design – increasingly attacked the disharmonious aspect of the piazza. By 1963, and a year after the deposal of Lauro from power by the Christian Democrats, *Roma* not only complained about building delays but began to doubt the very merits of the project: 'The road system and layout of the flower beds have turned out even worse [than the station]; the elongated piazza is not ... worthy of a large metropolis where important flows of tourists converge. Its unadorned arrangement appears more appropriate for a provincial town than for what is still considered the moral capital of the Italian South' (*Roma,* 4 January 1963). While the newspaper had welcomed the demolition of the nineteenth-century station back in 1956, it now openly acknowledged a general nostalgia for the old piazza: 'It is hoped that the present work will manage to alleviate the negative impact that one receives when casting a glance from the large piazza to the new station. The view is far worse than the old piazza for which Neapolitans have fond memories' (ibid.). To compound matters, the piazza's unimpeded view of Vesuvius – the one aspect of the new station's design that was generally celebrated – would rapidly become disfigured by private housing blocks that mushroomed around its lower slopes.

The new Piazza Garibaldi was now intersected by fourteen streets, six of which were main routes linking other parts of the city. The cleared space rapidly assumed the role of a giant road junction, which, as private transport rose, became increasingly congested. Moreover, the entrance to the Autostrada del Sole was located five hundred metres south-east, while a mile-long flyover erected in 1985 along Corso Novara directly linked Piazza Garibaldi with the Otto Calli district in the north of the city. The construction of the Centro Direzionale, to the north of the railway lines after 1985, and the gradual transfer of services and offices from the *centro storico* only provoked a further rise in transit across the piazza. It is not surprising, therefore, that during the 1970s and 1980s Piazza Garibaldi was associated with the mundane problem of traffic.

Both the redesigned piazza and the new central railway station are repeatedly overlooked in surveys of urban developments in Naples during the postwar period.[4] These tend to focus on the numerous architectural calamities perpetrated under the reign of Lauro. Clearly the publicly funded scheme did not possess the hallmarks of speculation or illegal building that characterized the era, nor did it alter the cityscape to the same extent as the new housing units that were then sprouting on the hills around the *centro storico*. While the general disinterest among historians can perhaps be inferred from the lukewarm public response to the new station at the time, the completion of the project nevertheless marked a significant moment in the modernization of the city's transport system and endowed Naples with a massive, indeed its largest, piazza.

Public representations of an unremarkable place

The public's perception of this '"hole" of vast dimensions' (Amato 1992: 91) has traditionally been closely tied to the social and economic character of the local area, popularly known simply as 'La Ferrovia' (The Railway), which incorporates the adjacent neighbourhoods of Vasto, La Duchesca and the northern part of the Mercato district. Station areas have historically held an ambivalent position in the modern city. While the railway represented the physical link with the rest of the Italian nation and a metaphor for unity (Mercurio 1994), the station itself inherited the role of the historic gateway. The construction of many stations involved the destruction of city walls, symbolically opening the way to expansion while obliterating the ancient boundaries of a clearly defined urban system. Heralded as a monument to modernity and urban progress (Alisio 1981: 78), albeit one which during the nineteenth century, at least in the Italian South, was mainly patronised by an affluent minority (Schram

---

4. No mention is made, for instance, by Dal Piaz (1985) or Galasso (1978), although see the short entry in Belfiore and Gravagnuolo (1994: 242–43). The dearth of research has been partially corrected by the recent publication of a pictorial architectural history of the central railway station, which coincided with the completion of the station's facelift in 2010 (Lenza 2010).

1997), the imposing architecture of the central railway station was at the same time typically situated in the poorest parts of the city and thus stood as physical testimony to the inherent socioeconomic contradictions of urban development. Moreover, the crowded station areas spatially embodied the impersonal and anomic experience of modern city life famously described by Georg Simmel in his essay 'The Metropolis and Mental Life' (Simmel 1950).

In Matilde Serao's vivid account of late nineteenth-century Naples, the station area was used as a yardstick for changes in the city. Before the Risanamento, the stranger arriving at the station had to face 'a dirty, foul-smelling city of narrow streets' (Serao 1994: 87) and risk robbery as he or she travelled along the port towards the salubrious neighbourhoods of Chiaia and Mergellina in the west. Twenty years later, Serao admitted that the station piazza had acquired 'a vastness worthy of a metropolis' and gave 'the curious onlooker a pleasant first impression' (ibid.: 88). However, she argued that both the piazza and the *Rettifilo* were an elegant 'windshield' to the deprivation in adjacent alleyways which regularly returned to infect the 'disembowelled' parts of the city:

> After nine o'clock in the evening, the stretch of the *Rettifilo* from Piazza Depretis to the station is traversed by few people, and despite the big electric lamps it becomes one of the most dangerous places in the city. ... During these hours only petty thieves, *camorristi,* former convicts and loose women roam the street – in the street that is supposed to serve the health and redemption of the Neapolitan people! (Serao 1994: 97)

The Mercato-Pendino area to the south of the *Rettifilo* and Piazza Garibaldi, as Serao noted, was especially poor. Developed in the early Middle Ages following the relocation of the city's central market, this district did not possess the vertical class stratification of other parts of the *centro storico* and was characterized by very low-quality housing. The post-Risanamento neighbourhoods of Vasto and Arenaccia, to the north of the central station, were planned in part as an alternative to the squalid and cramped slum tenements, but as a consequence of high rents, only a fraction of the seventy thousand people displaced by the demolitions found homes in these new quarters. Indeed most returned to what was left of their old districts, which only led to further overcrowding (Baculo 1979: 33). Although general living standards and consumption levels would rise over the course of the century – and despite further housing improvements, such as the Case Nuove (New Houses), built during Fascism to the immediate south of the station – the Mercato-Pendino district, in particular, would remain one of the poorest neighbourhoods in the city centre (Mingione and Morlicchio 1993; Morlicchio 2001).

More than anywhere else in Naples, the station area's economy revolved around the retail and wholesale sector which had intensified with the development of local road and rail networks. Many of the city's historic markets are still located around Piazza Garibaldi: Piazza Mercato, a regional centre for household items and furniture (although this role diminished with the development of suburban superstores in the 1980s), Lavinaio, one of the busiest food markets in the city, and La Duchesca, to the immediate west of the piazza, which has traditionally specialised in cheap clothes and general electronic goods. The piazza and its environs also attracted a high number of unlicensed street vendors, many selling contraband or stolen merchandise, as well as a more or less stable host of swindlers (such as thimbleriggers and the infamous '*paccottari*'),[5] which gave rise to periodic conflicts with shopkeepers.[6] In addition to this pervasive informal economy, during the postwar period, and particularly after the Merlin Law closed brothels in 1958, most street prostitution in Naples was concentrated along the pavements of Piazza Garibaldi and the *Rettifilo*.

However, it is important to point out that the informal activities of Piazza Garibaldi were rarely represented in a negative way but, on the contrary, were often considered the piazza's defining and inevitable character. For instance, amidst debates over the new layout of the piazza in 1963, a long article in *Il Mattino* (1 November 1963) focused on its illicit nocturnal activities. The article intended to introduce the reader, imagined as a resident from the middle-class suburb of Vomero, to 'the picturesque and at times humorous side of the piazza'. The piazza at night is described as an exotic place of prostitutes, illegal taxi drivers, hotel hawkers and itinerant pizza sellers. These are revealed to be part of a functional night economy: the sex workers are disciplined and keep within their boundaries, the '*autonoleggiatori*' offer an honest service and cost less than the official taxis, the '*affittacamere*' are the envoys of respectable local hostels, while the young dexterous '*pizzaiuoli*' are able to slip past the police into the station to offer travellers a taste of authentic Neapolitan pizza. During the daytime, on the other hand, life in the piazza is depicted as impersonal and drab: 'When all these people go to sleep, the railway piazza regains its normal appearance. The day lights up its vastness, but passersby are in too much of a hurry to look, or if they

---

5. The *paccotto* (package), part of modern Neapolitan folklore, is the art of duping a person into believing that he or she is buying an expensive watch (or, more commonly today, a mobile phone or video camera) at an astonishingly low price. By a sleight of hand, the packaged item is swapped for an identical box containing a stone or something of similar weight. Often the *paccottaro* (swindler) was, and still is, the first person one meets on exiting Naples Central Station.

6. In May 1974, for instance, a shopkeeper from La Duchesca was murdered after he and fellow proprietors had physically driven away unauthorized stallholders who had pitched their stalls in front of their premises (Pessetti 1977: 24).

stop, they start as usual to criticize the station, the traffic system, even the "*proboscide*". And so another day begins' (*Il Mattino,* 1 November 1963). This (bourgeois) enchantment with transgression is sanctioned by incorporating the various spatial practices into a local folkloristic discourse. The empty expanse, robbed of its picturesque nineteenth-century station, is rendered 'Neapolitan' by the presence of idiosyncratic activities which elsewhere would be considered undesirable.

Alongside its 'lumpen' elements, the piazza was also perceived, especially on the Left, as a working-class piazza due to the presence of the railway, trade union offices and political party offices in the immediate area. Following the death of Palmiro Togliatti in 1964, the local edition of *L'Unità* reported on the party's section next to the central station, where tourists and workers passed to pay their respects, while militants in the piazza publicly binned copies of a Monarchist newspaper that had insulted the dead Communist leader. When Piazza Garibaldi was not a source of newspaper debates on the state of the city's traffic and public transport, it was most regularly represented as a place of protest. The piazza was the traditional starting point for political marches and a chosen location for publicity stunts such as the blocking of traffic or the scaling of the Garibaldi monument, which was popularized by the Organized Unemployed Movement during the 1970s.

Most of the time, however, the station area was treated like any other part of the *centro storico.* The local press sometimes carried stories about crimes or municipal disinfection campaigns which took place around Piazza Garibaldi, but the piazza itself was never systematically associated with higher levels of illegality or rubbish. Only out-of-the-ordinary events were reported in any detail, as in the case of a particularly audacious armed robbery off the north-west corner of Piazza Garibaldi in 1967, which caused *Il Mattino* to exclaim: 'Such casual contempt of the law, which the robber displayed by pointing a gun at a woman's head in a crowded street during the middle of the day, does not have many precedents' (*Il Mattino,* 20 June 1967). According to the newspaper, what made the crime so incredible, apart from the robber's recklessness, was that it occurred in a busy shopping street in the centre of the city. Despite the area's less than salubrious credentials and its maze of alleyways, which offered the assailant his escape route, the place of the crime was not considered significant. From the late 1970s onwards, as the Camorra assumed near total control of the illegal economy, the station area was carved up between clans (the Giulianos in Forcella and the Continis in Vasto and Pendino). However, this trend affected the city of Naples as a whole, especially the central popular neighbourhoods and poor suburbs, and was not directly connected with Piazza Garibaldi.

From this social historical overview of the piazza, it is worth bearing in mind some key points before we turn our attention to the 1990s. First, Piazza Garibaldi rarely figured in debates about the city unless these concerned the question of traffic. Despite the initial hype in the 1950s, the symbolic significance of the new station and piazza did not extend beyond the original intentions of the project, which were to improve the rail service and the circulation of road traffic. Lauro's intention of incorporating the new space into a grand design of 'urban renewal' was eclipsed by the initiatives independently masterminded by his administration. Indeed his personal ambitions for Piazza Municipio as the tourist gateway to a modern Naples were pursued with far greater conviction. Second, the social dimension of the station area was seldom a cause for public alarm; rather, its promiscuous, unruly, picaresque aspect was sometimes considered part of its allure. Issues such as crime, urban decay and rubbish were considered citywide issues and not space-specific, and although some areas were classified as black spots, these were seldom stigmatized. It is significant that one of the few public spaces to be placed under the media spotlight during the 1950s and 1960s was Piazza Municipio: reports in the local press would bemoan the presence of street vendors and petty swindlers who spoiled the image of the city's seaward foyer. Third, it seems quite evident that the general public was not particularly fond of the new Piazza Garibaldi. Many planners continued to dream of a station relocated two kilometres to the east (see, for instance, Alisio, Izzo and Almirante 1987), while the present Piazza Garibaldi was considered a sort of urban miscarriage. Its vast dimensions during the 1960s were criticized as 'un-Neapolitan', and it would rarely feature in the city's symbolic cartography. Local bars and restaurants displayed photographs of the nineteenth-century central station, while postcard images of the piazza nearly always dated from the 1930s.[7] A nostalgic myth grew around the old station and its 'intimate' piazza. In 2000 an article in *Il Mattino* claiming to unearth the 'glorious history' of Piazza Garibaldi made no reference to the previous forty years. Instead, in a terse endnote, the vast cavity was considered the unfortunate but inescapable consequence of modernization (*Il Mattino*, 16 February 2000). Mario Isnenghi labels such upshots of modernity '*piazzali*': spaces 'where everything is too big, open, disproportionate, and where neither the buildings nor the passersby are to scale' (Isnenghi 1994: 8).

---

7. Although images of the present-day Piazza Garibaldi have been printed, these were extremely difficult to find during the second half of the 1990s and were never sold in the usual tourist outlets.

Chapter 12

Piazza Garibaldi as an Unregenerate Space (1994–2001)

Ingredients for a new place narrative

From the mid-1980s, the station area began to attract immigrants, firstly North and West Africans and later East Europeans and South and East Asians. Initially, this presence did not alter general attitudes to the area. Although the local press began to identify Piazza Garibaldi as one of the city's principal 'immigrant spaces', reports of troubling incidents, such as the arrest of North Africans involved in fights or the closure of overcrowded boardinghouses run by unscrupulous Neapolitans, were connected, if at all, with debates about immigration and not about the piazza itself. The significance of Piazza Garibaldi changed entirely with the inception of a discourse of urban regeneration under the Bassolino administration. Not only was it reconceived as the portal to a resurgent *centro storico,* but it also became the subject of intense debates over the control, use and shape of what was now widely perceived to be a problematic public space. Just as Piazza Plebiscito became the focus of debates about urban heritage and decorum after the G7 summit, Piazza Garibaldi was inseparable from the three interrelated issues of tourism, security and immigration, each of which shifted politically during the 1990s. In order to comprehend why the piazza became the subject of debates about Naples, it is to these three issues that I first turn.

Turismo

Piazza Garibaldi had long been associated with tourism. The central station was the arrival point for most visitors, and almost half the city's available beds were concentrated around the piazza. However, with the steady drop in tourists in Naples from the 1970s onwards, much of the piazza's accommodation was identified with the seamier end of the market. After the 1980 earthquake, numerous hotels were used to accommodate homeless families and were later turned into dormitories for immigrants looking for the cheapest sleeping arrangements.

One of the immediate aims of the Bassolino administration's strategy for regeneration was to resuscitate the city's moribund tourist industry. The general situation in the piazza, traversed in all directions by a continual flow of traffic and surrounded by rundown lodgings, was not consonant with this aspired revival. The local idea of urban cultural tourism targeted a more elite, higher-spending visitor. Over 60 per cent of foreign tourists stayed in four- or five-star hotels (Solima 1999: 26). This 'culturally conscious' group, it was argued, offered the greatest economic benefits to Naples: 'If the city moves away from this precious core of tourists, it falls into mass tourism comprised of transitory crowds, who create more problems than wealth' (Amato 1996: 29). The consumption of the 'art city', which was usually extended over a large area (unlike the 'leisure city', which often based itself around single attractions such as sports venues or amusement parks), demanded certain conditions. Apart from adequate hotels and efficient services, the urban cultural tourist needed to be guaranteed a clean and, above all, risk-free environment. Leisure facilities could be located in areas of urban decline if equipped with protective measures that concealed or bypassed possible danger, as in the case of the New York Yankees baseball stadium built on the edge of the Bronx (Eisinger 2000). The art city, on the other hand, could not fully function without eliminating risk or acquiring the approval and cooperation of its residents. Otherwise it turned into a destination for a different kind of intrepid, independent traveller, which was the reputation Naples earned itself during the 1980s, or a place of transit, as summed up by the commonplace: 'Before people went straight to the port to take the ferry to Capri'. Tourist regeneration in Naples under the Bassolino administration involved opening monuments, marking out itineraries (Comune di Napoli 1996) and providing safe and pleasant places (such as Piazza Plebiscito) where visitors were encouraged to linger. At the same time, however, this delicate process of renewal was hampered by persistent images among tourists and tour operators of Naples as a 'dangerous' and 'violent' city (Colella 1999; Solima 1999).

With the growing economic importance of tourism, visitors to Naples constituted a sort of 'virtual' urban class who, endowed with honorary citizenship, directly influenced debates about the city's transformation. If an aspect of Naples was deemed disagreeable to the imaginary tourist, then it was considered detrimental to the whole of the city. After the G7 summit, it became very common for local politicians and opinion makers to exclaim: 'a bad image for tourists'. Piazza Garibaldi became the testing ground for first impressions of the city and was therefore commonly labelled, like Piazza Plebiscito, a '*biglietto da visita*' (visiting card). This was a highly ambivalent term. While used rhetorically to suggest a favourable advertisement, *biglietto da visita* also referred to how the city actually presented itself to a newcomer. In this sense, Piazza Garibaldi lived up to its label: the multiple systems of commercial exchange in and around the piazza revealed a fundamental element of Neapolitan society. The fact that Piazza Garibaldi was continually reprimanded, as shall be seen, for failing to fulfil its diplomatic role reflected as much a redefinition of the city as an antipathy towards certain subjects and practices in the piazza itself.

Sicurezza

Although security has been a constant motif throughout the history of modern urban development (Cohen 1985), its prominence in political debates about the city at the end of the twentieth century (Petrillo 1996; Merrifield 2000; Bonnet 2004) can be seen to be the consequence of both a systemic crisis and a radical change in criminological thought. Increasing uncertainty and confusion in the face of economic and political restructuring translated into a diffuse sense of insecurity (Bouchard 1997; Landuzzi 1999a; Pitch 2000). Traditional forms of 'endogenous social control' (Palidda 1999: 95) such as the church, trade unions and political parties were increasingly divested of their former public roles or, in the case of the welfare state, were dismantled, often leaving the police forces and judiciary as the only stable, responsive institutions in the eye of public opinion. Contemporaneously, there was a consensual shift to the right in attitudes to criminal justice and social control policy (De Giorgi 2000: 21–48). The idea of penal welfarism, whereby crime was seen to have its roots in social conditions and offenders were to be rehabilitated back into society, was increasingly discredited and superseded by a vision of crime as a routine, rational activity that meant a greater stress on repressive strategies and protecting the real or potential victims of crime (Bouchard 1997; Lea 1997; Garland 2001). In Italy during the 1990s, '*sicurezza*' was conceived less in terms of defending the state (for instance from the threats of the mafia or political terrorism) and more in terms of protecting members of the public from everyday street crime or '*microcriminalità*', as it came to be labelled in Italian at the time. This was a vague concept that encapsulated everything from noise to drug dealing and which was popularly imagined as endemic to Italy's larger cities (Dal Lago 1999: 83). During the period, and especially in the North, collective mobilization took place specifically over the question of insecurity, as in the case of the night patrols and torch processions organized by 'citizen committees' comprising local residents, councillors and businesses (Sebastiani 2001). Attention focused on public spaces: from whole neighbourhoods to single streets and piazzas. These were the arenas where local 'identities' were defended and where claims about safety and order were made.

The Italian Communist Party had traditionally eschewed a politics of law and order that was not situated in a critique of the socioeconomic order. As the generic *'cittadino'* (citizen) increasingly assumed political precedence over the socially differentiated category of class following the party's dissolution after 1989 (Ignazi 1992), and with the PDS, the PCI's post-Communist offshoot, committing itself to a market-based economy, many on the Left started to introduce the question of *sicurezza* into a new idea of progressive politics. During its period in government between 1996 and 2001, the PDS (which from 1998 was renamed the Left Democrats (DS)) elaborated a number of foundational truths to vindicate its newfound enthusiasm for law and order. First and foremost, it was accepted that public feelings of insecurity really existed, and because these were greater than ever – even if due to heightened perceptions rather than an actual rise in crime – they had to be taken seriously (Fassino 2001). Second, insecurity affected, according to Luciano Violante, a former judge and the PDS-DS president of the Chamber of Deputies, the country's 'weakest citizens' (Palidda 2000: 192): therefore policies to combat it were conceived as a form of social solidarity. Third, as law and order was a central tenet of liberal democracy, it needed to be confronted democratically, for instance, by encouraging closer cooperation between public figures such as mayors and the police forces. Finally, as *sicurezza* was now considered a permanent problem, it could no longer be dealt with through emergency legislation but had to be addressed strategically through systematic policies.[1]

With the direct election of mayors after 1993, the governance of (in)security frequently rose to the top of local political agendas, both in cities controlled by the Centre-Right, like Milan, and those traditionally

---

1. By the end of the 1990s, the Left Democrats were placing as much, if not more, importance on the question of security as the Centre-Right opposition. In 1998 the party set up the research group 'Vivere Sicuri' (Living in Security) with its own website, which organized a series of public conferences. Significantly, after the Centre-Left lost the national elections in May 2001, this initiative fell silent.

run by the Left, such as Bologna.[2] As already noted in Chapter 3, Bassolino considered the question of security a fundamental principle of municipal citizenship and a priority for a new urban Left (Bassolino 1996b:
59–63). While he underlined the urgent need to deal with the Camorra
(although he considered this a regional rather than a specifically urban
problem[3]), he also recognized 'a feeling of widespread insecurity' in Naples (ibid.: 59). According to the mayor, the Left needed to refrain from
an 'overly social' vision of crime (ibid.: 60). Social exclusion could no
longer be regarded an excuse for illegal practices or delinquent behaviour. Rather, traditional methods of prevention had to be accompanied
by a greater emphasis on repression (ibid.). He also called for greater
political collaboration with the police forces, arguing that mayors should
play an important role because of their far-reaching 'knowledge of the
territory' (ibid.: 62).[4]

The centrality of security in municipal politics had a direct influence
upon the way in which the city and its problems were configured. As in
the rest of Italy, public attention in Naples focused on strategic places
perceived to be vulnerable to public disorder and crime. During the second half of the 1990s, nowhere was this more the case than in Piazza Garibaldi. The piazza possessed all the 'right' conditions: it was dirty, chaotic,
suffered from the city's worst noise and atmospheric pollution (Marciano
and Saulino 1995; Macaluso 1995) and was characterized by an array of
informal economic networks and marginal groups. It did not therefore
matter that crime levels in the station area had not markedly risen and
were in fact lower than other neighbourhoods in the city (Cantiere Sociale di Napoli 1999). Instead, Piazza Garibaldi became the principal '*zona
di degrado*' of the *centro storico*. The term '*degrado*' (degradation) was a
key concept in popular and political lexicons of the Italian city during the
1990s, after having first emerged into public discourse during the 1980s.
Like '*biglietto da visita*', its meaning was ambivalent. On the one hand, it
referred to urban decline and poor environmental conditions, but on the
other, it alluded to a moral degeneration of city life that was associated

---

2. For instance, Gabriele Albertini, the Forza Italia mayor of Milan (1997–2001), attempted to
import the ideology of 'zero tolerance' from New York to combat street crime (Foot 2001b). In Bologna, the Vitali administration's (1993–99) fixation with public security (to the point that it tried to
impose a night time ban on loitering in a central piazza in 1996 to ward off tramps and drug dealers)
preannounced the victory of the Centre-Right in 1999 (Monteventi and Ghedini 1999).

3. During much of the 1990s, the inescapable problem of organized crime in the city was not a
theme which constantly mobilized local policy or public opinion but was more often than not confronted with spectacular police and army 'blitzes' implemented by central government in emergency
situations.

4. For a description of local security policies in Naples, see Tedesco 2000.

with the presence of particular figures such as drug users, sex workers and, increasingly, immigrants. When this distinction was not made explicit, the term tended to be used to categorize and stigmatize parts of the city and to predict and objectify collective sentiments of insecurity.[5]

Immigrazione

During the course of the 1980s, immigration in Italy was considered largely a social and cultural phenomenon that was beginning to bear upon Italian society (Sciortino and Colombo 2004). With the Martelli Law of 1990, which established a legal framework on the matter, immigration became increasingly politicized, and in the wake of national moral panics such as the first 'invasion' of Albanians in 1991, it started to be publicly conceived as a social problem that needed to be regulated (Dal Lago 1999). Legislation after 1990 was primarily concerned with restricting entry and combating 'illegal' immigration in order to bring Italy into line with European Union directives on immigration management (Sciortino 1999). Although the Martelli Law, the Dini Decree (1995) and the Turco-Napolitano Law (1998) all issued amnesties for undocumented immigrants (not, of course, as charitable gestures but as a means of controlling the phenomenon), social and civil provisions were in comparison limited. The Turco-Napolitano Law, passed by the centre-left Prodi government, set out a series of rights for regular immigrants, but these were overshadowed by control mechanisms such as expulsions and detention centres. Some of the more progressive proposals of the original bill (including, significantly, the right to vote in administrative elections) were removed when the law was rushed in following public alarm surrounding a series of crimes involving immigrants during the summer of 1997 (Dal Lago

---

5. Although in the past '*degrado*', as a derivation of '*degradazione*', had occasionally been chosen from a selection of possible terms to describe some element of deterioration in the city, it was not until the 1980s that it began to be publicly used on a regular basis, in particular by environmentalists and urban critics such as Antonio Cederna in *La Repubblica,* and not until the next decade, and especially after *Tangentopoli,* that it was systematically deployed as a morally loaded label. In fact, in the Istituto della Enciclopedia Italiana's multivolume *Lessico Universale Italiano* (*Universal Italian Dictionary*), published between the late 1960s and early 1980s, '*degrado*' only appears in the 1985 supplement of new entries, where it is defined as '*deterioramento, degradazione: il d. dell'ambiente, di un edificio*' (deterioration, degradation: the d. of the environment, of a building). In Bassolino's 1996 book *La Repubblica delle Città, 'degrado'* is instead employed to evoke a negative past or the abject elements that obstruct the rehabilitation of Neapolitan identity. In sharp contrast, Maurizio Valenzi does not use the term once in his long discussion of the Communist-led administration formed after 1975, neither in reference to the 1973 cholera crisis nor to the problems that continued to afflict the city during his mayorship (Valenzi 1978). For an in-depth analysis of how '*degrado*' was constructed and employed by the media and politicians during the 1980s and 1990s in relation to the arrival and settlement of immigrants in the Esquilino neighbourhood next to Rome's Termini Station, see Mudu 2002.

1999).[6] The inclusionary rhetoric with which the Left differentiated itself from the Right was actually underpinned by a convergence in positions regarding immigration controls (Andall 2007).[7]

More than any other group, immigrants were a target of law-and-order offensives in Italian cities. Their conspicuous concentration in particular parts of cities (such as station areas), coupled with the unclear or mis-understood nature of their relationship with urban space, would often lead to these areas being labelled as 'dangerous' or 'at risk' (Landuzzi 1999b; Foot 2001a). While certain events, such as public disturbances and police arrests of irregulars, were used by the mass media and ac-knowledged experts on immigration to associate immigrants with urban decline (see, for example, Melotti 1993), neighbourhood committees, es-pecially in northern cities such as Turin (Foot 2001a) and Genoa (Petrillo 2000), played a significant role in turning subjective fears into political issues. Public protests by residents were sometimes coordinated by right-wing political parties like the Northern League but just as often involved political activists from the PDS who viewed themselves as working for the public good and preserving urban identities threatened by change (Fontana 2001). Committee members frequently possessed a mythicized sense of the past city. For instance, young professionals who had moved into Genoa's *centro storico* interviewed by Antonello Petrillo lamented the disappearance of the 'good thieves and prostitutes of Fabrizio de An-dré [a local folk singer]' and their substitution by new non-Italian inhab-itants (Petrillo 2000).

Negative representations of immigrants in public debates about the city cannot be solely explained in terms of social-cultural distance or plain prejudice. Immigrants were incessantly constructed as the 'other' by he-gemonic mono-ethnic notions of national and local identity but also, im-

---

6. Back in 1988, one of the Centre-Left's predecessors, the PCI, had presented a legislative proposal to the Senate to give immigrants the vote in local elections after three years of residence in Italy, but this was when the party was in opposition and a year before the first major case of public anti-immi-grant sentiment during the debate over the Martelli Bill (Andall 2007: 138). Significantly, the PDS party charter of 1991 made no explicit reference to immigration, despite (or perhaps due to) the fact that this had been a key topic in the press during the previous year. Instead, as Davide Pero points out, 'It is assumed [given the charter's general discussion of pluralism, solidarity and equality] that the PDS is a party which, at least in principle, is concerned also with the "new social subject" represented by the "new immigrants" and does care about the specificities of these citizens' conditions and status, along with the other parts of the population' (Pero 2001: 166).

7. The so-called 'Bossi-Fini' Law, approved in 2002 by the centre-right Berlusconi government, contained harsher sanctions regarding expulsion and detention and limited a series of rights such as family reunification. However, this was not technically a new law but a series of modifications to the Turco-Napolitano Law. The one key change was the introduction of the 'immigration contract', which essentially formalized an existing situation whereby an immigrant's status on Italian territory was bound to his/her (formal) employment. For a critical comparison of the two laws, see Dal Lago 2002.

portantly, by the political and legal constraints in which they were forced to live and work that excluded them from the rights enjoyed by Italians.[8] The legal disposition (and subsequent objectification) of immigrants as figures on the margins of society during the 1990s was reaffirmed by the political and popular use of terms such as '*extracomunitario*' (literally 'from outside the European Union' but essentially referring to any foreigner from a country markedly poorer than Italy[9]) and '*clandestino*' (undocumented immigrant). The fact that the immigrant was bound to the duty of work in order to 'earn' his or her status as a regular (Boutang 1997) meant that the foreign individual or group on a street corner in a visible state of economic inactivity was often automatically classified as a '*clandestino*' (and therefore a potential threat to urban security). Any analysis of the relationship between immigrants and urban space must therefore fully consider the political and legal frameworks that condition lived experiences and shape public representations. The resort to notions of 'ethnicity' or 'identity' alone, regardless of how they are understood, risks reifying cultural differences.

Naples first experienced modern immigration from non-Western countries in the late 1960s, with the arrival of small groups of Eritrean female domestic workers and Moroccan itinerant traders, but it was not until the second half of the 1980s that this became a sizeable, publicly recognized phenomenon.[10] According to statistics for the end of 1998, there were approximately 27,500 regular immigrants in the city, which included roughly 10,000 individuals who had applied for documents during the 1998 amnesty (De Filippo 1999). This figure did not account for irregulars, in other words, new arrivals or those whose documents had expired, or those who lived in Naples but were registered elsewhere.

---

8. Immigrants were subjected to a continual negotiation of their status with the Italian state. A regular immigrant by law had to posses a permit to stay, which needed to be renewed every one to four years (and every one to two years after the 2002 Bossi-Fini Law). After five years continual residence in Italy an immigrant could apply for a *carta di soggiorno* (residence card) (after 2002 this was raised to six years), which endowed a greater degree of legal stability and could only be removed in the event of a conviction for serious crime. The application for Italian citizenship remains an extremely drawn-out process and was made more difficult to acquire after legislation in 1992 that limited the principle of *jus soli* (Sciortino 1999). The consequences are manifold: without Italian citizenship, for instance, immigrants are not eligible for employment in the public sector.

9. For instance, Swiss or Norwegian nationals were not considered '*extracomunitari*', while Poles continued to be classified as such after Poland's entry into the European Union on 1 May 2004. Significantly, the term entered into popular usage at the end of the 1980s, as Italy began to negotiate its passage into Schengen, an agreement which would open the internal borders with fellow EU member states on the proviso that it sealed its external borders (Italy signed the agreement in 1990, which entered into effect in 1997). With the Eastern enlargement of the EU in 2004 and 2007, the term fell into disuse as its effectiveness as a selective moniker diminished and was finally rendered senseless with the expulsions of Romanian (i.e. EU) citizens by the centre-left government in late 2007.

10. For an early study of immigration in the Campania region, see Calvanese and Pugliese 1991.

Nevertheless, after Rome, Milan and Turin, Naples could be considered Italy's fourth 'immigrant city'.[11] Like the rest of Italy, this population was made up of many different national groups.[12] In contrast to northern Italian cities, large numbers of immigrants resided in the *centro storico* of Naples: in the station area itself as well as in popular neighbourhoods such as the Spanish Quarters, Montesanto and Sanità. Almost 70 per cent of immigrants in Naples, including the largest and oldest 'communities' (Sri Lankan, Philippine, Cape Verdean, Dominican and Somali), were employed in the domestic sector. The other main group, smaller but more visible, was engaged in informal commercial activities such as street trading. Despite the difficulties in finding regular work, the lower cost of living and housing meant that for many immigrants Naples was an ideal port of call prior to onward migration to northern Italy and the rest of Europe and acted as a suitable base for those employed in seasonal agricultural work in the region.

There has also been a general tendency, both nationally and locally, to view Naples as a relatively open and tolerant city for immigrants (Morlicchio 2001), because it, like the rest of the South, had experienced both mass emigration and discrimination in the past. The Neapolitan axiom '*l'arte d'arrangiarsi*' – 'the art of getting by (in the face of adversity)' – would often be attributed to the practical experiences of the city's new residents as evidence of their 'assimilation' into a distinct urban way of life. However, such a discourse also served to reiterate a subordinate social and economic position. Immigrants were more readily employed in the informal economy but were also the first to be laid off. While there was no local equivalent of a Northern League that employed overtly racist arguments and organized anti-immigrant campaigns, 'commonsensical' associations between immigrants and urban decline were as frequent in public debates in Naples as they were in the rest of Italy. Moreover, in terms of social services and support for immigrants, Naples did not possess the extensive voluntary networks and local government initiatives of some northern Italian cities. The 'integration' policies of the Bassolino administration were largely limited to providing information and funding 'intercultural' education programmes (Caponio 2005), and they tended to be informed by essentialist understandings of 'culture', 'community'

11, At the end of the 1990s, more immigrants lived in Naples than in any other city in the South (Bari: 5,000; Palermo: 16,000) and more than in Genoa or Bologna (both around 10,000), but far less than in Milan (86,000) and Rome (136,500) (based on calculations from statistics in Caritas di Roma 1999).

12. The principle countries of origin of the official population were, in descending order of numbers: Sri Lanka, The Philippines, Cape Verde Islands, Dominican Republic, Somalia, Tunisia, Peru, Albania, China, Algeria, Poland, Senegal, Ethiopia, Brazil and countries of the former Yugoslavia (Caponio 2005).

and 'ethnic identity' that were prevalent within the mainstream Italian Left (Pero 2001).

Despite the political rhetoric about a socially inclusive city, as non-Neapolitans and nonvoters, immigrants (unlike tourists) were not publicly perceived to be beneficiaries of regeneration. Just as immigration can be seen to constitute and reveal the limits of the nation-state (Sayad 2004), immigrants can be said to (negatively) define the boundaries of the 'city', its 'citizens', 'public space' and, ultimately, the very notion of 'urban regeneration'. The scooterist crossing Piazza Plebiscito, the pickpocket, the unruly *scugnizzo* were all ejected from official narratives of local identity but remained *de jure* 'Neapolitan'. The immigrant, rather, had to earn his or her place in this narrative through good behaviour or by displaying some appropriate form of ethnic identity which would ultimately reflect well on the host society's 'multicultural spirit'. Otherwise, the uncontrolled, unexplained, visible presence of immigrants in strategic places could become a hindrance to tourism and the city's revival.

Law and order in the post-G7 Piazza Garibaldi

The G7 summit in July 1994 was pivotal in redefining Piazza Garibaldi as a key public space in the city, just as it was with Piazza Plebiscito. It had the catalytic effect of merging debates about regeneration, tourism, security and immigration and projecting them onto a single place. The piazza was an important node during the event: it greeted participants and journalists who arrived at the central railway station and lay on the route of the motorcade that transported international statesmen and delegates from Naples airport to their hotels on the city's seafront. Its transformation had been considered the trickiest and most improbable of all interventions. Three billion lire (the same amount spent on Piazza Plebiscito) were used to clean the piazza and surrounding buildings, re-pave the road surface and lay out new green areas. Its unprecedented closure to private vehicles provoked chaos in the surrounding streets and (almost inevitably) brought protests from shopkeepers who claimed that the car park in the piazza was essential to their trade (*Il Mezzogiorno,* 9 April 1994).

The grooming of Piazza Garibaldi for the world event did not, however, simply mean tackling its traffic and shabby appearance but also involved stringent security arrangements. Shortly after preparations got under way, the summit's organizers were accused by a local anti-racist group of planning to expel immigrants from Piazza Garibaldi and the rest of Naples. During a debate on national radio about the impact that the G7 would leave on Naples, the prefect Improta responded that he merely wanted to remove street vendors from the city centre:

> First of all I don't like this phrase 'clean up', and it isn't the terminology used by the government or the security forces. Certainly, street vendors will not be allowed in the Royal Palace, Piazza Plebiscito or other areas connected with the delegations. Certainly, there will be severe measures to remove people who may in some way present *a distorted image of Naples.* They will have to adapt to certain rules because you know that these foreigners in order to survive often willingly sell objects in what I'd call an unlawful way, in the sense they occupy the city's pavements and this certainly *isn't a pleasant image. (Il Mattino,* 5 May 1994, italics added)

According to Improta, immigrants visibly involved in informal economic activities threatened the urban décor crafted for the event, this despite the fact that Neapolitan hawkers were often featured on postcards of 'real-life' Naples. Bassolino, who was also in the studio, hoped that expulsions would not be carried out:

> It would seem a wrong thing to do. Naples is, and should remain, an open city and must be able to present itself in the fairest way and in complete legality. But this must regard everybody, certainly not just immigrant workers, also because Naples has perhaps, among Italy's large cities, the greatest history of tolerance and friendship towards other peoples of the world. (*Il Mattino,* 5 May 1994)

Bassolino instead alluded to the city's alleged anti-racist disposition but simultaneously equated the question of immigration with the issue of law and order. In both responses, immigrants were conceived as non-Neapolitans and were therefore excluded from notions of local identity and the benefits of the G7 summit.

The prefect's justification of security measures led to angry reactions. The Communist Refoundation senator, Giovanni Russo Spena, declared solidarity with immigrants as fellow Campanians; the *centro sociale* Officina 99 organized a protest in Piazza Garibaldi itself; while Don Elvio Damoli, a local leader of the Catholic charity Caritas, expressed his growing doubts about the legitimacy of holding a summit of the richest nations in Naples:

> I wonder whether the prefect's attitude is right, but the more I think about it, the more it seems just an act of repression. … For years an infinite number of clearly irregular positions have been tolerated, and only now they decide to remove the *extracomunitari.* What's the purpose of this decision? I hope the G7 are more humane during their economic super-summit and spare attention for the poorest people. (*Il Mattino,* 4 May 1994)

Despite the controversy provoked by the radio debate, two weeks before the summit the administration issued a decree expelling all authorized and unlicensed street vendors – Neapolitan or immigrant – from the spaces connected with the event. The number of vendors in central Naples fluctuated between the city council's figure of about a thousand (*La Repubblica,* 21 June 1994) and the media's estimate of ten thousand (*La Repubblica,* 22 June 1994). According to the local press, immigrants constituted the overwhelming majority and were concentrated around Piazza Garibaldi. Newspapers spoke of a 'besieged' piazza whose appearance as a 'souk' threatened the very success of the summit (see *La Repubblica,* 21–22 June 1994). This was confirmed by the administration's assessor for 'Normality', Amato Lamberti: 'This is the period when the city is most congested with blacks, but in a few weeks' time they will disperse to work in the countryside. In the meantime, however, they will all have to move towards the periphery or neighbouring towns' (*La Repubblica,* 22 June 1994). As a countermeasure, Lamberti promised to create three ethnic 'souks' in city council–owned premises in the centre, east and west of the city (but away from Piazza Garibaldi). The condition was that immigrants sell 'authentic' products from their countries of origin, not the usual false goods bought in Naples, and that the markets become an attraction for tourists and Neapolitans. In other words, as with the city's monuments and neglected piazzas, immigrants needed to be '*rivalorizzati*' (reappraised). But after the hype of the summit subsided, and despite drawing up a deadline for applications for licences, these plans were shelved.

The empty piazza embodied most acutely the complimentary paradigmatic visions of the 'G7 city': *la città bella* (traffic and immigrant free) and *la città blindata* (militarily guarded). The failure of the event to permanently institute these two criteria in Piazza Garibaldi was measured in the local press by the speed with which it returned to 'normal'. Instead, the summit instigated a semipermanent monitoring of the piazza and its presumed problems.

The hasty facelift of Piazza Garibaldi did not bring about a lasting change to its appearance or function. Over the following years, various schemes were drawn up to improve the shape of the piazza. In 1996 the administration announced plans to reopen a system of subways under the piazza that would also provide an official place for street vendors to sell their wares away from the pavements. To this day, however, they remain closed.[13] The street layout, car parks and waiting areas for buses and taxis were reorganized in the vain attempt to solve the piazza's chaotic traffic. On occasions, the city council was forced to resort to emer-

---

13. In 2009, entrances to the metro station from the piazza were reopened after decades of closure, but the underground walkways remained closed.

gency measures to combat congestion and pollution. During September 1999, for instance, vehicles not equipped with catalytic converters were banned from the piazza, and control points were set up in the surrounding streets.

Given the limited effect of these few minor alterations, hopes switched to long-term infrastructural projects. In November 2000 plans for the renovation of the railway station were revealed by Grandi Stazioni, the same consortium that refurbished Rome's Termini Station for the 2000 Jubilee celebrations. The revamped building would include a new shopping centre, a four-star hotel and security measures such as protective fencing and close-circuit cameras. The intention was to transform the station into 'a centre for cultural and social meetings' that would relieve the '*degrado*' in the surrounding area (D'Angelo 2000: 19).[14] In early 2001 work started on extending the new underground line from Piazza Dante to Piazza Garibaldi, which, it was predicted, would eventually alleviate congestion around the central station but in the meantime turned most of the piazza into a patchwork of building sites and traffic channels. Finally, in 2004, plans were announced for a major refurbishment and pedestrianization of Piazza Garibaldi by the French architect Dominique Perrault, although this was not expected to commence until the completion of the new metro station scheduled for the end of 2012.

The aborted attempts at redesigning Piazza Garibaldi after the G7 summit were overshadowed by calls for greater controls in the piazza. In contrast to the closure of Piazza Plebiscito, imposed by an intransigent administration, political decisions regarding Piazza Garibaldi were greatly influenced by a vocal group of local hoteliers, shopkeepers and business associations. During the second half of the 1990s, a frequent figure to intervene in debates was Mario Pagliari, until 1999 the owner of the four-star Hotel Terminus next to the station and president of the Association of Hoteliers in Naples. In a letter addressed to Bassolino in 1998 published on the front page of the local section of *La Repubblica* (17 May 1998), Pagliari complained that police had been switched from Piazza Garibaldi to more monumental parts of the *centro storico* for the Maggio dei Monumenti festival. As the piazza was important for tourism, he urged that it receive equal attention. Bassolino's rejoinder to Pagliari in the same newspaper two days later laid down the administration's position on Piazza Garibaldi. He recognized the pressing issue of urban security in the area (singling out '*clandestini*' as both a physiognomically identifiable group and a potential source of crime) and promised to raise

---

14. Restructuring of the central railway station eventually began in 2005 and was completed in 2010. Although the new underground shopping centre includes a two-storey chain bookstore, it is too soon to say whether this has enhanced the station's role as a setting for 'cultural and social meetings'.

the issue at his impending meeting with the city's police forces. But more law and order was not enough. Rather, the public significance and function of the space needed to be transformed:

> Piazza Garibaldi in the heads of Neapolitans remains that muddle of things: a confusing and perhaps dangerous place, where somebody hurries past only when it is really necessary. Our main challenge ... is to change this very idea that Neapolitans have about this piazza, which must retain its social character and its role as a space of transit and meeting place but at the same time must become a lively and welcoming piazza. This is because, as Pagliari rightly points out, there is a considerable number of hotel beds in the surrounding area. The revaluing of Piazza Garibaldi is a very important goal for the whole city. Let's work together. (*La Repubblica*, 19 May 1998)

Bassolino argues that the autochthonous (Neapolitan) view of the piazza as a disordered space of transit needed to be changed for it to live up to its tourist potential. 'Let's work together' was therefore an invitation to Pagliari and Neapolitans but did not extend to immigrants who could not legitimately define the conditions of a 'lively and welcoming piazza'. The debate over the piazza was therefore set by Pagliari and expanded by Bassolino. On the very same day, the administration announced plans to transfer buses from under Hotel Cavour (the other four-star hotel in the piazza), which had waged a two-year campaign to have them removed. *La Repubblica* interviewed the proprietor and other hoteliers in the piazza, who affirmed the latent link with immigrants: 'We've got nothing against the *extracomunitari* ... if only their presence didn't provoke such noticeable disorder' (*La Repubblica*, 19 May 1998). Traffic and immigrants were therefore part of the same overall problem.

Self-proclaimed experts like Pagliari played an important role in framing what was at stake in Piazza Garibaldi. ASCOM, the association of shopkeepers, similarly pressed for a permanent police presence to protect businesses and residents. In 1999 its representative for the station area claimed that leniency in the past had forced 30 per cent of 'old residents' to abandon the area and in that year alone 15 colleagues had closed up shop and moved elsewhere (*Corriere del Mezzogiorno*, 4 November 1999). Managers of smaller hotels and local tour operators periodically organized night patrols to 'protect tourists' and monitored the piazza to inform the authorities of 'levels of *degrado*' (which ranged from rubbish to illicit activities). Like others, they refuted accusations of racism, claiming that they offered an essential public service in an area that had been abandoned by the city's authorities (*Il Mattino*, 1 December 1999).

Local councillors also applied pressure on the administration to intervene in the piazza. In 1999, in response to the lack of tangible progress and what it saw as a preoccupation with the city's more historic piazzas, the centre-right-controlled *circoscrizione* (district) of Mercato-Pendino backed a project by local maverick architect Aldo Loris Rossi to cover the tracks of the Circumvesuviana railway to the immediate south of Piazza Garibaldi. This would provide an area for the buses that congested Piazza Garibaldi, open the piazza to its 'citizens' and improve its appearance for the sake of investors and tourists. In an interview, the Forza Italia vice-president of the district council, Carmine Barbuto, argued that this project would only be effective if accompanied by greater police controls and the expulsion of all '*clandestini*':

> The piazza should be a *biglietto da visita* for all those who arrive by train. It cannot be left to the mercy of everyone. As a result of a lack of attention on the part of the institutions, there are a series [long pause] of 'lobbies' in Piazza Garibaldi, which not only belong to Neapolitan organized crime but come from [long pause] other countries. On exiting the station, people find themselves in the middle of a casbah. That's not Piazza Garibaldi. There has not been a proper commercial revival in the area, because there are so many *extracomunitari,* probably illegal in my opinion, who discourage both the Neapolitan and the citizen who comes from outside the city from investing in the area. (Interview with author, 5 May 2000)

The *extracomunitario* is explicitly singled out as a noncitizen whose presence has transformed the very meaning of the piazza. Councillors and local figures defined who constituted the 'public' and the rightful users of the piazza. Drawing on personal or perceived sentiments of disorientation, fear and loss, they elaborated a public discourse about insecurity.

Through public campaigns and the local media, these 'moral entrepreneurs'[15] were able to forge a general consensus of opinion that the piazza was dangerous, unappetizing to locals and visitors, and that, of all the groups present, immigrants were the principal hazard. This strongly influenced the administration's attitude to the piazza. For instance, following a series of complaints at the end of 1999, Massimo Paolucci, DS assessor for 'Mobility' (in other words, responsible for traffic and public transport), declared: 'The [immigrant] situation is terrible and we'll have to find some solution' (*Corriere del Mezzogiorno,* 2 December 1999). The administration was regularly pressured to step up police controls in the piazza for *its* citizens. For instance, following an intense public and media campaign at the end of 1999, in which every misdemeanour in the piazza was placed under the microscope, an emergency meeting between the city's police forces, prefect and administration led to the positioning of mobile police units in front of the station and on the south side of the

---

15. Alessandro Dal Lago defines moral entrepreneurs as 'a vanguard which assumes the task of rousing a passive and ignorant public opinion' (1999: 64).

piazza. In an interview, Raffaele Tecce, the Communist Refoundation assessor for 'Normality', described the situation in which the administration found itself:

> A feeling of insecurity which has grown among the population has certainly had an impact. The administration obviously has its sensors which are the many letters it receives and the district councils. Of course these are not scientific instruments like opinion polls but in the last five years that I've been assessor I have continually received letters from citizens who complain above all about the street markets and vendors. Today a wrong association is made: street vendors – *extracomunitari* – crime; and so the media has certainly captured a changing mood among people. Until five years ago, even though Piazza Garibaldi was chaotic and congested, it was nevertheless considered a dynamic piazza of the city. Today it is seen, in my opinion wrongly, as the centre of crime. (Interview with author, 2 June 2000)

There were isolated cases of collaboration between immigrant groups and the administration. The 3 Febbraio anti-racist association, which set up base in a street off Piazza Garibaldi at the end of 1999, and the local Senegalese Association, whose headquarters were located on the south side of the piazza, pressed the administration to sort out the position of street vendors most affected by police controls. In May 2000, Raffaele Tecce, under pressure from people within his own party, reproposed the idea of an 'interethnic' market. This was to be situated in Via Bologna, a side street off the northern edge of the piazza, with licensed places for seventy immigrants. The conditions were a regular permit to stay and the commitment to trading products from the immigrant's country of origin which were compatible with tourism (although it was not clear who of the five hundred or so immigrants were to be assigned a place and what constituted 'indigenous products'). During the subsequent debates with immigrant representatives, the local CGIL (Confederazione Generale Italiana del Lavoro) trade union and political organizations, doubts were raised over the location. The street's importance as a base of wholesale distribution for immigrants would be compromised, while the lack of prior consultation with residents risked damaging the working relationship that the mainly Senegalese had formed over the previous decade. The assessor insisted that the most important thing was to start immediately and promised that more markets would follow. The plan was, however, opposed at the district council meeting of San Lorenzo-Vicaria (with only one vote in favour from a Communist Refoundation councillor and the rest of the Centre-Left abstaining fearing residents' unrest). Instead, a provocative counterproposal by the small neo-Fascist party Fiamma Tricolore (Tricolour Flame) to relocate the market in Piazza Plebiscito was passed by the centre-right majority, with the support of two centre-left councillors (from the PPI and the SDI).

> The district council of San Lorenzo-Vicaria, … given that … Vicaria is one of the most
> rundown areas of the city, with a worrying presence of an arrogant and diffuse *micro-*
> *criminalità,* drug addicts, dealers, prostitutes and unruly immigrants; that the presence
> of a market would increase the ghettoization of an area that should represent the city's
> *biglietto da visita*; proposes that the street market for immigrants be located in Via
> Petrarca, Piazza del Plebiscito, Posillipo or the Chiaia-San Ferdinando district. (San
> Lorenzo-Vicaria District Council, Order of Business, 15 June 2000)

With only consultative powers, the district council could not block the
plan, and despite protests by a small group of residents, hoteliers and
district councillors, the street market opened at the end of July 2000.[16]
While it represented a courageous act in the face of a hostile 'public',
the market's impact was limited. It was much smaller than originally
planned, others did not follow and, significantly, it was located *off* Piazza Garibaldi. This isolated attempt at challenging public opinion and
addressing a situation of conflict was still bound to a need to legitimate the immigrant presence, exemplified by the assessor's insistence
on 'indigenous products'. Therefore, while individual members of the
administration attempted to integrate immigrants into projects of urban
renewal or, like Bassolino, disputed simplistic links between immigrants
and crime (*Corriere del Mezzogiorno,* 4 November 1999), the general
political slant did not contest, but rather often endorsed, the widely held
view that immigrants posed a problem for a permanent improvement of
the piazza.

Media representations of immigration and Piazza Garibaldi

During the second half of the 1990s, the local mainstream press played
a fundamental role in constructing a public discourse about Piazza Garibaldi. It transmitted the 'primary definitions' of hoteliers and politicians
and framed representations of the station area through a simplification
and dramatization of its perceived problems. For the first time since its
redesign in the 1960s, Piazza Garibaldi became a perpetual, and at times
obsessive, focus of attention. This was not due to a sudden increase in
actual events but because the piazza itself had become newsworthy: this
was the city's gateway ('*il biglietto da visita*') in the grip of social and
urban turmoil ('*degrado*') and was now inseparable from the question of
immigration.

---

16. During a roadblock, some residents demanded that the market at least be moved to the parallel
and much wider Corso Novara. As John Foot notes in his study of clashes over immigrants in Turin:
'Micro-conflicts often involve a simple request that the "problem" be moved elsewhere, perhaps even
a few hundred yards away' (Foot 2001a: 16).

Numerous studies have indicated how the Italian media's coverage of immigration during the 1990s became increasingly framed around questions of security and political responses to the phenomenon (Dal Lago 1999; Cotesta 1999; Sciortino and Colombo 2004). An analysis of the Turin-based newspaper *La Stampa* discovered that over 40 per cent of articles on immigration between 1992 and 2001 regarded themes of deviance or public order (with a noticeable peak at the end of the decade), 25 per cent dealt with legislation, while reports about immigrants' participation in the labour market, which had been central to initial debates about immigration during the late 1970s and early 1980s, practically disappeared (Sciortino and Colombo 2004). Positive representations of immigration, which amounted to a tiny proportion of news items,[17] tended to focus on its cultural contributions (such as cuisine and traditional festivals) to an emergent 'multicultural' society, but these were nevertheless subordinate to a dominant discourse that defined immigrants in terms of numbers, crime rates and citizens' feelings of security.

Early reports on immigration in the Neapolitan press often drew on the curiosity factor, and the coincidental accumulation of stories would occasionally warrant closer attention. In November 1980 one of the first discussions in *Il Mattino* about the non-Western foreign presence in Naples followed in the wake of previous reports of a robbery involving North Africans and the discovery of the body of a Somali who had starved to death in the port. The signs of a growing interest were cut short by a more extraordinary event: during the evening on the same day of the article's publication (23 November 1980), Naples was hit by an earthquake, and over the next few years very little was written on the subject of 'coloured workers'. At the end of the 1980s, a series of attacks on immigrant labourers in the agricultural area to the north of Naples, in particular the murder of South African political refugee Jerry Maslo in Villa Literno in 1989, attracted widespread media attention and triggered a national debate on racism in Italian society. At the local level, however, there was general consensus that Naples, unlike other cities, did not suffer such problems: 'Naples is not like Florence'[18] (*Il Mattino,* 23 March 1990); 'Naples does not show signs of intolerance. It's true that there are many immigrants and their numbers are increasing' (*La Repubblica,* 15 April 1990). During the heated discussions that preceded the 1990 Martelli immigration law,

---

17. A separate study of immigration-related news between 1991 and 1997 in five newspapers (*Corriere della Sera, Il Resto del Carlino, La Nazione, Il Messaggero* and *Il Mattino*) found that only 8 percent of the total 11,300 articles regarded cultural and social events involving immigrants, while only 5 percent concerned moments of cooperation or solidarity between Italians and immigrants (Cotesta 1999: 393).

18. Florence hit the headlines in spring 1990 following a series of violent assaults on immigrants.

newspapers in Naples began to spotlight immigrants in the station area. Overcrowded hotels were described as ghettoes after they were raided by police (*La Repubblica,* 15 April 1990), while there was also an increasing insistence upon the correlation between immigrants and crime: '*Camorristi* with black skin' (*Il Mattino,* 23 March 1990); 'Blacks are not always the victims' (*Il Mattino,* 25 April 1990). But although some reports saw this particular immigrant presence as having a deleterious impact on the city at large, Piazza Garibaldi itself was never considered at risk. Moreover, once the Martelli Law was passed, both the station area and immigration reverted to being mundane sources of news.

With the G7 summit in 1994, representations of Piazza Garibaldi abruptly changed. The G7 led to unprecedented media interest in the piazza and its possible role in a resurgent city, and, crucially, the piazza's fate was now indelibly tied to the question of immigration in Naples.[19] A new discourse about Piazza Garibaldi was accompanied by a series of discursive and stylistic breaks in the press's coverage. First, the topographical layout of many articles notably altered. Headlines and photographs were no longer simply descriptive tools but instant signifiers of the (problematic) relationship between the piazza and immigrants. For example, a report in *La Repubblica* (22 June 1994) about the cleanup of the station area for the G7 juxtaposes two images – a row of ceremonial guards and an immigrant peddler – to underline the opposition between the desired image of an orderly city and the unwanted presence of certain individuals. In an article about increased police controls in the piazza six years later (*Corriere del Mezzogiorno,* 16 February 2000), the headline 'The Prefect Fortifies Piazza Garibaldi' is placed above a photograph of a municipal policeman inspecting the car boot of a black African. The message is unequivocal: the controls will be rigorous, and nothing will be hidden from the eyes of the law.

Second, the vocabulary used to describe immigration shifted. Crude and racist expressions widely used by the press in the 1980s and early 1990s were either dropped ('chocolate-coloured skin', 'negro') or went out of fashion ('*vu'cumprà*'[20]), as the basic lexicon was whittled down to apparently neutral sounding denominations such as '*extracomunitario*', '*clandestino*' and '*immigrato*'. This quasi-legal and political terminology

---

19. Immigration and Piazza Garibaldi became inseparable topics of news. For example, during the last four months of 1999, over 90 per cent of articles about immigration in Naples in the local pages of *Il Mattino* concerned the station area. Conversely, over the same period, almost 70 per cent of news regarding Piazza Garibaldi made some form of reference to immigrants, even when the central subject was new parking arrangements or changes to the bus services.

20. '*Vu' cumprà*' was supposed to be the transcription of a North African pronunciation of the words '*Vuoi comprare?*' (Do you want to buy?). Once used to label all immigrants, the term was occasionally resurrected in the Neapolitan press in news stories involving West African street vendors.

6 MERCOLEDÌ 16 FEBBRAIO 2000   CRONACA/NAPOLI

Da domani tutta zona della stazione sarà presidiata dalle forze dell'ordine. Particolare attenzione agli extracomunitari

Il prefetto blinda piazza Garibaldi

Scatta il piano contro la criminalità: due camper mobili di polizia e vigili urbani

Controlli dei vigili urbani in piazza Garibaldi

Illustration 12.1. 'The Prefect Fortifies Piazza Garibaldi' (*Corriere del Mezzogiorno,* 16 February 2000).

was ultimately far more effective: not only did it circumvent the growing controversy that surrounded the casual use of derogatory nicknames during the early 1990s (Sciortino and Colombo 2004), but it established the otherness of immigrants as non-Italians (and non-Neapolitans). After 1994, racial imagery would instead be used to distinguish the flurry of Piazza Garibaldi from the rest of the city centre. Certain lower-class areas of the centre had themselves once been orientalized: the Forcella neighbourhood, for instance, was traditionally dubbed the 'Casbah'. After 1994, such labels would be almost exclusively reserved for Piazza Garibaldi. These included: 'miniature Africa' (*La Repubblica,* 27 October 1996); 'multiracial chaos' (*La Repubblica,* 20 May 1998); 'frontier zone swarming with people of every race' (*Il Mattino,* 12 September 1999); 'the dirty face of Naples' (*Il Mattino,* 3 May 2000) and 'African bidonville' (*Corriere del Mezzogiorno,* 3 May 2000).

This racialization of public space was combined with axiomatic discourses about immigration and stereotypes about Naples past, present and future to form a 'public idiom', in other words the negotiation of a style and the assumption of consensus between the writer and his/her targeted audience (Fowler 1991: 48). A detailed illustration of the public idiom used to depict Piazza Garibaldi is provided by an article published in *Corriere del Mezzogiorno* (1 December 1999) describing the weekly gatherings of Eastern Europeans in front of the central station, under the title: 'The Sunday meeting: five thousand *extracomunitari* exchange "parcels", embraces and letters'. The piece, written by Carlo Franco, a senior Neapolitan journalist who had made a name for himself reporting on the 1980 earthquake for *Il Mattino,* was part of a week-long campaign on Piazza Garibaldi that began with news about hoteliers' patrols in the station area and culminated with the news of a meeting between police forces to discuss law and order in the city centre.

The article opens with a commonsensical image of Piazza Garibaldi: 'It is the doorway to the city that has fallen into disrepute'. The initial impact of 'four to five thousand immigrants' on exiting the station is 'awesome'. While a Sunday crowd of Neapolitans and tourists of similar proportions in Piazza Plebiscito would be welcomed, in Piazza Garibaldi the throng becomes a menace. Franco sets up a basic opposition between 'us' (Neapolitans) and 'them' (immigrants), which enables him to speak on behalf of the city's indigenous inhabitants: 'Why do all the races of the world meet in piazza Garibaldi? To answer this mystery, we spent a day in the piazza, where we had the extraordinary experience of feeling foreigners in a city which we thought to know like the back of our hands.' Piazza Garibaldi, piazza only in name, is presented as a sort of open wound. Evocative expressions such as 'plague' and 'little Saigon' indicate its aberrant state. When immigrants leave at the end of the day, 'They let themselves be swallowed up by the immense city'. In other words, the issue is the assembly of immigrants *in Piazza Garibaldi,* and not their presence in Naples which is portrayed as an indomitable beast.

The investigation serves to answer a series of questions: 'What jobs do they do, what groups do they frequent?' The fact that 'no one, unfortunately, will ever know' allows the journalist to voice his own presumptions. No distinction is made between irregular and regular immigrants. Their presence in Piazza Garibaldi renders them all '*clandestini*', and therefore they have no legitimate claim to the space. The commercial activities are 'naturally unlawful'. The collective use of the makeshift postal service and market in the middle of the piazza raises suspicions that somewhere the Russian and Albanian (but not the local) mafia have a hand in the matter. While 'nobody controls and tries to understand the hidden dangers', the piazza is, at the same time, subject to a more sinister power.

The piazza is also a promiscuous space which seems to both lure and disturb the journalist. The younger women – nubile bodies with 'breathtakingly high miniskirts' – are no longer in the grasp of Italian men, who have been ousted by foreign rivals. The allusion to prostitution is implicit: the women wear heavy makeup, and kisses are conducted with 'excessive enthusiasm'. This is reiterated in the journalist's final climax: 'Everything and everybody become exchangeable goods'. But the presence of so many women autonomously assembled in public space, distant and unattainable, is at the same time threatening. The description bears semblance to the British tabloid press's portrayal of the Greenham Common peace protests in the 1980s, where groups of women protesters were represented as 'out of place', while the air base, objectively an eyesore, became part of a 'taken-for-granted landscape' (Cresswell 1996: 132). Similarly, the (ugly) Piazza Garibaldi, imagined as a pleasant gateway, is disturbed by hordes of foreign women. What the journalist 'sees' is translated into a consensual argument that links immigrants to the negative conditions in the piazza.

In the following day's edition of the paper, the same journalist 'returns' to gather the views of hoteliers and shopkeepers 'besieged' by immigrants and '*degrado*'. The unpleasant sights (and smells) of the previous article are intertwined within a new narrative about the plight of indigenous users. An unambiguous heading is employed: 'How can Piazza Garibaldi be saved?' Important figures are chosen and each is accorded a photograph: Mario Pagliari, Michele Cotuogno, the owner of Hotel Cavour, who has 'never left the trench', the heroic chemist who stays open at night, a bona fide Neapolitan pastry maker who threatens to close up shop and a young successful businesswoman who feels abandoned by her local professional association. Under a subtitle 'This is what we think', their responses are summarized. All call for more controls and commitment from the administration towards the problem of Piazza Garibaldi.

Paradigms raised by the veteran journalist were commonly replicated in the local media to interpret the piazza: a space of urban decay, invaded by outsiders, an obstacle to tourism, crime infested and dangerous. Carlo Franco's description of Piazza Garibaldi resembled Matilde Serao's chronicles of the 'bowels' of nineteenth-century Naples but devoid of the philanthropic guiding spirit and with a Neapolitan male angst substituting Serao's bourgeois paternalism. On other occasions, parody and sarcasm were deployed to heighten the drama: 'Greetings from the casbah! No this isn't the Medina of Tunis or the market in Algiers but Piazza Garibaldi, one of the postcards of Naples reduced to a wretched fair of street stalls. It's easy to imagine what sort of impression this had on the middle-aged Austrian tourist and his buxom wife who arrived yesterday with the overnight train' (*Il Mattino*, 15 September 1999). The northern European tourists unwittingly get off the train in the wrong continent. The colourful description in *Il Mattino* in 1963 of a 'Piazza Garibaldi by night' populated with virtuous deviants now appeared to be a comical anomaly of history. By the late 1990s, the space was no longer conceived as quintessentially Neapolitan. The nocturnal piazza was unanimously labelled an '*inferno*', while the situation hardly improved during the daytime.

There were few voices that countered the negative portrayal of immigrants in Piazza Garibaldi in the second half of the 1990s. The CGIL trade union, whose regional headquarters were located to the immediate north of the piazza, was accorded limited space in media debates about the piazza. Pleas for sensitive social policies and fairer treatment of immigrants nevertheless coincided with calls for stricter police controls, crime prevention measures and public-private investments to encourage the economic revival of the area. On rare occasions, Piazza Garibaldi would be used by the local press to represent the 'experience' of immigration in Naples, in other words, what they ate, wore or sold and what they thought about new legislation. In such cases, immigrants were typically at the mercy of the journalist's discretion. Indeed, reports often disclosed a fleeting encounter with the immigrant world: 'The trip around on a Vespa' (*La Repubblica,* 22 June 1994) or 'Let's pop over to Piazza Garibaldi' (*La Repubblica,* 16 February 1997).

The limited influence of the immigrant's voice was exemplified during the media's reaction in May 2000 to the police's arrest and assault of Abdou Dia Aziz, a Senegalese street vendor who had resisted the attempted confiscation of his merchandise. This event, which took place in Vomero and was uninteresting in itself, became newsworthy because locals had intervened to defend the street vendor, one of whom was arrested and spent a night in jail with the immigrant. Indeed, the pivot of the press's reporting of the story, which spanned four days, was Massimo Venditti: the honest and hard-working Neapolitan who immediately went to the defence of the unjustly treated Abdou. To add to the drama, the issue was also politicized. The left parties declared solidarity with Abdou and Massimo and censured the police's violence, while the right-wing opposition unconditionally defended the police force and called for a clampdown on illegal commercial activities. Amidst the controversy, two journalists from *La Repubblica* (19 May 2000) turned their attention to Piazza Garibaldi in order to investigate immigrants' trade in counterfeit items. They interviewed the president of the Senegalese Association, Pape Seck, who explained that 300,000 lire (150 euros) was given to new arrivals to help set them on their way. He confirmed that most bought their goods from the wholesalers around Piazza Garibaldi, to which the journalists added: 'most of them counterfeit brands'. From 'civil' Vomero and police brutality, attention switched to immigration, illegality and Piazza Garibaldi.

Pape Seck wrote a letter to *La Repubblica,* complaining that the article had insinuated the Senegalese Association's complicity with illegal commercial activities: 'I ask you to rectify the way in which you described the position of our association, which firmly rejects all illicit activities as well as every racist attempt to marginalize one of the communities which is collaborating with our city to create a peaceful and tolerant multiethnic society' (letter dated 19 May 2000, copy given to author during interview). Unlike Mario Pagliari's missive to the same paper, which had resulted in an immediate response from Bassolino, Seck's letter was not published nor was there any form of public or private apology from the journalists concerned. In spite of his references to 'our city' (ironically the Senegalese Association was located next door to the Hotel Terminus), the president had no public means of contesting the misinterpretation of his words. The local media did not conspire to silence the voices of immigrants: such voices were simply not included in the construction of consensual representations of Piazza Garibaldi. The press worked through and built on the opinions and statements of politicians, local public figures and the police. These 'primary definitions', in the words of Hall et al., 'command the field of signification relatively unchallenged' (1978: 69). Because the situation in Piazza Garibaldi was already considered dramatic, there was little concern for setting up alternative viewpoints. As noncitizens, immigrants forfeited their 'rights of reply' (ibid.).

Chapter 13

Mapping Immigrant Experiences In and Of Piazza Garibaldi

Extracomunitario is like extra-virgin olive oil: it's better quality. (Tunisian street vendor advertising wares in Piazza Gesù Nuovo, *centro antico,* 2000)

In stark contrast to Piazza Plebiscito, public representations of Piazza Garibaldi were obsessed with everyday details. While disruptive elements were ejected from the prophylactic representations of a civic Piazza Plebiscito, in Piazza Garibaldi these were repeatedly amplified as part of a call for 'regenerative' action. Immigrants in the piazza were at one level extremely visible – as bodies that were described, imagined and censured – but at the same time were absent as protagonists in public debates about the piazza's role as the gateway to the *centro storico.* Moreover, such debates very rarely referenced available statistics (which, for all their limitations, indicated a resident population in the three surrounding districts in 1998 of less than two thousand immigrants (Comune di Napoli 1999a) and a burgeoning immigrant economy around the piazza[1]), but rather depended more readily upon guesstimates and narratives of decline provided by 'indigenous' inhabitants and businesspeople.

---

1. Admittedly, it is difficult to estimate the number of immigrants in the station area during the second half of the 1990s. First of all, most spent a lot of their time in Piazza Garibaldi but lived elsewhere. Second, the piazza itself was divided between three districts: San Lorenzo-Vicaria, Mercato-Pendino and Poggioreale-Zona Industriale, which together covered a large swathe of the *centro storico* and the east of the city. The population of less than two thousand did not correspond to the actual number of immigrant residents who were either registered elsewhere or did not possess documents. Nevertheless, this figure is sobering compared to the claims of tens of thousands frequently made in the local press. Similarly, city council records concerning local economic activities in the station area refer to a much larger zone which comprises Piazza Mercato and Via Duomo to the west of Piazza Garibaldi. According to the assessor for 'Normality', Raffaele Tecce, there were approximately sixty registered immigrant businesses centred around Vasto and the northern edge of Piazza Garibaldi (interview with author, 2 June 2000).

Academic interest in Piazza Garibaldi during the 1990s also differed markedly to the discussions about Piazza Plebiscito. The piazza was not inextricably bound up with a debate about urban renewal under the Bassolino administration but instead provided a (depoliticized) site to describe, and more rarely to study, the phenomenon of immigration. The only local researcher to examine Piazza Garibaldi in any depth during the period was the geographer Fabio Amato at the Oriental Institute, who published two short accounts of immigrant street vendors in the area. The first study (Amato 1992), based on a month-long observation in the station area, concluded that the zone was undergoing a process of 'Africanization'. Observations were tested in a second inquiry (Amato 1997), and the central argument was adjusted to account for the arrival of new groups (Eastern Europeans and Chinese). On both occasions Amato admits the scientific limits of his descriptive surveys, claiming that they present a first stage prior to detailed analysis of what is a highly complex area (ibid.: 23). Although they are clearly limited in their scope (there is no reference to political and media debates and little discussion of non-economic uses of the space), the two studies are important as historical sources and, where appropriate, are compared with the findings of my own research.[2]

The pretext of this ethnography is not to reveal the unmediated, 'real' Piazza Garibaldi or to provide a definitive account of immigrants in the station area during the period but to examine uses of the piazza and unearth different points of view. Twelve semi-structured interviews were carried out with institutional figures, such as the Palestinian head of the CGIL immigrant bureau and individuals who had a long-standing relationship with the piazza, for example immigrant shop assistants. These dwelt on past and present relationships with the station area and discussed public representations of the piazza. In addition, visits to Piazza Garibaldi with immigrant 'guides' – a Pakistani (Madji), a Pole (Petra), a Guinean (Ousmanne) and a Senegalese (Diop) – lasting between one and five hours and leading to meetings and conversations with other people, sought to sketch the various relationships with the piazza, to understand the levels of significance attributed to the space and to gather thoughts over related issues such as security.

---

2. More recently there have been sympathetic literary portraits of Piazza Garibaldi, including Ermanno Rea's novel *Napoli Ferrovia* (2007), a personalized account of the station area, and Antonio Capuano's documentary film *Bianco e Nero alla Ferrovia* (2006), which recounts a day in the life of the piazza. The release of the DVD of this film was accompanied by a book with essays by local academics on immigration and Piazza Garibaldi (Rea et al. 2006). Most of these essays were somewhat journalistic in tone and did not critically engage with public discourses about the piazza.

All African and Asians met were male, while Poles and Ukrainians were predominantly female. Most were aged between twenty and forty years old. Many of the Eastern Europeans met in the piazza were undocumented and employed *al nero* (unofficial, cash-in-hand work) and so were not in a position to regularize their position. Petra, a part-time domestic worker who attended a 'cultural operator' course run by a social cooperative, had a *permesso di soggiorno* (residence permit). Madji, the Pakistani, and Ousmanne, the Guinean, had both applied for documents and were awaiting the outcome, while Diop, the Senegalese who had been in Naples for nearly ten years, possessed a *carta di soggiorno* that provided greater stability than the basic permit to stay, which required regular renewal.[3]

Each individual had a different migration project. Some intended to eventually return home, others planned to settle in Italy. Nearly everyone had come to Naples for economic reasons.[4] Abdoul, a Senegalese man employed as a technician and sales assistant in an Italian-owned shop which sold goods in bulk to street vendors, arrived in Naples in 1993 after a period in Milan. 'I came to Naples because here it was easier for an *extracomunitario clandestino* to find work. In Milan, after having worked for a period, I found myself doing nothing for three weeks. Back then I knew some Neapolitans who advised me to come down here, but I didn't know any Senegalese' (interview with author, 21 March 2000). Petra claimed that while most of her Polish compatriots came to the city for the (limited) economic opportunities, she was drawn by her 'curiosity' for Italy, although she ended up in Naples not by choice, but because she found work through an Italian job agency based in Poland. Most of the Africans and Pakistanis worked as street vendors or as porters for the nearby markets and wholesale stores. Some of the Senegalese worked (or had once worked, in the case of Diop who was now the president of a 'multi-ethnic' association) in shops in Vasto, to the immediate north of the piazza. All the Poles and Ukrainians were employed in the domestic or hotel sector. There were no Polish street vendors in the station area as compared to the mid-1990s, when they had semi-permanent pitches on Corso Garibaldi (Amato 1997: 21). Some of the immigrants who were undocumented or who had only ever lived in Naples hoped to move to the North to look for more stable forms of employment (like Madji, who

---

3. My collaboration with a volunteer-run drop-in centre offering free legal advice was essential for establishing contacts with undocumented immigrants and for overcoming the mistrust noted by Amato in his discussion of street vendors in Piazza Garibaldi (1997: 22).

4. The only exception was the Palestinian head of the immigrant service at the CGIL, who had come to Naples in 1981 to study at the university.

intended to join his brother in Bolzano as soon as he received his documents), while most of those who had spent time in the North said that they preferred Naples because it was less racist and more relaxed, despite the precarious economic situation and the hectic nature of everyday life.

The Piazza Garibaldi that emerged during fieldwork possessed an intricate order that was structured around overlapping boundaries and itineraries. This contrasted to the typical media images of the piazza as a permanently chaotic bazaar populated by an indiscriminate mass of '*clandestini*'. The immigrant presence altered according to the time of day and year. None of my informants had anything to do with the space at night. During the summer, and August in particular, the piazza was far less busy. Domestic workers were laid off by their employees and returned home, while many street vendors sold their wares on beaches or at inland festivals or went to work on the tomato harvest. West Africans and Asians (Chinese and Pakistanis) were concentrated on the north side of the piazza and in the streets of Vasto, while Eastern Europeans tended to stick to the south side when they visited the area, primarily on Thursdays and Sundays.[5] Maghrebis (principally Algerians and Tunisians in Piazza Garibaldi) were perhaps the most spatially dispersed, although they were more present on the north side.[6]

This 'ethnic'/national distribution tended to be reflected in the particular patronage of bars. A bar on the corner of Piazza Principe Umberto in Vasto had become a haunt for Maghrebis, the bars along the north side of Piazza Garibaldi were frequented by Africans and immigrant street vendors, while the pizzerias and bars on the south side and along Corso Lucci were meeting places for Poles. The area in front of the station was mainly a gathering place for Ukrainians but also, to a lesser extent, Poles, Moldovans, Romanians, as well as a few small groups of Pakistanis and Maghrebis. According to Poles met in the bars and pizzerias, this was the domain of new arrivals. One young Ukrainian male met under the *proboscide*, who had recently come to Italy after his mother found employment as a domestic worker, claimed that he worked all week but came every Sunday if only for half an hour: 'I don't know many people in the piazza, but it's a relaxing sort of place'.

The Duchesca market to the west of the piazza was a sort of interstice where Eastern Europeans, Maghrebis and West Africans all went to buy clothes and shoes. In the streets to the west and north of this market

5. According to an Italian friend of Petra, domestic workers meet on Thursday afternoons because this had been the traditional time off for waiters and domestic workers in Naples.

6. Amato noted in 1997: 'The Maghrebis are the ones who use the piazza the most: they meet in couples or in groups and discuss animatedly leaning on the steps of shops in the streets on the northern side of the piazza' (Amato 1997: 22).

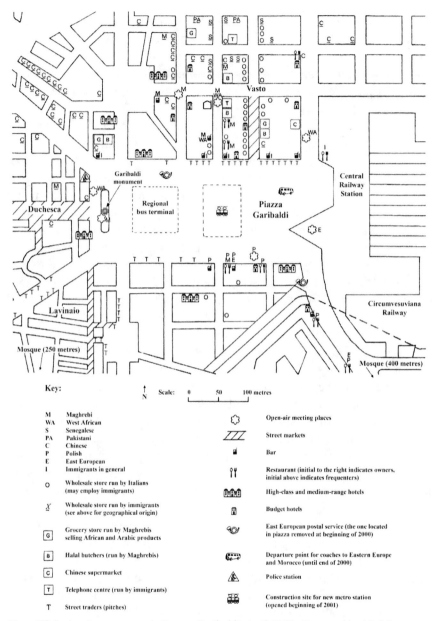

Map 13.1. Immigrant spaces in Piazza Garibaldi, April 2003. *Designed by Nick Dines.*

Key:

M	Maghrebi
WA	West African
S	Senegalese
PA	Pakistani
C	Chinese
P	Polish
E	East European
I	Immigrants in general
O	Wholesale store run by Italians (may employ immigrants)
X	Wholesale store run by immigrants (see above for geographical origin)
G	Grocery store run by Maghrebis selling African and Arabic products
B	Halal butchers (run by Maghrebis)
C	Chinese supermarket
T	Telephone centre (run by immigrants)
T	Street traders (pitches)

⬡	Open-air meeting places
▨	Street markets
⌿	Bar
⦵⦵	Restaurant (initial to the right indicates owners, initial above indicates frequenters)
🏨	High-class and medium-range hotels
🏨	Budget hotels
⏚	East European postal service (the one located in piazza removed at beginning of 2000)
🚌	Departure point for coaches to Eastern Europe and Morocco (until end of 2000)
△	Police station
🚋	Construction site for new metro station (opened beginning of 2001)

Scale: 0   50   100 metres   N

were concentrated most of the Chinese-owned wholesale shops (usually distinguishable by the red lanterns hanging outside), which sold clothes produced in local factories or cheap electrical and household items, such as alarm clocks and radios, imported from China. The spatial arrangement of the piazza was discernible during guided visits with immigrant informants. While Diop and Ousmanne remained in Vasto, three separate outings with Petra kept to the opposite side of the piazza. Madji was the most mobile because of his job as an 'international phone-line seller' (see below). Although he was the only one to cross the piazza, he still spent most of the time on the north side in the company of other Pakistanis and West Africans.

Just as the media often employed an elastic definition of Piazza Garibaldi that extended as far as the industrial zone of Gianturco (one mile to the east of the central railway station) when crimes were involved[7], so did immigrants possess multiple perceptions of 'Piazza Garibaldi'. For West Africans, for example, 'Piazza Garibaldi' encompassed the streets of Vasto, where their economy and meeting places were situated. For many Poles and Ukrainians who worked in private houses in suburbs or surrounding towns, the piazza was their principal contact with central Naples. Young Polish domestic workers living in Vomero referred to the piazza as 'the *centro storico*', where they would go to send parcels home or catch the coach to Poland. For them, it represented the quintessential Neapolitan space on account of the chaos and the incomprehensible dialect spoken by locals – characteristics that they did not associate with middle-class Vomero (interview with author, 12 March 1999).

For the majority of immigrants, Piazza Garibaldi was a multifunctional space. As well as providing a recreational place for meetings and refreshments, the piazza was a link with countries of origin. Polish and Moroccan coach lines and travel agencies operated in and around the piazza (although in 2001 most coaches were moved to the western district of Bagnoli, after work began on the new underground line). A thrice-weekly overnight bus service to Marseilles that connected with the ferry to Algiers departed from Piazza Principe Umberto. This provided the cheapest route to Algeria and was commonly used by Algerian 'suitcase traders', who rarely remained in Naples for more than a few hours (Peraldi 2007). Until the beginning of 2000, an informal delivery service with the Ukraine and Poland was run on Sunday mornings by an assortment of vans parked in the centre of the piazza (see figure 13.1). Despite accusations in the local media that this was a cover for the Russian and Albanian mafia, all those asked said that they regularly used the service. A middle-aged Polish man explained that it was quicker and cheaper than the official postal system. Parcels and money would arrive two days later at his family's doorstep in Poland. The man had never experienced any problems: he knew the driver and therefore trusted him. The situa-

---

7. In April 1999, a Japanese tourist was robbed and murdered by two young Poles outside the deserted Gianturco metro station after he had boarded the wrong train in the central station.

tion would change at Christmas and Easter, when demand increased and new drivers suddenly appeared offering extra services. According to the Pole, these were the types to be avoided. Following their removal at the start of 2000, the vans switched to an area in front of Campi Flegrei, Naples's second railway station, on the west side of the city, but shortly afterwards reappeared, albeit in fewer numbers, behind Hotel Terminus on the south-east corner of Piazza Garibaldi.

Piazza Garibaldi's traditional function as a transport hub had also been appropriated and renegotiated. Moroccan and Chinese hawkers used the piazza as an interchange as they moved across the province, while the regional bus to Villa Literno and the tomato fields, which departed from the centre of the piazza, was typically full of West Africans. The underground and suburban trains on Sunday mornings were crowded with East European women as they travelled in from other parts of the city and surrounding towns and villages. Strategically positioned at the heart of the region's public transport network, the piazza became the natural focal point for groups spread across a wide geographical area. A young Polish woman met in the piazza admitted: 'I don't know why we always come to this piazza, because, in fact, it's ugly. … But everybody meets here. I do as well, even though I might only stay a short while. Often in the afternoon I go for trips to Sorrento or Amalfi' (interview with author, 19 March 2000).

Illustration 13.1. The postal service in Piazza Garibaldi, September 1999. *Photograph by Roberta Valerio.*

The station area had also become a key residential space for immigrants due to the cheaper rents and the relatively easier task of finding housing. Many of the informants lived around Piazza Garibaldi. Ousmanne from Guinea used to live in Via Torino near the CGIL headquarters but had recently moved in with three Senegalese friends in an apartment on Corso Novara. Numerous Poles, on the other hand, lived around Porta Nolana, to the south of the piazza. Petra rented her flat in this area from a Neapolitan man whom she had befriended in 1996 under the *proboscide*. Other immigrants who had more stable forms of income or who lived with Neapolitans had moved out of the area. Some of the hotels were associated with a particular group. For instance, hotels Mignon and Dora were both predominantly patronized by Senegalese (Abdoul, the shop assistant, stayed in the latter for forty-five days when he first arrived in Naples), while Hotel Charlie in Via Milano was the preferred base for Algerian traders when they came to Piazza Garibaldi to buy goods. Abdoul explained: 'It's the cheapest area in the city centre, because when an immigrant comes down to Naples, he can find a hotel around the station for fifteen to twenty thousand lire a night. Instead, when he goes into the city he won't find that price. So perhaps this is one of the reasons why there are more immigrants around the station'.

The station area was also significant for religious purposes. Since 1998, a Polish mass had been celebrated every Sunday afternoon in a church on nearby Piazza Nolana, although most of those spoken to tended to go to the more established mass in Mergellina, on the other side of the city centre. Two of the city's three mosques were situated close to Piazza Garibaldi: one in Corso Lucci and the other to the north of Piazza Mercato (while the third was situated in Via Depretis, at the far end of the *Rettifilo*).

Piazza Garibaldi's principal function for immigrants was as an economic space which recalled its traditional role as a place of commercial exchange. Even for the Eastern Europeans, the piazza was a place where domestic jobs were advertised, bought and sold. Until the spring of 2000, the pavements on the northern edge of the piazza were brimming with street vendors. Although not strictly adhered to, there was a generally acknowledged 'ethnic' division of work: Pakistanis sold cheap *bijouterie* (either bought from Vasto, the traditional centre of jewellery wholesalers in Naples, or imported directly from Pakistan, as in the case of one individual who had acquired his permit to stay); Chinese sold electronic gadgetry or clothing items; a number of Maghrebis sold cassettes of Arabic songs (Amato 1992: 1997); while West Africans 'specialized' in counterfeit goods, such as caps, belts and CDs produced by Neapolitans. As Abdoul pointed out: 'Generally immigrants only sell cheap stuff. The

Senegalese mainly sell bootleg compact discs, like this one here! [pointing to his nephew who is in his shop] It's their role! When it comes to CDs, the Senegalese are the majority!'

As well as being the centre of 'ethnic businesses', such as African restaurants, grocery stores, halal butchers and hairdressers, Vasto was the heart of a wholesale economy that had developed around immigrants. This area attracted buyers from across Italy (Senegalese street vendors interviewed by Giuseppe Scidà in Catania referred to their trips to Naples to purchase wares (Scidà and Pollini 1993: 164)) and abroad, for instance Marseilles or Algiers (Coppola and Memoli 1997), and even as far afield as Dakar and Lagos.[8] Although Naples did not compare with Milan or Rome in terms of its immigrant population, it had nevertheless become a key node in a transnational trade network (Russo Krauss and Schmoll 2006; Peraldi 2007). Many Neapolitan '*ingrossisti*' employed immigrant assistants in order to maximize sales, as Abdoul explained: 'To make a shop work, of course you need either a Senegalese or a Moroccan, at least someone who speaks different languages! ... There's another fact too: when a Senegalese sees somebody from their country in the shop, he enters and at least tries to buy something. For this reason they prefer Senegalese: it's a way of attracting people'. Some immigrants had opened their own shops, such as two Senegalese-run stores in Via Torino specializing in African and Asian crafts, and the Chinese immigrants who had been longest in Naples had shops in Vasto (rather than in the area around Via Carriera Grande to the north-west of Piazza Garibaldi, where the majority of Chinese businesses were concentrated). From the end of the 1990s there had been a downturn in trade, partly due to increased police controls deterring immigrants away and partly because Rome had recently established itself as a new commercial centre, especially in the wake of an influx of Chinese wholesalers. The Neapolitan colleague of Abdoul, who had worked in the same shop for eight years, noticed a marked drop in business:

> There was much more work eight years ago. Now it's not even fifty per cent of what it was before. Business has decreased greatly. The piazza has lost its wholesale role. Most go to Rome, which has become the centre as far as the supply of merchandise is concerned. ... People still come from Sardinia and all parts of Italy to buy here. But they first go to Rome and then, if at all, come down here. (Interview with author, 21 March 2000)

Abdoul regarded the Chinese as his principle competitors in the wholesale economy. The bulk of the goods which he sold were imported from

---

8. During a trip to Senegal at the end of 2000, I met a trader in Dakar's Sandaga Market who sold shoes he had bought around Piazza Garibaldi in Naples.

China, but the same items were now being offered at cheaper prices in the recently opened Chinese stores in the vicinity.

The piazza was also the setting for ingenious entrepreneurial ventures. For instance, Madji, who was still awaiting regularization, earned about a hundred thousand lire (fifty euros) by buying up an international phone line on his mobile phone for a day, which he would proceed to sell to immigrants at one thousand lire a minute. Of all the immigrants met, he knew the most nationalities (North and West Africans, Pakistanis and Poles), and during the course of the four hours we spent together in the piazza he was repeatedly asked by passersby if he had a 'line' (to which he would reply 'No, perhaps tomorrow'). Elsewhere, a Pole set up a portable newspaper and magazine stand (in a suitcase) under the *proboscide* on a Sunday, stocking up on weekly visits to Poland.

Nearly all those workers who had been in Naples for a few years stressed the important contribution that immigrants had made to the local economy. A Senegalese met in Via Bologna exclaimed: 'Ten years ago there was nothing in Vasto. … Without us the area would die, and they know it'. Diop similarly stated: 'If you go to speak with the shopkeepers in Lavinaio, they'll tell you that they're happy if the immigrants put up their stalls, because they draw in people. Others come to buy' (interview with author, 17 March 2000). A middle-aged Polish male once employed as a domestic but who now worked intermittently as a decorator receiving eight hundred thousand lire a month (four hundred euros – the average wage for Eastern European domestic workers) extended this claim to a more general level: 'Those who pick tomatoes are Moroccans, Tunisians, Poles, Ukrainians. Without us there'd be no tomatoes. And who cleans the homes of Italians? Immigrants do' (interview with author, 12 March 2000). Petra argued that the Duchesca market depended on Polish and other immigrant clients: 'They live off our money. Many Poles come here because it's cheap, and they buy stuff which many Italians would never buy' (interview with author, 12 March 2000). The owner of a cantina where Poles met on Sundays conceded that immigrants were his main customers and claimed that he did not discriminate: 'three thousand lire a carafe of wine for foreigners, Poles and the lady who lives upstairs'.

There was a noticeable amount of interaction between immigrants and Neapolitans in the piazza. For males, this tended to correspond to the length of time spent in the area. Diop, who had worked for four years in the Italian warehouses to the north of Piazza Garibaldi, appeared to know most people in Vasto. Both Madji and Ousmanne, who had been in Naples for two and five years respectively, did not know any locals in the piazza, although they were acquainted with the various immigrant circuits.

In the case of Eastern European women, on the other hand, the amount of time spent in the city and legal status were not criteria for contact with locals. Their meetings on the station forecourt attracted an entourage of flirtatious middle-aged Neapolitan men, as well as North Africans. Various types of relationships were formed. Petra declared she was 'lucky' to have befriended the 'right' group but claimed that not all women had the same fortune. One man, who had become her close friend, rented her a flat, another had married a Polish woman and they now lived together in Forcella, while a third regularly took Ukrainian and Polish women on afternoon trips to the Amalfi Coast. For these men, who described themselves as 'former playboys', Piazza Garibaldi had always been a place of foreign liaisons: before the Eastern Europeans, the principal targets had been German, Scandinavian and American visitors. Indeed, one had previously been married to a Dane and another to an Australian, both of whom were met in Piazza Garibaldi.

Many immigrants, including those who spoke little Italian, had adopted local routines and had picked up Neapolitan habits and expressions. For instance, Madji greeted other immigrants and clients with the dialect salute 'ué guaglio!', while all those who invited me for coffee left hundred lire tips on the bar counter (something which was not usually done in northern or central Italy). Piazza Garibaldi had also been appropriated by immigrants as their principal space of protest in the city. Like the disoccupati organizzati, demonstrations for legal rights started or were carried out next to the Garibaldi monument. This was where collective demands were made and anger (for instance over the arrest of street vendors) was vented. Even though these protests were not explicitly directed at contesting dominant media representations of immigrants in Piazza Garibaldi, they were significant for opening up oppositional voices in political debates on immigration.[9] The piazza also occasionally became a place of group celebrations, something that had rarely been the case in the past. For instance, following Senegal's victory over France in the opening match of the 2002 World Cup, the traffic in the north-east corner was temporarily blocked as jubilant Senegalese supporters descended the streets of Vasto into Piazza Garibaldi.

The 'poly-national' presence in the piazza was marked by interconnectedness, juxtapositions and distance. Until recently, street vendors of different nationalities shared the same strip of pavement. On one ob-

---

9. Although many of the early protests were coordinated by Neapolitan left-wing groups such as the centri sociali and 3 Febbraio, some demonstrations were self-organized. The groups primarily involved in protests over the last two decades have been North and West Africans and South Asians. In June 2006, over one thousand Chinese marched for the first time from Piazza Garibaldi to the city hall in protest of a rise in robberies and the lack of support from public institutions.

served occasion, a Neapolitan *contrabbandiere* hid cigarettes in a steel
box which a Chinese hawker used as a seat, who in turn leant over to
borrow a feather duster from a neighbouring Senegalese without utter-
ing a word, while the Senegalese asked Madji, the Pakistani, who was in
conversation with myself, if he had a phone line. In contrast, there was
little contact between groups on the two opposite sides of the piazza
(although more Poles ventured north to visit the bars and shops than
their West African counterparts whose day-to-day existence was centred
on Vasto). Nobody actually remarked on this division, although one of
Petra's Neapolitan friends warned me to be careful before crossing the
piazza to the north side. Some informants referred to frictions between
different groups. Over half the Poles met complained that Ukrainians
were cutting the prices in the domestic sector.[10] The middle-aged man
met in the cantina claimed that Poles once had a good reputation as hard
workers but that this had changed since the Ukrainians arrived. His female friend stated that Ukrainian women were immediately recognizable
because they all had gold teeth (two of the three Ukrainian women I met
did, in fact, have gilded dentures). When asked, all Poles claimed to have
no close contact with their national neighbours, although Petra had met a
number of Ukrainians through her Neapolitan friends. At the same time,
she was enthusiastic about her new acquaintances met on the training
course for immigrants. During a visit to the Duchesca market, we met
one of her Somali colleagues. She admitted that she was more open than
her compatriots but that, aside from general prejudices and stereotypes,
there was no real tension between national groups. Indeed, the male Pole
who defended immigrant workers also included Ukrainians in his list.

The piazza was simultaneously a site of fears and desires. For all the
street vendors, the principal wish was to work in peace. A friend of Diop
believed that while Vasto perhaps appeared scruffy because of the pack-
ages and stalls lining the pavements, this was an accepted feature of local life. Abdoul claimed to be attached to the area but, like most of the
informants, he had nothing to do with it at night:

> I think it's a really nice area. It's a place where you can meet all nationalities. Let's say,
> a melting pot. This is the great thing about the station. But as for security, that's another
> issue. I don't like it at all. When I close up at the end of the day, I go away. I don't set
> foot here at night. I never pass by. … Those who frequent the station after midnight only
> come for sex and drugs. All the shops are closed. There are no services.

He later added that police controls had to concentrate on the criminal element: 'I don't say that there shouldn't be any controls. But these should

---

10. According to Fabio Amato, similar complaints were made by the Cape Verdeans and Sri Lankans
when the Poles first arrived in the early 1990s (interview with author, 14 April 2000).

concentrate on those who don't work, those who sell drugs, those who become petty criminals. Because, look, Neapolitans don't come here because of the dealers and delinquents. The station area is really dangerous'. All of the informants who touched on the subject were indignant about being labelled criminals. The real culprits were Neapolitans (and also Algerians and Tunisians, according to some of the Senegalese and Pakistanis). The head of immigration at the CGIL commented: 'The *degrado* in the piazza has existed for years. The immigrants have nothing to do with it. They haven't created the traffic or the smog. People come up with the same old story that they become drug dealers or prostitutes, but do you really think that these weren't around before immigrants arrived?' (interview with author, 23 March 2000). During the day, for most of those who regularly frequented it, the piazza was considered 'an easygoing place'. There were certain areas where one needed to be more vigilant. Petra told me to keep a watch on my bag as we wandered around the market. Madji also took me to an alleyway behind the Duchesca market to show me the place where Neapolitans and North Africans sold stolen goods. He recounted the story of a fellow Pakistani who would come to Piazza Garibaldi when he needed the phone service but who refused to meet Madji on the north side because he had been pickpocketed on more than one occasion.

Before the 2000 crackdown took place, many of the West African and Pakistani street vendors were wary about the police and complained about controls. Ousmanne preferred to sell at the weekend along the seafront, away from the potential danger of Piazza Garibaldi (although this area was also subject to police raids in the spring of 2000). During the week he worked instead as a porter for the shops and warehouses in Vasto. Madji argued that expelling the street vendors would only force more immigrants to revert to crime. Senegalese shop assistants in Via Bologna complained that police controls damaged the trade and the general economy of the area, while Abdoul, whose shop was located on Via Torino, remembered the G7 as a moment when immigrants had to lie low: 'Throughout that month, nobody set their stall up and nobody worked. It was real bad luck for all immigrants living in Naples. Those who had saved a bit of money got by. Others left and travelled to other cities'.

The extraordinary financial and security measures taken to militarize the city during the G7 summit could never be maintained in ordinary circumstances. Like Piazza Plebiscito, controls were not always very efficient. A common theme among both my immigrant interlocutors and those residents interviewed in the local press was that the police knew what was happening (a police station is actually located on the west side of the piazza) but did nothing to intervene. Controls in the piazza were characterized by what Salvatore Palidda terms the 'rules of disorder': ensuring that behaviour and activities do not provoke too many hostile reactions among the public or the excessive expansion of illegality (Palidda 1999: 90). Nevertheless, in the second half of the 1990s, immigrants were increasingly on the receiving end of law-and-order initiatives directly targeted at them *in Piazza Garibaldi*. For the few informants who had been present in Naples during the G7, Piazza Garibaldi was beginning to reassume the appearance of the *'città blindata'*.

Chapter 14

Exit Piazza Garibaldi

(Re)connecting Immigration and Urban Renewal

> Immigration is undeniably a subversive factor to the extent that it reveals in broad daylight the hidden truth and the deepest foundations of the social and political order we describe as national. Thinking about immigration basically means interrogating the state, interrogating its foundation and interrogating the internal mechanisms of its structuration and workings. Using immigration to interrogate the state in this way means, in the final analysis, 'denaturalizing', so to speak, what we take to be natural, and 'rehistoricizing' the state or that element within the state that seems to have been afflicted by historical amnesia. (Sayad 2004: 280)

The Algerian sociologist Abdelmalek Sayad's incisive comments about the power of immigration to lay bare the workings of the nation-state can be scaled down to think about the city. If immigrants are simply considered figures of 'integration', the corollary is that urban regeneration was an exclusively autochthonous matter and that immigrants, at best, were the passive beneficiaries of any improvements. If, on the other hand, they are recognized as active participants in urban life, then this raises some serious questions about the urban order promoted in Naples during the 1990s. Piazza Garibaldi corresponds to the 'broad daylight' referred to by Sayad, where immigrants 'denaturalized' the 'natural' ways in which the city was interpreted and 'rehistoricized' meanings about place that had been beset with 'historical amnesia'.

It is generally forgotten that the new Piazza Garibaldi which emerged after the demolition of the old station was greeted with dismay and bewilderment, and that illegal and informal activities were not a cause of collective angst but actually constituted, at times, a local folklore about the space. Such memories were sidelined after 1994, as the Bassolino administration, the local media and a host of moral entrepreneurs sought to resurrect the historically ambiguous (and unsuccessful) idea of the piazza as a *biglietto da visita*. The arrival of immigrants had reconfirmed the fluid, open-ended nature of the station area. But after the G7, their presence increasingly became a source of tensions, as attempts were made to ground the piazza in a new dominant narrative about Naples as a 'safe' and 'welcoming' city.

The detailed discussion of immigrant experiences *in* and *of* Piazza Garibaldi underlines the complex nature of the space. The piazza studied between 1999 and 2000 was characterized by a range of boundaries and itineraries, such as the discernible division between the north and south sides, which reflected a variety of divergent relationships with the station area. While it was a place of social interaction, it was not always a space of communication between different groups. Consensual images of Piazza Garibaldi as a dangerous, dirty or ugly place were internalized and reinterpreted. For instance, Abdoul intertwined his disdain for criminal practices with a positive image of the piazza as a 'melting pot'. Although immigrants did not share a common definition of the piazza, the space nevertheless accommodated a myriad of recreational and economic activities. Through its various functions, the station area was also 'symbolized' (Signorelli 1996). For many Eastern European domestic workers, for example, Piazza Garibaldi represented both the centre of Naples and the hub of their social life and, at the same time, a link with their countries of origin due to the presence of coach and postal services and improvised newspaper stands. It was this unmediated diversity of the piazza which many commentators regarded to be the central virtue of 'democratic' public space (Walzer 1986; Mitchell 1995). Indeed, in many ways it was as a result of the immigrants' multiple uses of the space that the traffic-congested gaping 'hole' was rendered a 'piazza'. This was not simply the 'gateway' to the *centro storico* but an opening to the diverse and alternative worlds that comprised the increasingly heterogeneous urban context of Naples.

However, there were two 'public spaces' to Piazza Garibaldi: that of the physical piazza and that of the discursive realm of debates. Immigrants' definitions of the piazza were usually excluded from this latter sphere, despite the fact that they were among its principal users. The complexities of the piazza were often reduced in public debates to a simple opposition between 'us' (Neapolitans and tourists) versus 'them' (immigrants and other 'undesirable' users). Formally 'noncitizens', immigrants were represented as an illegitimate public (Landuzzi 1999b). They were not conceived as civil individuals who *voluntarily* associated in public (Mitchell 1995) but as an incoherent mass of foreigners who physically took over the space. Activities normally connected with the private space of the home but which were carried out in the piazza – such as sleeping, drinking alcohol, eating dinner or going to the toilet – were highlighted by journalists to accentuate a sense of disorder and to further delegitimize the immigrant presence.

While immigrants continued, regardless, to appropriate and resignify urban space in Naples, they occasionally made themselves publicly heard through collective action and protest. It is significant that their mobilizations took place, or at least began, in Piazza Garibaldi. Although primarily concerned with specific political and legal issues, such as demanding the release of blocked documents, these struggles offered the chance to assert their right to the city and to project alternative definitions of immigration. As much as the Bassolino administration felt comfortable to talk multiculturally (albeit in a way that was often imbued with a crude understanding of cultural difference), it stopped short of embracing Piazza Garibaldi as a place that had been reconfigured by transnational movement. Ultimately, the administration's attempts to reposition Naples on the European and global stage were premised on an ethno-essentialist and sedentary vision of the city. According to Bassolino, Naples in the 1990s could capitalize on a more homogenous sense of local identity than Rome, Milan or Turin, where a far higher percentage of the population originated from other parts of Italy and had brought with them different traditions and affiliations (Bassolino 1996b: 15). Clearly, the idea that non-Italian groups of people and their descendents might also influence what it meant to live in Naples had yet to even enter the equation! Piazza Garibaldi instead demonstrates how immigration cannot be considered a separate, 'specialist' concern but is an integral element of contemporary Naples. 'Deprovincializing' urban regeneration, thus, does not simply mean comprehending 'more complex patterns' (Chambers 1994: 30) or exposing the 'virtual apartheid' (Balibar 2004) underpinning official narratives about the city's revival, but acknowledging the active role played by immigrants themselves – irrespective of their legal status – in reshaping Naples for good.

Part 4

An Alternative Idea of Public Space

The Centro Sociale *in Montesanto*

Chapter 15

Enter a Neighbourhood Park

In his 2007 book *I padroni della città,* a candid diagnosis of Italy's major cities, the Milanese journalist Curzio Maltese concludes his brief sojourn in a rubbish-strewn Naples waiting to interview the occupants of DAMM. Like many people before him, he finds himself unexpectedly struck by the picturesque surroundings.

> The true experts of Naples will laugh at this point, but the amphitheatre of the *centro sociale* DAMM in Montesanto is one of the most magical places in the city. You get a glimpse of the gulf from the poor side of the port. And yet it is a serene, almost happy, view. The laughter of children and the thud of a ball can be heard. I waited an hour with my notebook ready before it occurred to me to leave. (Maltese 2007: 70)

'True experts' would surely turn up their noses at the thought of a vernacular cityscape off the beaten heritage track being chosen above the countless monuments, many also with dramatic backdrops, that are testament to the city's glorious past. Maltese's discovery does not move beyond first impressions, because, in the end, no one from DAMM turns up. But its mere mention would appear enough to unsettle a local hierarchy of place. For not only was the place in question a *centro sociale* – which for the mainstream Italian press often conjured up images of extremism and marginalization – but it was situated in a *quartiere popolare*; and if there was one locale in the city centre that complicated the process of ennobling the image of Naples more than anywhere else, then this was it.

Diego Armando Maradona Montesanto (DAMM)[1] is based in a three-storey building inside a small park in Montesanto, a densely populated neighbourhood that climbs the lower slopes of Vomero Hill, on the western side of the *centro storico*. The two spaces form part of a larger

---

1. Like many *centri sociali,* the occupants and some journalists often wrote 'DAMM' in the lower case (i.e. 'Damm' or 'damm') which would suggest that the word was not simply an acronym but had assumed its own semantic autonomy. For the sake of clarity, I use the capitalized form 'DAMM' throughout this book.

structure, referred to here as the Ventaglieri Project, which was designed after a number of dwellings were demolished in the wake of the 1980 earthquake. This consists of a series of terraced gardens connected by a system of staircases and indoor escalators to a concrete esplanade and a primary school located at the foot of a thirty-metre cliff. When DAMM occupied the top of the site in 1995, the whole project, apart from the school, lay in a state of abandonment.

A study of DAMM offers the chance to examine a distinct example of a *centro sociale,* a form of collective organization with its origins in the political upheavals of the 1970s that became widespread in Italian cities during the 1990s and that over the last decade have been a source of fascination for academics and activists worldwide (Klein 2001; Hodkinson and Chatterton 2006). Through its occupation, DAMM sought to create and promote alternative ideas about public space in the particular setting of a popular neighbourhood. In doing so, it directly challenged widely held assumptions about the spontaneous and mercurial nature of politics in this part of Naples. Moreover, as it developed in concomitance and in dialectical relationship with the Bassolino administration, it consequently formulated one of the most powerful critiques of urban renewal in the *centro storico.*

We have already encountered traces of 'popular Naples' in Piazza Plebiscito and Piazza Garibaldi. Now we venture into the alleyways themselves, away from the constant glare of the media. Before analyzing the Ventaglieri Project and DAMM, it is necessary to examine the position of these districts and their inhabitants in planning debates and representations of the *centro storico.* The popular neighbourhoods continue, for the most part, to be dominated by a mix of petite-bourgeois, working-class, unemployed and precariously employed inhabitants. The principal forms of people's employment have traditionally been in the public sector, commerce, artisan workshops and small, often family-run firms producing garments or leather items such as bags, gloves and shoes. As already noted, the idea of the 'slum economy' – the communal survival system that simultaneously operated as a form of mythopoesis – had, by the 1970s, been largely eclipsed by an informal economy and, to a lesser degree, by illegal and semi-legal economies, such as the trade in contraband goods, that were usually, but not always, controlled by organized crime. In addition, while the working population was predominantly comprised of nonindustrial workers, there had always been, at least until the factory closures of the 1980s and early 1990s, a blue-collar minority that commuted out of the centre. The adjective 'popular' is therefore chosen here to underline the particular socioeconomic and cultural composition of the neighbourhoods, something which the terms 'working class' or 'inner city', often employed all too hastily by outside observers, simply fail to capture. As shall be explained below, 'popular' raises its own problems, especially in light of the demographic changes that took place in the final decades of the twentieth century, but given that it continues to be universally used in Naples to articulate a specific urban experience, it is a label that, with due caveats, is worth preserving.

Throughout the city's modern history, the *quartieri popolari* have held a very ambivalent position within urban narratives of Naples. While the bustling *vicoli* (alleyways) traditionally constituted metonyms of the city, for most of the twentieth century such scenes were under constant threat of demolition. Local authorities and planners responsible for the city's modernization were torn between 'the desire to eradicate the casbah of its poor quarters and the paralyzing fascination with a bimillenial urban system' (Macry 1994: 158). Similarly, the dwellers of these central neighbourhoods have either been at the centre or on the fringe of definitions of Neapolitanness, embodying both the city's perceived 'backwardness' and its 'vitality'. The reimaging of the *centro storico* during the 1990s raised new dilemmas. Above all, if Naples was to be marketed as a tourist and cultural capital, how should the reputation of its neighbourhoods as 'seething dens', as one travel writer in a British broadsheet joyfully described them (Elms 1998), be tackled?

Illustration 15.1. DAMM viewed from the Ventaglieri Park, October 2010. *Photograph by Nick Dines.*

Map 15.1. DAMM and surrounding area. *Designed by Nick Dines.*

Chapter 16

The Popular Neighbourhoods in the Twentieth Century

From *sventramento* to conservation: the neighbourhoods and urban planning

At the end of the nineteenth century, Matilde Serao famously argued that in order to improve the lives of the city's poor citizens, it was not enough to simply 'disembowel' the most squalid parts of Naples – the whole city would have to be rebuilt (Serao 1994: 11). Yet the street plan and buildings of those neighbourhoods not involved in the Risanamento have hardly changed over the last hundred years.[1] Besides the construction of the Rione Carità district and the new buildings erected on bomb sites after the Second World War, other large-scale programmes of modernization remained on paper. For example, throughout the twentieth century, master plans continued to propose a trunk road parallel to the central artery Via Roma, which would have demolished parts of the Spanish Quarters and Montesanto. According to the logic of these plans, the network of narrow alleyways blocked the development of the city's infrastructure and hindered economic growth.

The unchecked dilapidation of much of the centre's housing stock was aggravated by the 1980 earthquake, but while funds were allocated to repair the worst-hit buildings, the reconstruction itself concentrated on the city's run-down suburbs. The then-mayor Maurizio Valenzi argued that improved conditions in the suburbs would enable a further reduction in

---

1. Montesanto and the Spanish Quarters remain practically the same as they were three centuries ago. If one compares a present-day layout with an eighteenth-century map of the area, the only major change is the narrowing of Piazza Montesanto, which followed the construction of the funicular and the Cumana railway station at the end of the nineteenth century.

the residential population of the *centro storico*: a necessary precondition for eventual improvements to the old neighbourhoods (Valenzi 1987: 51). The few projects in the *centro storico* itself, such as the Ventaglieri Project, were small-scale schemes and were not envisioned as part of a comprehensive renovation plan for the *centro storico,* to the disappointment of many of the planners involved.[2] These projects nevertheless evolved amidst intense debates about the future of the city centre. In the immediate aftermath of the earthquake, an array of experts and politicians advanced various proposals, some of which had been concocted in the past but were now mooted with greater conviction. Francesco Compagna, a local intellectual and former national minister for public works, advocated the demolition of large sections of the worst-hit neighbourhoods and the construction of a new satellite city for two hundred thousand inhabitants near Villa Literno, twenty-five kilometres to the northwest of Naples (Compagna 1981). Others, such as the architectural historian Cesare de Seta, called for a protection of the *centro storico,* albeit following the removal of particularly damaged and historically insignificant tenements (De Seta 1983). While building inspectors issued eviction orders to hundreds of households, the earthquake victim committees provocatively called for public housing blocks to be erected in the old city (one of their battle cries was '167 in the centre!' which referred to the social housing law of 1962), but given the emergency situation, these same groups ultimately found themselves resisting the 'deportation' of families from the central neighbourhoods.

During the second half of the 1980s, largely as a result of the limited public interventions in the city centre after the earthquake, the popular neighbourhoods were the focus of a showdown between heritage campaigners who called for the protection of the *centro storico* in its entirety and various interest groups who pressed for its redevelopment. These divergent, incompatible positions came to ahead with the Regno del Possibile, a detailed project launched in 1986 by a consortium of construction firms with the active participation of academics and politicians, which proposed the wholesale transformation of the old neighbourhoods (Studi Centro Storico Napoli 1988). Buildings categorized as structurally unsafe and of little historical value would be replaced or removed to make way for much-needed green areas, schools, leisure facilities and car parks. In addition, a new service sector would be developed, including the construction of conference centres, which, it was claimed, would

---

2. As one of the architects who coordinated the reconstruction programme in the *centro storico* recalled in 1986: 'We knew that we did not have sufficient conceptual and executive instruments or the time at our disposal to consider a large-scale project, which since the ruinous experience of the Risanamento had never possessed the right conditions to come into being' (Ferulano 1986: 88).

allow for the economic recovery of the whole of Naples. The project essentially represented a blueprint for demolition and a lucrative opportunity for an insatiable building industry. Large swathes of the Spanish Quarters, Montesanto and Sanità were to be razed. In the area around Via Ventaglieri in Montesanto, whole blocks and streets were to disappear to give way to a car park next to the underground station, while the fronts of other buildings were to be pulled down to allow for the widening of alleyways. Significantly, the Ventaglieri Project was one of the few sites to be left untouched, because it was legally bound to the post-earthquake reconstruction programme.

Promoters of the Regno del Possibile insisted that the social composition of the *centro storico* would not be dramatically altered but would be preserved for the city's benefit. Residents would instead be guaranteed the same standard of living enjoyed in more modern parts of the city (Siola 1988: 197). Work would be staggered over a period of fifteen years to allow for the temporary removal of residents who would then be rehoused in modern accommodation in their neighbourhoods of origin. Supporters declared that the transformation of the *quartieri* also aimed to entice the middle classes back to the *centro storico,* which would help revive the local artisan industry and prevent the centre from becoming more of a 'ghetto' (Corsi 1989: 4). With the backing of powerful politicians in central government such as the Christian Democrat Paolo Cirino Pomicino, the administration was urged to adopt the plans. While the Regno del Possibile clearly appeared to be incubated in the political climate of the post-earthquake period (Dal Piaz 1987; Barbagallo 1997),[3] it also reflected the growing trend across Italy during the 1980s that saw businesses attempt to dictate the planning agenda of cities (Indovina 1993).

Significantly, the local PCI and trade unions were not against the proposals in principle and agreed with the project's supporters that inaction would be the worst possible outcome (Compagnone 1989).[4] Nevertheless, many on the Left were suspicious that the consortium hoped to overturn the public planning process. It was stressed that any major rebuilding programme would have to be administered by the governing institutions in consultation with residents, and concern was raised over

---

3. Francesco Barbagallo sees the Regno del Possibile as representative of the rampant corruption of the 1980s, arguing that the assignment of a further twelve billion lire to the reconstruction of earthquake-hit areas in the national budgets of 1987 and 1988 was instrumental to the development of the project (Barbagallo 1997: 100).

4. Gerardo Chiaromonte and Giorgio Napolitano, key figures on the right wing of the Communist Party in Naples, initially gave their endorsement to the Regno del Possibile, only to retract it as the project became embroiled in controversy.

the undemocratic idea of shifting populations from their homes.[5] The most steadfast opposition, however, did not come from politicians, but from a coterie of local intellectuals, heritage groups such as Italia Nostra and the Napoli 99 Foundation, and nationally renowned architects like Pier Luigi Cervellati, the mastermind behind Bologna's *centro storico* plan. Together this 'civic alliance' mobilized to save Naples from the bulldozers. Opponents feared the destruction of a unique urban environment, although some appeared more preoccupied about the fate of the old buildings than their inhabitants (Craveri 1989: 50). Largely as a result of this public protest, which had also alerted international interest in the affair, the local administration refused to switch planning decisions to central government, and the Regno del Possibile remained a dead letter. The conclusion to the episode would be celebrated by many local commentators as one of the few political high points in an otherwise ignoble decade (Barbagallo 1997).[6]

The campaign against the Regno del Possibile signalled a growing concern for the city's historical patrimony, and although the spectre of demolition would never be entirely vanquished, this opposition represented a decisive public rejection of restructuring projects.[7] But it must be said that the war of positions triggered by the Regno del Possibile also produced a forced dichotomy whereby the neighbourhood residents themselves were either totally absent or merely instrumental to respective ambitions. Despite the deterioration of conditions and the infamy brought about by the earthquake, neither conservation nor redevelopment was necessarily in tune with everyday issues of collective consumption or local place attachments. Indeed, the rhetorical slogan '167 in the city centre!' of the earthquake victim committees in the early 1980s was as much an anathema to the heritage groups as it was to the construction firms. That an enlightened minority was seen to defeat the Regno del Possibile on behalf of the rest of the city may have made for an inspiring tale, but it did so by also establishing an ideological meta-narrative about urban heritage that sought to liberate the neighbourhoods from their fastidiously contradictory nature.

---

5. The whole affair provoked a fierce debate at the PCI provincial congress in 1989, which led to the marginalization of two party members involved in the project: the head of the faculty of architecture at Naples University, Uberto Siola, and the economist Massimo Lo Cicero (Barbagallo 1997: 103–4).

6. For a reassessment of the affair, see Demarco 2007. Although Demarco's account often smacks of biased revisionism, it importantly details how from the late 1990s onwards, various exponents of the Centre-Left (and principally the DS) started to reconsider the project a missed opportunity.

7. The *Neonapoli* plan for the metropolitan area of Naples, launched personally by the Christian Democrat 'boss' Pomicino at the end of 1990 and which also proposed redevelopment in the *centro storico,* was again met with strong opposition and led to the formation of the Assizes of Palazzo Marigliano (see Chapter 3).

On the back of this 'civic resistance', but also in the wake of *Tangentopoli* which stigmatized grandiose redevelopment schemes, the general consensus of political opinion by the 1990s was to conserve rather than demolish the *centro storico*'s fragile fabric. During the election campaign for mayor in 1993, both Antonio Bassolino and Alessandra Mussolini gave reassurances that the Spanish Quarters, which had continued to be the focus of architectural competitions (see, for instance, Alisio, Izzo, and Almirante 1987), would not be destroyed (*Il Mattino,* 3 December 1993). Under the Bassolino administration, the *centro storico* was no longer considered the impediment to the city's modernization but the vehicle for urban recovery. Its size and diversity became Naples's principal asset. The first Bassolino administration drew up a plan to document the type and period of every built structure, with the aim of restoring and modernizing buildings at the same time as preventing 'poor repair work or inappropriate use that might compromise their distinctive characteristics' (Comune di Napoli 1999b: vi). The lack of action during previous decades had seen the proliferation of illegal alterations to buildings such as front porches, windows, balconies and extra floors (Laino 2001). While it was impossible to completely eradicate self-build practices, planning permission for independent construction in the *centro storico* in any form and for whatever reason was firmly rejected. For example, Vezio De Lucia recalls the public outcry after he prevented a school in the Sanità neighbourhood from constructing a greenhouse in its courtyard (De Lucia 1998: 35–36). Meanwhile, the idea of trunk roads through the old city, at the top of the planning agenda for most of the twentieth century, was ditched in favour of traffic controls in the centre and investment in the public transport network, which included the completion of an extensive underground network.

Conservation of the past, however, faced the same timeworn set of problems, namely what to do about the widespread urban decay and poverty in the popular neighbourhoods. Perhaps the most ambitious response to this dilemma was the EU-sponsored URBAN initiative, which after 1996 coordinated a series of interventions in the Spanish Quarters and the Sanità (Comune di Napoli 1997; Laino 1999; Nanetti 2001). With the declared objective of 'integrating' the two neighbourhoods with the rest of the city (Comune di Napoli 1997), the scheme combined measures aimed at alleviating social and economic marginality, such as 'street tuition' for school dropouts and financial support for local artisans, with environmental improvements. In the Spanish Quarters, this involved the conversion of a former nursery into a multi-purpose space that would house a neighbourhood police station, a job centre for young people and a family advice clinic (Comune di Napoli 1999c); the redesign of five small piazzas; and the repaving of alleyways adjoining Via Roma. The two neighbourhoods were selected partly on the basis of existent associative experiences that participated in the project's planning and delivery but also 'because they constitute[d] two places of particular significance in the city's history' (Comune di Napoli 1997: 5). Physical regeneration was therefore integrated with the administration's desire to recuperate and market the city's past, and indeed some interventions were targeted as much at tourists as at residents. A restored eighteenth-century palace in the Sanità, for instance, was planned to house a museum dedicated to the comic actor Totò, who was born in the district.[8] As a multilevel approach to neighbourhood renewal, URBAN signalled a departure from the top-down megaplans of the previous decade (Nanetti 2001). Rather than being expected to yield results on its own, the programme was envisaged as part of a wider set of planning tools and social policies that shaped urban governance in the 'problem' areas of the city centre. Nevertheless, its achievements often fell short of the original objectives. A negligible number of new jobs was created, while property prices and rents rose disproportionately in the areas that had been refurbished (Laino 2001). Moreover, the impact of certain measures was limited or short-lived due to the finite funding and lack of coordinated management. Some of the redesigned piazzas, for instance, were inaugurated before completion and, once out of the limelight, were left to deteriorate. According to one commentator and participant in URBAN, this reflected an increasingly 'Bassolinian' influence upon the programme, whereby immediate and physically visible transformations assumed precedence over the experimental approach and mundane social questions (ibid.).[9]

Although the whole of the *centro storico* was formally accorded protection – and in spite of URBAN's ambitions to improve two neighbourhoods – the *quartieri* were otherwise rarely incorporated into broad visions of a regenerated Naples. They did not feature in the facelift for the G7 summit in 1994, nor were they included in the official 'Streets of Art' established for tourists in the *centro antico* and around Piazza Plebiscito. A typical accusation, and one initially used as an expedient to politically attack Bassolino, was that the neighbourhoods were being ignored. In November 1994, during the UN conference on organized crime, when Naples (and Piazza Plebiscito) once again became a focus of international

---

8. The Totò Museum was originally supposed to be completed in late 1998, but at the time of writing in late 2011 it had still not opened due to the lack of a lift and a legal dispute with neighbouring residents.

9. An emphasis upon visual impact was also a key element of the 'Sirena' (Mermaid) project, which from 2002 funded the restoration of façades of historic palaces and tenements mainly in the central popular neighbourhoods.

attention, shopkeepers from the Spanish Quarters mounted photographs along Via Roma to denounce the number of scaffolded buildings in their area that were still awaiting earthquake repairs.[10] In the meantime, tenement blocks continued to crumble. In 2000, following the partial collapse of a building in the Spanish Quarters near to the proposed site of a new metro station, an assessor in the Bassolino administration and member of the post-DC Margherita Party proposed an amendment to the master plan, backed by local construction firms, that would permit redevelopment in the surrounding area. Despite its minor proportions, the plan triggered a wave of outrage among the same heritage groups and intellectuals who had fought the Regno del Possibile during the 1980s, and it was subsequently withdrawn (Laino 2001). The incident indicated the degree of public consensus against demolition during the Bassolino era and how meddling with the issue was tantamount to political suicide, but it also suggested that as long as the neighbourhoods remained in a physically precarious state and were peripheral to narratives about a new Naples, they would forever be caught between conflicting external interests.

From lumpen rabble to uncivil citizens: shifting representations of the popular classes

Like any urban setting, the central neighbourhoods of Naples elude general, univocal classifications (Shields 1996). Nevertheless, due to the particularities of these districts and their apparent aporetic effect upon Western models of urban modernity, the temptation to elicit all-embracing images, whether around communal responses to poverty, peculiar cultural practices or through allegations about the pervasive presence of organized crime, has always been great. In popular discourse and literature, the neighbourhoods have often been considered constitutive of a relentlessly unique local urban culture and thus tend to be placed beyond the realms of historical contingency, geographical commensurability and social relations. Such representations clearly do not hold up to closer, dispassionate analysis. For instance, Pier Paolo Pasolini's famous celebration of the indomitable resistance of the Neapolitan poor to the consumerist ideology of Italian society (Pasolini 1976) not only idealized the old neighbourhoods as timeless and undifferentiated but, by overlooking the disparate forms of consumption that took place within them, lost sight of the ways in which inhabitants critically engaged with national mass culture.[11] The

---

10. It should be noted that most of the remaining scaffolding from the 1980 earthquake was removed over the course of the first Bassolino administration.

11. For a critique of Pasolini's writings on cultural 'integration', see Foot 2001b.

so-called '*l'arte d'arrangiarsi*' (the art of getting by), described by one commentator as the 'rearranging [of] available elements as props for an unstable urban existence' (Chambers 1996: 56), was nearly always formulated around idiosyncratic activities (such as the *granita* seller in Piazza Plebiscito) that evaded 'the controls and behavioural rules imposed by organized work' (De Matteis 1994: 142) rather than around more mundane forms of survival that were as burdensome and unexciting as anywhere else. Meanwhile, the common conflation with organized crime, which on occasions led to the outright criminalization of certain districts and all that went on within them, invariably failed to consider the ways in which the Camorra and crime were stigmatized by many residents themselves (De Matteis 1993; Pardo 1996).

As already noted, social scientists from the 1970s onwards sought to comprehend and categorize the 'otherness' of the neighbourhoods' inhabitants and, in doing so, refuted or complicated the long-held arguments about a backward slum society. Studies advanced contrasting and at times diametrically opposed arguments: from Thomas Belmonte's emphasis on people's rejection of morals in favour of cunning and force in the negotiations of daily life (Belmonte 1989) to Italo Pardo's focus on neglected elements such as entrepreneurialism and autonomous strategies for dealing with bureaucracy (Pardo 1996). Yet there remained a tendency to cast the micro-neighbourhoods at the centre of inquiry as part of a larger, sociologically homogenous milieu. Anthropological research during the early 1990s by local scholars indicated a more heterogeneous and stratified 'popular Naples'. Both Grilli (1992) and De Matteis (1993) demonstrated how the life paths of residents and their relationship with the 'community' varied according to the level of family ties, on the one hand, and the extent of informal extra-kin networks, on the other. The alleyways were a much more dynamic and contradictory domain: 'They represent a universe where choices can be made and where people can carve out their own space associating or disassociating themselves from others' (De Matteis 1993: 160).

Moreover, the demographic composition of the central neighbourhoods at the end of the twentieth century was more cosmopolitan than implied by the label '*popolare*' and in spite of the social dislocation accelerated by the 1980 earthquake. First, although it is true that the exodus to the new residential districts during the postwar period radically changed the layered socio-occupational structure of the *centro storico,* this was not a uniform process, and some neighbourhoods such as Montesanto retained a more cross-class composition than others and included working-class residents who commuted to outlying factories such as Italsider in Bagnoli and Alfasud in Pomigliano d'Arco. Second, from the early 1990s on-wards there was a steady rise of middle-class residents from surrounding districts who bought and renovated apartments often on the upper floors of buildings. Like the earlier 'pioneers' of the 1970s, such as political activists and intellectuals, these new inhabitants were attracted by the relatively cheap property and the cultural and social facilities offered by the *centro storico*. The increasing popularity of the centre, especially amongst young people, also led to a rise in outsiders using restaurants, bars and theatres located in the neighbourhood areas. The influx of new owner occupiers and visitors would fuel a property boom at the end of the 1990s and start to generalize a process of gentrification that had been previously confined to a few pockets and desirable historic buildings (F. Amato 2006).[12] Third, the settlement of immigrants in the *centro storico* from the late 1980s, many of whom were sublet *bassi* and other poor-quality accommodation, further undermines the notion of an immutable popular identity. Some national groups became associated with specific neighbourhoods, such as Sri Lankans in the Sanità and Cape Verdeans in Montesanto.

While we must be wary of sweeping definitions that gloss over internal differences, this should not mean disavowing the distinctiveness of the central neighbourhoods and their populations. Rather than an accurate empirical description, the idea of the 'popular neighbourhood' is better understood as a category used locally to make sense of social structures and urban cultures that are seen to set it apart from other areas of Naples and from other cities. On this point, the reflection of Michael Herzfeld regarding the persistence of the 'Mediterranean' as a construct in anthro-pological research is especially helpful:

> [C]ultural-area categories have an existence by virtue of being articulated. ... They exist in the sense that they are representations of something experienced in the phenomenal world. ... To deny [the Mediterranean's] existence is as obtuse as to treat it as an obvi-ous fact that needs no further comment. These apparent ontological truisms become interesting ... when we ask who makes them and why. (Herzfeld 2005: 47)

The Neapolitan popular neighbourhoods are a similarly obdurate phe-nomenon. But at the same time as they are articulated as a 'fact' (Herz-

---

12. A similar process of middle-class return occurred in other Italian cities where the *centro storico* had been abandoned after the war, for instance in Genoa (Petrillo 2000) and Palermo (Gerbino 2000). One of the residents of the Pallonetto interviewed in Piazza Plebiscito had moved to the neighbour-hood from Vomero in 1980: 'My parents were Communists and they took this demagogic decision to move into a *quartiere popolare*. But you're always richer than the others, and so integration is never a hundred per cent. It's as if you were always in the territory of others' (interview with author, 25 July 1999).

feld 2005), both by long-standing residents and by the middle classes and foreign immigrants who have recently moved into them, they are also a conceptual battleground where various meanings about urban life are advanced and repelled. In other words, the challenge is not just to reconsider such districts as more complex but to grasp how place identities, particularly in the face of demographic change and urban renewal, are continually constructed through social relations.

What is of interest here is how the 'indigenous' inhabitants – the very 'popular' classes who bestow their name to the districts – have been conceived in local left-wing political discourse. The Neapolitan poor embody an abject paradigm in the historical development of communist thought. Although Marx paid little attention to Naples itself, the figure of the *lazzarone* – the classic Neapolitan lower-class rogue – appears in a famous passage of *The Eighteenth Brumaire of Louis Bonaparte,* where Marx describes, with unusual literary fervour, the assorted components of the 'lumpenproletariat' (Marx 1984; Stallybrass 1990). This pre-political mass was adjudged to side with any authoritarian power that was able to guarantee its immediate needs, and when these were not met, its prerogative was to revolt. The inherently reactionary nature of the lumpenproletariat was seen to be confirmed in Naples by the *popolo*'s participation in the violent suppression of the Neapolitan Republic of 1799 and the revolutionary uprising of 1848 (Hobsbawm 1959; Allum 1973; Engels 1977). Throughout the twentieth century, the popular neighbourhoods in Naples posed a political challenge for the Left. From exile in Paris in 1936, the agronomist Emilio Sereni argued that the Neapolitan *sottoproletariato* had hindered the advancement of the working class with its mores, habits and forms of struggle. Its participation in strikes before the First World War had led to these degenerating into riots that were violently quashed by employers and the government (Sereni 1938). Writing more than three decades later on her experiences as a local PCI parliamentary candidate, Maria Antonietta Macciocchi attempted to unpack the thorny relationship between proletariat and lumpenproletariat. Almost heretically, she empathized with the psychological isolation of working-class residents in the city centre who were tormented by the realization that the freedom and adventure of a precarious existence without bosses had been forsaken for the discipline of industrial labour.

> The worker, sealed up in his factory, is like a cloistered monk who has cut himself off from the world of others and renounced that life. In doing this, he is aware above all of having renounced the air, the environment, the rules and the means of *the secular life,* the philosophers of which are the *lazzari,* as the sub-proletariat is called. (Macciocchi 1973: 185, original italics)

At one extreme, then, the lumpenproletariat represented a contagion that undermined an organized workers movement, while at the other it offered a form of resistance to a moral conformity centred around industrial work. This contradictory dynamic, however, was lost on those, especially among the Neapolitan PCI leadership dominated by middle-class intellectuals, who reduced the notion of the *sottoproletariato* to a solely derogatory label (Lay 1981; Pardo 1993) or used it as a catchall for any resident who was not a member of the industrial working class (Pugliese 1998). In such cases, the social and political predicaments posed by the neighbourhoods were overlooked or downplayed. Their material conditions simply needed to be improved.

Studies of the postwar political system in Naples have examined the extent to which inhabitants of the popular neighbourhoods, regardless of their class position, were regarded as fodder for votes, first blatantly by Lauro (who offered packets of pasta in the place of Louis Bonaparte's sausages) and, later, more systemically by the Christian Democrats (Allum 1973; Chubb 1982). The PCI's relationship with this electorate was directly affected by its moral opposition (and lack of access) to the clientelistic system as well as its exclusion from the management of central state funds. Despite being at times suspicious of a politically backward mob, it nevertheless saw the neighbourhood poor as a group through which it could build support. Their contribution to the PCI's success in the 1975 local elections indeed proved that the nonindustrial working classes were not inherently self-interested or politically opportunistic. Some commentators saw this same electorate as chiefly responsible for the eventual downfall of the Valenzi administration in 1983. Judith Chubb (1982) argues that the urban poor's support was oriented to short-term material goals which were not satisfied. Italo Pardo takes a different angle: the administration's insistence on honest government impressed but ultimately alienated many voters from the *quartieri* as a result of 'local Communists' inability to understand in non-negative terms modes of behaviour, exchange and production that [were] strongly informed by a high degree of individuality and independence' (Pardo 1993: 90). While the demise of the left-wing administration cannot be solely blamed on the fickleness of the popular masses (for in fact the PCI suffered some of its heaviest electoral losses in working-class districts over the period and, as explained in Chapter 3, there were underlying political reasons that precipitated the end of its experience in local government), it is also true that many Communists in Naples still considered industrial development as the economic panacea for the city and a means of forging collective class consciousness. This directly affected the party's attitude towards the large swathes of nonindustrial and precarious working classes in the *centro storico*. Beneath the froth of electoral success lay the scum.

In the 1990s this attitude appeared to change. The ideological trans-formation of the post-Communist Left and its search for wider social constituencies, the direct election of the mayor which changed the rela-tionship with voters and, above all, the focus on the revival of the *centro storico* as a route to economic recovery spelt a shift in the representation of the neighbourhoods and their inhabitants. Bassolino aimed to build cross-class consensus around a moderate political agenda which drew on hitherto neglected issues of culture, legality and civic pride. Where the 'popular classes' had once been defined in socioeconomic terms (in 1980 he had contrasted their 'precarious equilibrium' and 'self-regulation of poverty' to an organized combative working class (Bassolino 1980: 28)), they were now addressed simply as 'Neapolitans', 'citizens', 'young people' or (in the case of nonvoters) as 'children' (Bassolino 1996b). The personal popularity of Bassolino was actually very strong in the *quar-tieri*; in fact, on the mayor's reelection in 1997, traditionally right-wing districts such as San Lorenzo registered the highest levels of converted voters (Savino 1998).

At the same time, the reimaging of the *centro storico* as a site of cultural heritage effectively excluded those long-standing relationships with the built environment that did not accord with officially promoted visions of the area. Bassolino claimed that prior to its renovation, the *centro storico* represented 'the city's abandoned heritage' (Bassolino 1999: 13). This was echoed by Mirella Barracco, president of Napoli 99, who argued that the Monumenti Porte Aperte programmes in the early 1990s had enabled Neapolitans to 'suddenly gain awareness' of the *centro storico* that was no longer the 'inaccessible ghetto' that it was in the 1980s (Barracco 1999: 78–79). While anthropologists have indicated how residents of the popular neighbourhoods had long taken pride in their city (Provitera, Ranisio, and Giliberti 1978: 45, 52–54; Belmonte 1989: 41–42; Pardo 1993: 88), the suggestion here was that certain people did not possess the *correct* awareness. In a debate with local intellectuals over how to insti-gate 'civic-minded behaviour' among Neapolitans (and especially with regard to pedestrianized zones), the vice-mayor Riccardo Marone argued that educational programmes and controls should focus on those neigh-bourhoods 'where cultural sensitivity was lower' (Colella 1999: 36). The URBAN initiative offered an opportunity to structurally transform two neighbourhoods of the *centro storico* both for residents and city users, but it was hoped that, with the right training, it would lead to a greater respect of the public realm. According to Elisabetta Gambardella, the DS president for the local district council, the Spanish Quarters not only suffered from insufficient hygienic and social facilities, as well as crime and unemployment, but from 'a lack of belonging and a sense of resentment' (Montalto 2000: 166), which was exemplified by the habit among old women of throwing bags of rubbish from their windows into the streets below: 'It is pointless modernizing a building, rearranging a street and making a piazza beautiful if the citizen is not willing to show respect' (ibid.: 167). Significantly, both Marone and Gambardella distinguished the *quartieri* from the 'civic-minded' upper-middle-class neighbourhood of Chiaia.[13] It would seem that while there was an absence of *class* consciousness according to PCI orthodoxy, certain Neapolitans now lacked *civic* consciousness.

Although not explicitly part of an official political position (of course, Bassolino could not afford to alienate a large section of voters), a tendency to reframe (and confirm) the 'lowness' of the neighbourhood residents within a discourse about decorum surfaced in debates over public space, especially concerning those places associated with regeneration. This was demonstrated in Piazza Plebiscito, where the young assailants of *La Montagna del Sale* (identified as *scugnizzi* and therefore from the *quartieri*) were repelled by 'civic guards'. Piazza Bellini, on the edge of the *centro antico* and close to Montesanto, was another significant case. The city's first pedestrianized piazza symbolized the beginning of the reclamation of the *centro storico*. A line of bars, some hosting cultural associations and bookshops, were opened along one side and became a popular nocturnal haunt for young Neapolitans and the local cultural and political elite, as well as, significantly, hosting Bassolino's election campaign in 1993. Besides this new group of users, the piazza itself attracted '*ragazzi dei quartieri*' (neighbourhood kids) who would congregate at night on scooters to smoke weed. With the return of the 'abject', tensions rose. At the end of October 1999 a habitué of one of the bars was murdered in the piazza after a violent argument. The fact that the victim was killed by his partner did not prevent a public outcry among bar owners and their illustrious clients (see *Corriere del Mezzogiorno,* 31 October – 5 November 1999), who blamed the neighbourhood youths for general disturbances and called for a permanent police presence in the piazza. Their unruly presence was considered 'out of place'. Amato Lamberti, the Green Party president of the Province of Naples (and former assessor in the first Bassolino administration), exclaimed: 'The other day I suddenly noticed that the piazza had been taken over by groups of lowbrows,

---

13. Gambardella stated: 'The problem is all over Naples, but if I'm around Via dei Mille or Piazza dei Martiri [in Chiaia], I certainly won't notice this lack of education, which is perhaps due to the area's wealth, a more efficient refuse collection, but certainly the result of a common sense of respect towards the city, which is perhaps lacking among the inhabitants of the *quartieri*' (Montalto 2000: 168).

drug dealers and lumpenproletarians. ... Piazza Bellini was once the perfect place to observe the multifarious world of young people. But now, under the eyes of everyone, it has been engulfed by the *degrado* of the surrounding areas' (*Corriere del Mezzogiorno,* 3 November 1999).

In terms of tourism, the *quartieri* remained a source of attraction and repulsion. On the one hand, they contributed to the vitality of the *centro storico* and therefore potentially represented an asset, but on the other, their association with illegality and transgression also offered a negative image for tourists. In a front-page article of the *Corriere del Mezzogiorno* entitled 'Fascinating Ambiguity' (25 April 2000), Attilio Wanderlingh (the owner of one of the bars in Piazza Bellini who had organized a public meeting after the murder) claimed that tourists who visited the *centro storico* were apprehensive about wandering into alleyways. Admitting that a full-fledged tourist city might provoke further social and spatial divisions in the centre, Wanderlingh argued that this could be abated 'if we instead tried to revive and ennoble the most authentic popular traditions and translate them into occasions which attract tourists and encourage social reintegration'. In perhaps an extreme and isolated but nevertheless indicative case, two streets in the Spanish Quarters were specially lit (and patrolled by municipal police) on the same evening in spring 2000 on which the new lighting in Piazza Plebiscito was inaugurated. Visitors therefore had the chance to observe an alleyway scene at night with the assurance that they were not in any danger.

Inside the *quartieri* themselves, the administration introduced various measures aimed at socially 'integrating' the populations with the rest of the city. In 1998, two electric minibus lines provided the Spanish Quarters with their first ever public transport service. *La Repubblica* (20 December 1998) quipped that this 'autonomous republic' had finally bowed to the authority of the state (although for the first week the buses had to be escorted by police cars in order to unblock the route). On occasions, the administration also attempted to regulate public behaviour and collective practices. Apart from increasing the police presence in areas associated with petty crime, for instance in front of the funicular station in Piazza Montesanto, it took more affirmative action, such as attempting to bar the traditional pyres of old furniture built by children in neighbourhood piazzas in mid-January for the annual Feast of Saint Anthony. These were replaced with official bonfires lit and cordoned off by the fire brigade (De Matteis 1995). However, in general, it would seem that the *quartieri* were left to their own devices. Some of the more drastic measures backfired or were simply not a success (as in the case of the bonfires). A crackdown on contraband cigarette sellers at the beginning of 1994 led to a mass revolt and had to be abandoned. Due to the lack of formal employment, the Bassolino administration was forced to maintain, to a certain extent, a laissez-faire policy towards illegal and semi-illegal activities.[14]

Attempts to quell, or at least censure, aberrant forms of collective behaviour mostly took place in those spaces with strongly classified symbolic boundaries, where transgression was more likely to be experienced. Hence, while complaints would sometimes be voiced over the motorized incursions into Piazza Plebiscito or over the mass infringement of the 1999 motorcycle helmet law in the city's main streets, the apparent total disregard for the highway code in the *quartieri,* where one-way and no-entry signs appeared little more than colourful additions to the urban landscape, would proceed unabated and unnoticed.[15] Where formal legal boundaries were ineffectual, these boundaries were replaced by unofficial norms and codes which regulated the social organization of urban space and redefined the 'place' of transgression. This is why the common association of the 'illegal' car park with disorder is meaningless. Anyone who has parked a car in the *quartieri* will know that there are intricate rules and pecuniary obligations governing the temporary occupation of the roadside.

Bassolino insisted that the conservation of the *centro storico* directly implied the preservation of its social composition (although the same claim was made by the supporters of the Regno del Possibile), whereas for most of the twentieth century the inhabitants of the popular neighbourhoods were viewed in urban plans and political strategies as simply displaceable. However, they also presented a dilemma for the regeneration of the *centro storico*: while they embodied a quintessential aspect of Naples and Neapolitanness, certain forms of behaviour were considered damaging to attempts at reimaging the city. Although this dilemma was most apparent in symbolic sites, as improvements to the *quartieri* were carried out debates about the meaning of the city and universal appeals to civicness spread accordingly. This was also intimated in Bassolino's argument for involving local young people and children in the cultural programmes in the *centro storico*: 'In these areas we have to build a new

---

14. Contraband cigarette selling in the city plummeted from 1999 onwards, not due to repression on the part of the local administration, but because navigation in the Adriatic Sea was blocked for the duration of the Kosovo war in spring 1999, and controls were subsequently increased in the Straits of Otranto to prevent the arrival of refugees, which simultaneously shut off the principal tobacco smuggling route.

15. The wearing of motorcycle headgear, which in some neighbourhoods was once associated with hired killers wanting to conceal their identity, was now more commonly a sign of non-indigenous residents (the author included) or outsiders visiting the area. The 'refusal' to wear helmets among some dwellers of the *quartieri* cannot be simply understood as a disdain for the law but reflects a particular relationship with the *motorino.* This was less a personal form of transport for getting from point A (home) to point B (work) than a rapid (and often shared) instrument for negotiating social networks and movement within the neighbourhood (Rossi-Doria 1999: 161–63).

mentality and introduce a system of rules which is best achieved by investing in the younger generations' (Bassolino 1996b: 67).

Montesanto and the Ventaglieri Project

The idea of the historic popular neighbourhood is less likely to bring to mind Montesanto than the Spanish Quarters, Sanità, Forcella or Mercato, where images of crime (all are, or have been, closely associated with the Camorra) jostle with figures of folklore and culture such as the actor Totò or the playwright Eduardo De Filippo. Montesanto does not possess the (in)famous reputation of these neighbourhoods, nor is it as sprawling or physically dense. Nevertheless, the area was as much threatened with *sventramento* during the twentieth century as the other areas, and it plays its own part in *centro storico* myths.[16] More than any other central neighbourhood, Montesanto is a place of daily transit for thousands of people who use its transport systems. After Piazza Garibaldi, it is home to the most important public transport hub in the *centro storico,* with the funicular to Vomero and the terminus of the Cumana and Circumflegrea railway serving the suburbs and towns to the west of Naples, both located in Piazza Montesanto, and the Montesanto metro station in nearby Piazza Olivella. It has long been more socially heterogeneous. There is a larger amount of higher-quality housing stock compared with the Spanish Quarters or the Sanità, while the presence of a university faculty building, one of the busiest hospitals in the city centre and the Teatro Bracco (reopened in 1999 and specializing in mainstream Neapolitan productions) attract a wider variety of users. It is also visited by outsiders for its fruit, vegetable and fish markets, clothes shops, specialist shops such as comic stores and international delicatessens, and cheap pizzerias. The impact of immigration over the last two decades has been particularly noticeable in the area. Of the various national groups present in Montesanto during the 1990s (which included Sri Lankans and Dominicans), Cape Verdeans were the most numerous and appeared to be the more 'integrated' in the daily life of the neighbourhood. They frequented the bars and pizzerias around Piazza Montesanto as well as their own spaces, such as a small telephone centre off Via Ventaglieri. Evidence of their interaction with the 'indigenous' community could be seen from the condolence notices put up along Via Ventaglieri following the death of a Cape Verdean child.

---

16. Pignasecca and Piazza Montesanto have traditionally been considered the haunts of pickpockets and petty thieves. Myth has it that Pignasecca derives its name from the pine tree on which thieves once hung their booty. The tree was said to have dried up in the face of sinful acts.

Illustration 16.1. Via Montesanto, October 2010. *Photograph by Nick Dines.*

Like all the central neighbourhoods, Montesanto does not exist administratively and, as such, does not possess official borders. Most of it is situated in the Avvocata district that also comprises Materdei, a mainly middle-class residential area of early twentieth-century housing blocks more similar to Vomero than the city centre, while its southern edge lies in the Montecalvario district that includes the Pignasecca Market area (sometimes considered part of Montesanto) and the upper reaches of the Spanish Quarters. To complicate matters, Montesanto is in turn divided into smaller quarters, usually consisting of a few streets, although these, for the most part, are only recognized by local inhabitants. Prior to the earthquake, a study in the area calculated the population of Montesanto to be just under ten thousand (Provitera, Ranisio and Giliberti 1978).[17] Taking into consideration the fact that the dispersal caused by the earth-quake plus the ongoing, steady exodus from the city centre, especially of young families, was partially offset by professionals, immigrants and students moving into the neighbourhood, the population during the Bas-solino era can be estimated to have dropped to roughly eight thousand.

DAMM and the Ventaglieri Project are located in the hilly northern section of Montesanto, between the subquarters of Ventaglieri and Tarsia. A study of this micro-area conducted in 1983 and published in the Confindustria[18] journal *Orizzonti Economici,* provides a detailed social portrait of the zone as well as a glimpse of attitudes about the area's re-furbishment following the earthquake. According to its author, Gennaro Biondi, the area, like most of the *centro storico,* had been subjected to a disorderly development (Biondi 1983: 80). Although dotted with shops and artisans' workshops, it was primarily a residential area of approxi-mately three thousand inhabitants. Most spent the day elsewhere, either in the nearby Pignasecca Market or the *centro antico.* There was there-fore less of an 'alleyway life' than in other neighbourhoods. The physical state of buildings varied from street to street. Former courtiers' palaces lined the principal arteries of Via Ventaglieri and Salita Tarsia. While the upper floors had recently attracted many residents from outside the neighbourhood (in particular, students, intellectuals and left-wing politi-cal militants who were drawn by the area's proximity to the centre and the university and because rents offered better value for money), many of the ground-floor spaces had long been converted into *bassi,* which had not only caused overcrowding but had disfigured the 'architectural dignity' of buildings (ibid.). Nevertheless, most living quarters met mini-mum standards. They all had running water and washing facilities, and most had hot water, gas and a telephone. One street – Via Avellino a Tar-sia – was, however, in a particularly bad physical state. This hugged the edge of a precipice that overlooked Vico Lepri ai Ventaglieri. Together, these two alleyways demarcated the zone that had been chosen for a re-construction project. 'Here the buildings are nearly all derelict and living

---

17. The population of Avvocata dropped from 59,892 in 1951 to 28,798 in 1997, while the figure for Montecalvario over the same period dropped from 52,492 to 22,309 (Comune di Napoli 1999a). In 1997, Montecalvario had 29,745 inhabitants per square kilometre and Avvocata 28,798 per square kilometre, the second and third highest densities of the city's 29 districts (ibid.).

18. This is the General Confederation of Italian Industry, the principle employers' organization in Italy.

conditions are at the limits of decency. … The sense of abandonment is immediately perceptible, and this is accompanied by a general sense of disaffection among inhabitants' (ibid.: 81). These conditions, according to Biondi, justified demolition. Although the residents were said to have voiced their allegiances to the neighbourhood, Biondi claims that they did not manifest resistance to the thought of transferral to another part of the city.

What Biondi described in 1983 was not actually caused by the earthquake. The area in question had been beset with problems such as unstable buildings and subsidence long before 1980. In June 1967, an empty dwelling in Vico Lepri ai Ventaglieri undergoing repairs crumbled to the ground. Although there were no casualties, over 150 residents from neighbouring blocks were evacuated as a precautionary measure. *Il Mattino* viewed the incident as a symbol of administrative negligence towards the *centro storico* and demanded immediate improvements to buildings at risk. The 'helpless', 'forgotten' residents who gathered their possessions in the street and slept in parked cars were compared with coolies, pariahs and Vietnamese refugees (*Il Mattino,* 13 July 1967). Back in 1963, *L'Unità* had instead recognized a rebellious streak among the same residents, who were collecting a petition to protest at the lack of a refuse collection (12 January 1963). The street was also mentioned on more than one occasion by Macciocchi during her travels around the city in 1968 as the place where she became involved with the plight of eighty families who had received eviction orders from their building after waiting eight years to be rehoused (Macciocchi 1973: 115–16). In each case, the Ventaglieri area, tucked away in a far corner of the city centre, was portrayed as a marginal place, ignored by local authorities.

A plan to intervene in the area was first proposed in 1979 after an uninhabited building collapsed in Via Avellino a Tarsia and an unstable edifice was evacuated in Vico Lepri ai Ventaglieri. The 1980 earthquake worsened the situation. Those who had been made homeless the previous year now had no hope of returning to their former homes and were instead joined by other families evicted from neighbouring buildings. Many were rehoused in a requisitioned block of flats near Pomigliano d'Arco, fifteen kilometres to the east of Naples. Although the new accommodation was usually more spacious and salubrious to what people had been accustomed to in Montesanto, relocation was often a traumatic experience. Social networks were shattered and fragile economic equilibria destroyed, while those who had steady work suddenly found themselves commuting every day back to the city centre. One former resident of Vico Lepri ai Ventaglieri remembers the adverse effect that displacement had upon his family:

If we hadn't gone to Pomigliano, my sister wouldn't have gone off the rails [nb this is a reference to heroin addiction], I'd never have gone to Germany because we had a decent enough place to live in, and I could always work with my father even if it did mean working for cash in hand. ... Instead it was just a tremendous effort. You worked elsewhere, you came home late and so you never saw anything. ... It was the same story for many families. (Interview with author, 17 January 2003)[19]

Less than two months after the earthquake, as if a curse had befallen the area, a boiler exploded in an undamaged building at the end of Vico Lepri ai Ventaglieri, which led to yet more evictions. With the support of the local branch of the PCI, these families proceeded to occupy a private religious school in Piazza Montesanto, and after initially refusing the administration's various offers of housing outside Naples, they were eventually forced to accept temporary housing in requisitioned holiday apartments in the coastal resort of Baia Domizia, fifty kilometres to the north-west of Naples. A local carpenter was among those sent to the seaside:

They put us and fifteen other families in a residence. We were housed in a wing that was rented out during the summer months. The owners of the other apartments were not affected. We never got on because they were owners and we were 'earthquake victims'. I could never stand that phrase. What does 'earthquake victim' mean? Someone who's had less luck than someone else. (Interview with author, 25 January 2003)

This protracted upheaval guaranteed the area's inclusion in the 1981 reconstruction programme, although work did not ultimately commence until 1984 by which time eviction orders had been lifted and numerous dislodged families had managed to return to their homes. The project site represented the largest post-earthquake intervention in the *centro storico*. Whereas most of the other few schemes concentrated on the construction or restoration of individual buildings, the official aim here was to provide the area with public facilities that would eliminate 'situations of *degrado*' (Dispoto 1991: 100). Among the proposals were a terraced park, a theatre and parking spaces in converted caves in the tuff escarpment. The levelling of the tenement blocks would, according to one planner, make amends for the ancient gardens and orchards that had been lost during the intense spate of building in the sixteenth century (Ferulano 1986). The construction of new residential units was not a plausible option because

19. The interviews in this section were conducted as part of the AHRB-funded project 'Memory and Place in the Italian Twentieth-Century City' between 2002 and 2004. My research on Naples examined memories of the 1980 earthquake in Montesanto and the Spanish Quarters and involved the production of a sixty-one-minute documentary film entitled *Fuggifuggi Memories of an Earthquake* (2004). Extracts of this film can be viewed at the insu^tv website: http://www.insutv.it/domenicaut/memorie-del-terremoto-del-1980.

these would create, it was argued, serious health and safety risks in an already overcrowded area (Ferulano 1991). Giovanni Dispoto, who oversaw the design of parks in the reconstruction programme, wrote of the project: 'In the vast cleared space, the task was to formulate a multifunctional project that would restore the historical value of the landscape, increase the minimal level of services and green space in the area and offer an urban "void" in a congested part of the city' (Dispoto 1991: 100). In retrospect, the idea of a liberated 'void' seems somewhat nonchalant in light of the consequences that this provoked. The clearance of the area in 1984 foresaw the transferral of approximately 250 families, the majority of whom were rehoused in new flats in the city's working-class suburbs such as Ponticelli or in towns around Vesuvius. Rather than responding to the needs of a small community, planners saw the project as a one-off occasion to experiment in the centre of Naples. The supervisor of the post-earthquake schemes in the *centro storico,* Giancarlo Ferulano, saw the metamorphosis of the zone as a positive development and, like Biondi, claimed that people were happy to leave: 'Although this operation led to the definitive transfer of households to other localities, this was willingly accepted and sometimes endorsed by the inhabitants who were by now exasperated by their living conditions' (Ferulano 1991: 106).

In actual fact, many residents had been, unsurprisingly, opposed to the scheme. Shortly following the project's announcement in 1981, a campaign, with the active backing of the local PCI branch, was organized with the principal objective of preventing as many people as possible from leaving the neighbourhood. After initially advancing a deliberately provocative plan for five tower blocks on the site that would have accommodated all the displaced households, attention turned to challenging the provisions of the scheme. Mario Pochet, a Montesanto resident and leader of the PCI on the local district council, recalls the episode:

> It was a long battle that lasted two years. In the end, the theatre was scrapped. There had been a lot of publicity and heated exchange over the issue in the local press in which our branch argued that if you really need a theatre, there's the Bracco Theatre down the road, which is closed. If you really want a theatre, you can reopen the Bracco, but whatever you do, don't build another one here. It would be more appropriate to save some of the condemned buildings and bring back some of the original residents. ... We also suggested they build a school, because there had never been a state school in the area. Given the nature of the project, why had they never thought of building one? So as a result of this two-year battle we eventually reached a compromise whereby the school was built, and in place of the theatre, five or six buildings were saved.' (Interview with author, 25 January 2003)

According to Pochet, the campaign's principal adversaries were the engineers who had organized contracts for the project and were keen not to lose their fee. However, he also noted that opposition to the scheme inevitably involved confrontation with the Valenzi administration, which had coordinated the reconstruction programme. In other words, the dispute was also between people from the same political party. This reflected the hostility among many grassroots PCI activists towards the local government's limited action in the *centro storico* after the earthquake (Belli 1986). More generally, it indicated dissonant attitudes about the central popular neighbourhoods, not only from different institutional perspectives, but from within the Left itself. On the one hand was a campaign born out of residents' place attachments and presumptions that an intervention in the area would at least serve local collective needs. On the other was the top-down technical vision of planners, many of them young and idealistically committed to working in the public sector (Corona 2007), whose goal was to recuperate the architectural and environmental 'dignity' that had been lost over the centuries. The proposed facilities, in particular the theatre, were conceived for a general public rather than the local inhabitants alone. A traditionally peripheral and problem-prone area would be transformed into a unique visitor attraction. But despite changes being made to the scheme,[20] the project ultimately illustrated the inevitable social disruption caused by demolition in the *centro storico*. Those not lucky enough to be allocated one of the few apartments in the spared buildings were instead offered the choice of a new life in a new and more distant periphery. At a micro level, it stood as a sign of what would have happened on a much grander and devastating scale had the Regno del Possibile gone ahead. But it also indicated the ambiguity that lay behind the idea of a 'historically sensitive' approach to redeveloping the popular neighbourhoods.

Writing in 1991, Giancarlo Ferulano declared that the Ventaglieri Project, once complete, would feature terraced gardens, secluded pergolas, panoramic viewpoints, as well as a system of covered escalators linking the two levels of the neighbourhood. Unfortunately, the scheme met the same fate as many other post-earthquake interventions in Naples, which suffered from cursory, ill-conceived planning decisions and protracted, uncontrolled work that turned into opportunities to siphon public money (Dal Piaz and Apreda 1993; Barbagallo 1997). According to a DAMM activist and local resident, the work in Montesanto was drawn out even further because the Camorra had managed to guarantee locals employment on the site. The fenced-off area was once again forgotten by the city's authorities:

---

20. The modifications to the original project were interpreted by its authors as a purely technical matter (the theatre would have provoked unsustainable levels of congestion), and no reference was made to the residents' campaign (Ferulano 1991).

It's as if this thing never existed. I basically discovered it by chance even though I lived only a few metres away – but it was closed off. I remember one evening when these gigantic lorries arrived carrying the escalators and had to spend over an hour manoeuvring into the alleyway. Everyone knew that they were part of some project, but nobody knew what it was about. Residents had been moved out. My brother was sent to Sant'Anastasia [a town near Vesuvius]. Anyway, the area was abandoned. In fact young people and children used to call it the '*sgarrupato*', which means broken, and some still do. (M., interview with author, 1 August 1999)

The bulk of the infrastructure was completed by 1993, but only the school became operative. Other proposed facilities, such as a library and workshops, never materialized, while the abandoned green spaces were variously used as a rubbish tip, a receptacle for stolen items and a shooting gallery for heroin users. Like many of the reconstruction schemes in Naples, the Ventaglieri Project remained officially closed due to a lack of finances, management skills and political will in local government (Dal Piaz and Apreda 1993). At the beginning of 1994, Antonio Bassolino inaugurated a number of post-earthquake parks in the outer suburbs as part of his first hundred-days plan. The mayor considered these openings as symbolic gestures that signalled a breach with the past, because they 'demonstrated that it was possible to do many things even with few resources – often at zero cost – using the personnel of the administration in a new way and creating a different relationship with the city' (Bassolino 1996b: 17). However, the neglected project that would eventually be christened the Ventaglieri Park was not among the new structures opened to the public.

Chapter 17

Diego Armando Maradona Montesanto (DAMM)

Collective Action over Public Space in Montesanto

The Italian *centri sociali* and radical urban politics in the 1990s

On 25 August 1995 a group of local residents and students broke into the top end of the Ventaglieri Project and occupied the former deaf insti-tute that had been saved from demolition. The three-storey building was duly declared a '*centro sociale occupato autogestito*' (occupied and self-managed social centre), and the adjacent terraced park was hastily cleaned and prepared for an inaugural public party.

In 2001 there were over one hundred *centri sociali* across Italy, from more than a dozen in cities such as Milan and Rome to single examples in small provincial towns.[1] At a very generic level, *centri sociali* are dis-used, privately or publicly owned buildings such as factories, warehouses and schools often (but not always) located in working-class districts, which are occupied and transformed by groups of predominantly young people for social, cultural and political activities. They are characterized by activists' insistence on autonomous collective organization and di-rect democracy. A regular *assemblea di autogestione* (self-management meeting) held by the group of occupants and sometimes open to sympa-thetic members of the public determines the specific direction of the *centro sociale*. Practical and theoretical issues are debated, activities within and beyond its boundaries are planned and means of financial self-support are proposed.

---

1. Mudu (2004) estimated that over 250 *centri sociali* were occupied between 1985 and 2003, al-though many of these occupations were short lived. Only 18 per cent were located in the Italian South. For in-depth discussions of Italian social centres in English, see Dines 2000; Ruggiero 2000; Wright 2000; Mudu 2004 and Montagna 2006.

The *centri sociali* have their roots in the radical political and cultural upheavals of the 1970s (Lumley 1990; Balestrini and Moroni 1997). The occupation of buildings in the city during this decade were a means of creating autonomous spheres and solidarity networks among young people unrepresented (and unrepresentable) by traditional forms of organization. Their demands were no longer defined in purely quantitative terms, such as a roof over heads, but as the need to reappropriate and self-organize social space and time. They also often became refuges for far-left organizations such as Autonomia Operaia and remnants of the New Left parties such as Lotta Continua (Lodi and Grazioli 1984). During the 1980s, *centri sociali* represented bastions of cultural and social opposition to the mass retreat into the private domain. They organized assistance to combat the rise of heroin addiction and played an important role in peace and anti-nuclear protests (Dines 1999). Although a few of the original *centri sociali* have 'resisted' through to the present, such as Leoncavallo in Milan (first occupied in 1975, although forced to change premises on three occasions), they did not become a widespread national phenomena until the beginning of the 1990s. The nationwide Pantera student movement of 1990, which led to month-long occupations of universities across Italy and was also specifically instrumental in the reclaiming of nocturnal public spaces in the *centro storico* of Naples, had an influential role that stimulated a revisiting and reappraisal of past traditions and fostered new forms of protest. During the first part of the decade, with the recently dissolved Communist Party facing a membership crisis especially among younger people, the *centri sociali* became laboratories of counter-hegemonic political projects and the bases for cultural and recreational activities that were either inexistent or inaccessible in the rest of the city. Alternative forms and modes of cultural production were practiced and promoted, such as the experimentation with information technologies and music. Rap groups formed by activists, like 99 Posse that came out of the experience of Officina 99 in Naples, helped popularize the issue of *centri sociali* (Wright 2000).

The *centri sociali* in the 1990s were not simply a residue of the 1970s, nor were they merely a collective expression of 'post-material society' (Melucci 1984). Past traditions and practices were reformulated within shifting contexts – structural transformations to the urban built environment and labour market, the rise of new technologies and the presence of new social actors such as immigrants – which in turn generated new forms of collective action. Many *centri sociali* assumed more offensive positions than in the past. During the course of the 1990s they were instrumental in political mobilizations over immigrant rights (where left parties were initially absent), the organization of anti-war demonstrations and, at the beginning of the following decade, 'anti-globalization' protests (for instance, they played a key role in the organization of the protests against the G8 summit in Genoa in July 2001). Conventional forms of protest such as the *corteo* (march) were interwoven with new strategies, such as the civil disobedience tactics adopted by the '*Tute Bianche*' (White Overalls) movement,[2] while different methods of communication (in particular Internet and video) combined with the more traditional plethora of publications, newspapers and leaflets in creating extensive alternative circuits of information. Whereas in the 1970s the *centro sociale* was conceived primarily as a venue for social gatherings, during the 1990s the term simultaneously referred to the occupied building, the group of occupants, a form of collective action, as well as a broadly counter-hegemonic identity.

However, since their outset, *centri sociali* have been complex, contradictory phenomena that defy singular definitions. All the irreconcilable contradictions of the 1970s – the 'here and now' and the 'revolutionary', irony and dogma, personal politics and collective action, spiritual retreat and confrontational violence – as well as potentially conflicting currents such as punks and *autonomi* 'flowed' into the *centro sociale* (Lodi and Grazioli 1984; Zaccaria 1997). During the 1990s, the *centri sociali* would become increasingly distinguishable on political grounds (the majority were Communist, although these diverged between classic Marxist-Leninist and more heterodox Autonomist positions, followed by anarchist centres and others that considered themselves leftist but claimed to be 'non-ideological');[3] over their relationship with institutions (hostile, pragmatic or strategic); over their principal objectives (cultural, social or

2. The 'White Overalls' refer to the clothing worn by activists from a number of northern Italian and Roman *centri sociali* during direct-action protests – such as the scaling of the walls of immigrant detention centres – and more traditional demonstrations. Emphasis was placed on the communicative impact of this attire, which at the same time concealed the individual identity of protesters (Centro sociale Leoncavallo 1999: 41). In 2001, following the anti-G8 protests in Genoa, the *Tute Bianche* were disbanded, and most of those involved formed themselves into a new group, the *Disobbedienti* (Disobedients).

3. Nicola Montagna has noted the continuation of three distinct movement networks after 2001: 'The Libertarians refuse any kind of formalization of their structures and dialogue with state institutions, but also with movements that they judge too moderate. ... The Antagonists and Antimperialists feel themselves legitimate inheritors of the autonomist movements of the 1970s and base their analyses of the social system on Marxist class categories. The Disobedients reclaim the heretical Marxist tradition and argue that Western capitalist economies have been experiencing a transitional period from Fordism to post-Fordism' (Montagna 2006: 297). Since 1990, a handful of neo-Fascist occupied spaces have existed, primarily in Rome, with the most notable example currently being Casa Pound, a condominium occupied in 2003 in the multiethnic neighbourhood of Esquilino. It goes without saying that besides the act of squatting, these scattered and usually short-lived experiences have had very little in common with *centri sociali* (despite the mainstream press's insistence on calling them 'right-wing *centri sociali*'): their organizational structure is hierarchical; their energies are focused on a few activities, namely organizing concerts and providing housing for homeless Italian families; and

political) and over their ability to attract a critically engaged public. At the same time, these tensions would often be present within individual *centri sociali,* leading in some cases to internal groups breaking away and creating new occupations.

It would also be possible to trace some general geographical variations. The majority of available literature as well as national media interest during the 1990s focused on the long-established post-autonomist *centri sociali* in Milan and, to a lesser degree, Rome and Turin.[4] Leoncavallo in Milan was considered by many to be the archetypal *centro sociale,* especially after it became the centre of national media attention during a violent eviction in 1989, but in reality it reflected a particular tradition and agenda. At the end of the 1990s, Leoncavallo, together with centres in the Veneto region, opened dialogues with left-wing parties with the aim of building strategic alliances and elevating their impact on society (Centro Sociale Leoncavallo 1999).[5] This provoked a deepening of existent divisions and led to a major split between former allies. The strategies, agendas and language of Neapolitan *centri sociali* contrasted to those in the North. Two of the city's most active *centri sociali* in the 1990s, Officina 99 and lo Ska ('Laboratorio Occupato di Sperimentazione di Kultura Antagonista'), both drew on the Marxist-Leninist tendency within Autonomia Operaia and forged a close relationship with the radical faction of the Organized Unemployed Movement. During the 1990s, the two considered themselves part of the '*area antagonista*' in contradistinction to the various *centri sociali* in the North that had sought working alliances with institutions, while in 2001 they were key protagonists in the regional 'NoGlobal Network'.[6] In contrast to Officina 99 and lo Ska, DAMM did not consider political ideology a means for mobilization and was not aligned with any other *centro sociale* in Italy, although it did participate in anti-war and anti-globalization networks alongside other local *centri*

---

activities tend to be confined behind closed doors due to widespread hostility (for an overview, see Di Tullio 2006).

4. More recently, as *centri sociali* have become an established phenomena of sociological inquiry, research has included southern Italy. See, for instance, Festa (2003) on Naples and Piazza (2007) on Catania.

5. In 1999, these *centri sociali* coordinated a series of spectacular direct actions against immigrant detention centres across Italy, which led, for the first time, to debates over the matter in the mainstream press. As with numerous other protests, the involvement of individual members of parliament (from Communist Refoundation and the Green Party) ensured a greater public impact.

6. For a detailed discussion of Neapolitan *centri sociali,* see Dines (1999) and Festa (2003). The NoGlobal Network was set up to contest the OECD Global Forum on E-government held in Naples in March 2001. The term 'no-global' was subsequently deployed by the Italian mainstream press and politicians as a generic appellative to describe the international anti-globalization movement as well as all *centri sociali* activists in Italy. With the mass anti-globalization protests from the end of 1999 onwards and the movement against the war in Kosovo and later in Iraq, lo Ska and Officina 99 began to collaborate more actively in broad networks that included left parties and the peace movement.

sociali from 1999 onwards. Its links with the past were less direct. Activists claimed to feel affinity with the neighbourhood-based campaigns of the early 1970s and their tactics of self-reduction of prices of goods and services, as well as the ludic and ironic elements of the 1977 student movement, rather than the more explicitly ideological traditions. But, as in the other two cases, it was first a Neapolitan and second a national tradition that was recuperated.

The Italian *centri sociali* have rightly been described as forming 'a heterogeneous archipelago' (Montagna 2006). Some observers have seen them as also comprising a particular 'social movement' (Ruggiero 2000; Berzano and Gallini 2000), partly to endow them with sociological significance so as to counter their common portrayal in the mainstream Italian press and some academic circles as marginalized, subversive and drug ridden.[7] While the *centri sociali* do indeed resonate with many of the traditional theoretical debates about urban social movements, be it the direct challenge to the socioeconomic structuring of the city (Castells 1983), the formulation of alternative codes and symbols (Melucci 1984) or the interplay between social conflict and group identity (Castells 1997), their depiction as a specific 'movement' not only overlooks their often irreconcilable differences but also risks reifying their politics into the physical spaces of squatted buildings. It would be more accurate and appropriate to conceive *centri sociali* as a particular praxis (commonly bound around the organizational principle of self-management and the critical reshaping of the built environment) and as 'movement actors' (Montagna 2006) that have made important contributions to a range of political struggles and experiences, from the Italian Zapatista movement to anti-racist campaigns and, as in the case of DAMM, to a radical critique of urban regeneration.

The category of youth has been used to encompass the diversity of the *centri sociali*. As a biological, cultural and sociological concept, youth is identified as a particular passage in life distinguished by a set of presumed idiosyncrasies such as a propensity for transgression, experimentation and innovation which enable and legitimate certain forms of social action, including the occupation of urban spaces. In the past, the *centri sociali* were examined within an 'area of youth movement' in order to interpret the transformations of a post-1968 'generation' (Lodi

---

7. For instance, in an entry on Italian rap music in the *Encyclopedia of Contemporary Italian Culture*, the *centro sociale* is described as an 'occupied drop-in centre' for 'marginalized youth and the socially disaffected' (Moliterno 2000: 496–97). Research carried out jointly by *centri sociali* and sociologists in Milan discovered that users were not markedly different in terms of employment and education to nonusers, thus contradicting the social stigma usually associated with them (Guarnieri Gomma 1996).

and Grazioli 1984). However, a similar approach to examining the phenomena in the 1990s would be reductive and would miss the dynamic nature of the *centri sociali*. Activists are only classifiable as 'youths', or rather '*giovani*', because the sociocultural threshold of adulthood in Italy has risen since the 1970s, largely due to delayed entry into the job market and secure employment (Cristante 1995). In fact, the majority of activists in the *centri sociali* in Milan and Naples were, on average, in their late twenties and thirties (Guarnieri Gomma 1996; Dines 1999). More important, the notion of 'youth' was not a basis of a *centro sociale*'s identity, which, according to Lodi and Grazioli, had been the case during the early 1980s; rather, the basis of this identity was intersected by other factors such as political orientation and social class.

The focus of my interest here is the *centro sociale*'s relationship with the city. The appropriation and transformation of built space is a constant feature and is the platform from which activists deal with outsiders. Don Mitchell has argued that in spite of the rise of information technologies, material public space remains fundamental for alternative collective action 'to arise and contest issues of citizenship and democracy' (Mitchell 1995: 117). He argues that the 1989 Tiananmen Square protests would not have become such a momentous political and media event if the physical space had not been taken over in the first place (ibid.: 123). Unlike Tiananmen Square, the *centro sociale*'s occupation of space is not linked to a brief, intense period of protest but involves the laborious construction, over a daily basis, of an alternative agenda and discursive arena. For much of the time, the *centro sociale*'s presence in the city is ignored. It is during key episodes, such as the initial occupation and attempted (or successful) evictions or organized political protests and cultural events, that it may become a focus of public attention. The *centro sociale* is not simply an alternative autonomous sphere but a place 'that allows [collective action] to be seen … where it can represent itself to a larger population … where it becomes a public' (ibid.: 115).

The *centro sociale*'s relationship to the built environment is conceived in various ways. For Officina 99 and lo Ska, the urban dimension was the place where political struggles were conducted. Officina 99 was based in an abandoned factory occupied in May 1991 in the eastern industrial suburb of Gianturco. The choice of this run-down industrial location was primarily symbolic: a stimulus to conspicuously project alternative notions of urbanity in the shadow of the high-rise development of the Centro Direzionale. Lo Ska, on the other hand, occupied an unused university building close to Piazza Gesù Nuovo in February 1995. Its location in the *centro antico,* a few yards from a number of tourist attractions such as the Monastery of Santa Chiara, gave the space greater visibility and enabled

it to play on the contradictions and consequences of the area's revaloriza-
tion during the 1990s. Activists were briefly involved in the organization
of protests of removal workers who had been evicted from their traditional pitches in Piazza Gesù Nuovo following the city council's decision
to turn part of the piazza into a tourist coach park. However, the attempts
of both *centri sociali* to build a closer rapport with locals were ultimately
undermined by their explicitly militant political agenda.

In the case of DAMM, it was the social reality of the Montesanto
district that influenced the form of many of its initiatives and elicited a
more pragmatic approach. This was also used by activists to distinguish
themselves from other *centri sociali*. 'When you work in a neighbourhood you have to confront its contradictions. … Officina would never
have been the same Officina if it had been located in a neighbourhood
like Montesanto' (L., interview with author, 11 July 1999). By occupying the Ventaglieri Project, DAMM set about reconfiguring and investing meaning into a planned environment that had been left in the lurch
but that now found itself in a resurgent city centre. The contradictions it
faced were many indeed.

The following analysis of DAMM draws on written material produced
during the occupation (posters, leaflets and short books), extended periods of participant observation (including attendance at weekly meetings)
and in-depth interviews with principal activists. Living a few hundred
metres from the Ventaglieri Park, I frequently attended recreational activities and built a close, daily rapport with a number of occupants. As
observers have noted, *centri sociali* have traditionally eschewed analysis
by others (Ruggiero 2000; Berzano and Gallini 2000). It must be stressed
that I do not claim to offer a definitive historical study of the first six
years of DAMM, which was and continues to be a contradictory and
fragmented experience. Rather, by exploring the various registers – from
the communicative rhetoric of leaflets to the more reflective accounts of
publications and personal positions discussed in interviews – the aim
here is to concentrate on the emergence of alternative ideas about public
space in the *centro storico*.

The creation of a *centro sociale* in Montesanto

The occupation of DAMM was initially provoked by the lure of the
project's incongruous position in the heart of Montesanto. The site was
in a state of total dereliction. The unused escalators had been vandal-
ized, and the incomplete top gardens were littered with used syringes.

The three-storey '*palazzina*' had been planned as a sports centre but was never consigned to the city council because of numerous structural irregularities. All its doors were off their hinges and its windows smashed. The reclamation of the space was at first seen as a sort of epic challenge rather than a form of political protest, as evinced in the personal account of one of DAMM's activists:

> This park was in the middle of my neighbourhood: ten thousand unguarded square metres, two buildings, the odd flower bed and flights of steps that wound around a tuff mountain. … I'd often go to have a look at the place. At the time I was running a Theatre of the Oppressed workshop at Officina 99, and once I took the guys along and we spoke about occupying it. I wasn't the type to hang around, but I didn't have any firsthand experience of occupations. … On that first occasion we fantasized, but I continued to look for people. Every so often I'd go back to the park with some dreamer, until one day I went with the right person. His name was Fiore. We were there one early morning in May after a night spent wandering the city, and we saw the sunlight shine through the sea of discarded syringes and rubbish. The Yellow Giant wanted to live and spoke to us through this dunghill. Fiore decided he wanted to make a film. He had some spare reels. 'I'm up for it, let's occupy!' (Braucci 1998)

The choice of name, Diego Armando Maradona, aimed to appeal to everybody. This was a *centro sociale* named in honour of Naples's idolized hero, who had recently left the city. A mock shrine on a nearby street corner painted after the first championship in 1987 depicting the Argentinian footballer in the arms of the city's preeminent patron saint, San Gennaro, was featured on the homepage of DAMM's website. The name underlined a distaste for the political sloganeering considered endemic among orthodox *centri sociali*. More significant, it reflected a wish for open dialogue with the neighbourhood, as one of its first leaflets announced: 'Maradona has returned to Naples to play with Neapolitans'. It inevitably attracted the attention of the national and local media, which viewed the experience as a modern folkloric curiosity rather than a form of political action. The national edition of *Corriere della Sera* ran a report on the *centro sociale* a month after the occupation, noting: 'Everyone loved [Maradona], nobody has forgotten him, and many still have his photo on their walls' (22 September 1995). The reference to the footballer was, however, soon assimilated into the acronym DAMM.[8]

The northern part of Montesanto had a history of collective urban activism. Gennaro Biondi's 1983 survey of the area mentioned two significant political experiences: the Mensa dei Bambini Proletari (Working-class Children's Refectory), founded by political militants and intellectu-

---

8. For a philosophical and sociological reflection on the significance of Maradona for Naples and Neapolitans, see Dini and Nicolaus (1991).

Illustration 17.1. Mural of Maradona in the Spanish Quarters, April 2002. *Photograph by Nick Dines.*

als in 1973 and located one hundred metres from DAMM,[9] and the city's first *comitato di quartiere* (neighbourhood committee) between 1972 and 1973. One could also add the local section of the PCI, which mobi-

---

9. The association, which survived on donations from private donors and limited funds from the city council, provided daily hot meals and a place to meet and play for over a hundred children from

lized residents after the earthquake and often found itself in conflict with the left-wing administration.[10] While none of these experiences directly influenced the creation of DAMM, the occupation of the space, as well as informal contacts with past activists such as Mario Pochet and the nationally famous cultural critic Goffredo Fofi,[11] who had been involved with the Mensa, acted to resurrect this local radical tradition. As Dolores Hayden argues: 'An ordinary urban neighbourhood will also contain the history of activists who have campaigned against spatial injustices. ... Every city and town has ... landmarks where territorial struggles have been waged' (Hayden 1995: 39). The Ventaglieri Project was one such landmark. If it had not been for the campaign led by Pochet, the *palazzina* later occupied by DAMM would not have existed. But while this past battle had been almost entirely concerned with questions of collective consumption, DAMM oriented its action also around less immediately material issues such as the self-management of space and the politics of place representation.

It is possible to divide the history of DAMM between 1995 and 2001 into three general phases. The first few months between 1995 and 1996 were a period of mobilization. Large weekly meetings of up to fifty people put forward a myriad of ideas and projects. Adjustments to the bare *palazzina,* such as rewiring and basic decorating, were carried out by activists themselves, and equipment was gradually installed, including makeshift theatre seating and lighting, in order to convert the building into a base for activities. Following this initial moment of chaotic euphoria, from 1996 to 1998, the occupation steadily developed. A daily programme of social and cultural activities was funded by frequent concerts and other social events, a core group of activists emerged and important contacts were made with public figures in Naples. From 1999 to 2001,

---

the local area (Stazio and Traiola 1981: 137). In addition, it served as a local base for organized unemployed and feminist groups (Fofi 1999), regularly organized political and cultural debates, and participated in neighbourhood events such as the pedestrian campaigns in 1978 to reclaim the steps behind Montesanto funicular station (Capasso, Niego and Vittoria 1982).

10. Going even further back in time, one could also include the so-called 'Montesanto Federation', a leftist organization within the PCI that famously split from the party at the end of 1943 in dispute with Togliatti's reformist line of national unity of anti-Fascist forces and his rejection of socialist revolution (Amyot 1981).

11. Goffredo Fofi (born in 1937 in Gubbio (Umbria)) has been a charismatic figure on the Italian Left since the early 1960s, making his name as a prolific essayist, film critic, script writer, biographer, political activist and all-round polemicist (see his autobiography, Fofi 1999). During the 1960s and 1970s he collaborated with New Left journals such as *Quaderni Piacentini* and *Ombre Rosse* and was later active in the extra-parliamentary organization Lotta Continua. He has spent his life between Milan, Rome, Palermo and Naples, where he was one of the protagonists of the Mensa dei Bambini Proletari. During the last two decades he has set up and edited (or co-edited) a series of often short-lived cultural journals with a focus on the Italian South. These include *La Terra Vista dalla Luna, Dove sta Zazà* and the current publication *lo Straniero.*

DAMM appeared to consolidate its organizational strengths, concentrating on activities considered most important (such as the campaigns to improve the park), and renounced the more ambitious and popular public events, which were considered an excessive expenditure of energies and not financially worthwhile.

The occupation evolved out of a confluence of individual experiences. Some activists had previously been involved with Officina 99 but had clashed with its explicitly political orientation, while others joined DAMM with proposals for social projects in the local area. In 1999 there were approximately twenty core activists, while about one hundred people had participated at some stage in the occupation. This was a socially heterogeneous group comprised of university students, unemployed graduates, skilled and manual labourers, social workers, actors and writers, all of whom were in their twenties or thirties. Nearly all were Neapolitan: some were natives of Montesanto itself and possessed an intimate knowledge of the local area, a few moved into the neighbourhood after 1995, while others lived in residential districts such as Vomero and Soccavo.

The group of occupants possessed a range of skills and expertise, from metalwork and rudimentary electrical engineering to graphic design and video production, as well as a series of contacts with professionals such as theatre performers and sports instructors. These various resources were put to use in the organization of a wide range of weekly activities: a *ludoteca* (play space) and *doposcuola* ('after-school') that offered recreational activities and extra tuition for local primary school children,[12] a women's health group, a medical advice centre, martial arts such as Aikido, meditation evenings and yoga, dance lessons, theatre workshops and an all-day cinema. A boxing gym on the top floor which trained local youths broke away from DAMM in 1998 and continued to operate separately until early 2001. These activities were not simply a means of animating the empty *palazzina* but were conceived as a critique on the availability, accessibility and quality of similar services in the city. Over a short space of time, DAMM also became known for its publications and cultural productions. Besides a constant flow of leaflets and posters that were handed out at events and pasted on the walls around the *centro storico,* three books were self-published (two reflections on the

---

12. The 'after-school' was one of the most successful and popular activities organized by DAMM. It ran three days a week between 1996 and 2000 and involved ninety children from a primary school in the adjacent Tarsia quarter. During the first year it offered assistance with homework, but the emphasis later switched to developing a series of art workshops and organizing games in the park. The basic costs of materials and refreshments were met by the children's families who paid five thousand lire (€2.50) a month (DAMM 1998).

occupation (DAMM 1998, 2000) and a play script (DAMM 1999)), a website was designed (although this was rarely updated[13]), while in 1999 a short-lived newsletter, *Il Ventagliere,* was distributed free at DAMM and around Montesanto. The *palazzina* became the venue for independent theatre and cabaret, as well as performances written, directed and performed by occupants themselves. A number of short films were made, including one shot during the occupation in 1995 and a film-noir parody that was presented at the Venice Film Festival in 1996.

Many of DAMM's initiatives were targeted at local residents. After discovering that 'cobret', a smokable derivative of heroin, was being consumed in the park, DAMM organized a public-awareness campaign. Local children and teenagers became regular users of the *centro sociale* and sometimes helped out with the organization of activities, particularly in the case of film productions. This said, many of DAMM's habitués came from outside the neighbourhood. An open-door policy was also adopted because DAMM saw itself as a providing a window for the rest of the city on the particular situation in Montesanto. However, activists were publicly scathing of nonlocal visitors who were only interested in attending cheap social events and consuming cut-price alcohol.

Out of the collective enthusiasm sparked by the occupation, there emerged divergent positions about which direction DAMM should take. Some of the original occupants, influenced by the spatial theories and practices of the situationists, first conceived DAMM as a sort of 'detourned' space for cultural experimentation and played on the peculiarities and absurdities of the abandoned structure. This 'current' existed alongside a more explicitly political approach, which sought to devise alternative discourses about the city through a programme of social activities. The significance of the term *'centro sociale'* was also perceived in different ways. One activist argued that DAMM loosely belonged to a libertarian current of *centri sociali* in contradistinction to the historic experiences in the North, such as Leoncavallo and the *'autonomi'* of Officina 99, while another disputed its relevance altogether, preferring the more malleable term *'zone multiple autogestite'* (multiple self-managed zones):

> I don't see why the *centro sociale* has to be the exclusive reference when it comes to struggles. ... In fact, DAMM is called a "self-managed zone", but this doesn't mean anything. What is written [on the wall] does not necessarily correspond to who you are. Of course, if you have to explain to someone who asks 'What's that place?', you reply 'a *centro sociale* occupato'. (M., interview with author, 1 August 1999)

---

13. At the time of writing, this website was hosted at the following address: http://isole.ecn.org/damm.

The accommodation of internal differences was nevertheless considered to be a principal source of DAMM's vitality and distinctiveness: 'We refused to assume a single identity, and therefore we haven't affixed symbols to our actions. Even though a symbol is easier: you accept it or reject it because you can imagine what's behind it' (leaflet entitled 'If you managed to live this space today…', summer 1997).

The weekly meeting was the sacrosanct arena in which potentially divisive issues such as funds from outside donors or the illegal status of the occupation were confronted, leaflets were discussed and written, and decisions were made. Tensions would sometimes reach a boiling point, whereupon (in a uproarious mêlée of Italian and Neapolitan dialect) individuals would be variously accused of middle-class idealism, anti-democratic boorishness, acquiescence or extremism. However, group solidarity was maintained by a universal adherence to the collective management and defence of the space, and those seen to exploit the occupation for personal gain were reprimanded and sometimes ostracized (as occurred in the case of the manager of the boxing ring). There was also consensus over the greater emphasis given to the quotidian, practical and local significance of the occupation: 'We are an occupied space in a *quartiere popolare* which is working in this neighbourhood, confronting the contradictions and the real needs, separating the human requests from those of the consumer, embracing the former and scorning the latter' (untitled leaflet, January 1996).

In spite internal differences, as a collective, DAMM assumed a pragmatic attitude towards mediation with institutions but was generally hostile to any form of interference. During its early phase, DAMM was courted by left-wing organizations, in particular Communist Refoundation. These approaches were rebuffed as purely opportunistic given that nobody had ever taken any interest in the Ventaglieri Project prior to their arrival. At the same time, activists were aware that the ill-defined identity of DAMM, together with its popularity, made it vulnerable to assimilation:

> In contrast to other *centri sociali,* we are truly social, which makes us likeable in the eyes of the city. But when it comes to the powers that be, the newspapers and middle classes, this likeableness is as much a result of our weak identity. And we don't want to be liked by these people. … We're not talking about hoisting red flags or setting absolute formulas but a bit of identity (i.e. who we are) is also built reflecting on the things that happen here every day. We must not be shy or frightened to bring them out in public. (Leaflet entitled 'Why only an illegal DAMM makes sense', January 1997)

As DAMM grew in confidence and formulated its own flexible cultural-political identity, it took a less dismissive and defensive approach to its encounters with the world that lay beyond Montesanto and its user base. It began to offer itself as a public forum for debates on a range of issues, from the development of the third sector in Naples to the NATO war in Kosovo.[14] Following the arson attack on the Roma camps in the run-down suburb of Scampìa in June 1999, it hosted and participated in meetings with voluntary groups and representatives from unions and left-wing parties in order to organize a protest campaign. It also forged close links with professionals such as town planners and educationalists who provided support and expertise (for instance in the running of the after-school activities). A number of 'allies', such as the town planner Daniela Lepore and Goffredo Fofi, endorsed the occupation in the local media which contributed to its public impact in the city. Fofi, for instance, wrote a full-page article for *Corriere del Mezzogiorno* in which he welcomed DAMM's endeavour to confront the contradictions in the *centro storico* through its self-management of an abandoned structure: '[DAMM is a] novel laboratory which must learn to resist the alarms or pressures from above and continue to produce an alternative culture from below, which in the present climate is increasingly rare' (*Corriere del Mezzogiorno,* 10 June 1998).[15] These outsiders also played an important role in securing resources for DAMM. In particular, Fofi's close contacts with cultural operators, publishers and the film industry were not only instrumental in bringing national writers and performers to DAMM but also opened up career opportunities for individual activists. Some published work in reviews edited by Fofi himself, such as *lo Straniero* and *Poco di Buono* (Braucci 1998; Peppicelli 2000), while a novel written by a DAMM activist set in the loosely fictional neighbourhood 'Santo' and narrating the interwoven lives of a drug addict and a novice *camorrista* (Braucci 1999a) received enthusiastic reviews in the national press. However, links with outsiders that affected the running of the occupation were negotiated collectively; and sometimes offers of support (for instance from the Neapolitan film director Pappi Corsicato) were refused on the grounds that they compromised autonomy.

For the most part, DAMM did not have to contend with a hostile administration. Following his victory in 1993, Antonio Bassolino declared that he would take a tolerant attitude to the *centri sociali* in contrast to the

---

14. DAMM was highly critical of the development of the third sector, a common topic of discussion, which, it argued, removed critical autonomy, made service organizations dependent on public handouts and diminished the possibilities of constructive conflict (DAMM 2000).

15. Besides these 'allies', the three mainstream local newspapers (*Il Mattino, La Repubblica* and *Corriere del Mezzogiorno*) were generally approving of DAMM. It was sometimes seen as beneficial to the local community, as in the case of its opening of the park: 'The children of Maradona save the garden' (*La Repubblica,* 24 August 1996) or through its 'discovery' of the heroin-based drug 'Cobret' (*Il Mattino,* 3 November 1996). However, most interest focused on its cultural production: 'The poor film goes to the Venice festival in the name of Maradona. ... Never before in Italy has a *centro sociale* produced fiction' (*La Repubblica,* 14 July 1996).

aggressive approach of administrators in other cities, such as the Northern League mayor of Milan, Marco Formentini, who had run part of his
election campaign on a promise to evict Leoncavallo. 'My opinion on the
matter is exactly the opposite of Formentini's. Young people have the right
to their spaces. If anything, the task of the council is to link them to the
rest of the city' (*La Repubblica,* 7 December 1993). At the beginning of
the occupation in 1995, it transpired that the *palazzina* was supposed to
have housed a municipal archive, but despite a protest by local intellectuals who called for the occupants to be removed (*La Repubblica,* 4 October
1995), this idea was dropped after a more suitable site was found. Although there were various rumours over the following years that the city
council intended to repossess the *palazzina,* which led to solidarity action
from the other *centri sociali* in the city, these never materialized, and most
of the time it seemed that the local authorities had relinquished all interest in the building. In fact, DAMM repeatedly accused the administration
of assuming an indifferent position to the whole Ventaglieri Project. The
few official attempts at recuperating the park were deemed halfhearted.
When Bassolino paid his only public visit to the site in August 1997 to in-
augurate the hastily fixed escalators, DAMM and some in the local press
accused him of using the event to launch his reelection campaign:

> On 8 August the mayor came to inaugurate the escalators, which are only one important
> part of the structure, despite the fact that the builders have left the work unfinished and
> no decision has been made regarding the management of the park. ... Our relation-
> ship with the administration is inevitable but informative, even if disagreeable for the
> slowness and inefficiency, and seeks to ensure minimum guarantees of maintenance to
> provide the basis for developing a free zone that, through the participation of others, is
> able to experiment rules and practices which arise from the needs and contradictions
> of those who implement them. ... Don't vote. Occupy the post-earthquake structures.
> Support and participate in the self-management of the Ventaglieri Park. (Leaflet entitled
> 'About the self-management of the Ventaglieri Park', September 1997)

Although DAMM invited the public to collaborate with its management
of the Ventaglieri Project, it nonetheless admitted that constant mediation
with the administration was necessary if conditions in the park were to
be permanently improved. It was through this confrontation that DAMM
elaborated and put into action a more politically incisive way of thinking
about public space in the *centro storico* of Naples.

Redefining public space in a popular neighbourhood

The experience of DAMM did not just revolve around the activities in the
palazzina but was marked by its relationship to the surrounding structure

of the park and escalators. This was a unique space. The park itself was one of only a very few green spaces in the *centro storico,* enjoying a particularly picturesque location with views over Vomero Hill and the Gulf of Naples. DAMM earned the accolade of being 'the most beautiful *centro sociale* in Italy' (Dazieri 1996).

The clear-up, re-use and restitution of public spaces to the neighbourhood was considered a central aspect of DAMM's purposive action. With the occupation in August 1995, the upper gardens were immediately cleared of syringes, and during the following summer, DAMM called on the services of a group of international volunteers, who spent a week tidying them. It sought to encourage increased usage of the space by organizing regular events for local children, such as treasure hunts, and flyposting the neighbourhood with information about the park. The first issue of *Il Ventagliere* printed a map of the entire project, which indicated the recovered zones around DAMM and the '*degrado*' (in other words the abandoned areas) that encroached on the new school below. DAMM assumed the role of 'counter planner'. It reappropriated an abandoned structure that had once ambitiously sought 'to trigger a process of urban restructuring of the *centro storico*' (Ferulano 1991: 107) and reinvested the remnants with new meaning. Hence, the flights of steps and various levels of the escalator system were turned into a regular venue for concerts and theatre performances.

Illustration 17.2. The Ventaglieri Park, October 2010. *Photograph by Nick Dines.*

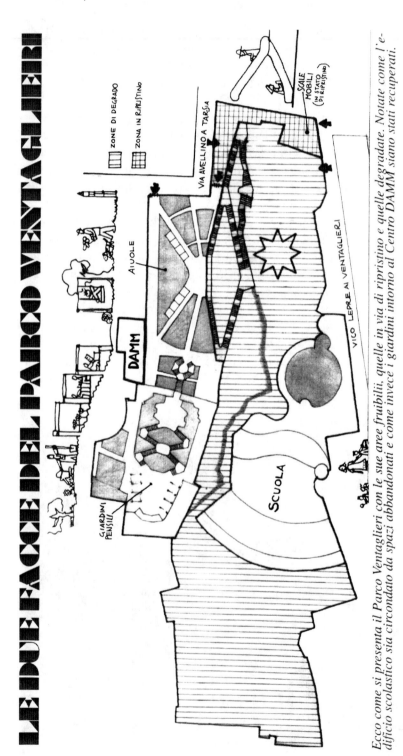

Map 17.1. 'The two sides to the Ventaglieri Park' (*Il Ventagliere*, no. 1, March 1999).

Ecco come si presenta il Parco Ventaglieri con le sue aree fruibili, quelle in via di ripristino e quelle degradate. Notate come l'e-dificio scolastico sia circondato da spazi abbandonati e come invece i giardini intorno al Centro DAMM siano stati recuperati.

The post-earthquake project was not officially opened and rechristened the Ventaglieri Park until the summer of 1997. The working escalators connected the upper and lower quarters of Montesanto and were especially handy for the young children from Tarsia who attended the school at the base of the project and older residents who shopped in Pignasecca. However, the inadequate arrangements, in particular the understaffing and the lack of equipment and facilities (there were no litter bins, and the only toilet was situated in the *palazzina*), meant that DAMM, which continued to possess keys to the park and escalators, remained the principal, and at times only, operator in the whole complex.

With their daily presence and intimate knowledge of the place, DAMM occupants pressurized the city council by highlighting a string of problems and proposing possible solutions. It took direct forms of action, such as encouraging users to phone city hall to demand the city council's intervention and at one point threatened to lock the top (and main) access to the park. It even set up a parallel organization – the Pelé Committee (after the Brazilian footballer) – with the intention of opening a channel of dialogue with the administration and, in the summer of 1997, submitted a detailed, deliberately overambitious, scheme for the renovation and utilization of the space. Proposals included exploiting the free floor space in the escalator structure for a children's bookshop, a theatre and a meeting place for local associations. According to the plan, the city council would complete the work and provide the necessary funds for the committee to run a 'no-profit' programme of events. However, DAMM made it clear throughout that it had no intention of permanently occupying these structures: 'Most of the management proposals were not realistic. Nobody ever thought about assuming the responsibility of organizing cultural activities in the park. They were always a way of attracting the administration's attention' (L., interview with author, 19 July 1999).

At the end of 1998 and little over a year after Bassolino's inauguration of the park, DAMM convened a *comitato di quartiere* following the sudden, unexpected closure of the escalator service and after a return of heroin addicts to the park. Up to fifty, mainly middle-class, local residents met regularly in the park for almost a year to discuss the situation and to draw up a list of recommendations that were subsequently presented to the district council. DAMM activists found themselves at odds with many of the participants' views, as it became clear that they were primarily concerned about the escalator service and less interested in the park as a public place. Some were more bothered about unruly children playing on the escalators than the city council's absence. But as a result of its stronger organizational position, DAMM claimed that it was able to steer the debate away from questions of security and surveillance and on to more concrete proposals regarding the space's management. In a public leaflet, it cuttingly remarked upon the motives of the committee and its rift with the local population:

> The committee was composed of the neighbourhood's elites: university professors, doctors, artists, an ex-assessor of the Bassolino administration. ... Sometimes a few women from the surrounding houses would approach only to immediately retreat. ... With the opening of the escalators, as sudden and as mysterious as their closure, the committee disbanded, as the social reasons for its existence disappeared. (DAMM 2000)

Activists were nevertheless aware of DAMM's limited influence on the administration. After 1998, occupants participated in the local district council's special commission on the park, and although this local public assembly came to accept the mediating role of DAMM, it was considered ineffective given its restricted powers and lack of competence. 'They know we're the only ones who make serious proposals. They listen to us, but they don't have the expertise. They've always proposed banal things – like flowers – but you can't maintain an intransigent position and deride them all the time' (L., interview with author, 19 July 1999).[16]

Through its campaigns to improve the park, DAMM questioned the city's organization under the Bassolino administration and the implications of its urban renewal programme. At the heart of the conflict were divergent definitions of the Ventaglieri Park as a public space. From 1993, the administration stressed the importance of providing recreational areas in a city with the lowest amount of green space per inhabitant in Italy. But although plans were made to liberate large tracts of land on the city's outskirts, more prestigious parks like the Villa Comunale were restored and, significantly, other post-earthquake public projects were opened, the administration did not commit itself to the management of a green space in a central neighbourhood. Instead of responding to the more mundane needs of the park, such as structural repairs to walls and stairways, its sporadic interest in the park tended to focus on its peculiar properties and how these could be applied to a more general strategy of regenerating the *centro storico*. The escalator system, in particular, was considered a unique innovation in the city. At its inauguration, Bassolino declared to the press: 'This is another stage in the revival of the neighbourhoods

---

16. The only event organized by the council in the park during the period was an open-air concert in the summer of 1998 on the concrete esplanade at the bottom of the park (in other words the area not used by DAMM). The district council itself became increasingly frustrated at the lack of response from city hall. Its DS president, Elisabetta Gambardella, complained in interview with a local newspaper: 'There's the Ventaglieri Park, which is a "green lung" of fundamental importance for the neighbourhood. But only if they give me some money to cover the costs and guarantee a team of gardeners will the *circoscrizione* accept the responsibility of managing the space. Tell this to the mayor.' (*Corriere del Mezzogiorno,* 21 March 1999).

that requires maximum attention. This escalator system may represent a model to pursue for a hilly city' (*Il Mattino,* 8 August 1997).

Indeed, a month after Bassolino's visit, a proposal was announced by the assessor for urban maintenance, Antonio Amato, for another escalator link between the Ventaglieri Park and the lower end of Vomero and the Viviani Park.[17] According to Amato, the 2.5 billion lire plan would give residents of the (more affluent) districts above the *centro storico* quick access to the public transport terminals in Montesanto (*Corriere del Mezzogiorno,* 1 October 1997). But, as with numerous other projects, this particularly extravagant plan was almost immediately shelved. According to DAMM, it confirmed that the administration was evading its more immediate responsibilities of managing the Ventaglieri Park: 'This arrogant and ridiculous declaration confirmed to those who still harboured doubts or hopes that the city council was washing its hands of the affair' (DAMM 2000). In an article in *Corriere del Mezzogiorno,* Daniela Lepore, one of DAMM's 'allies', saw the project as a symptom of overambitious and unrealistic planning strategies for Naples:

> The design of a new elaborate link between two malfunctioning parks really seems a 'solution in search of a problem'. I would modestly suggest, although I fear in vain, an alternative approach. For example: try to understand why projects full of good intentions end up as disasters; experiment with more realistic organizational and formal remedies; involve people in projects such as the guys from DAMM, the Viviani Park association, neighbourhood groups and potential users. Perhaps this idea of green space is more banal and less ambitious, but on the other hand the public might be able to understand it better and therefore love and look after it. (*Corriere del Mezzogiorno,* 9 October 1997)

Ultimately, the Ventaglieri Park's location in a popular neighbourhood meant that the space remained a low priority. In Rosa Russo Iervolino's 2001 election brochure, the park was listed as one of the 'green lungs' opened under the Bassolino administrations, but the only information provided was its size: eight thousand square metres (Napoli con Iervolino 2001: 19). As a functional space constructed after the earthquake, it simply did not possess the symbolic import of a monumental piazza or a historic green space that warranted closer attention. In stark contrast, the restoration in 1999 by the Milanese architect Alessandro Mendini of the Villa Comunale, the park laid out by the Bourbons in the eighteenth century along the seafront of Chiaia, was a daily focus of attention of the media and administration. Public opinion was divided over

---

17. Parco Viviani, also part of the post-earthquake reconstruction programme and opened at the beginning of 1994, is located close to DAMM but on the Vomero side of Corso Vittorio Emanuele, the early nineteenth-century ring road that marks the outer boundary of the popular neighbourhoods of the *centro storico.*

the postmodern design of the new fencing and multicoloured chalets. The height of the controversy came with the discovery that one of these chalets blocked the Villa Pignatelli's historic view of the island of Capri, at which point Bassolino personally intervened to order its removal. For DAMM activists, the Villa Comunale represented the antithesis of the park in Montesanto:

> Let's zoom onto another place, the Ventaglieri Park located in the heart of the city and defined as a "neighbourhood space", or, in other words, of little interest to the city. The reason for this definition is mysterious; logically it could refer to the fact that it is only used by residents of surrounding neighbourhoods and therefore only of interest to a minority. In Naples, 'Take the children to the Villa Comunale' is a family proverb, and since the family is the fundamental nucleus in this extremely Catholic country, so the Villa of Via Carracciolo becomes the place of majority interest and therefore susceptible to scandals and controversies which attract the public's attention, especially in the lead-up to an election campaign. ... The truth of the matter is that the entire structure [of the Ventaglieri Park] was a horrendous case of speculation and was built with shoddy and unsuitable materials, which the present administration wants to forget and whose motto is 'It's not my responsibility'. (Braucci 1999b)

The public debates over the Villa Comunale centred upon issues of aesthetic taste rather than on the social implications of the new design. Neither the supporters nor the opponents of the restoration questioned the principle of enclosing the space (which was required to formally turn it into a park). The unfenced edges of the Villa Comunale, apart from allowing permanent access (to a space that had long been a well-known gay cruising area in Naples), had previously been used as seating by Sri Lankan and Filipino immigrants who attended a Catholic service in a nearby church. According to DAMM, this propensity to 'enclosure' led to the suppression of a truly interactive social space. 'Public gardens are destined to become empty, identical and hostile to any kind of spontaneous socialization. The usual method is to close them, as in the case of the Villa Comunale, ignoring the uses of those who live around them' (*Il Ventagliere* No.1, March 1999).

The Ventaglieri Park was not simply conceived by DAMM to be in need of material improvements but as a site that was constituted by its different publics and their overlapping uses and meanings of public space. The official definition of the 'park' as an enclosed place with fixed sets of rules was therefore considered anomalous. Moreover, activists pointed out that the Ventaglieri Project had never been planned as a 'park', but as a link between two streets, and it was on these grounds that they successfully campaigned to extend the opening hours of the escalators to comply with people's spatial routines in the neighbourhood. The occupation promoted multiple and often discordant uses of the whole complex.

The 'participation' of certain users did not always reflect the intentions of activists. For instance, theatrical performances in the *palazzina,* attended by mainly nonlocal users, were sometimes interrupted by the incursions of children from the park. In order to negotiate their daily presence in a popular neighbourhood, DAMM had to endure continual problems: regular theft, damage to the structure and equipment, insults and derision, as well as complaints from neighbours over noise levels during open-air events. 'We ask ourselves when the thefts will end but they'll never stop. Before we were a lot more anxious. We couldn't sleep. Every day something would happen. … Now we've calmed down a bit. But it depends on the period. D'Agostino [local teenager], for instance, seems a lot more respectful' (L., interview with author, 11 July 1999).

The modus operandi of DAMM was to try to critically accommodate social and cultural differences. The endemic problem of urban poverty, considered specific to Naples and the Italian South, was not regarded a tinderbox for political struggles (as it may have been by Officina 99 or lo Ska) but as the impetus to engage with individuals.

> An experience like DAMM could be repeated in Messina or Palermo – where there's poverty: that makes the difference. It's true that here they buy these big cars and stereos, but they remain economically and culturally poor. We don't delude ourselves that things will change, but we know that this experience will have a significant impact on one out of ten people. (M., interview with author, 1 August 1999)[18]

However, due to the more affluent social background of some occupants and the knowledge acquired through university education of many others, the (desired) attempts at establishing equal-based, interactive relationships with local residents, especially the 'rowdy' teenagers, were often limited. Most at DAMM were nevertheless aware of the various symbolic and material barriers between themselves and the park's local users (as well as within the group of occupants itself), and it was for this reason that it claimed to adopt a pragmatic, rather than a politically idealistic, attitude towards the occupation.

Through its campaign over public space and with its intimate knowledge of the surrounding area DAMM made a point of combating negative representations of local users and residents. When one of DAMM's activists had first tried to muster interest in the occupation, the idea of squatting in the neighbourhood did not carry much appeal:

---

18. For instance, in 2000, after DAMM and an occupied centre in Berlin organized an exchange between groups of teenagers from Montesanto and the Berlin suburb of Kreuzberg (with the aid of a EU youth project grant), one of the young Neapolitan participants decided to move to Germany to search for work.

I spoke to a lot of people. I had a meeting with the anarchists at the Louise Michel Circle near the Montesanto metro station. They said, 'That's not possible. You can't occupy that space.' So I replied, 'I don't want to create a *centro sociale* closed in on itself but one that's open to the neighbourhood'. 'No way! Not the neighbourhood! It's full of shit people!' I remember various comments: 'They used to spit in my face outside the metro!' 'At Tien'A'Ment [a "libertarian-punk" *centro sociale* in Soccavo closed by police in 1996] we'd go from house to house in shirts and ties, but it was no use because the people were shits!' (M., interview with author, 1 August 1999)

DAMM reserved the greatest animosity for a cultural and political ruling elite (often generally defined as the 'bourgeoisie'), which it accused of trying to impose a singular vision of the city and denying difference. According to one activist, the common association of the popular neighbourhood with '*degrado*' meant that the Ventaglieri Park was a priori labelled as a dangerous place (L., interview with author, 11 July 1999). DAMM's publications and leaflets were scathing of those parents who prevented their children from using the park, in particular the participants of the *comitato di quartiere,* which had convened over the escalator service: 'Only three of the families responded to our request by taking their children to the park. With the end of their parents' brief season of activism, the other children lost the last opportunity to use this strange place which they had learnt to fear' (DAMM 2000).

Unlike Piazza Plebiscito or Piazza Garibaldi, the Ventaglieri Park was seldom the focus of newspaper debates about public space. Its marginal location reduced the level of media interest. But on the rare occasions in which it did hit the headlines, comments bordered on the vitriolic. At the end of September 1997, the local press complained that the recently inaugurated escalators had become the favourite loitering place for gangs of local children and that the city council had done nothing to deter their misuse (*Corriere del Mezzogiorno,* 27 September 1997). A few days later, an editorial by the left-leaning intellectual Massimo Galluppi entitled 'The Problem of a New Civic Consciousness: The Ventagliere [sic] Escalators' appeared on the front page of *Corriere del Mezzogiorno.* Galluppi used the case to reflect on what he considered the city's deep-rooted backwardness as well as to question the achievements of the Bassolino administration:

The 'new' Naples has not been able to assimilate the idea that besides public efficiency, individual discipline is necessary if we want to change the face of the city. From this point of view the episode of the escalators in Via Ventaglieri is the metaphor of a common destiny. In a city that has not recognized the bourgeois revolution and which has never possessed a bourgeoisie worthy of its name, the superficial hedonism [here Galluppi is referring to the administration's promotion of leisure events such as those organized in Piazza Plebiscito] constitutes an obstacle to the formation of a modern civic consciousness, which needs to be created if one accepts the idea that the use of force is necessary but not sufficient to bring the terrible children of Montesanto to reason. It is a long and difficult job, which somebody sooner or later will have to do. Who and how, for the moment, nobody knows. (*Corriere del Mezzogiorno*, 1 October 1997)

The same words, 'terrible children', were used to describe the climbers of the *Montagna del Sale* in Piazza Plebiscito. But in Montesanto no attempt was made to 'civilize' the transgressors. Galluppi claimed that nobody was seeking to bring these children to 'reason'. It was perhaps fitting that he made no reference to DAMM. According to DAMM, the playful appropriation of the escalators was considered a means of making sense of an 'alien' structure in the neighbourhood (DAMM 1998). Through its everyday experience with children, DAMM mocked the administration's words of commitment to young Neapolitans. Shortly prior to election in 1993 Bassolino had declared that he would personally oversee a 'Children of Europe Project', which would aim to 'take [children] off the streets, send them to school and fill their free time with sports and cultural activities' (*Il Mattino*, 3 December 1993). DAMM turned this idea of 'right' and 'wrong' places on its head:

They declare that their objective is to remove children from the streets. For the moment they remove the street with controls and automobiles, tourists and flower boxes, walls and gates, police and *vigili urbani*. ... But every day, children regain terrain in the city. They require spaces and want to decide on their own how to use them. (Leaflet entitled 'Children at risk don't exist', spring 1999)

In sharp contrast to Bassolino's vision of young people as good citizens in the making – but also to Santucci's recollections of childhood in Piazza Plebiscito as being marked by innocence and harmony – children were here seen to actively and autonomously redefine public space. Indeed, their appropriations of urban space potentially held the most politically potent commentaries on the organization of the city. One can sense in the position of DAMM (or at least those involved with the *doposcuola*) the influence of the late British anarchist Colin Ward, who gave a lecture at the Mensa dei Bambini Proletari in 1997 and whose book *The Child in the City* (1978) was translated into Italian by a DAMM activist in 1999. Ward sees the child's use of space as the only true international culture but also as one which is continually ignored, excluded and regulated. Despite restraints imposed by planners and local authorities, children will nevertheless continue to adapt the urban realm: 'A city that is really concerned with the needs of its young will make the whole environment accessible to them, because whether invited to or not, they are going to use the whole environment' (ibid.: 73). By ridiculing the Bassolinian idea of Naples as a 'city of children' (DAMM 1998, 2000), DAMM exposed the glibness of public pronouncements about cultivating a civic consciousness among young Neapolitans. For all the talk of a common project, children were continually separated into the compliant and the incorrigible, the vulnerable and the disruptive, which recalled the age-old binary conceptualization of children as angels or devils (Valentine 2004) but at the same time mirrored the traditional dualistic representation of Neapolitan society that was now increasingly articulated in terms of the civil and uncivil. Indeed, Massimo Galuppi appears, almost cathartically, to lay the burden of two hundred years of failed civilization upon the shoulders of a few errant ten-year-olds. Sliding down the escalators backwards, they only further distance themselves from an imminent citizenship that is already way beyond their grasp.

Chapter 18

Exit DAMM

The Constitutive Role of Collective Action upon Public Space

The experience of DAMM in Montesanto represents an attempt at the collective self-management of public space in central Naples. As such, it sharply contrasted to the daily forms of informal negotiation and resistance, variously labelled under the maxim '*arrangiarsi*', which were considered typical of the popular neighbourhoods. The occupation, without a doubt, made a positive impact on the abandoned post-earthquake project. It must be remembered that until August 1995 the structure did not exist as a public space. DAMM's constructive presence attracted an array of users who would not have otherwise visited the site:

> A heterogeneous use has been consolidated, characterized by young people and children from the neighbourhood who are usually expelled from this type of space. DAMM constitutes their only reference in the park and ... together with them has pursued an exhausting daily course to establish rules of coexistence and respect towards places and other people. The daily activities, the political initiatives and the cultural events organized by the centre have also drawn thousands of people to this place, attracting the city's attention and encouraging its use by people from outside the neighbourhood. (Untitled leaflet, spring 1999)

DAMM sought to promote a pluralistic vision of public space which celebrated in a not uncritical way the social and cultural diversity of the city. For instance, it purposely organized joint concerts of alternative rock groups and the *neo-melodici*[1] to cater for the divergent tastes of locals and outside users. It established contact with immigrant groups in the

---

1. The *neo-melodici* are singers from the city's popular neighbourhoods and working-class suburbs who rework themes of traditional Neapolitan songs. The lyrics are almost exclusively in Neapolitan, and their immense popularity (with at least three local private television channels solely dedicated to showing their videos) is confined to Naples and its hinterland. For a general journalistic overview of the phenomenon, see Vacalebre 1999. For a more in-depth analysis from an anthropological perspective, see Pine 2008.

area. During 2001 it provided lodging to two Cape Verdeans from Montesanto who had been evicted from their homes, and during the summer it organized a party in the park with the local Cape Verdean community and immigrant organizations. Through its involvement with schoolchildren DAMM encouraged activities in the park – such as treasure hunts and the design of murals – which were not possible in the street, were either discouraged or deemed irrelevant at school and were banned from other open spaces such as the restored Villa Comunale. At the same time, by engaging with 'difficult' users (in particular the aggressive male teenagers) and pursuing 'sustainable' forms of conflict, DAMM confronted the representations of certain inhabitants as '*scugnizzi*' or 'lumpenproletarian lowbrows' (as they were described by the president of the province of Naples Amato Lamberti) and defended errant forms of behaviour which the administration was trying to reform. In its own words, DAMM acted as a buffer against the 'normalization' of the *centro storico* and counteracted the political inaction and social exclusivity that lay beneath the rhetoric of a 'progressive city' advanced by the Bassolino administration (DAMM 1998, 2000).

DAMM had many limits and shortcomings. While it encouraged mixed uses of the Ventaglieri Park and formed ongoing relationships with children and young people, activists acknowledged that they lacked the engaged support of many other locals, especially adults, who preferred to avoid the park. Formulating and sustaining a collective urban project in a *quartiere popolare* was fraught with difficulties. The social contradictions in the area prevented the elaboration of far-reaching political and social agendas (although this might also be seen to be the inevitable corollary of an explicitly territorial project), while numerous events and some of the language (such as the regular pillory of the 'bourgeoisie' and its cultural conformity which at times resembled Pasolini's diatribe against the nefarious impact of consumer society upon popular culture) targeted a different (nonlocal) audience. Furthermore, the possibilities for projecting itself into a wider public sphere were restricted. Forms of activity were episodic, underfunded, and at times weakened by ambivalent attitudes to 'allies' and distrust towards other political and social organizations in the city. In addition, DAMM admitted that the administration was mainly indifferent to its campaigns to improve the park, although this reflected as much the peripheral position of the structure as a weakness on the part of DAMM.

However, it would be futile to assess the *centro sociale* in terms of 'success'. DAMM was not born with the aim of directly challenging the urban politics of Bassolino. This emerged out of its management of various spaces of the Ventaglieri Park. Moreover, it did not consider itself a force specifically geared to pressing for urban change but as an experimental space promoting *convivenza* (coexistence) at a micro-level. As such, DAMM represented a radical politics of place that challenged official attempts to frame public space within an ambiguous vision of the 'good city' (Amin 2006). By situating itself critically between, on the one hand, the administration, construction firms and associative experiences with their particular (class) interests and, on the other hand, the park's users, DAMM actively contested the simplistic, culturally insensitive representations of popular neighbourhoods that spoke, often peremptorily, of '*degrado*' or 'incivility'. Perhaps its most important achievement, over and above its campaigns and political struggles, was to invest an abandoned space with collective meaning. As one activist asserted: 'Since we've been here people call the park "DAMM" or "the *centro*"' (L., interview with author, 19 July 1999). The occupation contributed to the radical tradition of the area by offering a new possible path of action:

> Politics is not something confined to Palazzo San Giacomo [the city hall]. It's here in the alleyway in front of DAMM, it's your relation with your surroundings. ... What do I care about assessors and the mayor? In two years' time nobody will remember them. ... Perhaps in five years time somebody in Messina will want to start up a *centro sociale*. The existence of a historical example of struggle like DAMM may help them. (M., interview with author, 1 August 1999)

Ultimately, as the Ventaglieri Park's principal 'representative', DAMM confronted the marginal role assigned to the *quartieri popolari* during the process of urban regeneration. It managed to construct a degree of political consensus among users as well as the local press by exploiting the paradoxical absence of an administration that had prioritized the provision of parks and the resurrection of the *centro storico*. In contrast to the administration's crude statistical vision of green space and its ad hoc approach to urban renewal in the neighbourhoods, DAMM experimented and promoted on an ongoing basis a 'more specialist, needs-based approach' (Greenhalgh and Worpole 1995: 21). In terms of concrete and lasting achievements, DAMM may not have made a difference to the life of Montesanto, let alone the city as a whole, but it was significant as a model for an alternative vision of the city and as a form of political action that was explicitly conceived through the reuse of urban space. The fact that DAMM's demands for mundane repairs to the Ventaglieri Park were often ignored reflected the priorities of the administration's regeneration agenda and at the same time underlined the limited scope of 'citizen participation' in building a new, more 'inclusive' city. The popular neighbourhoods nevertheless continued to be both a constitutive and disruptive element in the history of Naples. DAMM succeeded in channelling their *aporia* into a political critique of urban change.

Conclusion

*Rethinking Urban Change in
Late Twentieth-century Naples*

By the end of the 1990s, the widespread optimism prompted by Antonio
Bassolino's election had begun to abate amid accusations of a concentration of power around the mayor and an overemphasis on symbolic
policies (Esposito 1999; Allum and Cilento 2000). Nevertheless, after
Bassolino left the helm of the city to run as the Centre-Left's presidential
candidate in the regional elections of April 2000, there was a general
consensus among political observers and the mainstream media that his
reign in Naples had marked a turning point in the city's fortunes. Some
argued that the city had reached its lowest ebb in the early 1990s and that
therefore things could not have got much worse, but that the Bassolino
administration proved very capable in steering Naples out of crisis (Geremicca 1997). The city's immense debts were trimmed and the squander-
ing of public resources curtailed. The investment of council bonds on the
New York Stock Exchange released funds for the purchase of a new fleet
of public buses, which not only saw Naples pioneer new financing methods ahead of the rest of Italy but also indicated a newfound faith among
former Communists in the benefits of a globalized market economy
(Boccia 1996). By reasserting the principle of legality in everyday life,
a greater sense of order was established and the central streets became
more manageable both for pedestrians and vehicles. Indeed, a new cliché
emerged that many drivers now *did* stop at red lights.

The administration's commitment to rehabilitating the *centro storico*
not only represented a victory for the cultural associations that had campaigned against its demolition during the 1980s but also provided a boost
for the city's moribund tourist industry. After reaching an all-time low
in 1993, there was a notable increase in Italian and foreign tourism to
Naples, especially in the wake of the publicity surrounding the G7 summit and later after the establishment of cheap flight connections with
European capitals and the reinstatement of the city on the Mediterranean

cruise circuit.[1] Most people, however, only stayed a few days, and their sojourns were concentrated in certain periods and to specific parts of the city. Furthermore, the city barely rivalled the popular destinations in the province of Naples such as the seaside resorts of Sorrento, Capri and Ischia, while the archaeological sites of Pompeii and Herculaneum far outnumbered the museums of Naples in terms of visitors (Solima 1999: 91).

Urban regeneration obviously had its limits. Naples remained one of Western Europe's poorest cities. Although the administration was successful in generating a perception of change, its urban strategies did not have a great socioeconomic impact on the city as a whole. Despite climbing a few places in the various pseudo-scientific 'quality-of-life' league tables of Italian cities (albeit still rooted, like most of the South, in their bottom half) and receiving an A1 investment grade from the credit rating agency Moody's in November 1995,[2] Naples continued to be afflicted by unemployment, crime, inadequate housing, as well as a precarious subsoil weakened by years of overbuilding. A disaster in the northern suburb of Secondigliano in January 1996, where the sudden collapse of a main street into a giant sinkhole led to eleven deaths, provided brutal contrast to the celebrated trope of the heritage city. Bassolino himself was well aware of the limitations of local government and insisted that structural improvements required a new systematic approach at national level to economic development in the South (Bassolino 1996b). This said, throughout the 1990s (and indeed beyond) the cultural and symbolic reevaluation of the *centro storico* was promoted as the groundwork for the city's resurgence, especially as the ambitious large-scale projects such as the construction of an extensive urban rail network and the redevelopment of Bagnoli progressed slowly or, in the case of the latter, showed little sign of materializing.

This book, however, has provided a different perspective on urban regeneration in Naples that has been less concerned to measure its ultimate 'success' or to substantiate the sophistic claim that 'it was all a question of image'. Rather, regeneration has been seen as a multidimensional process, embedded within a set of historical, political, social, economic and

---

1. In 1995 there were 610,000 registered arrivals in the city (the highest figure in ten years) and 1,290,000 presences. 'Arrivals' refer to the number of guests booking into accommodation and 'presences' to the total number of overnight stays. Based on this set of statistics, the revival was still far below the levels registered during the 1960s and 1970s. In the peak year of 1964 there were 1.1 million arrivals and 2.7 million presences (Amato 1996).

2. This upper-medium rating, which was higher than that of Barcelona or Montreal and preceded the emission of the council bonds, was awarded largely on the basis of budgetary planning and controls introduced by the Bassolino administration (Boccia 1996).

linguistic conjunctures that advanced and sought to activate ideas about transforming the city. By examining three sites in the *centro storico,* the analysis has been able to consider the pivotal role of public space in regeneration strategies and to grapple with issues such as traffic, heritage, immigration and grassroots collective action that are either omitted or brushed over in more sweeping accounts of the period. Moreover, a focus on public space has challenged orthodox evaluations of regeneration as well as culturalist explanations of urban life in Naples, because it has necessarily confronted questions of difference and conflict. Each of the three micro-studies raised its own conclusions regarding specific topics. In this final chapter I want to draw together and reflect upon some common themes: first, the shifting role of places within narratives about the urban environment; second, the ruptures inherent within the administration's idea of a new Naples as a 'city of citizens'; and third, the significance of examining and understanding each site as a 'contested space'.

The intricate histories of everyday places in the city shake up the self-assuredness and complacency with which certain discourses about public space (for instance, the use of the term *'degrado'*) are constructed. The three spaces examined in this book were all peripheral to debates about Naples prior to the mid-1990s. Piazza Plebiscito had been a car park and a link in the city's road network. Piazza Garibaldi, a public transport hub and traffic junction, was rarely a cause for public concern. And before the occupation of DAMM in 1995, the Ventaglieri Project languished in a state of abandonment. Apart from a few architectural and tourist accounts of Piazza Plebiscito, there was scant literature about the history of the three spaces. This meant conducting a sort of archaeological dig to retrace 'buried' representations from the past. Thus, for instance, by perusing newspaper reports from the 1950s and 1960s it was possible to unearth public responses to the establishment of the car park in Piazza Plebiscito, debates over the new station and enlargement of Piazza Garibaldi, and reactions to the crumbling state of the Ventaglieri district of Montesanto. During the 1990s, regeneration narratives about public space rekindled previous layers of meaning, for instance Lauro's vision of Piazza Garibaldi as the gateway to the *centro storico,* while redefining or erasing certain legacies, such as the car-park period in Piazza Plebiscito, which after 1994 was construed as a thirty-year void. The G7 summit signalled a watershed for Piazza Plebiscito and Piazza Garibaldi, not only for the physical changes that it brought about (which were actually limited in the case of the latter) but, more important, because it precipitated a shift in public attitudes about the two spaces.

At the same time, the twists and turns in dominant representations about the *centro storico* ran up against those meanings and uses that were closely bound up with the configuration, location and social mi-lieu of the three spaces and which tended to reproduce themselves over the course of time. Piazza Plebiscito's immense dimensions meant that through history it remained a venue for organized events but also, given its ongoing associations with power, a focus of political protest. During the nineteenth and twentieth centuries the colonnade continually served as a *pissoir* and dormitory and, due to the proximity of two populous neighbourhoods, remained the busier side of the piazza. During a visit to the city in 1850, the German writer Ferdinand Gregorovius observed groups of idle *lazzaroni* lolling on the colonnade's steps in the full view of the Royal police (Ramondino and Müller 1992: 50). Over 150 years later, a local journalist complained about gangs from the Spanish Quar-ters congregating in the same area and disturbing the 'high-class *movida*' and tranquillity of Piazza Plebiscito (*La Repubblica,* 7 August 2001). The discrepancy between a new narrative framework and enduring routines was also apparent in Piazza Garibaldi. Indeed, long before the arrival of immigrants during the 1980s, the station area had been the centre of an informal commercial economy and a place where strangers mingled. Within a much shorter span of time, DAMM's occupation and campaigns over public space recalled the tradition of popular struggles over urban issues in the immediate surrounding area.

These intriguing combinations do not simply provide a backdrop to the 'real' issues that occurred during the Bassolino era. On the contrary, recognizing the accretion and persistence of preexisting meanings (with-out denying the contemporaneous emergence of new ones) alongside the ways in which these were officially selected, suppressed or inverted is es-sential to a more penetrating analysis of the transformation of the *centro storico*. Taken-for-granted truths about urban change are revealed to be contingent and situated. Hence, the incontrovertibility of the traffic-free Piazza Plebiscito is undermined less by the counter-axiom that this was merely a 'window dressing' operation than by the fact that the car park itself had been assigned a similar redemptive role back in the 1960s.

Each study examined the practical implications of political discourses about public space. Piazza Plebiscito and Piazza Garibaldi represented two conflicting visions: a desire for social interaction in the former and a commitment to safety and order in the latter. Both, however, involved the drawing up of boundaries around appropriate behaviour and defini-tions about an acceptable public. In the case of DAMM, these boundaries were far more flexible, which reflected activists' attempts to self-manage a space in accordance with its users but also underlined the marginal position of the popular neighbourhoods in regeneration strategies for the *centro storico*. In the light of the three spaces, rhetorical pronouncements by the administration and local media about 'returning' the city to its citizens often appeared more exclusive than inclusive. Dominant ideas about the *centro storico* as the site of cultural heritage, a source of civic pride and the city's principal tourist attraction tended to directly favour certain groups, such as tourist operators and conservationists, but also, at a more general level, they privileged those people whose cultural values and habits were seen to comply with the project of improving Naples. There was certainly a revanchist tone to discussions about urban change that emphasized the 'rediscovery' of historic buildings, the 'reclamation' of public space and the 'recuperation' of local identity. Such talk chimed more readily with the higher-educated, affluent inhabitants of middle-class districts such as Vomero than with many of the residents in the central neighbourhoods themselves.

It would be too simplistic, however, to describe the reimaging of central Naples as part of a new bourgeois cultural vision (Zukin 1995). Some of Bassolino's most vociferous opponents were shopkeepers (around Piazza Plebiscito) and small hoteliers (around Piazza Garibaldi) whose immediate interests stood in opposition or were not met by the administration's policies (although it might be argued that these were merely exemplary of a local *unenlightened* petty bourgeoisie). Moreover, the vitality of 'popular' Naples was, in its right manifestations, considered one of the *centro storico*'s unique assets. Certainly, many cultural initiatives were aimed at a narrow public, such as jazz performances in the Ospedale Militare Park in the Spanish Quarters or avant-garde theatre in the piazzas of the *centro antico,* but frequent, large, open-air events such as pop concerts, often sponsored by the city council, targeted a much wider audience.

Rather, regeneration was articulated in terms of a renewed citizenship based around ideal Neapolitans. The deployment of citizenship by the post-Communist Left in Naples during the 1990s coincided with its reuse at a global level, both as an expansive category informed by different claims for rights and recognition and as a 'vehicular idea' adopted by transnational institutions and corporations to proclaim 'social responsibility' and to legitimate neoliberal restructuring.[3] The citizenship con-

---

3. For a discussion on the rise of discourses about 'corporate citizenship' and 'social responsibility' during the 1990s, see Sadler 2004, especially pages 858 to 861. 'Vehicular idea' has been coined by Gregor McLennan and Thomas Osborne to describe the role that certain concepts play in contemporary informational capitalism. '[Vehicular ideas] are designed as problem-solving devices, something that will simply "move things along" and take us from A to B. This sense of movement and transitoriness is important in the world of vehicular ideas, because that world is accepted as an ever-modernizing one, one in which things do not keep still, and one in which it is a good moral and political quality to be able to shift one's sense of values and organization practice' (McLennan and Osborne 2003: 53–54). Citizenship can be considered to operate as a vehicular idea when it is employed as an organizing discourse by people in positions of power (and obviously not when it is used as a general political or philosophical category). Indeed, one could detect a degree of 'vehicularity' in Bassolino's

ceived by Bassolino was neither purely the result of political bandwag-
oning nor a 'third-way' compromise. Instead, it signalled the attempt by
the Centre-Left to formulate a new political identity, to redefine its relationship with the city and to respond to a change in administrative and
economic circumstances. But while it might have silenced the language
of class, the administration's definition of citizenship ultimately recodified age-old distinctions between 'modern' and 'backward' sections of
the population and created new forms of exclusion and stigmatization.
Hence, immigrants, as noncitizens, had few possibilities of participating
in debates about Piazza Garibaldi and were often considered the cause
of feelings of insecurity, while some Neapolitans, such as the indecorous
residents of the popular neighbourhoods, were marginalized from promoted notions of collective identity. Besides pursuing a particular model
of urban development, it is important to understand that regeneration in
the *centro storico* also represented a sort of civilizing process, but one
which in order to function had to omit a priori the reprobate and nonin-
digenous. This saw the Centre-Left often abandon a soberly critical, if
perhaps ideologically blinkered and economically determinist, analysis
of urban life for a more visceral discourse about 'civicness' and 'civility' that offered peremptory answers to social and cultural dilemmas and
which in turn prevented it from positively contemplating *other,* nonconforming relationships with the city.

Although certain groups and types of behaviour were ejected from discourses about a new Naples, they were nevertheless very present in public
space. Each site was subject to episodes of conflict, daily minor infractions
and unintended uses. Meanings about place were internalized, manipu-
lated and resignified. Like anywhere else, these processes were structured
by overlapping variables, such as class, age, gender and ethnicity/nation-
ality that were in turn intersected by other factors, such as the type and
extent of social networks, levels of cultural capital, employment and legal
status, length of residence, affective attachments to place and so on. In
other words, it would be as reductive to generalize about immigrants' or
women's experiences of the city as it would be to speak of a specific popular or middle-class culture of public space. Thus divergent ideas about
Piazza Garibaldi not only existed between hoteliers and immigrants but
also between immigrants themselves, who possessed different relationships with the station area. Similarly, while it is commonly acknowledged
that women are more likely to raise concerns about safety (Pain 2001),
these differed according to competing values about public space. Franca

---

deployment of the term, which also sought to 'move things along', particularly with regards to urban
regeneration.

Pastore in the tourist observatory lambasted the entry of all motorcycles into Piazza Plebiscito, because the potential danger that they posed was inextricably bound up with a desire to safeguard decorum, while the mothers from the Pallonetto – out on the frontline – only chided those fellow locals who passed too closely to their children, given that their own motorized relationship with the piazza held practical benefits. Issues of gender and personal safety were far more pronounced in Piazza Garibaldi, where the visible presence of single-gender gatherings served as an aggravating factor in the media's sentencing of the piazza and where fears about security clampdowns were shared by immigrant men and women alike. Meanwhile, the frolics of neighbourhood youngsters on *La Montagna del Sale* and the Ventaglieri escalators disrupted the panegyric about Neapolitan children as future citizens and, along with the barbed responses in the local press, exposed the prescriptive, colonial ambitions of certain interventions.[4]

The particularities of place were a further 'axis of differentiation' (Pain 2001: 911). The extent to which certain activities and practices became a source of friction also depended on the position of spaces within public debates. While the incursions of *motorini* in Piazza Plebiscito sometimes led to a media outcry, the races and wheelie competitions in the alleyways of the *quartieri* would go by unnoticed. Similarly, the congregation of Eastern European women in front of the railway station in Piazza Garibaldi was considered threatening, unlike, for instance, the raucous groups of Cape Verdeans who would regularly meet to drink beer on the pavements of Piazza Montesanto.

Certain groups and places were in fact subject to greater controls during the 1990s, especially immigrants in Piazza Garibaldi and those involved in informal economic activities. However, the total eradication of disorder only occurred under extraordinary circumstances, when Naples was transformed into a 'fortress city' for the G7 summit; but such levels of control could not be maintained on a daily basis. Genuine public space can never be a closed realm. Rather, it is the site where alternative ideas about the city are incubated and where people struggle to claim their place in the city, not as generic 'citizens' but as individuals and groups with differ-

---

4. The notion of regeneration as a kind of colonialism might sound somewhat far-fetched, but if we consider that a central trope of colonialism was that of an empty territory to be filled (and civilized), then the association becomes less tenuous. I certainly do not want to suggest that there was something exceptional or extreme about the case of Naples. Numerous similar situations can be identified across Europe over the last three decades. For example, the construction of the Olympic Park in Stratford, East London, has been officially lauded as the regeneration of a desolate wasteland which erases this same area's recent history as, inter alia, a place of work. Most of the small businesses that previously existed on the site had involved traditional 'dirty' occupations, such as car repairs, and were therefore incompatible with the prospect of a post-industrial future based around leisure and services (Raco and Tunney 2010).

ent desires and fears, needs and resources, who continually challenge the boundaries and definitions of a reinvigorated citizenship.

This book has considered separate instances of collective action, from the self-management of DAMM to demonstrations in Piazza Plebiscito and Piazza Garibaldi that subverted dominant place narratives about these latter two spaces. My ultimate aim has not been to evaluate the effectiveness of such acts but to configure a broader and more nuanced idea of spatial conflict that can intervene in our approach to thinking and writing about Naples as well as the contemporary city at large. Hence, the composite notion of contested space framing each study takes into account collective action alongside sociocultural habitus and transgression. These three elements are imbricated in the politics of public space and the ways in which it is perceived and used by people. So, examining the daily infringements of symbolic boundaries in Piazza Plebiscito provides insights into dissonant relationships with heritage space and how these might then be mobilized into forms of protest, as in the case of the occupation of the church by the organized unemployed. Exploring how immigrants reappropriate Piazza Garibaldi as a social, economic and cultural space also indicates the strategies by which they confront and elude the restrictions placed upon their presence and movement around the city. Finally, an analysis of squatting and redefining public space in Montesanto is not about championing the *centro sociale* as an enticing model of radical urban politics (an indiscriminate appraisal that DAMM itself disputed); rather it crucially needs to address the occupation's interaction with the lived experiences and political histories of 'popular' Naples – a social environment that, as one occupant of DAMM recalled, other local (anti-capitalist) activists had scorned as 'full of shit people'. It was these multivarious relationships and conflicts, and not just the repertoires and cycles of collective struggle, that rendered the administration's take on citizenship impracticable as a political design. A more realistic and operative, if difficult, urban project needed to commence from the recognition of the city's incongruous complexities rather than tie itself to preconceived ideas about inclusivity which, as I have shown, so often ended up bemoaning and forsaking the messy pluralism of Naples.

An incisive understanding of regeneration in the *centro storico* therefore needs to examine its unintended consequences and the active part played by different people in remaking urban space, otherwise one risks sketching a speculative portrait of experiences of the period or, worse still, reproducing the responses of privileged observers and their value-laden descriptions of the city. Such an approach also problematizes the apparently neutral turns of phrase – such as 'the retrieval of Piazza Plebiscito' or 'multiethnic Piazza Garibaldi' – that have punctuated academic accounts of the period. More generally, when critics use the piazza to extol the richness of public life in Italian cities, they need to ponder on the multiple conflicts and uncomfortable contradictions that this study has brought to light. A far more interesting and provocative history of public space lies at the interface between urban plans and policies and their contestation in everyday circumstances. No matter how 'unique' its history or 'errant' its inhabitants, Naples should never be considered exempt from such an approach. Dipesh Chakrabarty (2002) has spoken about the 'pain' felt by some Indian academics in their attempts to understand the recalcitrance of many city dwellers to embrace the advance of bourgeois modernity. This was rarely a quandary in Naples, where 'misuse' of the public realm was often summarily denounced by commentators as uncivil or illegal. My intention throughout this book has not simply been to contemplate the positions of the subaltern, downtrodden or un(der)represented but to probe assumptions about the unequivocal virtuosity of building 'citizen cultures', a strategy that acquired currency during the institutional and political crises of the early 1990s and which unwittingly influenced – and indeed continues to influence – popular definitions about urban change and development.[5]

Coda: looking back from beyond the downfall

The election of Rosa Russo Iervolino as mayor in May 2001 saw the spotlight move away from the cultural regeneration of the *centro storico* towards the day-to-day running of the whole city. From now on, far less prominence was accorded to individual public spaces in debates about the state and future of Naples. Nonetheless, the car-free Piazza Plebiscito remained a main venue for civic events, televised extravaganzas and public art. Controversy occasionally flared up over issues about inappropriate behaviour and the piazza's revitalization, as in early 2006 when the entrance to a pub that had recently opened under the colonnade was walled up by the neighbouring prefect on the legal grounds that it contravened building regulations (although for those who applauded the decision it

---

5. The correlation between a behavioural ideal of citizenship and regeneration continues to be advanced with conviction, as exemplified in a recent pamphlet by Amato Lamberti, a criminologist and assessor during Bassolino's first term: 'It is undeniable that there exists a deficit of "civility" regarding various forms of social and interpersonal behaviour, the use of public spaces, respect for the basic rules of civil coexistence as well as people's relationships with the state and its representatives. This blemishes, almost like a curse, the lifestyles of Neapolitans, irrespective of their social or class status. ... [T]oday, if Naples wants to be firmly placed on the map of global tourism and to host major media events, it needs to present itself with a clean face that is both decorous and skilfully adorned, especially if it wants to harness its monumental and cultural patrimony' (Lamberti 2008: 111).

had primarily breached standards of taste). Piazza Garibaldi continued to be a major social and economic base for the city's immigrants as well as a periodic source of news about crime and public security. A 2004 plan to redesign Piazza Garibaldi after the eventual completion of the new metro station envisaged much of the piazza pedestrianized with new green spaces and public facilities but also foresaw the removal of the 'multiethnic' street market set up by the city council in 2000. If this grand project goes ahead, and the current hostile climate towards immigration does not abate, one can expect the area's restructuring to become a flashpoint of contention.[6] Meanwhile, in the northern reaches of Montesanto, DAMM proceeded to organize social and cultural activities, albeit with less of the intensity of the late 1990s, and together with other local associations pursued its campaign for the upkeep of the park and escalators. In 2008, the city council finally conceded use of the three-storey building to its occupants on a rent-free tenancy agreement, which de facto legalized the status of the *centro sociale* and signalled a recognition of its constructive role in the neighbourhood.[7]

Of course, these brief vignettes do not capture the complex, intersubjective dynamics inherent to each space, nor do they account for the possible shifts in meaning and function over the last decade. However, this is not the place, nor is it my intention, to open a new chapter on the *centro storico* in the current era. Rather, here I want to offer some final remarks about the recent dramatic shift in public narratives about Naples and the extent to which this has affected interpretations of the city in the 1990s.

Over the last few years Naples has been cast as a city in free fall. The eruption of a new Camorra war at the end of 2004 and the deterioration of the rubbish crisis in late 2007 effectively extinguished the last vestiges of national and international acclaim that both Naples and Bassolino had received during the previous years. These two calamities sat alongside a host of more 'mundane' concerns, from rising street crime and a cocaine pandemic to the demise of the vibrant cultural scene and nightlife that had characterized the *centro storico* in the 1990s. Worryingly, there was also a marked rise in racist attacks, some of them particularly clamorous, such as the pogrom of Roma camps in the eastern suburb of Ponticelli in May 2008: this in a city that was supposedly immune to such sentiments on account of its 'welcoming spirit'. In the meantime, it was widely held

---

6. An official computer-animated video of the new Piazza Garibaldi can be viewed at: http://www .youtube.com/watch?v=sFI9EYPd26w&feature=related. For a critique of the redevelopment plans, see the 2007 video *Piazza Garibaldi: migranti 2*, produced by immigrants and media activists from the *centro sociale* Officina 99 at www.insutv.it/domenicaut/piazza-garibaldi-migranti-2.

7. For an overview of recent social initiatives and campaigns in the Ventaglieri Park, see http:// www.parcosocialeventaglieri.it/.

that the signs of political rebirth augured in late 1993 had turned sour. Following the municipal and regional elections of 1997 and 2000, the centre-left coalition became increasingly unwieldy as new centrist forces came aboard or jumped ship from the centre-right opposition. This not only meant accommodating a plethora of forces with divergent interests in the ruling executives, but, given the greater dependence of parties upon public funding for their survival, it also led to a scramble for salaried posts in local public agencies (Allum and Allum 2008). The forceful return of party (and sometimes national[8]) interference in administrative affairs (by no means confined to Naples or to the Centre-Left) went hand in hand with the reemergence of forms of personalized patronage and clientelism, which in turn further reduced the possibilities of meaningful popular participation in decision-making processes. To top it all, the Naples region was hit particularly hard by the economic downturn and recession of the late 2000s, with a swathe of temporary or permanent layoffs from small firms and large factories, which was compounded by the absence of a serious attempt on the part of both the Prodi and Berlusconi national governments to tackle the structural weaknesses of the Italian South.

Since 2006, the tribulations of Naples have been a fashionable topic for the Italian publishing industry, with various intellectuals and journalists chronicling the city's decline and providing their take on 'what went wrong'. Most of the authors are, or have been, associated with the Left. Self-assured and often self-righteous, their tones vary from angry and resigned to snooty and sarcastic, as they all seek to lay the city bare and confront uncomfortable truths. The publishers, for their part, have opted for eye-catching, uncompromising titles such as *Naples in the Blood* (Fo et al. 2006), *We Are Naples* (Bocca 2006), *Naples of Many Betrayals* (Scotto di Luzio 2008), *Shame* (Durante 2008) (the original is written in Neapolitan dialect with an Italian subtitle)[9], *Naples, Stark and Still* (Masullo and Scamardella 2008), *The Days of Shame* (Imarisio 2008) and *The Rubbish Caste* (De Stefano and Iurillo 2009). All the books are targeted at a general rather than an academic audience and, with a couple of exceptions (Fo et al. 2006 and Demarco 2007), do not burden themselves with citations

---

8. For instance, according to a party colleague and former economic advisor of Antonio Bassolino, Isaia Sales, in 2005 Francesco Rutelli and Piero Fassino (then respective leaders of La Margherita and the DS) signed an agreement that obliged Bassolino to hand two posts in the regional executive as well as the presidency of the assembly to the UDEUR (a centrist party electorally strong in the Campania region formed from a group that had defected from the Centre-Right in 1998) in order to consolidate the centre-left alliance at a national level in prospect of the forthcoming 2006 general election (*Corriere del Mezzogiorno,* 22 September 2008).

9. It should be noted that, despite its title, *Scuorno (Vergogna)* by Francesco Durante is the one book that makes a concerted attempt to distance itself from the catastrophic rhetoric about Naples, although the discussion of the city's various crises is still full of clichés about Naples's exceptionality.

or bibliographies. Instead, they draw on personal opinions, anecdotes and experiences, the paraphrased or unreferenced deliberations of others and, in a few cases, journalistic investigations and interviews conducted by the authors themselves.

One of the recurrent themes in these publications is that, despite its ups and downs, Naples has remained at a standstill. Nobody is blunter than veteran journalist Giorgio Bocca: 'You return to Naples after five or ten years and nothing has changed: the anarchy and criminal alliances are still the same' (Bocca 2006: 119). The philosopher Aldo Masullo, who was briefly mooted as the Left's mayoral candidate in 1993 before Bassolino stepped into the frame, sees the familist communitarian spirit and historic absence of a sense of civicness as the root cause of the city's immobility and current sorry state (Masullo and Scamardella 2008: 50–54). Marco Demarco, editor of *Corriere del Mezzogiorno,* attempts a more subtle reasoning: behind the peaks of enthusiasm and dips of despair that perpetuated after the Second World War, the city endowed itself with shock absorbers, such as illegality, welfare dependence, a rent-based economy and the *gattopardismo*[10] of the professional classes, which acted to stabilize local society (Demarco 2007: 19–20). 'The direct election of the mayor', argues Demarco, 'should have favoured a government free of obstacles and, consequently, the transformation of the city. Instead this stability yielded a static situation' (ibid.: 20).

Over and above the spurious (and provincial) idea that Naples sits outside the 'normal' course of history, the authors present a somewhat desolate scenario. There are no escape routes from this eternally damned place, no obvious solutions for such an unearthly metropolis. In the few cases where remedies are offered, these are vague and not particularly original. With the end of the prospect of a proletarian revolution, Giorgio Bocca now pins his hopes on young people 'who are fed up with leading the lives of thieves and liars [and] who want to be citizens in a civil country' (Bocca 2006: 132). Civility, however, is conceived as a final resting place and not a transformative strategy – something that was instead intrinsic to the journalist's erstwhile socialist beliefs – and so it is likely that Bocca's hopes will remain in vain.

The other common thread in these recent texts is an all-out attack on Antonio Bassolino as the person singly most responsible for the degeneration of Naples and local politics. Instead of maintaining his promise to revive both, some critics claim that he merely replaced the old regime with himself (De Stefano and Iurillo 2009: 26) and strengthened his grip

---

10. *Gattopardismo* refers to the political idea and practice of granting reforms provided they do not alter the existing state of affairs.

on power by establishing a network of cronies and lobbies (Demarco 2007: 89–98). Throughout the 2000s, Bassolino continued to exert a major influence on the city, swaying agendas of cultural policy and urban development (ibid.: 125–33), while Iervolino, for all her honesty, was considered out of her depth in the role of mayor (Bocca 2006: 34). But as regional governor, Bassolino's overall record was disappointing: costly commissions and consultancies, many of dubious worth, proliferated, EU structural funds were inefficiently used and did not induce economic growth, while the rubbish crisis exposed mismanagement of the highest order. The *Corriere della Sera* journalist Marco Imarisio, who reconstructs the city's *annus horribilus* of 2008, laments that 'the man who was supposed to renew everything is [now] doomed to be the emblem of the impossibility of change' (Imarisio 2008: 141).[11]

At a broader level, the Left is rebuked for its ingenuity and redundancy in the face of Naples's predicaments (although the right-wing opposition, sidelined and bereft of ideas, is never seriously taken into consideration). 'The Left' is usually portrayed as an amorphous entity, reflecting more the personal bias of the author than a specific party or line of thought. This is particularly evident in the semi-biographical essay by Adolfo Scotto di Luzio (2008), a young lecturer who had left Naples for a post at Bergamo University in northern Italy, in which the enlightened bourgeoisie, the Bas-

---

11. After weathering calls for his resignation throughout 2008 (thanks in part to his collaboration with the Berlusconi government in forcing through a stopgap solution to the rubbish crisis in May of the same year), Bassolino remained in his post until the end of his mandate in 2010. In the meantime, the Province of Naples would fall to the Centre-Right in June 2009, which would be followed by the same coalition's conquest of Campania in the regional elections of March 2010 (the Centre-Left's unsuccessful candidate on this occasion was Vincenzo De Luca, mayor of Salerno). Bassolino has, for the moment at least, taken a back seat in local politics. In 2009 he set up the Sudd Foundation with the intention of supporting research on the Mezzogiorno, and in early 2011 he published an account of his experiences as mayor and regional governor. Interestingly, the book's finale vindicates the lasting role of his administration's cultural policy in creating a more 'sophisticated idea about Naples' (Bassolino 2011: 176). In May 2011, against the expectations of most pundits, Luigi De Magistris, a former prosecutor and candidate of the anti-corruption centre-left party 'Italy of Values', backed by the Federation of the Left (that included Communist Refoundation and the Party of Italian Communists) and a radical group of independents, was elected mayor of Naples with a landslide 65.4 per cent in the run-off, beating Berlusconi's candidate Gianni Lettieri. This was not only a defeat for the Centre-Right, but also for Bassolino's and Iervolino's Democratic Party whose candidate Mario Morcone, a former prefect, had come third in the first-round vote. De Magistris had in fact campaigned hard against both the Centre-Right and the incumbent mayor, promising a decisive change in direction in local administrative affairs, just as Bassolino had vowed back in 1993. Much of the attention in the months following this extraordinary election was consumed by the resurgent rubbish crisis and the new administration's plans to maximize differentiated waste collection in the city. It is too early to assess the new mayor's vision for Naples (and it would appear that government cuts to local budgets will severely restrict the room for manoeuvre), but it is notable that in the area of cultural policy, De Magistris has already expressed a desire to move away from highbrow contemporary art towards more grassroots and 'traditional' forms of culture (*Corriere del Mezzogiorno,* 10 July 2011). What this might entail in terms of everyday urban experience, only time will tell.

solino administration, Christian Socialists, hippies and the *centri sociali* are indiscriminately gathered under the same banner. All are guilty of entertaining romanticized and speciously progressive clichés about the city's history, the Mediterranean, and, above all, the popular classes. This is a matter about which Scotto di Luzio declares intimate knowledge, having once been an active member of Proletarian Democracy and a participant of the Pantera student movement in the early 1990s. But like many other disillusioned Neapolitans, especially those fellow middle-class youths who chose to move into the *centro storico* in the 1990s, it is clear that Scotto di Luzio has a bee in his bonnet and that his biting cynicism does not put him in very good stead to appreciate the differences and mutations on 'The Left', least of all to recognize that during the 1990s its institutional post-Communist variant had begun to revise its notions of progress.

The main objection that I want to raise against these books is not that the city's problems are overstated or that certain criticisms (such as the stagnation of administrative politics) are not valid. Rather, it is that teleological and retrospective visions of the downfall of Naples neglect the entangled processes at play and leave little room for measured, critical analysis. Urban history is reduced to the words and deeds of politicians and other local public figures, and to a series of major events, scandals and tragedies. The notion of the 'Neapolitan Renaissance' is evoked simply in order to be ridiculed or to express a sense of betrayal. Yet the principal charges (for instance, that cultural policies amounted to a rarefied form of bread and circuses) are neither unique to Naples, for they are common criticisms in many cities across the world, nor are they novel, but rather they echo accusations that were already being levied during the 1990s. I would go even further to argue that the current polemics actually bear many similarities with the regeneration narratives of the Bassolino era in the way that they replicate the same perfunctory descriptions of urban change[12] and continue to unquestioningly espouse loaded terms such as '*identità*', '*cultura*' '*senso civile*' and '*cittadino*'.

Most important, the authors tend to endorse a picture of the 1990s as essentially devoid of social conflict. Scotto di Luzio, for one, believes that 'For many years no one raised their voice. The fascination with the "renaissance" captivated everybody' (Scotto di Luzio 2008: 112). The inhabitants of Naples are at best passive, at worst, complicit observers, but are never active participants in the transformation of their city. Moreover, the ease

---

12. Examples include the 'liberat[ion of] Piazza del Plebiscito from cars and poisonous smog' (De Stefano and Iurillo 2009: 15) and 'the retrieval of the *centro storico* from the clutches of *degrado*' (Demarco 2007: 177). The latter quote actually refers to Bari so as to underline that even the southern Adriatic port had achieved more than Naples. The point is that the significance of the *centro storico* and the implications of its recuperation are not queried but simply presumed to be positive.

with which 'Neapolitans' are collectively summoned is rarely placed into doubt, be they chips off a monolithic block or separated into the honest and the corrupt. Indeed, it is telling that next to no attention is paid to the presence of immigrants in the city.[13] This is no mere hairsplitting: it simply underlines how the 'Renaissance' and its aftermath are unproblematically conceived as 'indigenous' affairs.

It appears, therefore, that it is not so much the city than the formulation of certain debates that are stuck in a rut. In the weary world of pop-urbanism, with its cargo cults and pet arguments, very little has actually altered over the last twenty years bar the final assessment. Whether regenerate or degenerate, Naples persists as an *extraordinary* city, caught between the greener grass of elsewhere and parochial readings of its urban culture.

13. Marco Imarisio is the one author to deal with the issue in any depth, although he only concentrates on two episodes that occurred in 2008: the arson attacks on the Roma camps in Ponticelli in May and the odyssey of ninety, mainly West African, immigrants evacuated from a dilapidated building in the western suburb of Pianura in July.

Glossary of Italian Terms

Abusivo	Illegal, unauthorized, unlicensed
Arte dell'arrangiarsi	Art of getting by
Assessore/i	Assessor(s), member(s) of the executive cabinet with responsibility in a particular area (e.g. planning)
Autonomo/i	Autonomist(s); either an original member of, or broadly influenced by the late 1970s extra-parliamentary Leftist movement Autonomia Operaia. The term is used by the mainstream media and politicians to generally label users of the *centri sociali* irrespective of their different political positions
Autostrada del Sole	The 'Motorway of the Sun': the motorway linking Milan with Naples via Bologna, Florence and Rome.
Basso/i	Ground floor dwelling(s) in the *centro storico* of Naples
Biglietto da visita	Visiting card, business card
Borghesia illuminata	Enlightened bourgeoisie
Borgo	Village, historic suburb
Camorrista/i	Member(s) of the Camorra (Neapolitan criminal organization)
Carabiniere/i	Member(s) of the national gendarmerie that is part of the armed forces but with authority over the civilian population
Carro/i gru	Municipal tow truck(s) (for parking offenders)
Carta di soggiorno	Residence card
Casa/e del popolo	'House(s) of the People'; community centre(s) associated closely with the Communist and Socialist Parties
Centro antico	Ancient centre
Centro Direzionale	Administrative and business district
Centro/i sociale/i	Social centre(s)
Centro/i storico/i	Historic centre(s)

Circoscrizione	Administrative district that existed in the city of Naples from 1980 to 2005 (in 2005 the city's twenty-one *circoscrizioni* were reorganized into ten larger 'municipalities')
Città bella	Beautiful city
Città blindata	Fortress city
Cittadinanza	Citizenship
Cittadino/i	Citizen(s)
Civico	Civic
Civile	Civil
Clandestino/i	'Illegal' (i.e. undocumented) immigrant(s)
Comitato/i di quartiere	Neighbourhood committee(s)
Comune	Municipality, administrative territory, town hall
Contrabbandiere	Contraband cigarette seller
Cuccagna	Cockaigne; the main attraction during Carnival in late eighteenth-century Naples
Degrado	Degradation, blight
Doposcuola	After-school
Extracomunitario/i	Person(s) without citizenship of a member state of the European Union
Ferrovia	Railway
Festa/e dell'Unità	Annual fundraising festival(s) organized by the PCI (by the PDS between 1991 and 1998 and by the DS after 1998)
Fiore all'occhiello	A feather in one's cap, showpiece
Giunta	Mayor's executive cabinet
Granita	Crushed ice drink
Identità	Identity
Immigrato	Immigrant
Incivilmento	Civilizing
Intervento Straordinario	State-funded industrialization programme in the Italian South
Isola/e pedonale/i	Pedestrian zone(s)
Largo/ghi	Open space(s), piazza(s)
Lazzaroni (or Lazzari)	Historic term for the various lower-class people who lived by their wits on the streets of Naples and who were known to be staunch supporters of the monarchy

Ludoteca	Play space
Maggio dei Monumenti	'May of the Monuments'; annual art and urban-heritage festival coordinated by Naples City Council after 1994
Magliaro	Door-to-door vendor of poor-quality fabrics
Mani Pulite	'Clean Hands'; national anti-corruption trials which began in early 1992 and struck at the highest levels of Italian politics and business
Microcriminalità	Petty crime, street crime
Monumenti Porte Aperte	'Monuments Open Their Doors'; festival organized by Napoli 99 Foundation between 1992 and 1994
Motorino/i	Small-engine motorcycle(s)
Napoletanità	Neapolitanness
Paccottaro/i	Swindler(s) who seek(s) to convince a buyer that he/she is purchasing a high-value item such as a video camera
Palazzina	Small block; the three-storey building occupied by DAMM
Paravento	Windshield
Parcheggiatore/i abusivo/i	Unauthorized parking attendant(s)
Passeggiata	Stroll, promenade
Pentapartito	The five-party alliance consisting of the DC, PSI, PSDI, PRI and PLI that dominated Italian politics in the 1980s and early 1990s until all five parties were decimated by the *Mani Pulite* trials
Permesso di soggiorno	Residence permit
Piano nobile	Floor of a building where the noble classes once lived
Piazzale/i	Large piazza(s), forecourt(s)
Popolare	Popular; used to describe the lower-class population of Naples
Popolino	Little people, populace; local term used to describe the popular classes
Popolo	People
Proboscide	'Elephant's trunk'; popular name for the canopy extending from Naples central station into Piazza Garibaldi
Quartiere/i popolare/i	Popular neighbourhood(s)
Ragazzacci	Bad lads

Recupero	Reclamation
Regno del Possibile	'Realm of the Possible'; a major redevelopment scheme in the *centro storico* during the 1980s
Rettifilo	Straight line; popular name for the late nineteenth-century boulevard Corso Umberto I
Rianimazione	Revitalization
Riflusso	Reflux; the mass retreat into private life following the widespread collective action of the 1970s
Rigenerazione	Regeneration
Rinascimento Napoletano	Neapolitan Renaissance
Riqualificazione	Upgrading
Risanamento	Healing, urban renewal; title of the late nineteenth-century building programme following the 1884 cholera epidemic
Rivalorizzato	Revalued, reappraised
Salotto/i	Salon(s), exclusive meeting place(s)
Scudetto	Shield awarded for winning Serie A
Scugnizzo/i	Neapolitan street urchin(s)
Serie A	The top national league of Italian football
Sicurezza	Security
Società civile	Civil Society
Sottoproletariato	Sub-proletariat, lumpenproletariat
Spiazzo/i	Clearing(s)
Sventramento	Disembowelment, urban clearance
Tangentopoli	'Bribesville'; the system of political corruption that came to a head in the 1980s and early 1990s but also commonly used to describe the period of the *Mani Pulite* trials
Tangenziale	City ring road
Turismo	Tourism
Variante/i	Alteration(s) to an urban plan
Vetrina	Shop window, showcase
Vicolo/i	Alleyway(s)
Vigile/i urbano/i	Municipal police officer(s) with responsibility for traffic
Vu' cumprà	Literal transcription of non-Italian pronunciation of '*Vuoi comprare?*' (Do you want to buy?); derogatory term used for immigrant street traders

Bibliography

Agustoni, A. 2000. *Sociologia dei luoghi ed esperienza urbana*. Milan: Franco Angeli.

Alisio, G. 1981. *Napoli e il Risanamento. Recupero di una Struttura Urbana*. Naples: Guida.

Alisio, G., Izzo, A. and Almirante, R. 1987. *Progetti per Napoli*. Naples: Guida.

Allum, F. and Allum, P. 2008. 'Revisiting Naples: clientelism and organized crime'. *Journal of Modern Italian Studies* vol. 13, no. 3: 340–365.

Allum, F. and Cilento, M. 2001. 'Antonio Bassolino: From Mayor of Naples to President of Campania' in *Italian Politics: A Review, Volume 16. Emerging Themes and Institutional Responses,* eds. M. Caciagli and A. S. Zuckerman. Oxford: Berghahn, 119–32.

Allum, P. A. 1973. *Politics and Society in Post-war Naples*. Cambridge: Cambridge University Press.

Allum, P. A. 2003. 'The politics of town planning in post-war Naples'. *Journal of Modern Italian Studies* vol. 8, no. 4: 500–527.

Amato, F. 1992. 'Africani a Piazza Garibaldi'. *La città nuova* vol. 7, no. 1–2: 91–95.

Amato, F. 1997. 'Il suq di piazza Garibaldi a Napoli'. *Africa e Mediterraneo* no. 1: 20–23.

Amato, F. 2000. 'La circolarità commerciale degli immigrati nel napoletano'. *Afriche e oriente* vol. 2, no. 3/4: 53–57.

Amato, F. 2006. 'Il centro storico di Napoli tra rinascita e fine apparente'. *Storia Urbana* no. 113: 59–75.

Amato, F., Cattedra, R., Memoli, M. and Ventriglia, S. 1995. 'L'immigrato extracomunitario tra emarginazione e integrazione: Italia, Mezzogiorno, Campania'. *Terra d'Africa* no. 4: 129–96.

Amato, P. 2006. 'Il vuoto e l'abitare' in *Aporie napoletane. Sei posizioni filosofiche,* P. Amato et al., Naples: Edizioni Cronopio, 105–34.

Amato, P., Borrelli, G., Di Marco, G. A., Martone, A., Moroncini, B. and Zanardi, M. 2006. *Aporie napoletane. Sei posizioni filosofiche*. Naples: Edizioni Cronopio.

Amato, V. 1996. 'Dinamiche del turismo a Napoli'. *Orizzonti Economici* no. 82: 16–29.

Amaturo, E., ed. 2003. *Capitale sociale e classi dirigenti a Napoli*. Rome: Carocci.

Amin, A. , ed. 1994. *Post-Fordism: A Reader*. Oxford: Blackwell.

Amin, A. 2006. 'The Good City'. *Urban Studies* vol. 43, no. 5/6: 1009–23.

Amin, A. and Graham, S. 1997. 'The Ordinary City'. *Transactions of the Institute of British Geographers* vol. 22, no. 4: 411–29.

Amyot, G. 1981. *The Italian Communist Party: The Crisis of the Popular Front Strategy*. London: Croom Helm.

Andall, J. 2007. 'Immigration and the Italian Left Democrats in government (1996–2001)', *Patterns of Prejudice* vol. 41, no. 2: 131–53.

Astarita, T. 2005. *Between Salt Water and Holy Water: A History of Southern Italy*. New York: Norton.

Atkinson, R. 2003. 'Domestication by Cappuccino or a Revenge on Urban Space? Control and Empowerment in the Management of Public Spaces'. *Urban Studies* vol. 40, no. 9: 1211–45.

Augé, M. 1995. *Non-Places: Introduction to an Anthropology of Supermodernity*. London: Verso.

Aymard, M. 1999. 'Spazi' in *Il Mediterraneo. Lo spazio la storia gli uomini le tradizioni,* edited by F. Braudel. Milan: Bompiani, 123–44.

Baculo, A. 1979. *Napoli. Rilievi e problemi di intervento pubblico nel centro storico. Quartieri Porto-Pendino-Mercato.* Naples: Facoltà di Architettura dell'Università di Napoli.

Bagnasco, A. 1977. *Tre Italie. La problematica territoriale dello sviluppo italiano.* Bologna: il Mulino.

Baldini, G. 2002. 'The direct election of mayors: an assessment of the institutional reform following the Italian municipal elections of 2001'. *Journal of Modern Italian Studies* vol. 7, no. 3: 364–79.

Baldini, G. and Legnante, G. 2000. *Città al voto. I sindaci e le elezioni comunali.* Bologna: il Mulino.

Baldwin, P. C. 1999. *Domesticating the Street: The Reform of Public Space in Hartford, 1850–1930.* Columbus: Ohio State University Press.

Balestrini, N. and Moroni, P. 1997. *L'Orda D'Oro 1968–1977. La grande ondata rivoluzionaria e creativa, politica ed esistenziale.* Milan: Feltrinelli.

Balibar, E. 2004. *We, the People of Europe?: Reflections on Transnational Citizenship.* Princeton: Princeton University Press.

Banfield, E. 1958. *The Moral Basis of a Backward Society.* New York: The Free Press.

Barbagallo, F. 1997. *Napoli fine Novecento. Politici Camorristi Imprenditori.* Turin: Einaudi.

Barbagallo, F. 1999. *Il Potere della Camorra (1973–1998).* Turin: Einaudi.

Barbiani, L., ed. 1992. *La Piazza Storica Italiana. Analisi di un sistema complesso.* Venice: Marilio.

Barletta, L. 1997. 'Un esempio di festa: il Carnevale' in *Capolavori in Festa. Effimero Barocco a Largo di Palazzo (1683–1759),* catalogue of exhibition held at Palazzo Reale, Naples (20 December 1997–15 March 1998). Naples: Electa, 91–104.

Barracco, M. 1999. 'Alla ricerca dell'identità perduta. Intervista con Fabio Amato'. *Quaderni del Circolo Rossi* no. 14: 77–81.

Bassolino, A. 1980. *Mezzogiorno alla Prova. Napoli e il Sud alla Svolta degli Anni Ottanta.* Bari: De Donato.

Bassolino, A. 1996a. 'Imparare dalle città' in *Verso un rinascimento napoletano,* A. Bassolino, F. Ceci, E. Cicelyn, G. Fofi and D. Lepore. Naples: Liguori Editore, 49–67.

Bassolino, A. 1996b. *La repubblica delle città.* Naples: Donzelli.

Bassolino, A. 1999. 'Salpando verso l'Europa. Intervista con Fabio Amato'. *Quaderni del Circolo Rossi* no. 14: 13–16.

Bassolino, A. 2011. *Napoli Italia.* Naples: Guida.

Bassolino, A., Ceci, F., Cicelyn, E., Fofi, G. and Lepore, D. 1996. *Verso un rinascimento napoletano.* Naples: Liguori Editore.

Basson, S. 2006. "Oh Comrade, What Times Those Were!' History, Capital Punishment and the Urban Square'. *Urban Studies* vol. 43, no. 7: 1147–58.

Bauböck, R. 2003. 'Reinventing Urban Citizenship'. *Citizenship Studies* vol. 7, no. 2: 139–60.

Becchi, A. 1984. 'La città ambigua: economia e territorio a Napoli' in *Napoli "Miliardaria". Economia e lavoro dopo il terremoto,* edited by A. Becchi. Milan: Franco Angeli, 9–35.

Becchi, A. 1994. 'Napoli vista dal comune'. *Meridiana* no. 21: 233–60.

Belfiore, P. and Gravagnuolo, B. 1994. *Napoli. Architettura e urbanistica del Novecento.* Bari: Laterza.

Belli, A. 1986. *Il labirinto e l'eresia. La politica urbanistica a Napoli tra emergenza e ingovernabilità.* Milan: Franco Angeli.

Belli, A., ed. 2007. *Non è così facile. Politiche urbane a Napoli a cavallo del secolo.* Milan: Franco Angeli.

Bellucci, P., Maraffi, M. and Segatti, P. 2000. *PCI, PDS, DS. La trasformazione dell'identità politica della sinistra di governo.* Rome: Donzelli.

Belmonte, T. 1989. *The Broken Fountain,* 2nd ed. New York: Columbia University Press.

Benjamin, W. 1978. *Reflections: Essays, Aphorisms, Autobiographical Writings.* New York: Harcourt Brace Jovanovich.

Berdini, P. 2000. *Il Giubileo senza città. L'urbanistica romana negli anni del liberismo.* Rome: Riuniti.

Berg, L. D. 2004. 'Scaling knowledge: towards a *critical geography* of critical geographies'. *Geoforum* no. 35: 553–58.

Berger, J. and Mohr, J. 1975. *A Seventh Man: The Story of Migrant Workers in Europe.* Harmondsworth: Penguin.

Berman, M. 1986. 'Take it to the Streets: Conflict and Community in Public Spaces'. *Dissent* vol. 33, no. 4: 476–85.

Berzano, L. and Gallini, R. 2000. 'Centri Sociali Autogestiti a Torino'. *Quaderni di Sociologia* vol. 44, no. 22: 50–79.

Bevilacqua, P. 1996. 'New and Old in the Southern Question'. *Modern Italy* vol. 1, no. 2: 81–92.

Bianchini, F. 1993. 'Remaking European cities: the role of cultural policies' in *Cultural Policy and Urban Regeneration: The West European Experience,* edited by F. Bianchini and M. Parkinson. Manchester: Manchester University Press, 1–20.

Biondi, G. 1983. 'Il ruolo di "Avellino a Tarsia" nel riassetto del centro storico di Napoli'. *Orizzonti Economici* no. 38: 79–82.

Bocca, G. 1992. *L'inferno. Profondo Sud, Male Oscuro.* Milan: Mondadori.

Bocca, G. 2006. *Napoli siamo noi. Il dramma di una città nell'indifferenza dell'Italia.* Milan: Feltrinelli.

Boccia, F. 1996. *I buoni obbligazionari comunali: che cosa sono e perche convengono.* Milan: Il Sole-24 Ore libri.

Bodo, G. and Viesti, G. 1997. *La Grande Svolta. Il Mezzogiorno nell'Italia degli anni novanta.* Rome: Donzelli.

Bonnet, F. 2004. 'The aftermath of France's last moral panic and its sociology'. *International Journal of Urban and Regional Research* vol. 28, no. 4: 948–51.

Bonnett, A. 1996. 'The Transgressive Geographies of Daily Life. Socialist Pathways within Everyday Urban Spatial Creativity'. *Transgressions: A Journal of Urban Exploration* no. 2/3: 20–37.

Borriello, M. 1961. 'La nuova Stazione di Napoli Centrale' in *Itinerari F.S. Guida del Compartimento Ferroviario di Napoli,* edited by R. Tornincasa. Naples: Manifatture di Pompei, 173–93.

Bouchard, M. 1997. 'Le risposte possibili alla criminalità diffusa' in *Storia d'Italia (Annali 12: La criminalità),* edited by L. Violante. Turin: Einaudi, 1033–53.

Bourdieu, P. 1977. *Outline of a Theory of Practice.* Cambridge: Cambridge University Press.

Bourdieu, P. 1984. *Distinction: A Social Critique of the Judgment of Taste.* London: Routledge.

Bourdieu, P. 2005. 'Habitus' in *Habitus: A Sense of Place,* edited by J. Hillier and E. Rooksby. Aldershot: Ashgate, 43–49.

Boutang, Y. M. 1997. 'Une forme contemporaine du salariat bridé' in *Les Lois de l'Inhospitalité. Les politiques de l'immigration à l'épreuve des sans-papiers,* edited by D. Fassin, M. Morice and C. Quiminal. Paris: La Découverte et Syros, 127–43.

Brancaccio, L. 2000. 'Il comune di Napoli nel passaggio del 1993. Reti, potere, politiche, interessi', unpublished PhD thesis, University of Trent.

Brancaccio, L. 2003. 'Gerarchia e differenziazione al vertice del potere cittadino' in *Capitale sociale e classi dirigenti a Napoli,* edited by E. Amaturo. Rome: Carocci, 155–73.

Braucci, M. 1998. 'Bodhisattva. Sulla creazione di una zona autogestita'. *Lo Straniero* no. 3: author's original copy and therefore no page numbers.

Braucci, M. 1999a. *Il mare guasto.* Rome: Edizioni e/o.

Braucci, M. 1999b. *Dottori della Villa Comunale e Misteri del Parco Ventaglieri,* unpublished manuscript.

Broccolini, A. 1998. 'La ritualità festiva del borgo: la festa della "Nzegna", Santa Lucia e la Madonna della Catena' in *Il Borgo di Santa Lucia. Trasformazione urbana e tradizioni. Immagini fotografiche 1870–1950,* edited by the Archivio Fotografico Parisio. Bracigliano: Cecom, np.

Bucaro, A. 1989. 'Architetture e spazi urbani: i tre fori napoletani'. *Agorà. Le piazze storiche dell'Italia meridionale e insulare* vol. 2, no. 4: 26–31.

Bull, A. C. 2005. 'Democratic Renewal, Urban Planning and Civil Society: The Regeneration of Bagnoli, Naples'. *Southern European Society and Politics* vol. 10, no. 3: 391–410.

Bull, M. J. 1996. 'The great failure? The Democratic Party of the Left in Italy's transition' in *The New Italian Republic: From the Fall of the Berlin Wall to Berlusconi,* edited by S. Gundle and S. Parker. London: Routledge, 159–72.

Burke, P. 1986. *The Historical Anthropology of Early Modern Italy: Essays on Perception and Communication.* Cambridge: Cambridge University Press.

Cacciapuoti, S. 1972. *Storia di un operaio napoletano.* Rome: Riuniti.

Caglioti, D. L. 1994. *Il guadagno difficile. Commercianti napoletani nella seconda metà dell'Ottocento.* Bologna: il Mulino.

Calaresu, M. 2007. 'From the street to stereotype. Urban space, travel and the picturesque in late eighteenth-century Naples'. *Italian Studies* vol. 62, no. 2: 189–203.

Caldeira, T. P. R. 2000. *City of Walls: Crime, Segregation, and Citizenship in São Paulo.* Berkeley: University of California Press.

Calvanese, F. and Pugliese, E. 1991. *La Presenza Straniera in Italia. Il Caso della Campania.* Milan: Franco Angeli.

Caniglia, C. 1993. 'Andare a piedi a Napoli: il caso di Piazza del Plebiscito' in *Lo spazio pedonale,* edited by R. Gerundo and A. M. D'Amato. Naples: Edizioni Graffiti, 19–26.

Canniffe, E. 2008. *The Politics of the Piazza: The History and Meaning of the Italian Square.* Aldershot: Ashgate.

Cantiere Sociale di Napoli 1999. *Un anno vissuto paurosamente. Disordine, crimine, repressione e pietà nell'Italia del 1998. Cronologia degli eventi.* Naples: Carta.

Capasso, A. 1993. 'La pedonalizzazione di piazza del Plebiscito' in *Lo spazio pedonale,* edited by R. Gerundo and A. M. D'Amato. Naples: Edizioni Graffiti, 47–49.

Capasso, A., Niego, A. and Vittoria, E. 1982. *Lo spazio pedonale e la città.* Naples: Società Editrice Napoletana.

Caponio, T. 2005. 'Policy Networks and Immigrants' Associations in Italy: The Cases of Milan, Bologna and Naples'. *Journal of Ethnic and Migration Studies* vol. 31, no. 5: 931–50.

Cappelli, O. 1978. *Governare Napoli. Le sinistre alla prova nella capitale del Mezzogiorno.* Bari: De Donato.

Cappelli, O., ed. 1998. 'Governo e partiti a Napoli negli anni Novanta. Verso un "presidenzialismo metropolitano"?'. Special issue of *Nord e Sud* vol. 45, no. 4/5: 1–165.

Cappelli, O. 2001. 'La resistibile ascesa del sindaco-presidente. Bassolino, i media e gli intellettuali'. *Meridione* vol. 1, no. 2: 16–54.

Cappelli, O., ed. 2003a. *Potere e società a Napoli a cavallo del secolo. Omaggio a Percy Allum.* Naples: Edizioni Scientifiche Italiane.

Cappelli, O. 2003b. 'La "cosa" napoletana. Le trasformazioni di un partito di massa' in *Potere e Società a Napoli a Cavallo del Secolo. Omaggio a Percy Allum,* edited by O. Cappelli. Naples: Edizioni Scientifiche Italiane, 181–218.

Caritas di Roma., ed. 1999. *Immigrazione. Dossier Statistico '99.* Rome: Anterem.

Carr, S., Francis, M., Rivlin, L. G. and Stone, A. M. 1992. *Public Space.* Cambridge: Cambridge University Press.

Cassano, F. 1996. *Il Pensiero Meridiano.* Bari: Laterza.

Cassano, F. 2009. *Tre modi di vedere il Sud*. Bologna: il Mulino.

Castells, M. 1983. *The City and the Grassroots*. London: Edward Arnold.

Castells, M. 1997. 'Citizens movements, information and analysis. An interview'. *City* no. 7: 140–155.

Cattedra, R. and Memoli, M. 1992. 'I luoghi degli immigrati'. *La città nuova* vol. 7, no. 1–2: 66–80.

Cavola, L. and Vicari, S. 2000. 'Napoli fra emergenza e governabilità: il monito della riqualificazione urbana'. *Rassegna Italiana di Sociologia* no. 4: 517–38.

Cederna, A. 1956. *I Vandali in Casa*. Bari: Laterza.

Cederna, A. 1991. *Brandelli d'Italia. Come distruggere il bel paese*. Rome: Newton Compton.

Centro Sociale Leoncavallo 1999. 'Laboratorio Nord-Est'. *Derive Approdi* no. 18: 41–43.

Cerase, F. P., Morlicchio, E. and Spanò, A., eds. 1991. *Disoccupati e disoccupate a Napoli*. Milan: CUEN.

Cervellati, P. L. 1991. *La città bella. Il recupero dell'ambiente urbano*. Bologna: il Mulino.

Chakrabarty, D. 2002. *Habitations of Modernity: Essays in the Wake of Subaltern Studies*. Chicago: University of Chicago Press.

Chambers, I. 1994. *Migrancy, Culture, Identity*. London: Routledge.

Chambers, I. 1996. 'Naples: the emergent archaic' in *Strangely Familiar: Narratives of Architecture in the City,* edited by Borden, I., Kerr, J., Pivaro, A. and Rendell, J. London: Routledge, 42–45.

Chubb, J. 1980. 'Naples Under the Left: The Limits of Local Change'. *Comparative Politics* vol. 13, no. 1: 53–78.

Chubb, J. 1982. *Patronage, Power and Poverty in Southern Italy*. Cambridge: Cambridge University Press.

Cicelyn, E., ed. 1998. *Bandiere di Maggio: Napoli, Piazza del Plebiscito, 24 aprile–7 giugno 1998*. Naples: Cronopio.

Cioffi, J. W. and Höpner, M. 2006 'The Political Paradox of Finance Capitalism: Interests, Preferences, and Center-Left Party Politics in Corporate Governance Reform'. *Politics Society* vol. 34, no. 4: 463–502.

Clifford, J. 1986. 'Introduction: Partial Truths' in *Writing Culture: The Poetics and Politics of Ethnography,* edited by J. Clifford and G. E. Marcus. Berkeley: University of California Press, 1–26.

Cohen, J. and Arato, A. 1992. *Civil Society and Political Theory*. Cambridge: MIT Press.

Cohen, S. 1985. *Visions of Social Control*. Cambridge: Polity Press.

Cohn, B. 1987. *An Anthropologist among the Historians and Other Essays*. Delhi: Oxford University Press.

Colella, P. 1999. 'Forum: Cittadini e Istituzioni a Napoli'. *Il tetto* no. 215: 25–76.

Compagna, F. 1981. *Dal terremoto alla ricostruzione*. Naples: Edizioni Scientifiche Italiane.

Compagnone, S. 1989. 'Il progetto che non c'è. Intervista a Berardo Impegno'. *NdR* no. 6: 31.

Comune di Napoli. 1996. *Napoli. Le vie dell'Arte. Progetto Museo Aperto*. Naples: Cosmofilm.

Comune di Napoli. 1997. *Il Quartiere, Un Bene Comune. Programma Urban U.E. Quartieri Spagnoli Rione Sanità*. Salerno: Arti Grafiche Boccia.

Comune di Napoli. 1999a. *Bollettino di Statistica. Maggio – Agosto 1998*. Naples: F.lli De Siena.

Comune di Napoli. 1999b. *Variante al piano regolatore generale. Centro storico, zona orientale, zona nordoccidentale. Sintesi informativa*. Naples: F.lli De Siena.

Comune di Napoli. 1999c. *Programma Urban. I Quartieri Spagnoli*. Salerno: Arti Grafiche Boccia.

Comune di Napoli. 2000. *Le elezioni a Napoli dal 1946 al 1997*. Naples: SISTAN.

Comune di Napoli. 2005. *La occupazione a Napoli ai censimenti dal 1951 al 2001*. Naples: SISTAN.

Comune di Napoli. 2007. *La popolazione di Napoli ai censimenti dal 1951 al 2001*. Naples: SISTAN.

Cooper, D. 1998. 'Regard between strangers: diversity, equality and the reconstruction of public space'. *Critical Social Policy* vol. 18, no. 4: 465–92.

Coppola, P. 1999. 'Nuovi abitanti, nuove mixités. Napoli: tracce di una città meticcia' in *Immigrazione e Multicultura nell'Italia di Oggi Vol. II. La cittadinanza e l'esclusione, la "frontiera adriatica" e gli altri luoghi dell'immigrazione, la società e la scuola*, edited by C. Brusa. Milan: Franco Angeli, 414–22.

Coppola, P. and Memoli, M. 1997. 'Per una Geografia indiziaria: alcune indagini sugli immigrati a Napoli' in *Immigrazione e Multicultura nell'Italia di Oggi. Il territorio, i problemi, la didattica*, edited by C. Brusa. Milan: Franco Angeli, 363–79.

Coppola, P., Sommella, R. and Viganoni, L. 1997. 'Il paesaggio urbano napoletano tra immagine e mercato' in *Studi geografici in onore di Mario Fondi*, edited by M. Mautone. Naples: Edizioni Scientifiche Italiane, 65–91.

Corona, G. 2007. *I ragazzi del piano. Napoli e le ragioni dell'ambientalismo urbano*. Rome: Donzelli.

Corsi, E. 1989. 'Contro l'immobilismo. Intervista a Enzo Giustino'. *NdR* no. 6: 3–6.

Corsi, E. 1994. 'Il palco che avanza'. *Napoli Guide: Piazza Plebiscito* vol. 7, no. 21: 28–30.

Cotesta, V., ed. 1999. 'Mass media, conflitti etnici e immigrazione'. *Studi Emigrazione* vol. 36, no. 135: 387–497.

Craveri, P. 1989. 'Napoli addio?'. *NdR* no. 6: 50–51.

Crawford, M. 1995. 'Contesting the Public Realm: Struggles over Public Space in Los Angeles'. *Journal of Architectural Education* vol. 49, no. 1: 4–9.

Cresswell, T. 1996. *In Place/Out of Place: Geography, Ideology, and Transgression*. Minneapolis: University of Minnesota Press.

Cristante, S. 1995. *Matusalemme e Peter Pan. Vecchi, adulti e giovani nella società di fine secolo*. Genoa: Costa and Nolan.

Cuoco, V. 1995. *Saggio Storico sulla Rivoluzione di Napoli del 1799*. Naples: Procaccini.

Dainotto, R. M. 2003. 'The Gubbio Papers: historic centers in the age of the economic miracle'. *Journal of Modern Italian Studies* vol. 8, no. 1: 67–83.

Dal Lago, A. 1999. *Non-persone. L'esclusione dei migranti in una società globale*. Milan: Feltrinelli.

Dal Lago, A. 2002. 'Guardiani e Cagnolini. Appunti sulla deriva a destra'. *Rivista del Manifesto* no. 30: 7–9.

Dal Piaz, A. 1985. *Napoli 1945 – 1985. Quarant'anni di Urbanistica*. Milan: Franco Angeli.

Dal Piaz, A. 1987. 'L'epicentro Napoli'. *NdR* no. 2: 3–7.

Dal Piaz, A. and Apreda, I. 1993. 'Area Napoletana: Gli interventi straordinari tra "emergenze" ed "occasioni"' in *La città occasionale*, edited by F. Indovina. Milan: Franco Angeli, 103–50.

DAMM. 1998. *Montesanto, Napoli: Prove di convivenza al confine tra due città*. Naples: DAMM edizioni autogestite.

DAMM. 1999. *Storia spettacolare di Guyelmo el Pesado che voleva rovesciare il mondo*. Naples: DAMM edizioni autogestite.

DAMM. 2000. *Un, due, tre! Non si muove una foglia. Politiche (a)sociali della città progressista*. Naples: DAMM edizioni autogestite.

D'Angelo, A. 2000. 'Il "modello" Termini'. *Linea Diretta. Mensile per il personale per il gruppo FS* vol. 4, no. 1: 16–21.

Dardi, C. 1992. 'Elogio della piazza' in *La piazza storica italiana. Analisi di un sistema complesso*, edited by L. Barbiani. Venice: Marilio, 47–61.

Davis, J.A. 1998. 'Casting Off the "Southern Problem": Or the Peculiarities of the South Revisited' in *Italy's 'Southern Question': Orientalism in One Country*, edited by J. Schneider. Oxford: Berg, 205–24.

Davis, J. A. 1999. 'The Neapolitan Revolution 1799–1999: Between History and Myth'. *Journal of Modern Italian Studies* vol. 4, no. 3: 350–58.

Davis, M. 1990. *City of Quartz: Excavating the Future in Los Angeles.* London: Verso.

Dazieri, S. 1996. *Italia Overground. Mappe e reti della cultura alternativa.* Rome: Castelvecchi.

De Filippo, E. 1999. 'Le donne immigrate in Campania' in *défilé,* edited by L. Mastrodomenico. Naples: L'ancora, 87–107.

De Fusco, R. 1996. *Storia, progetti e "parole" su Napoli. Scritti brevi (1979–1996).* Naples: Fausto Fiorentino.

De Giorgi, A. 2000. *Zero Tolleranza. Strategie e pratiche della società di controllo.* Rome: Derive Approdi.

De Luca, G. 1987. *I problemi urbanistici di Napoli. Un progetto possibile.* Naples: Ste Edizioni.

De Lucia, V. 1989. *Se questa è una città.* Rome: Riuniti.

De Lucia, V. 1998. *Napoli Cronache urbanistiche 1994–1997.* Milan: Baldini & Castaldi.

De Matteis, S. 1991. *Lo specchio della vita. Napoli: antropologia della città del teatro.* Bologna: il Mulino.

De Matteis, S. 1993. 'Storie di famiglia. Appunti e ipotesi antropologiche sulla famiglia a Napoli'. *Meridiana* no. 17: 137–62.

De Matteis, S. 1994. 'Le culture del popolo e l'arte di arrangiarsi'. *Micromega* no. 3: 142–52.

De Matteis, S. 1995. 'Le lingue mute di Napoli'. *Dove sta Zazà* no. 6/7: 16–17.

De Mauro, T. and Mancini, M. 2000. *Dizionario Etimologico della Lingua Italiana.* Milan: Garzanti.

De Seta, C. 1981. *Napoli.* Bari: Laterza.

De Seta, C., 1983. *Dopo il terremoto la ricostruzione.* Bari: Laterza.

De Stefano, B. and Iurillo, V. 2009. *La Casta della Monnezza. Dall'emergenza rifiuti alla crisi finanziaria, il ritratto di un Paese e di una classe politica sotto inchiesta.* Rome: Newton Compton.

Delanty, G. 2000. 'The resurgence of the city in Europe?: the spaces of European citizenship' in *Democracy Citizenship and the Global City,* edited by E. F. Isin. London: Routledge, 79–92.

Delli, S. 1994. *Le Piazze di Napoli. Tradizioni popolari e storia, arte e urbanistica. Un viaggio attraverso i palcoscenici naturali di una "città nobilissima".* Rome: Newton Compton.

Demarco, M. 2007. *L'atra metà della storia. Spunti e riflessioni su Napoli da Lauro a Bassolino.* Naples: Guida.

DETR (Department of the Environment, Transport and the Regions). 1999. *Towards an Urban Renaissance: Final Report of the Urban Task Force UK.* London: HMSO.

DETR (Department of the Environment, Transport and the Regions). 2000. *Our Towns and Cities: The Future: Delivering an Urban Renaissance.* London: HMSO.

Desideri, P. 1995. *La città di latta: favelas di lusso, autogrill, svincoli stradali e antenne paraboliche.* Genoa: Costa e Nolan.

Desideri, P. and Ilardi, M, eds. 1996. *Attraversamenti. I nuovi territori dello spazio pubblico.* Genoa: Costa e Nolan.

Dines, N. 1999. 'Centri sociali: occupazioni autogestite a Napoli negli anni novanta'. *Quaderni di Sociologia* vol. 43, no. 21: 90–111.

Dines, N. 2000. 'What are 'Social Centres'?: A Study of Self-managed Occupations during the 1990s'. *Transgressions: A Journal of Urban Exploration* no. 5: 23–39.

Dines, N. 2001. 'Urban Change and Contested Space in Contemporary Naples', unpublished PhD thesis, University College London.

Dines, N. 2005. 'Una visione post-comunista del rinnovamento urbano: spazio pubblico, sicurezza e cittadinanza nella Napoli di Bassolino' in *Polis e panico I. Tra vulnerabilità e immunizzazione,* edited by A. Petrillo. Avellino: Elio Sellino Editore, 87–109.

Dines, N. 2009. 'The disputed place of ethnic diversity: an ethnography of the redevelopment of a street market in East London' in *Regenerating London. Governance, Sustainability and Community in a Global City,* edited by R. Imrie, L. Lees and M. Raco. London: Routledge, 254–72.

Dines, N., Cattell, V., Gesler, W. and Curtis, S. 2006. *Public Spaces, Social Relations and Well-being in East London.* Bristol: Policy Press.

Dini, V. and Nicolaus, O., eds. 1991. *Te Diegum. Genio sregolatezza & bacchettoni.* Milan: Leonardo.

Dini, V., Esposito, R. and Nicolaus, O. 1993. 'Il mare bagna Napoli'. *Micromega* no. 4: 29–40.

Dispoto, G. 1991. 'I Parchi e gli spazi verdi del PSER'. *Architettura Quaderni* no. 6: 100–103.

Di Tullio, D. 2006. *Centri sociali di destra. Occupazioni e culture non conformi.* Rome: Castelvecchi.

Doria, G. 1992. *Piazza del Plebiscito.* Naples: Fausto Fiorentino.

Dunford, M. and Greco, L. 2006. *After the Three Italies: Wealth, Inequality and Industrial Change.* Oxford: Blackwell.

Durante, F. 2008. *Scuorno (Vergogna).* Milan: Mondadori.

Eisinger, P. 2000. 'The Politics of Bread and Circuses: Building the City for the Visitor Class'. *Urban Affairs Review* vol. 35, no. 3: 316–33.

Elden, S. 2001. 'Politics, philosophy, geography: Henri Lefebvre in recent Anglo-American scholarship'. *Antipode* vol. 33, no. 5: 809–25.

Elias, N. 1995. 'Technization and Civilization'. *Theory, Culture and Society* vol. 12, no. 3: 7–42.

Elms, R. 1998. 'Take the Plunge'. *The Sunday Times,* 1 March.

Engels, F. 1977. 'The Latest Heroic Deed of the House of Bourbon' in *Collected Works of Karl Marx and Friedrich Engels, 1848, Vol. 7: Demands of the Communist Party in Germany, Articles, Speeches,* edited by L. Golman. New York: International Publishers, 142–43.

Esposito, G. 1973. *Anche il Colera.* Milan: Feltrinelli.

Esposito, R. 1999. 'Morte di una stagione napoletana'. *Micromega* no. 1: 11–19.

Fabian, J. 1983. *Time and the Other: How Anthropology Makes Its Object.* New York: Columbia University Press.

Fabietti, U. 1995. *L'identità etnica.* Rome: Carocci.

Fassino, P. 2001. *Sicurezza e Giustizia. Conversazione con Paolo Borgna.* Rome: Donzelli.

Fassino, P. and Garavini, S. 1992. *C'eravamo tanto amati.* Rome: Roberto Napoleone.

Fazio, M. 1977. *Il destino dei Centri Storici.* Florence: La Nuova Italia.

Featherstone, M. 1991. *Consumer Culture and Postmodernism.* London: Sage.

Ferrara, L. 1997. *E' qui la festa 1970–1997. Disoccupati organizzati a Napoli.* Naples: Ulisse Edizioni.

Ferrari, M. 1993. 'Pedonalizzazione e mobilità automobilistica' in *Lo spazio pedonale,* edited by R. Gerundo and A. M. D'Amato. Naples: Edizioni Graffiti, 27–32.

Ferulano, G. 1986. 'La sperimentazione nel centro storico'. *Urbanistica* no. 83: 88–89.

Ferulano, G. 1991. 'Il comparto centro urbano'. *Architettura Quaderni* no. 6: 104–109.

Festa, F. A. 2003. 'L'alchimia ribelle napoletana' in *Potere e Società a Napoli a Cavallo del Secolo. Omaggio a Percy Allum,* edited by O. Cappelli. Naples: Edizioni Scientifiche Italiane, 381–423.

Fine, R. 1997. 'Civil Society Theory, Enlightenment and Critique'. *Democratization* vol. 4 no. 1: 7–28.

Fisdall, C. and Bozzolla, A. 1977. *Futurism.* London: Thames and Hudson.

Fo, J., Di Maio S., Sorace, S., Sinicatti, E., Genovese, M., Canova, S., Calabria, D. and Napolitano, A. 2006. *Napoli nel sangue.* Naples: Edizioni Voce dei Voci.

Fofi, G. 1999. *Le nozze coi ficchi secchi.* Naples: L'ancora.

Fofi, G. 2009. *La vocazione minoritaria: Intervista sulle minoranze.* Rome: Laterza.

Fontana, I. 2001. *Non sulle mie scale. Diario di un cittadino alle prese con l'immigrazione clandestina e l'illegalità*. Rome: Donzelli.

Foot, J. 1996. 'The "Left Opposition" and the crisis: Rifondazione Comunista and La Rete' in *The New Italian Republic: From the Fall of the Berlin Wall to Berlusconi*, edited by S. Gundle and S. Parker. London: Routledge, 173–88.

Foot, J. 2001a. 'The Creation of a "Dangerous Place": San Salvario, Turin, 1990–1999' in *The Mediterranean Passage: Migration and New Cultural Encounters in Southern Europe*, edited by R. King. Liverpool: Liverpool University Press, 206–30.

Foot, J. 2001b. *Milan since the Miracle. City: Culture and Identity*. Oxford: Berg.

Forgacs, D. 1990. 'The Italian Communist Party and Culture' in *Culture and Conflict in Postwar Italy: Essays on Mass and Popular Culture*, edited by Z. G. Barański and R. Lumley. Basingstoke: Macmillan, 97–114.

Forni, E. 2002. *La città di Batman. Bambini, conflitti, sicurezza urbana*. Turin: Bollati Boringhieri.

Foucault, M. 1979. *Discipline and Punish: The Birth of the Prison*. Harmondsworth: Penguin.

Fowler, R. 1991. *Language in the News: Discourse and Ideology in the Press*. London: Routledge.

Fraser, N. 1992. 'Rethinking the Public Sphere: A Contribution to the Critique of Actually Existing Democracy' in *Habermas and the Public Sphere*, edited by C. Calhoun. Cambridge: MIT Press, 109–42.

Fratta, A. 1986. *Centro Storico e Città Futura*. Naples: Gruppo Mezzogiorno dei Cavalieri del Lavoro.

Fratta, A., Volpe, T. and Vajro, M. 1970. *Napolitutto*. Naples: Edizioni Scientifiche Italiane.

Furbey, R. 1999. 'Urban "regeneration": reflections on a metaphor'. *Critical Social Policy* vol. 19, no. 4: 419–45.

Fyfe, N. R. 1996. 'Contested visions of a modern city: planning and poetry in postwar Glasgow'. *Environment and Planning A* vol. 28, no. 3: 387–404.

Galasso, G. 1978. *Intervista sulla storia di Napoli*. Bari: Laterza.

Galasso, G. 1994. 'Il perimetro del potere'. *Napoli Guide: Piazza Plebiscito* vol. 7, no. 21: 17–19.

Gambardella, A. 1990. *Piazza Mercato a Napoli. Architettura e sviluppo urbano del Borgo orientale*. Genoa: Sagep.

Garland, D. 2001. *The Culture of Control: Crime and Social Order in Contemporary Society*. Chicago: University of Chicago Press.

Gartman, D. 2004. 'Three Ages of the Automobile: The Cultural Logics of the Car'. *Theory, Culture & Society* vol. 21, no. 4/5: 169–95.

Genoino, C. T. 1989. 'Suonatori ambulanti nelle province meridionali. Archivi della polizia borbonica e postunitaria dell'ottocento'. *La Ricerca Folklorica. Contributi allo studio della cultura delle classi popolari* no. 19: 69–76.

Gerbino, G. 2000. 'Identità, appartenenze territoriali e politiche pubbliche urbane: il caso del centro storico di Palermo'. Paper presented at 'Localismi e Globalizzazione' conference at Istituto Universitario Suor Orsola Benincasa. Naples, 16 June.

Geremicca, A. 1977. *Dentro la città. Napoli angoscia e speranza*. Naples: Guida.

Geremicca, A., ed. 1997. *Napoli. Una Transizione Difficile*. Naples: Guida.

Gerundo, R. and D'Amato, A. M., eds. 1993. *Lo spazio pedonale*. Naples: Edizioni Graffiti.

Ghirelli, A. 1976. *La Napoletanità*. Naples: Società Editrice Napoletana.

Giannetti, D. and Mulé, R. 2006. 'The Democratici di Sinistra: In Search of a New Identity'. *South European Society and Politics* vol. 11, no. 3: 457–75.

Giglia, A. 1997. *Crisi e ricostruzione di uno spazio urbano. Dopo il bradisismo a Pozzuoli: una ricerca antropologica su Monteruscello*. Milan: Guerini.

Ginsborg, P. 1990. *A History of Contemporary Italy: Society and Politics, 1943–1988*. London: Penguin.

Ginsborg, P. 1998. *Storia d'Italia 1943–1996: Famiglia, Società, Stato.* Turin: Einaudi.

Ginsborg, P. 2001. *Italy and Its Discontents: Family, Civil Society, State, 1980–2001.* London: Allen Lane.

Gleijeses, V. 1968. *La Piazza del Plebiscito in Napoli.* Naples: Edizioni del Delfino.

Goddard, V. A. 1997. *Gender, Family and Work in Naples.* Oxford: Berg.

Gómez, M. V. 1998. 'Reflective Images: The Case of Urban Regeneration in Glasgow and Bilbao'. *International Journal of Urban and Regional Research* vol. 22, no. 1: 106–21.

Goss, J. 1997. 'Representing and re-presenting the contemporary city'. *Urban Geography* no. 18: 180–88.

Governa, F. 1997. *Il Milieu Urbano. L'identità territoriale nei processi di sviluppo.* Milan: Franco Angeli.

Gramsci, A. 1978. *Quaderno 22. Americanismo e fordismo.* Turin: Einaudi.

Gramsci, A. 1982. *La Questione Meridionale,* 3rd ed. Rome: Riuniti.

Greenhalgh, L. and Worpole, K. 1995. *Park Life: Urban Parks and Social Renewal.* London: Comedia.

Gribaudi, G., 1997. 'Images of the South: the *Mezzogiorno* as seen by Insiders and Outsiders' in *The New History of the Italian South: The Mezzogiorno Revisited,* edited by Lumley, R. and Morris, J. Exeter: University of Exeter Press, 83–113.

Gribaudi, G., 1999. *Donne, uomini, famiglie. Napoli nel novecento.* Naples: L'ancora.

Gribaudi, G., 2008. 'Il ciclo vizioso dei rifiuti campani'. *Il Mulino* vol. 53, no. 1: 17–33.

Grilli, L. 1992. 'Nei vicoli di Napoli. Reti sociali e percorsi individuali'. *Meridiana* no. 15: 223–47.

Guarnieri Gomma, E., ed. 1996. *Centri Sociali: Geografie del Desiderio.* Milan: Shake Edizioni.

Guidoni, E. 1989. 'Le piazze storiche dal progetto alla ricerca'. *Agorà. Le piazze storiche dell'Italia meridionale e insulare* vol. 2, no. 4: 3–7.

Gundle, S. 2000. *Between Hollywood and Moscow: The Italian Communists and the Challenge of Mass Culture, 1943–1991.* Durham and London: Duke University Press.

Habermas, J. 1989. *The Structural Transformation of the Public Sphere: An Inquiry into a Category of Bourgeois Society.* Cambridge: Polity Press.

Hall, S. 1991. 'Old and New Identities, Old and New Ethnicities' in *Culture, Globalization, and the World System,* edited by A. D. King. London: Macmillan, 19–68.

Hall, S. 2003. 'New Labour's Double-shuffle'. *Soundings* no. 24, 10–24.

Hall, S., Critcher, C., Jefferson, T., Clarke, J. and Roberts, B. 1978. *Policing the Crisis: Mugging, the State, and Law and Order.* London: Macmillan.

Hall, T. 1997. '(Re)placing the city: Cultural relocation and the city as centre' in *Imagining cities: Scripts, Signs, Memory,* edited by S. Westwood and J. Williams. London: Routledge, 202–18.

Hall, T. and Hubbard, P., eds. 1998. *The Entrepreneurial City: Geographies of Politics, Regime and Representation.* Chichester: John Wiley and Sons.

Harney, N. 2006. 'Rumour, migrants, and the informal economies of Naples, Italy'. *International Journal of Sociology and Social Policy* vol. 26, no. 9/10: 374–84.

Harney, N. 2007. 'Transnationalism and Entrepreneurial Migrancy in Naples, Italy'. *Journal of Ethnic and Migration Studies* vol. 33, no. 2: 219–32.

Harvey, D. 1985. *Consciousness and the Urban Experience: Studies in the History and Theory of Capitalist Urbanization.* Baltimore: John Hopkins University Press.

Harvey, D. 1989a. *The Urban Experience.* Oxford: Blackwell.

Harvey, D. 1989b. 'From Managerialism to Entrepreneurialism: The Transformation in Urban Governance in Late Capitalism'. *Geografiska Annaler, Series B, Human Geography* vol. 71, no. 1: 3–17.

Harvey, D. 1990. *The Condition of Postmodernity: An Enquiry into the Origins of Cultural Change.* Oxford: Blackwell.

Hass-Klau, C., Crampton, G., Dowland, C. and Nold, I. 1999. *Streets as Living Space: Helping Public Places Play Their Proper Role.* London: Landor.

Hayden, D. 1995. *The Power of Place: Urban Landscapes as Public History.* Cambridge: MIT Press.

Hellman, S. 1996. 'Italian Communism in the First Republic' in *The New Italian Republic: From the Fall of the Berlin Wall to Berlusconi,* edited by S. Gundle and S. Parker. London: Routledge, 72–84.

Herzfeld, M. 1991. *A Place in History – Social and Monumental Time in a Cretan Town.* Princeton: Princeton University Press.

Herzfeld, M. 2005. 'Practical Mediterraneanisms: Excuses for Everything, from Epistemology to Eating' in *Rethinking the Mediterranean,* edited by W. V. Harris. Oxford: Oxford University Press, 45–63.

Herzfeld, M. 2006. 'Spatial Cleansing: Monumental Vacuity and the Idea of the West'. *Journal of Material Culture* no. 11: 127–49.

Herzfeld, M. 2009. *Evicted from Eternity: The Restructuring of Modern Rome.* Chicago: University of Chicago Press.

Hillier, J. and Rooksby, E., eds. 2005. *Habitus: A Sense of Place.* Aldershot: Ashgate.

Hobsbawm, E. J. 1959. *Primitive Rebels: Studies in Archaic Forms of Social Movement in the 19th and 20th Centuries.* Manchester: Manchester University Press.

Hodkinson, S. and Chatterton, P. 2006. 'Autonomy in the city? Reflections on the social centres movement in the UK'. *City* vol. 10, no. 3: 305–15.

Hubbard, P. 1996. 'Urban Design and City Regeneration: Social Representations of Entrepreneurial Landscapes'. *Urban Studies* vol. 33, no. 8: 1441–61.

Iaccarino, L. 2005. *La rigenerazione. Bagnoli: politiche pubbliche e società civile nella Napoli postindustriale.* Naples: L'ancora.

Iacuelli, A. 2008. *Le vie infinite dei rifiuti. Il sistema campano.* Rome: Rinascita.

Ignazi, P. 1992. *Dal PCI al PDS.* Bologna: il Mulino.

Imarisio, M. 2008. *I giorni della vergogna. Cronaca di una emergenza infinita.* Naples: L'ancora.

Improta, U., et al. 1994. *I Grandi della Terra e l'effetto Napoli.* Naples: Fausto Fiorentino.

Imrie, R. and Raco, M., eds. 2003. *Urban Renaissance? New Labour, Community and Urban Policy.* Bristol: Policy Press.

Indovina, F. 1993. 'Strategie e soggetti per la trasformazione urbana, anni '80', in *La città occasionale. Firenze, Napoli, Torino, Venezia,* edited by F. Indovina. Milan: Franco Angeli, 11–43.

Isin, E. F., ed. 2000. *Democracy Citizenship and the Global City.* London: Routledge.

Isin, E. F. and Siemiatycki, M. 1999. 'Fate and Faith: Claiming Urban Citizenship in Immigrant Toronto', Working Paper, Joint Centre of Excellence for Research on Immigration and Settlement, Toronto, no. 8.

Isin, E. F. and Turner, B. S., eds. 2002. *Handbook of Citizenship Studies.* London: Sage.

Isnenghi, M. 1994. *L'Italia in piazza. I luoghi della vita pubblica dal 1848 ai nostri giorni.* Milan: Mondadori.

Jacobs, J. 1961. *The Death and Life of Great American Cities.* London: Penguin.

Jäggi, M., Müller, R. and Schmid, S. 1977. *Red Bologna.* London: Writers and Readers.

Julier, G. 2005. 'Urban Designscapes and the Production of Aesthetic Consent'. *Urban Studies* vol. 42, no. 5: 869–87.

Kearns, G. and Philo, C., eds. 1993. *Selling Places: The City as Cultural Capital, Past and Present.* Oxford: Pergamon.

Kerzer, D. I. 1980. *Comrades and Christians: Religion and Political Struggle in Communist Italy.* Cambridge: Cambridge University Press.

Klein, N. 2001. 'Squatters in White Overalls'. *Guardian,* 8 June.

Koff, S. Z. and Koff, S. P. 2000. *Italy: From the First to the Second Republic.* London, Routledge.

Kymlicka, W. and Norman, W. 1994. 'Return of the Citizen: A Survey of Recent Work on Citizenship Theory', *Ethics* vol. 104, no. 2: 352–381.

Laino, G. 1984. *Il Cavallo di Napoli: I Quartieri Spagnoli.* Milan, Franco Angeli.

Laino, G. 1999. 'Il Programma Urban in Italia', *Archivio di studi urbani e regionali* no. 66: 69–97.

Laino, G. 2001. 'Il cantiere dei Quartieri Spagnoli di Napoli'. *Territorio* no. 19: 25–32.

Lamberti, A. 2008. *Napoli: Dov'è l'uscita?* Naples: Graus editore.

Landry, C. and Bianchini, F. 1995. *The Creative City.* London: Demos.

Landuzzi, C. 1999a. *L'inquietudine urbana. Tre percorsi per leggere il cambiamento.* Milan: Franco Angeli.

Landuzzi, C. 1999b. 'Insicurezza urbana e illegittimità spaziale dell'immigrato'. *Sociologia urbana e rurale* no. 60: 75–93.

Lattuada, P. 1997. 'La macchina a festa: un'esperienza ricostruttiva tra filologia e technologia' in *Capolavori in Festa. Effimero Barocco a Largo di Palazzo (1683–1759),* catalogue of exhibition held at Palazzo Reale, Naples (20 December 1997–15 March 1998). Naples: Electa, 135–138.

Lay, C. 1981. *Il terremoto quotidiano.* Naples: Loffredo.

Lea, J. 1997. 'Post-Fordism and Criminality' in *Transforming Cities: Contested Governance and New Spatial Divisions,* edited by N. Jewson and S. MacGregor. London: Routledge, 42–55.

Lees, Loretta. 2003. 'Visions of 'urban renaissance': the Urban Task Force report and the Urban White Paper' in *Urban Renaissance? New Labour, Community and Urban Policy,* edited by R. Imrie and M. Raco. Bristol: Policy Press, 61–82.

Lees, Lynn H. 1994. 'Urban Public Space and Imagined Communities in the 1980s and 1990s'. *Journal of Urban History* vol. 20, no. 4: 443–65.

Lefebvre, H. 1991. *The Production of Space.* Oxford: Blackwell.

Le Galès, P. 2002. *European Cities. Social Conflicts and Governance.* Oxford: Oxford University Press.

Lenza, C., ed. 2010. *La stazione centrale di Napoli. Storia e Architettura di un palinsesto urbano.* Milan: Electa.

Leonardi, R. and Nanetti, R. Y. 2008. *La sfida di Napoli. Capitale sociale, sviluppo e sicurezza.* Milan: Guerini.

Leonetti, E. and Napoli, A. 1996. *Antonio Bassolino.* Naples: Tullio Pironti.

Leontidou, L. 1996. 'Alternatives to Modernism in (Southern) Urban Theory: Exploring In-Between Spaces'. *International Journal of Urban and Regional Research* vol. 20, no. 2: 178–95.

Lepore, D. 1995. 'Napoli: Le Cose che non Convincono'. *La Terra Vista dalla Luna* no. 7: 26–33.

Lepore, D. 2007. 'Il riuso dell'area di Bagnoli' in *Non è così facile. Politiche urbane a Napoli a cavallo del secolo,* edited by A. Belli. Milan: Franco Angeli, 105–46.

Lepore, D. and Ceci, F. 1997. *Arcipelago Vesuviano. Percorsi e Ragionamenti intorno a Napoli.* Lecce: Argo.

Levi, M. 1996. 'Social and Unsocial Capital: A Review Essay of Robert Putnam's Making Democracy Work'. *Politics and Society* vol. 24, no. 1: 45–55.

Locatelli, V. 1989. 'Spazio urbano e architettura contemporanea. Cinque interviste e dieci piazze del mondo' in *Le piazze. Storia e progetti,* edited by F. Nuvolari. Milan: Electa, 35–58.

Lodi, G. and Grazioli, M. 1984. 'Giovani sul territorio urbano: l'integrazione minimale' in *Altri Codici,* edited by A. Melucci. Milan: Feltrinelli: 63–127.

Lovering, J. 1995. 'Creating Discourses Rather Than Jobs: The Crisis in the Cities and the Transition Fantasies of Intellectuals and Policy Makers' in *Managing Cities: The New Urban Context,* edited by P. Healey, S. Cameron, S. Davoudi, S. Graham and A. Madani-Pour. Chichester: John Wiley and Sons, 109–26.

Low, S. 2000. *On the Plaza: The Politics of Public Space and Culture*. Austin: University of Texas Press.

Low, S. and Lawrence-Zúñiga, D. 2003. *The Anthropology of Space and Place: Locating Culture*. Oxford: Blackwell.

Lumley, R. 1990. *States of Emergency: Cultures of Revolt in Italy from 1968 to 1978*. London: Verso.

Lumley, R. 1996. *Italian Journalism: A Critical Anthology*. Manchester: Manchester University Press.

Lumley, R. and Morris, J., eds. 1997. *The New History of the Italian South: The Mezzogiorno Revisited*. Exeter: University of Exeter Press.

Luongo, E. and Oliva, A. 1959. *Napoli com'è*. Milan: Feltrinelli.

Lupo, S. 1996. 'The changing Mezzogiorno: Between representations and reality' in *The New Italian Republic: From the Fall of the Berlin Wall to Berlusconi*, edited by S. Gundle and S. Parker. London: Routledge, 247–260.

Macaluso, M. 1995. 'Inquinamento da traffico autoveicolare a Napoli'. *Orizzonti Economici* no. 76: 63–72.

Macciocchi, M. A. 1973. *Letters from Inside the Italian Communist Party to Louis Althusser*. London: NLB.

Macry, P. 1988. *Ottocento: Famiglia, elites e patrimoni a Napoli*. Turin: Einaudi.

Macry, P. 1994. 'Alla ricerca della normalità'. *Micromega* no. 3: 153–61.

Macry, P. 1997. 'The Southern Metropolis: Redistributive Circuits in Nineteenth-century Naples' in *The New History of the Italian South: The Mezzogiorno Revisited*, edited by R. Lumley and J. Morris. Exeter: University of Exeter Press: 59–82.

Macry, P. 1998. 'Bassolino, per esempio. I piccoli passi di Napoli'. *Il Mulino* vol. 43, no. 2: 341–52.

Makagon, D. 2004. *Where the Ball Drops: Days and Nights in Times Square*. Minneapolis: University of Minnesota Press.

Maltese, C. 2007. *I padroni delle città*. Milan: Feltrinelli.

Mancini, F. and Gargano, P. 1991. *Piedigrotta. Nel segno della tradizione. I luoghi le feste le canzoni*. Naples: Guida.

Marcelloni, M. 1979. 'Urban movements and political struggles in Italy'. *International Journal of Urban and Regional Research* vol. 3, no. 2: 251–68.

Marciano, E. and Saulino, C. 1995. 'Inquinamento acustico da traffico'. *Orizzonti Economici* no. 76: 73–76.

Marcus, G. and Fischer M. 1999. *Anthropology as Cultural Critique: An Experimental Moment in the Human Sciences*, 2nd ed. Chicago: University of Chicago Press.

Marone, R. 2002. *Una sfida in Comune*. Naples: Tullio Pironti Editore.

Marrone, T. 1996. *Il Sindaco. Storia di Antonio Bassolino*. Milan: Rizzoli.

Marshall, T. H. 1950. *Class, Citizenship and Social Development*. Cambridge: Cambridge University Press.

Marx, K. 1984. *The Eighteenth Brumaire of Louis Bonaparte*, 3rd ed. London: Lawrence and Wishart.

Masotti G. 1990. *I giorni neri. Il raid di Firenze e i veleni del razzismo*. Florence: Ponte alle Grazie.

Massa, P. 2002. 'Lo spazio simbolico: riflessioni su alcuni luoghi della memoria popolare napoletana' in *Cultura popolare a Napoli e in Campania nel novecento*, edited by A. Signorelli. Naples: Edizioni del Millennio, 75–83.

Massey, D. 2007. *World City*. Cambridge: Polity Press.

Mastrostefano, E. 1969. *La città parla. Napoli*. Naples: Morano Editore.

Masullo, A. and Scamardella, C. 2008. *Napoli siccome immobile*. Naples: Guida.

Maturo, C. 1999. *Dicette 'o pappecce*. Naples: Legambiente.

McLennan, G. and Osborne, T. 2003. 'Contemporary "Vehicularity" and "Romanticism": Debating the Status of Ideas and Intellectuals'. *Critical Review of International Social and Political Philosophy* vol. 6, no. 4: 51–66.

McNeill, D. 1998. 'Writing the New Barcelona' in *The Entrepreneurial City: Geographies of Politics, Regime and Representation,* edited by T. Hall and P. Hubbard. Chichester: John Wiley and Sons: 241–52.

McNeill, D. 1999. *Urban Change and the European Left: Tales from the New Barcelona.* London: Routledge.

McNeill, D. 2000. 'McGuggenisation? National identity and globalisation in the Basque country'. *Political Geography* no. 19: 473–94.

McNeill, D. 2003. 'Mapping the European Urban Left: The Barcelona Experience'. *Antipode* vol. 35, no. 1: 74–94.

Melucci, A., ed. 1984. *Altri Codici: Aree di Movimento nella Metropoli.* Bologna: il Mulino.

Melotti, U. 1993. 'Migrazioni internazionali, povertà e degrado urbano: il caso italiano e le esperienze europee' in *La residualità come valore. Povertà urbane e dignità umane,* edited by P. Guidicini and G. Pieretti. Milan: Franco Angeli, 193–225.

Mercurio, F. 1994. 'Le ferrovie e il Mezzogiorno: i vincoli "morali" e le gerarchie territoriali (1839–1905)'. *Meridiana* no. 19: 155–93.

Merrifield, A. 1996. 'Public space. Integration and exclusion in urban life'. *City* no. 5/6: 57–72.

Merrifield A. 2000. 'The Dialectics of Dystopia: Disorder and Zero Tolerance in the City'. *International Journal of Urban and Regional Research* vol. 24, no. 2: 473–89.

Merriman, P. 2006. '"Mirror, Signal, Manoeuvre": assembling and governing the motorway driver in late 1950s Britain' in *Against Automobility,* edited by S. Böhm, C. Jones, C. Land and M. Paterson. Oxford: Blackwell, 75–92.

Mezzadra, S. and Ricciardi, M. 2005. 'Una scienza neutra per migranti assimilati e scontenti'. *Il Manifesto,* 10 May.

Miles, M. 1997. *Art, Space and the City: Public Art and Urban Futures.* London: Routledge.

Miles, M. and Paddison, R. 2005. 'Introduction: The Rise and Rise of Culture-led Urban Regeneration'. *Urban Studies* vol. 42, no. 5/6: 833–39.

Miller, T. 1993. *The Well-Tempered Self: Citizenship, Culture, and the Postmodern Subject.* Baltimore: Johns Hopkins University Press.

Mingione, E. and Morlicchio, E. 1993. 'New Forms of Urban Poverty in Italy: Risk Path Models in the North and South'. *International Journal of Urban and Regional Research* vol. 17, no. 3: 413–27.

Minolfi, S. and Soverina, F. 1993. *L'incerta frontiera: Saggio sui consiglieri comunali comunali a Napoli 1946-1992.* Naples: Edizioni Scientifiche Italiane.

Mitchell, D. 1995. 'The End of Public Space? People's Park, Definitions of the Public, and Democracy'. *Annals of the Association of American Geographers,* vol. 85, no. 1: 108–33.

Moe, N. 2002. *The View from Vesuvius: Italian Culture and the Southern Question.* Berkeley: University of California Press.

Moliterno, G. ed. 2000. *Encyclopedia of Contemporary Italian Culture.* London: Routledge.

Montagna, N. 2006. 'The de-commodification of urban space and the occupied social centres in Italy'. *City* vol. 10, no. 3: 295–304.

Montalto, M. 2000. 'Il Progetto Urban a Napoli: i Quartieri Spagnoli ed il Rione Sanità', unpublished degree thesis, Faculty of Sociology, Federico II Naples University.

Monteventi, V. and Ghedini, R. 1999. *Guazzaloca 50.69%. Perché Bologna ha perso la sinistra.* Rome: Luca Sossella Editore.

Moore, D. S. 1998. 'Subaltern Struggles and the Politics of Place: Remapping Resistance in Zimbabwe's Eastern Highlands'. *Cultural Anthropology* vol. 13, no. 3: 344–81.

Morlicchio, E. 2001. *Spatial Dimensions of Urban Social Exclusion and Integration: The Case of Naples, Italy.* Amsterdam: URBEX.

Mudu, P. 2002. 'Gli Esquilini: Contributi al dibattito sulle trasformazioni nel rione Esquilino dagli anni settanta al duemila' in *I Territori di Roma. Storie, Popolazioni, Geo-*

grafie, edited by R. Morelli, E. Sonnino and C. M. Travaglini. Rome: Università di Roma Sapienza/Tor Vergata/Tre: 641–80.

Mudu, P. 2004. 'Resisting and Challenging Neoliberalism: The Development of Italian Social Centers'. *Antipode* vol. 36, no. 5: 917–41.

Musatti, R. 1955. 'Concorso nazionale per la Stazione di Napoli'. *L'Architettura. Cronache e Storia* no. 1: 27–35.

Nanetti, R. Y. 2001. 'Adding Value to City Planning: The European Union's Urban Programmes in Naples'. *South European Society and Politics* vol. 6, no. 3: 33–57.

Napoli con Iervolino. 2001. *Una città in cammino.* Naples: Grafica Times.

Nare, L. 2009. 'The making of 'proper' homes: Everyday practices in migrant domestic work in Naples'. *Modern Italy* vol. 14, no. 1: 1–17.

Newman, J. and Clarke, J. 2009. *Public, Politics and Power: Remaking the Public in Public Services.* London: Sage.

Nicolini, R. 1996. *Napoli Angelica Babele. Diario di un anno.* Milan: Rizzoli.

Niola, M. 2003. *Il Purgatorio a Napoli.* Rome: Meltemi.

Nocera, V., ed. 2008. *La grande crisi d Napoli. Sette conversazioni sul momento difficile che vivono la Campania e Napoli.* Naples: Tullio Pironti editore.

Nuvolari, F., ed. 1989. *Le piazze. Storia e progetti.* Milan: Electa.

Officina 99-lo Ska. 2000. *Appello per un "contromaggio" dei movimenti.* Naples, self-published leaflet.

Pace, S. 2004. 'Through the Looking-Glass: Research on the Italian City in Historical Perspective' in *Italian Cityscapes: Culture and Urban Change in Contemporary Italy,* edited by R. Lumley and J. Foot. Exeter: Exeter University Press, 15–28.

Paddison, R. and Sharp, J. 2007. 'Questioning the End of Public Space: Reclaiming Control of Local Banal Spaces'. *Scottish Geographical Journal* vol. 123, no. 2: 87–106.

Pain, R. 2001. 'Gender, Race, Age and Fear in the City'. *Urban Studies* vol. 38, no. 5/6: 899–913.

Palermo, M. 1975. *Memoria di un comunista napoletano.* Parma: Guanda.

Palestino, M. F. 2003. *MiraNapoli. La costruzione dell'immagine urbana negli anni '90.* Naples: Clean edizioni.

Palidda S. 1999. 'Polizia e immigrati: un'analisi etnografica'. *Rassegna italiana di sociologia* vol. 40, no. 1: 77–114.

Palidda, S. 2000. *Polizia postmoderna: Etnografia del nuovo controllo sociale.* Milan: Feltrinelli.

Palumbo, B. 2001. 'Campo intellettuale, potere e identità tra contesti locali, "pensiero meridiano" e "identità meridionale"'. *La Ricerca Folklorica/Erreffe* no. 43: 117–33.

Palumbo, B. 2003. *L'Unesco e il campanile. Antropologia, politica e beni culturali in Sicilia orientale.* Rome: Meltemi.

Pardo, I. 1993. 'Socialist visions, Naples and the Neapolitans: value, control and representation in the agency/structure relationship'. *Journal of Mediterranean Studies* vol. 3, no. 1: 77–98.

Pardo, I. 1996. *Managing Existence in Naples: Morality, Action and Structure.* Cambridge: Cambridge University Press.

Pardo, I. 2009. 'Dynamics of Exclusion and Integration: A Sobering View from Italy' in *Beyond Multiculturalism: Views from Anthropology,* edited by G. B. Prato. Farnham: Ashgate, 103–22.

PCI (Partito Comunista Italiano). 1977. *Almanacco PCI '77.* Rome: PCI.

PCI (Partito Comunista Italiano). 1978. *VII Conferenza operaia del Partito Comunista Italiano. Napoli 3–5 marzo 1978.* Rome: Riuniti.

PCI (Partito Comunista Italiano). 1986. *Il Sud grande polo turistico mediterraneo e internazionale: atti del convegno nazionale del PCI: Napoli, 29–30 novembre 1985.* Bari: Edizioni del Sud.

Pasolini, P. P. 1976. *Lettere luterane. Il progresso come falso progresso.* Turin: Einaudi.

Pasotti, E. 2000. *Agenda, Trust and the Mobilization of Consensus: The Rise and Fall of Leadership in Naples,* paper presented at the annual meeting of the Italian Political Science Association, Naples, 28–30 September.

Pasotti, E. 2004. *From clients to citizens: Public opinion mobilization in Naples,* unpublished PhD thesis, Columbia University.

Pelliciardi, G. 2008. 'Communist Rock Party. Trent'anni di concerti alle feste comunali dell'Unità di Correggio. Una lunga avventura entrata nella storia della musica rock dal vivo in Italia' in *Correggio Mon Amour. Storia di storie della musica rock in una città della provincia emiliana,* edited by M. Colarossi, L. Levrini, L. Pergreffi and F. Tavernelli. Correggio: Lucio Lombardo Radice Editore, 136–58.

Pepicelli, R. 2000. 'Napoli: la palla al piede'. *Poco di buono* vol. 1, no. 0: 4–5.

Peraldi, M. 2007. 'The Station of Alicante is the Centre of the World: Wars at the Borders and Peace in the Market along the North African Routes to Europe'. *History and Anthropology* vol. 18, no. 3: 389–404.

Pero, D. 2001. 'Inclusionary rhetoric/exclusionary practice: an ethnographic critique of the Italian Left in the context of migration' in *The Mediterranean Passage: Migration and New Cultural Encounters in Southern Europe,* edited by R. King. Liverpool: Liverpool University Press, 162–85.

Pessetti, M. 1977. 'La Duchesca. Chi ruba, chi imbroglia, chi vende'. *Il Napoletano* vol. 4, no. 6: 22–26.

Petrillo, Agostino. 1996. 'L'insicurezza urbana in America'. *aut aut* no. 276: 71–92.

Petrillo, Antonello. 2000. 'Insicurezza, rappresentazioni del territorio e costruzione di identità locali in rapporto ai flussi migratori'. Paper presented at 'Localismi e Globalizzazione' conference at Istituto Universitario Suor Orsola Benincasa, Naples, 16 June.

Petrusewicz, M. 1998. *Come il Meridione divenne una Questione. Rappresentazioni del Sud prima e dopo il Quarantotto.* Catanzaro: Rubbettino.

Philo, C. and Kearns, G. 1993. 'Culture, history, capital: a critical introduction to the selling of places' in *Selling Places: The City as Cultural Capital, Past and Present,* edited by G. Kearns and C. Philo. Oxford: Pergamon, 1–32.

Piazza, G. 2007. 'Quali concezioni e pratiche politiche nei centri sociali in Italia? Un'analisi comparata delle occupazioni a Catania'. Paper presented at the annual Italian Society of Political Science (SISP) conference, University of Catania, 20–22 September.

Pine, J. 2008. 'Contact, Complicity, Conspiracy: Affective Communities and Economies of Affect in Naples'. *Law, Culture and the Humanities* no. 4: 201–23.

Pinnarò, G. and Pugliese, E. 1985. 'Informalization and Social Resistance: The Case of Naples' in *Beyond Employment: Household, Gender and Subsistence,* edited by N. Redclift and E. Mingione. Oxford: Blackwell, 228–47.

Piperno, F. 1997. *Elogio dello spirito pubblico meridionale: genius loci e individuo sociale.* Rome: Manifesto Libri.

Pitch T. 2000. 'I rischi della sicurezza urbana'. *ParoleChiave,* no. 22/23/24: 71–97.

Pred, A. 1995. *Recognizing European Modernities: A Montage of the Present.* London: Routledge.

Provitera, G., Ranisio, G. and Giliberti, E. 1978. *Lo Spazio Sacro. Per un'analisi della religione popolare napoletana.* Naples: Guida.

Pugliese, E. 1998. 'Postfazione' in *Ci dicevamo analfabeti. Il movimento dei disoccupati napoletani degli anni Settanta,* F. Ramondino, 2nd ed. Lecce: Argo, 191–98.

Putnam, R. D., Leonardi, R. and Nanetti, R. Y. 1993. *Making Democracy Work: Civic Traditions in Modern Italy.* Princeton: Princeton University Press.

Rabitti, P. 2008. *Ecoballe. Tutte le verità su discariche, inceneritori, smaltimento abusive dei rifiuti.* Rome: Aliberti Editore.

Raco, M. and Tunney, E. 2010. 'Visibilities and Invisibilities in Urban Development: Small Business Communities and the London Olympics 2012'. *Urban Studies* vol. 47, no. 10: 1–23.

Ragone, G. 1997. 'Napoli oggi tra luci e ombre'. *Quaderni di Sociologia* vol. 41, no. 14: 5–19.

Ramondino, F. 1998. *Ci dicevamo analfabeti. Il movimento dei disoccupati napoletani degli anni Settanta,* 2nd ed. Lecce: Argo.

Ramondino, F. and Müller, A. F. 1992. *Dadapolis. Caleidoscopio Napoletano.* Turin: Einaudi.

Ranieri, U. 1994. *Battaglie riformiste a Napoli.* Rionero in Vulture: Calice Editori.

Ranisio, G. 2003. *La città e il suo racconto. Percorsi napoletani tra immaginario e reale.* Rome: Meltemi.

Rao, A. M. 1999. 'Popular Societies in the Neapolitan Republic of 1799'. *Journal of Modern Italian Studies* vol. 4, no. 3: 358–69.

Rea, E. 1995. *Mistero napoletano.* Turin: Einaudi.

Rea, E. 2003. *La Dismissione.* Milan: Rizzoli.

Rea, E. 2007. *Napoli Ferrovia.* Milan: Rizzoli.

Rea, E., Niola, M., Zaccaria, A. M., Amato, F., Miranda, A. and Perrella, S. 2006. *Voci e volti dei nuovi napoletani. Il futuro comincia alla Ferrovia: scene da una metropoli alla ricerca di una nuova identità.* Rome: Fandango Libri.

Reichl, A. J. 1999. *Reconstructing Times Square.* Lawrence: University Press of Kansas.

Remotti, F. 1996. *Contro l'identità.* Rome: Laterza.

Rendell, J. 2002. *The Pursuit of Pleasure: Gender, Space and Architecture in Regency London.* London: The Athlone Press.

Riall, L. 2000. 'Which road to the south? Revisionists revisit the Mezzogiorno'. *Journal of Modern Italian Studies* vol. 5, no. 1: 89–100.

Robb, P. 1998. *Midnight in Sicily.* London: Harvill Press.

Roberts, P. 2000. 'The Evolution, Definition and Purpose of Urban Regeneration' in *Urban Regeneration: A Handbook,* edited by P. Roberts and H. Sykes. London: Sage, 295–315.

Robinson, J. 2006. *Ordinary Cities: Between Modernity and Development.* London: Routledge.

Rose, N. 2000. 'Governing cities, governing citizens' in *Democracy Citizenship and the Global City,* edited by E. F. Isin. London: Routledge, 95–109.

Rossi, U. 2004a. 'New Regionalism Contested: Some Remarks in Light of the Case of the Mezzogiorno of Italy'. *International Journal of Urban and Regional Research* vol. 28, no. 2: 466–76.

Rossi, U. 2004b. 'The Multiplex City: The Process of Urban Change in the Historic Centre of Naples'. *European Urban and Regional Studies* vol. 11, no. 2: 156–169.

Rossi-Doria, M. 1999. *Di mestiere faccio il maestro.* Naples: L'ancora.

Rossomando, L. 2002. *La Voragine. Una cronaca dalla periferia di Napoli.* Rome: Riuniti.

Rowe, P. G. 1997. *Civic Realism.* Cambridge: MIT Press.

Ruggiero, G. 1996. *Le Piazze di Napoli.* Rome: Tascabili Economici Newton.

Ruggiero, V. 2000. 'New social movements and the 'centri sociali' in Milan'. *The Sociological Review* vol. 48, no. 2: 167–85.

Russo Krauss, R. 2005. *Geografie dell'Immigrazione. Spazi multietnici nelle città: in Italia, Campania, Napoli.* Naples: Liguori Editore.

Russo Krauss, R. and Schmoll, C. 2006. 'Spazi insediativi e pratiche socio-spaziali dei migranti nella città sud-europea: il caso di Napoli'. *Studi Emigrazione* vol. 43, no. 163: 699–719.

Rustin, M. 1986. 'The Fall and Rise of Public Space. A Postcapitalist Prospect'. *Dissent* vol. 33, no. 4: 486–494.

Sabetti, F. 1996. 'Path Dependency and Civic Culture: Some Lessons from Italy About Interpreting Social Experiments'. *Politics and Society* vol. 24, no. 1: 19–44.

Sadler, D. 2004. 'Anti-corporate Campaigning and Corporate "Social" Responsibility: Towards Alternative Spaces of Citizenship?'. *Antipode* vol. 36, no. 5: 851–70.

Salierno, G. 1972. *Il sottoproletariato in Italia: Per un approccio politico e metodologico al problema dell'alleanza tra classe operaia e 'Lumpenproletariat'.* Rome: La nuova sinistra.

Savarese, L. 1983. *Un'alternativa urbana per Napoli. L'area orientale.* Naples: Edizioni Scientifiche Italiane.

Saviano, R. 2006. *Gomorra. Viaggio nell'impero economico e nel sogno di dominio della camorra.* Milan: Mondadori.

Savino, R. 1998. 'L'immagine del sindaco. La personalizzazione della politica a Napoli'. *Nord e Sud* vol. 45, no. 4/5: 29–47.

Savitch, H. V. and Kantor, P., eds. 2002. *Cities in the International Marketplace: The Political Economy of Urban Development in North America and Western Europe.* Princeton: Princeton University Press.

Savonardo, L. 2003. *Cultura senza élite. Il potere simbolico a Napoli nell'era Bassolino.* Naples: Edizioni Scientifiche Italiane.

Sayad, A. 2004. *The Suffering of the Immigrant.* Cambridge: Polity Press.

Schmoll, C. 2004. 'Une place marchande cosmopolite. Dynamiques migratoires et circulations commerciales a Naples', unpublished PhD thesis, Université Paris X.

Schneider, J. and Schneider, P. 2003. *Reversible Destiny: Mafia, Antimafia, and the Struggles for Palermo.* Berkeley: University of California Press.

Schram, A. 1997. *Railways and the Formation of the Italian State in the Nineteenth Century.* Cambridge: Cambridge University Press.

Scidà, G. and Pollini, G. 1993. *Stranieri in città. Politiche sociali e modelli d'integrazione.* Milan: Franco Angeli.

Sciortino, G. 1999. 'Planning in the Dark: The Evolution of Italian Immigration Control' in *Mechanisms of Immigration Control: A Comparative Analysis of European Regulation Policies,* edited by G. Brochmann and T. Hammar. Oxford: Berg, 233–54.

Sciortino, G. and Colombo, A. 2004. 'The flows and the flood: the public discorse on immigration in Italy, 1969–2001'. *Journal of Modern Italian Studies* vol. 9, no. 1: 94–113.

Scotto di Luzio, A. 2008. *Napoli dei molti tradimenti.* Bologna: il Mulino.

Sebastiani, C. 2001. 'Comitati cittadini e spazi pubblici urbani'. *Rassegna Italiana di Sociologia* vol. 41, no. 1: 77–114.

Sennett, R. 1974. *The Fall of Public Man.* Cambridge: Cambridge University Press.

Serao, M. 1994. *Il Ventre di Napoli. Ieri, l'altroieri e...oggi.* Naples: Luca Torre.

Sereni, E. 1938. *Napoli.* Naples: Libreria Pisacane.

Sheller, M. and Urry, J. 2000. 'The City and the Car'. *International Journal of Urban and Regional Research* vol. 24, no. 4: 737–57.

Shields, R. 1996. 'A Guide to Urban Representation and What to Do About It: Alternative Traditions of Urban Theory' in *Re-presenting the City: Ethnicity, Capital and Culture in the 21st Century Metropolis,* edited by A. D. King. Basingstoke: Macmillan, 227–52.

Sibley, D. 1995. *Geographies of Exclusion: Society and Difference in the West.* London: Routledge.

Signorelli, A. 1996. *Antropologia Urbana. Introduzione alla ricerca in Italia.* Milan: Guerini.

Signorelli, A., ed. 2002. *Cultura popolare a Napoli e in Campania nel novecento.* Naples: Edizioni del Millennio.

Simmel, G. 1950. 'The Metropolis and Mental Life' in *The Sociology of Georg Simmel,* edited by K. Wolff. New York: The Free Press, 409–24.

Siola, U. 1988. 'Per una politica di piano' in *Rigenerazione dei Centri Storici. Il Caso Napoli Vol. 1,* edited by Studi Centro Storico Napoli. Milan: Edizioni Sole-24 Ore, 195–220.

Sitte, C. 1965. *City Planning According to Artistic Principles.* London: Phaidon Press.

Smith, N. 1992. *The New Urban Frontier: Gentrification and the Revanchist City.* London: Routledge.

Smith, S. J. 1995. 'Citizenship: all or nothing'. *Political Geography* vol. 14, no. 2: 190–93.

Snowden, Frank. M. 1995. *Naples in the Time of Cholera, 1884–1911.* Cambridge: Cambridge University Press.

Soja, E. W. 1989. *Postmodern Geographies: The Reassertion of Space in Critical Social Theory.* London: Verso.

Solima, L. 1999. 'Turismo culturale e sviluppo economico'. *Quaderni del Circolo Rossi* no. 14: 82–100.

Sorkin, M., ed. 1992. *Variations on a Theme Park: The New American City and the End of Public Space.* New York: Hill and Wang.

Soysal, Y. N. 2007. '"The Banality of Good": The new transnational normativity of the good citizen', paper presented at School of Public Policy evening seminar, University College London, 8 February.

Staeheli, L. A. and Mitchell, D. 2007. 'Locating the public in research and practice'. *Progress in Human Geography* vol. 31, no. 6: 792–811.

Stallybrass, P. 1990. 'Marx and Heterogeneity: Thinking the Lumpenproletariat'. *Representations* no. 31: 69–95.

Stallybrass, P. and White, A. 1986. *The Politics and Poetics of Transgression.* Ithaca: Cornell University Press.

Starr, D. A. 2005. 'Recuperating cosmopolitan Alexandria. Circulation of narratives and narratives of circulation'. *Cities* vol. 22, no. 3: 217–28.

Stazio, M. L. and Traiola, S. 1981. *Vedi Napoli...* Milan: Gammalibri.

Stevenson, D. 2004. '"Civic Gold" Rush: Cultural Planning and the Politics of the Third Way'. *International Journal of Cultural Policy* vol. 10, no. 1: 119–31.

Studi Centro Storico Napoli., ed. 1988. *Rigenerazione dei Centri Storici. Il Caso Napoli (2 Vols.).* Milan: Edizioni Sole-24 Ore.

Tarrow, S. 1996. 'Making Social Science Work across Space and Time: A Critical Reflection on Robert Putnam's Making Democracy Work'. *American Political Science Review* vol. 90, no. 2: 389–97.

Tedesco, E. 2000. 'Sicurezza Urbana e Convivenza Civile. L'esperienza di Napoli'. *Archivio di Studi Urbani e Regionali* vol. 31, no. 68: 75–93.

Tornincasa, R. 1961. *Itinerari F.S. Guida del Compartimento Ferroviario di Napoli.* Naples: Manifatture di Pompei.

Trani, G. 2004. 'L'immigrazione in Campania nel 2003' in *Immigrazione Dossier Statistico 2004,* edited by Caritas/Migrantes. Rome: New Anterem, 423–30.

Trigilia, C. 1992. *Sviluppo senza autonomia. Effetti perversi delle politiche nel Mezzogiorno.* Bologna: il Mulino.

Trigilia, C. 1994. 'Dai comuni medievali alle nostre regioni'. *L'indice* no. 3: 36.

Trigilia, C., ed. 1995. *Cultura e sviluppo. L'associazionismo nel Mezzogiorno.* Catanzaro: Meridiana Libri.

Urry, J. 2004. 'The "System" of Automobility'. *Theory, Culture & Society* vol. 21, no. 4/5: 25–39.

Vacalebre, F. 1999. *Dentro il vulcano. Racconti neomelodici e altre storie dal villaggio locale.* Naples: Pironti.

Valentine, G. 2004. *Public Space and the Culture of Childhood.* Aldershot: Ashgate.

Valenzi, M. 1978. *Sindaco a Napoli.* Rome: Riuniti.

Valenzi, M. 1987. 'Sindaco nel terremoto'. *NdR* no. 2: 48–51.

Vandelli, L. 1997. *Sindaci e miti. Sisifo, Tantalo e Damocle nell'amministrazione locale.* Bologna: il Mulino.

Vercellone, C. 1996. 'The Anomaly and Exemplariness of the Italian Welfare State' in *Radical Thought in Italy: A Potential Politics,* edited by P. Virno and M. Hardt. Minneapolis: University of Minnesota Press, 81–95.

Verdicchio, P. 1992. 'The Subaltern Written/The Sublatern Writing: Pasolini's "Gennariello" as Author'. *Pacific Coast Philology* vol. 27, no. 1/2: 133–44.

Viale, G. 1996. *Tutti in taxi. Demonologia dell'automobile.* Milan: Feltrinelli.

Villari, S. 1995. 'Tra neoclassicismo e restaurazione: la chiesa di San Francesco di Paola' in *Pietro Bianchi 1787–1849. Architetto e archeologo,* edited by N. Ossanna Cavadini. Milan: Electa, 129–39.

Villone, M. 2001. *Dialoghi con la mia città.* Naples: Guida.

Viviani, D. 1998. *Piazza del Plebiscito. Guida tra storia, arte e leggenda della piazza più famosa di Napoli.* Naples: Edizioni Teamidea.

Wacquant, L. 1999. '"Tolleranza zero", il credo americano si diffonde'. *Le Monde Diplomatique,* Italian edition, April.

Wacquant, L. and Bourdieu, P. 1999. 'The Cunning of Imperialist Reason'. *Theory, Culture, and Society* vol. 16, no. 1: 41–58.

Walzer, M. 1986. 'Pleasures and Costs of Urbanity'. *Dissent* vol. 33, no. 4: 470–75.

Wanderlingh, A. and Corsi, E. 1987. *Storia fotografica di Napoli 1945/1985. Quaranta anni di immagini della tua città.* Naples: Intra Moenia.

Wanderlingh, A. 1988. *Maurizio Valenzi. Un romanzo civile.* Naples: Sintesi.

Ward, C. 1978. *The Child in the City.* London: Bedford Square Press.

Ward, S. V. 1998. *Selling Places: The Marketing and Promotion of Towns and Cities, 1850–2000.* London: Spon.

Weintraub, J. 1995. 'Varieties and Vicissitudes of Public Space' in *Metropolis: Center and Symbol of Our Times,* edited by P. Kasinitz. New York: NYU Press, 280–319.

Whyte, W. H. 1980. *The Social Life of Small Urban Spaces.* Washington D.C.: The Conservation Foundation.

Williams, R. 1983. *Keywords: A Vocabulary of Culture and Society.* Oxford: Oxford University Press.

Wilson, E. 1991. *The Sphinx in the City: Urban Life, the Control of Disorder, and Women.* London: Virago Press.

Wright, S. 2000. '"A Love Born of Hate": Autonomist Rap in Italy'. *Theory Culture Society* vol. 17, no. 3: 117–35.

Young, I. M. 1990. *Justice and the Politics of Difference.* Princeton: Princeton University Press.

Zaccaria, A. 1997. 'Cari compagni e compagne dell'altra sponda! Dibattito nel movimento: impresa sociale, soggetti e forme del conflitto'. *vis-à-vis* no. 5: 212–37.

Zinn, D. L. 2007. 'I Quindici Giorni di Scanzano: identity and social protest in the New South'. *Journal of Modern Italian Studies* vol. 12, no. 2: 189–206.

Zolo, D., ed. 1994. *La cittadinanza. Appartenenza, identità, diritti.* Bari: Laterza.

Zukin, S. 1988. *Loft Living: Culture and Capital in Urban Change.* London: Radius.

Zukin, S. 1995. *The Culture of Cities.* Oxford: Blackwell.

Index

Marotta, Gerardo, 7–8, 65, 65n10, 66
Marseilles, 214
Marshall, Thomas Humphrey, 57–58
Martelli Law, 190, 191n6, 202, 203
Martone, Mario, 41n1
Martusciello, Antonio, 145
Marx, Karl, 242
Marxist-Leninism, 67, 258, 259
Masaniello, 109
Maschio Angioino, 34, 37, 110, 120, 136
Maslo, Jerry, 202
Massey, Doreen, 14–15
Masullo, Aldo, 295
Mattino, Il, 19, 19n, 53, 279; on DAMM,
    269n15, 275; on heritage, 126; on
    immigration, 202, 202n17, 203, 203n19;
    on motorization in Naples, 123n5, 124,
    125, 126; on Piazza Garibaldi, 182–3,
    184, 195, 198, 203n19, 204, 205, 206;
    on Piazza Plebiscito, 128, 131, 132, 133,
    136, 143, 144, 145, 146; on the popular
    neighbourhoods, 237, 251
mayor, -s (post-1993), 9, 12, 50, 77, 81, 188,
    189; direct election of, 9, 39, 50, 67, 78,
    188, 244, 295
mayoral season, 9, 50
McLennan, Gregor, 288n
McNeill, Donald, 46
media, 12, 13, 14, 21, 64, 102, 166n2,
    184, 275, 292n; analysis, 19–20, 286,
    and the Bassolino administration,
    23, 50, 52, 80, 84, 134, 284; and the
    centri sociali, 259, 263, 293n6; and
    cities, 40, 190n; and DAMM, 269;
    Naples and the international, 10, 24,
    53; and Piazza Garibaldi, 199, 200,
    201, 203–8, 210, 212, 214, 219, 223,
    290; and Piazza Plebiscito, 129, 131,
    138, 146, 148, 157, 168, 290; and the
    popular neighbouhoods, 230, 278;
    representations of immigration, 191,
    196, 201–8, 219; and rhetoric about
    Naples, 9, 25, 41, 173, 287–88. *See also*
    representation, Naples newspapers
Mediterranean, 32, 285, 297; as an
    anthropological construct, 241;
    metropolis, 17, 46–47
mega-projects, 44, 55, 238
memory; of Bassolino administration, 25; of
    Bourbon kingdom, 66n11; dissociation
    of cars from, 155; of local radical
    traditions in Montesanto, 263–65; of
    Neapolitan Revolution, 8, 65, 66, 66n; of
    1980 earthquake, 128, 251–53; of 1987
    Scudetto victory, 128, 163; the piazza as
    a place of, 107; in/of Piazza Plebiscito,
    111, 136, 138, 155, 163; urban, 31, 32,
    39, 44, 66. *See also* forgetting

men; in Piazza Garibaldi, 205, 206, 211,
    212, 214, 216, 218, 219, 220; in Piazza
    Plebiscito, 123, 151; and public space,
    94, 103, 165n
Mendini, Alessandro, 275
Mensa dei Bambini Proletari, 263–64, 264n,
    279
Mercato (Naples central district), 33n, 34,
    68, 180, 181
Mercato (Naples central neighbourhood),
    37, 248. *See also* Pendino
Mercato-Pendino district council,199, 209n
Mergellina (Naples central neighbourhood),
    34, 181, 216
Merz, Mario, 142n8
Messina, 277, 283
metro rail system, 22, 53,125, 177, 196n,
    197, 214, 214n, 215, 235, 237, 239, 248,
    278, 293. *See also* LTR (Rapid Tram
    Line), public transport
Mezzogiorno. *See* South (Italian)
middle class, -es, 3, 4, 7, 11, 24n18, 33, 47,
    61, 64, 69, 70, 72, 83–84, 103, 167, 206,
    243, 268, 273, 295; and motorization,
    123–24, 126, 127, 168; neighbourhoods
    in Naples, 34, 34n, 35, 60–61, 75, 75n,
    77, 158, 182, 214, 249, 288; progressive,
    66, 71, 154; and public space, 89, 90,
    94, 95, 167n, 183, 278, 282, 289; and
    relocation to the *centro storico,* 235,
    241, 241n, 242, 250, 297; upper, 34,
    47n6, 110, 245. *See also* bourgeois urban
    culture, enlightened bourgeoisie, Vomero
Milan, 12, 19n, 32n, 33n, 47n7, 49, 49n10,
    69–70, 116n3, 127, 229, 265; *centri
    sociali* in, 256, 257, 259, 260n, 261,
    270, 275; and immigration, 173, 193,
    193n11, 211, 217, 225; and the Italian
    Communist Party, 68; and motorization,
    124; piazzas in, 108; and the politics of
    security, 188, 189n2
military parades, 119, 120, 121, 137, 156
Mina, 177n
Mitchell, Don, 261
mobility, 45, 51n14, 90, 110, 123, 124, 133,
    199, 247n15; 291; the right to, 81, 112;
    transnational, 74n, 225
modernity, 1, 2, 3, 6, 60n, 110, 181, 292;
    Naples's perceived disconnection from,
    3–4, 17, 96, 239; Naples's relationship
    with, 4, 17, 35, 60, 66, 78, 124, 135, 184
Moldovans, 212
Molise, 48
Monarchists, 35, 36, 68, 121, 121n2, 124,
    177, 183. *See also* Lauro, Achille
Monastery of Santa Chiara, 38, 261
Montagna del Sale, La, 142–144, 145–46,
    156, 159–60; controls around, 143; and
    the discourse about citizenship, 144; as

symbol of Naples, 142–43; and uncivil behaviour, 143, 245, 279, 290

Montagna, Nicola, 258n3

Montecalvario (Naples central district), 33n, 37, 249, 250n17

Monteoliveto (former central neighbourhood), 35

Montesanto (Naples central neighbourhood), 14, 20, 22, 102, 229, 245, 248–54, 266, 267, 268, 273, 276, 277n, 281, 283, 286, 291, 293; demolition and evictions in, 233, 235, 251; everyday life in, 248; history of activism in, 263–65, 265n; immigrants in, 193, 241, 248, 282; location and layout of, 233n, 249–50; public transport in, 233n, 246, 248, 265n9, 275, 278; reputation of, 248, 279; socio-demographic structure of, 240–41, 250, 262. *See also* DAMM, Piazza Montesanto, Ventaglieri Park

Montesanto funicular railway, 233n, 246, 248, 265n9

Monti, 18n9

Montreal, 285n2

monument, -s, 3, 33, 35, 37, 106, 111, 120, 167, 180, 196, 197; -ality, 18, 18n9, 165; everyday and festive uses of, 12, 18n9, 38, 128; and ideas about heritage, 29, 37; 'misuse' of, 139n; national, 120, 121; perceptions of Piazza Plebiscito as a, 131, 133, 135, 137, 139, 141, 155, 160, 162, 166; in and around Piazza Garibaldi, 180, 183, 219; the popular neighbourhoods perceived as lacking, 229, 275; restoration and reopening of, 53, 55, 65, 74, 120n2; and urban regeneration, 9, 186, 292n. *See also* Maggio dei Monumenti, Monumenti Porte Aperte, restoration

Monumenti Porte Aperte, 39, 65, 66, 244

Moore, Donald, 16

moral entrepreneurs, 199, 199n, 223

Morcone, Mario, 296n

Moroccans, 192, 214, 215, 217, 218

Mostra d'Oltremare, 72

mothers, 212; and Piazza Plebiscito, 137, 152, 154, 155, 162, 165n, 167, 290

motorcycle, -s, 123n4, 155, 160, 207; as an environmental solution to traffic congestion, 142; as an object of transgression, 105n, 134, 247; pedestrianized areas breached by, 12, 141–42, 142n7, 151, 151n, 152, 153, 157, 160, 162, 167, 194, 247, 290; police controls on, 153, 157, 164; as a source of incivility, 134, 142, 156, 158, 167; as an urban accessory with practical and social benefits, 164, 165–66n, 247n15, 290. *See also* automobile, conduct

motorization, 92, in Naples, 124, 125, 127n, 141

motorway, 37, 91, 125, 127, 180; as a contested space, 105

Mudu, Pierpaolo, 256n

multiculturalism, 43, 44, 86, 193, 194, 202, 225

multiethnicity, 20, 44, 196, 200, 208, 211, 258n3, 293. *See also* markets

Musatti, Roberto, 179

museum, -s, 43, 44, 116; -city, 32, 55n21; -ification, 30, 116; in Naples, 34, 54, 115, 179, 238, 238n8, 285

Mussolini, Alessandra, 10, 50n12, 51, 237

Naples; as backward, 5, 36, 78, 231, 240, 278; as blacklisted and outcast, 2, 23–24, 96; as the capital of the Italian South, 3, 178, 179; as a 'city built by crime', 24; as a 'city of children', 279; as a 'city of citizens', 80, 286; as a city of dirt and disorder, 3, 82, 131, 139, 146, 181; as a city in perpetual crisis, 7; as a city of political malpractice, 3, 66; as civically deficient, 21, 60–61, 62, 64, 66, 96, 245n; as a 'cultural capital', 65, 73, 82, 131, 231; as a dangerous city, 186; in decline, 7, 8, 9, 25, 293–94; as an enigma, 69–70; as an enormous, seething city, 32, 62; enthusiasm for the purported 'aberrant' nature of, 3–4, 11, 96–97; as folkloristic, 5, 82, 139, 182n5, 183; as a former capital city, 34, 61; as immobile and timeless, 4, 61, 105, 295; and its internal differences acknowledged or denied, 6, 13, 17–18, 33, 61, 87, 97, 241, 278, 286; measured against other European cities, 1, 2, 54; as a morally and civically rehabilitated city, 11, 51, 66, 86, 116, 131, 146, 238; the negative reputation of, 2, 3, 9, 37, 53, 186; as a 'new' city, 9, 11, 13, 15, 16, 56, 57, 84, 140, 157, 168, 173, 239, 278, 286, 289; as a politically progressive city, 10–11, 72–73, 78–79; as a politically reactionary city, 68, 242; the positive reputation of, 5, 13, 73, 168; as a preindustrial city, 3, 96; as a promiscuous and permissive city, 96, 105–6, 164; as a resurgent city, 9, 115, 203; revisionist histories of, 4; as a socially inclusive city, 82, 106, 194, 283; as a tolerant and open city, 13, 173, 193, 195, 202, 212, 224, 293; as a tourist city, 55, 231; as an unplanned city, 35–36; urban and political history of, 32–39, 50–55, 59–67, 68–77, 108–112. *See also* ordinary city

Naples Campi Flegrei railway station, 215

population; of the *centro storico,* 33, 33n,
35, 37; of immigrants in Naples during
the 1990s, 192–93, 209, 209n, 217,
233–34; of Montesanto, 250, 250n7; of
Naples, 3, 32, 32n, 35, 37, 70, 81, 225,
230
porosity, 4, 96
port (of Naples), 34, 36, 37, 120n2, 181,
186, 202, 229
Portici, 175n
Porto (Naples central district), 33n
Posillipo (Naples central district), 33n, 34,
127, 201
postcards, 195; of Piazza Garibaldi, 184,
206; of Piazza Plebiscito, 139–40, 161
postcolonialism, 2, 6
post-Communism, 25, 78, 83n, 188, 284,
297, and the jettisoning of class analysis,
76, 188, 244; and politics of citizenship,
78, 288, and popular classes, 244–45.
See also Bassolino, Antonio, Democratic
Party of the Left, Left Democrats, market
post-Fordism, 40, 258n3
post-industrial society, 46, 102, 290n
poverty, 4, 24n8, 31, 41, 69, 90, 94, 181,
192, 195; in the *centro storico,* 3, 8,
15, 31, 35; in Naples, 8, 17, 18, 32,
35, 37, 61, 70n16, 85, 109, 183, 233,
239, 285; and Piazza Garibaldi, 181;
and Piazza Plebiscito, 122–23; in the
popular neighbourhoods, 33, 68, 70, 72,
229, 231, 237, 239, 241, 242, 243, 244,
277; and public space, 91, 96. *See also*
unemployment
power, 2, 4, 5, 18, 90; on display in Piazza
Plebiscito, 21, 119, 287; relations in the
centro storico, 31; relations in Naples,
7, 60, 84, 242; relations in urban public
space, 16, 60, 94, 99, 104, 105, 107
Pozzuoli, 17, 103–4
Pred, Allan, 2
privatization, 3, 75, of urban space, 91, 92
Prodi, Romano, 142, 190, 294
Proletarian Democracy (DP), 75n, 76, 297
prosperity, 42, 44, 72, 162, 186, 195,
245n; and car ownership, 123, 124; and
gentrification, 241n
prostitution, 33, 90, 94, 181, 182, 190, 191,
201, 205–6, 220, 221
protests, 52, 68, 110, 191, 206; organized by
centri sociali, 257, 258, 258n2, 259n5–6,
261, 262, 269, 270; in/over Piazza
Garibaldi, 183, 194, 195, 201, 219,
219n, 225; in/over Piazza Plebiscito, 13,
102, 122, 127, 132, 134, 144–45, 146,
147, 148, 152, 153, 153n, 154n, 157,
160, 167, 287, 291; over redevelopment
schemes for the *centro storico,* 38, 65,

236, 191, 206; over refuse disposal, 23,
251; unemployed, 4, 12, 74, 101
Province of Naples, president of, 245, 282,
296n
public space, 1–3, 9, 13, 21, 44, 45, 56,
88–99, 106, 107n15, 108, 111, 116, 154,
165, 270, 283; connections between
citizenship and, 2, 89; constituted by
conflict, 1, 93, 94, 99–100, 261, 290,
291, 292; constituted by difference, 2,
89, 224, 274, 276, 281; 'decline' of,
3, 89–93, 98; definition of, 2–3, 89;
genealogy of, 89–91; and immigration,
172, 173, 194, 204, 289; material and
symbolic boundaries in and around, 97,
100, 104, 144, 167, 182, 194, 212, 224,
247, 287, 291; media debates about,
184, 185, 278; methods of analysis of,
15, 19–20, 103–4, 149n; and Naples, 88,
96–98; and the popular classes, 245, 277,
291; versus private space, 1, 61, 89, 90;
reclamation and revival of, 3, 39, 43, 73,
93–96, 98, 135, 257, 288; redefinition
of, 67, 85, 106, 194, 230, 262, 279;
regulations in, 1, 92, 138, 246, 247, 279;
and urban regeneration, 13, 116, 165,
166–67, 286. *See also* contested space,
piazza
public toilets, 137, 149, 273
public transport, 20, 31, 81, 124, 127, 131,
237; and Piazza Garibaldi, 183, 199,
215, 286; and Piazza Plebiscito, 133; and
the popular neighbourhoods, 246, 248,
275. *See also* buses, metro rail system,
railway
Puglia, 48, 175
punks, 258, 278
Putnam, Robert, 59–60

Queen Elizabeth II, 73

railway, 36, 171, 175, 177, 180–81, 183,
199, 215, 233n1, 248, Circumvesuviana,
175n, 199; Cumana, 233n, 248. *See also*
metro rail system, Naples central station
rap music, 102, 146, 257, 260n
Rauschenberg, Robert, 152, 163
Rea, Ermanno, 210n2
Reagan, Ronald, 95n6
Reclaim the Streets, 96
referenda, 59, 68, 71, 79, 133
reform, 8, 39n, 51, 61, 76, 79, 295n; local
electoral, 9, 50, 67, 79, 83
reformism, 53, 69, 76, 78, 84n, 90, 92,
265n10, 282
Regno del Possibile, 38, 234–36
representation, 16, 18n10, 25, 65, 75, 86,
239, 261; of the *centro storico,* 14,
15, 17, 20, 32, 103, 230, 244, 283; of